Richard F. Brown

COMPLETE BOOK OF

WOODWORKING

COMPLETE BOOK OF

WOODWORKING

by Rosario Capotosto

OUTDOOR LIFE
HARPER & ROW

New York, Evanston, San Francisco, London

DEDICATION

To my wife, Jennie, and sons, August,
Michael and Raymond, who have always
been very helpful (and patient) with
my woodwork and photography activities.

ACKNOWLEDGEMENTS

The author wishes to acknowledge his grateful appreciation
to John W. Sill for his help, advice and tireless effort in preparation of this book, and to Jeffrey Fitschen for his creative
contribution in the design of the book.

Copyright © 1975 by Rosario Capotosto
Published by Book Division, Times Mirror Magazines, Inc.

Library of Congress Catalog Card Number: 74-27319
ISBN: 06-010613-1

Second Printing, 1975

Manufactured in the United States of America

ontents

SECTION **1**

INTRODUCTION

**1. Woodworking—
An Absorbing Craft**   2

2. Why wood?   9
Workability, Durability, Beauty,
Availability

SECTION **2**

FROM FOREST TO WORKBENCH

3. Wood Facts   14
Wood Cells, Growth Rings, Springwood
and Summerwood, Sapwood and Heart-
wood, Hardwood and Softwood, Surface
Characteristics, Grain, Figure, Texture,
Color

4. Lumber   22
Cutting Methods, Seasoning, Lumber
Defects

5. Kinds of Wood   27
Selection and Suitability, Wood Suitability Tables, Wood Identification

6. Plywood   40
Description, Kinds of Plywood,
Plywood Types, Special Surfaces

7. Manufactured Wood   46
Hardboard, Speciality Hardboard,
Particleboard

8. Plastic Laminates   57
Construction, Sizes and Grades

SECTION **3**

SHOPPING FOR MATERIALS

9. Lumber Sizes and Surfaces   60
Lumber Dimensions, Rough Lumber,
Surfaced Lumber, Board Feet, Linear
Feet, Square Feet

10. Lumber Grading   65
Softwood Grading, Softwood Grade
Chart, Hardwood Grading, Hardwood
Grade Chart, Plywood Grading Hard-
wood Plywood Grades, Softwood
Plywood Grades, Softwood Plywood
Grading Chart

11. Buying Lumber   70
Determine Needs, Economizing,
Lumber Terms

12. Where to Buy Lumber   74
Lumber Yard, Home Improvement
Center, Lumber Supermarket, Hard-
wood Lumber Yard, Mail Order

13. Speciality Items   78
Legs, Turnings, Carvings

SECTION **4**

TOOLS AND THE WORKSHOP

14. The Workshop   82
Shop Location, Shop Planning, The
Workbench, Bench Tops, Tool
Storage, Lighting and Power, Wiring

15. Tools for your Shop   100
Selection, Which Tools First?
Minimal Kit, Expanded Kit

16. Buying Tools   103
Tool Quality, Finish, Design, Construction, Safety

17. Hand Tools   108
Layout and Measuring, Cutting,
Boring, Fastening, Holding, Miscel-
laneous

18. Portable Power Tools   114
Saber Saw, Portable Circular Saw,
Portable Drill, Portable Sanders,
Router, Power Plane, Impact Tool

19. **Stationary Power Tools**   137
Circular Saw, Circular Saw Blades,
Radial Arm Saw, Band Saw, Jig Saw,
Drill Press, Bench Sander, Sander/
Grinder, Jointer, Shaper, Wood Lathe,
Grinder, Multi-Purpose Tool

SECTION **5**
TECHNIQUES WITH TOOLS

20. **Measure and Layout**   190
Rules, Squares, T Bevel, Marking
Gauge, Other Tools, Drawing Irregular
Shapes

21. **Sawing**   200
Hand Saw, Saber Saw, Portable
Circular Saw, Jig Saw, Band Saw,
Circular Saw, Radial Arm Saw

22. **Surfacing and Shaping**   242
Chisel, Plane, Spokeshave, Surform,
Jointer, Router, Shaper

23. **Drilling**   278
Hand Drill, Portable Electric, Drill
Press

24. **Sanding**   290
Abrasives, Hand Sanding, Power
Sanding

25. **Fastening**   300
Hammers, Nailing, Nails, Screws,
Screwdrivers, Other Fasteners,
Miscellaneous Hardware

26. **Wood Turning**   316
Cutting Actions, Lather Chisels,
Basic Cuts, Faceplate Turning, Lathe
Techniques Applied

SECTION **6**
CONSTRUCTION TECHNIQUES

27. **Woodworking Joints**   334
Butt, Rabbett, Dado and Groove,
Lap, Miter, Mortise and Tenon,
Dovetail

28. **Gluing and Clamping**   346
Glue Selection, Kinds of Glue, Gluing
Procedure Clamping

29. **Working with Plywood**   358
Cutting, Joints, Fasteners, Gluing,
Assembling, Installing, Drawers,
Shelves, Cabinet Backs, Edge Treat-
ments

30. **Working with Hardboard**   370
General Techniques, Practical
Applications

31. **Working with Particleboard**   376
General Techniques, Joints, Edge
Treatments Typical Project

32. **Working with Molding**   380
Uses, Mitering a Molding, Coping a
Molding, Blended Moldings, Blind
Nailing

33. **Bending Wood**   386
Lamination, Kerfing, Self-Forming,
Using a Form

34. **Paneling Walls**   398
Existing Walls, Furring, Installing
Panels, Moldings, Other Paneling

35. **Applying Plastic Laminates**   406
Cutting, Applying Cement, Applying
the Laminate, Trimming, Special
Techniques

36. **Using Ready Mades**   414
Legs, Dowels, Spindles, Drawers,
Ceiling Beams, Clock Case Kit

37. **Wood finishing**   426
Sanding, Bleaching, Filling, Sealing,
Staining, Topcoats, Woodgraining

INDEX   437

INTRODUCTION

Woodworking— An Absorbing Craft

It can be said with little likelihood of argument that woodworking is one of the most absorbing and rewarding of all the crafts.

Examine a piece of wood. Feel its texture and warmth, observe its color, figure, and distinctively beautiful grain pattern. See it for what it is: a fine example of nature's wonderful, intricate artistry. But don't stop here!

Put a sharp-edged tool to the wood—a plane, a chisel or even a pocket knife and make a slicing cut. Listen to the crisping sound, see the curling shaving so gracefully emerge and enjoy the wonderful aroma of freshly cut wood. Can you resist the urge to go further: to shape and form the wood into some item of beauty or utility? Not likely!

Woodworking is a craft that will provide a new experience with every article you make.

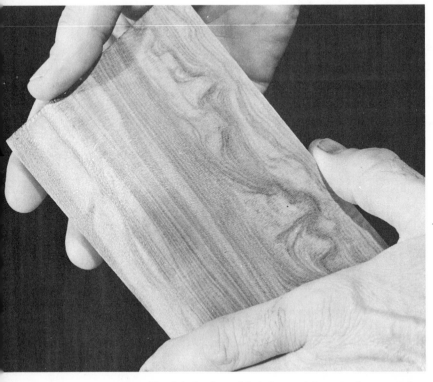

The beauty of wood is but one of its many fine properties; it boasts many more.

If you haven't yet experienced the joy of woodworking, try this— you'll soon get the bug.

Accordingly, your enjoyment and sense of accomplishment will increase in proportion to your effort.

Wood is easy to work with, so don't cling to any preconceived notion that you may not possess the required talents to turn out reasonably good work, at the very least. The modern power tools at your disposal will put skill in your hands and enable you to do fine woodwork that may equal or even surpass the quality of some high-priced manufactured items.

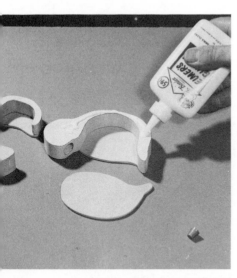

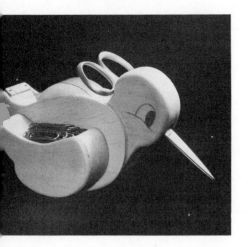

It doesn't matter how small you start in woodworking, each project you work on will add knowledge and skills; enable you to progress from the simple to the more complex.

This "homemade" transformation from bleak to beauty is a fine example of what can be accomplished by applying basic skills in working with wood. There aren't too many professional carpenters around who would dare tackle such a project. Nor could many homeowners afford their price tag.

The 45-ft redwood rail was constructed by lap joining and gluing short lengths of 2 x 12 lumber to form a continuous angular piece. This was then sawed and planed to shape.

THE BASIC OPERATIONS IN WOODWORKING

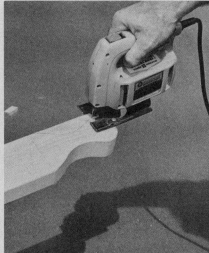

Planning and layout are the first steps in any project. Rough sketches are developed into drawings with dimensions which are then transferred to the stock. Cutting the stock to size or required shape is easily done with any one of a number of types of saws like the saber saw, center photo, or table and radial arm saws, or many hand saws. Surfaces are shaped and smoothed with power tools such as the shaper, router, jointer or with hand tools like the plane, chisel, or spokeshave.

Many jobs require the use of the drill to bore holes for dowel joints, screw pilot holes or just plain holes as needed. Power drills perform this function with ease and speed. Sub or final assemblies are joined with nails, screws or excellent modern glues which are strong and quick setting. Sanding is the final step of construction. It removes tool marks and smooths the raw wood in preparation for finishing. It can be done either by hand or with several different types of power sanders.

There are actually very few operations involved in woodworking: layout, sawing, shaping, boring, smoothing, and joining. These are the basics and each of them can be learned, if not altogether mastered, with practice and experience. There are many techniques, of course, and these you can apply as you learn to use the various tools and discover their potentials.

Working with tools and wood is a gratifying way to utilize spare time. It affords an outlet for your creative impulse—the satisfaction of making something useful with your own hands. Meanwhile, the diversion relieves the pressure of everyday living in this topsy-turvy world.

Beyond the diversionary aspects, the realities of our present economy practically dictate that you become involved in woodworking. The oppressive situation which prevails today—skyrocketing costs for hired labor coupled with slap-dash mediocre workmanship—has brought about a significant change in our lifestyle. We are, in ever increasing numbers, compelled to become "do-it-yourselfers" in an effort to offset the high costs and to achieve satisfactory work results.

You too can join the ranks of the millions of Americans who have realized that spare time woodworking pays off financially. You can save a lot of money by making your own repairs, maintaining and improving your home and property yourself and by making furniture as well.

You are undoubtedly painfully aware of the high prices demanded for general carpentry services. Consider for example the installation of a lockset on a door; a simple task requiring the boring of three holes, essentially, and the driving of a few screws. The price tag for such a job currently runs a minimum of 25 dollars. The replacement of a single damaged piece of house siding or the installation of a few ordinary shelves will cost at least as much, usually more.

If you decide to farm out to a tradesman any job requiring custom fabrication such as cabinetry, built-ins, book shelf modules, a room divider or a patio deck and the like, your budget will really be hard hit. Major remodeling projects such as wall paneling or attic and basement finishing can be unbearably expensive and frequently quite unsatisfactory in quality particularly if the work is contracted to unscrupulous home improvement gypsters.

These and many others are the kinds of jobs which you can do on your own. In many instances you'll need to rely only on the use of a few basic

A hobby in woodworking is the best medicine for shaking off the tensions of modern-day high pressure living and a fine way to keep involved with small-fry.

You'll not only save money by maintaining your home and making your own repairs; you will very likely do a more thorough job than would be done by hired help which in general is rather slipshod.

The professional price quotation for interior remodeling jobs run quite high mainly due to the cost of labor. You can save at a ratio of about 7 or 8 to 1 by doing it yourself.

portable power tools or perhaps simple hand tools.

Building supply dealers have geared up to the do-it-yourself trade because that's where the action is today. They're anxious for your business and the competition is keen so you'll frequently have the opportunity to take advantage of the numerous sales in progress on construction lumber, wall paneling, room divider components, redwood decking modules and countless other items. If you have a room in need of redecorating, shop around for a good buy on materials and consider the possibility of a dramatic treatment with prefinished wall paneling instead of the usual ritual of painting. A project of this nature can be accomplished with few tools and little in the way of prior experience. On the dealer's free literature racks you'll find excellent suggestions for product use and plans and instructions which are made available by the various materials manufacturers.

Furniture making is another facet of woodworking which offers a great potential for both creativity and economy. You, like many others, may harbor a misconception about this. You may believe that furniture making is a specialty reserved mainly for the professional craftsman. The fabrication of detailed, complex pieces does indeed require the talents of a highly skilled and experienced woodworker, without question. But all furniture is not complex. If you start out by tackling simple projects you'll soon discover that skill in woodworking is cumulative. Just as the master craftsman acquires his talents bit by bit through experience, so will you.

Numerous items of furniture or accessories lend themselves for fabrication in stages from the simple to the more complex. You'll find that with minor additions to a basic unit you can gradually increase the degree of professionalism of a finished product. Consider the possibilities in a project such as a coffee table: A set of ready made legs attached to a board which has been cut to the desired size results in a serviceable table made in quick time and at small expense. If a shallow box-like frame is made and installed between the legs and the top, the table will then have an "apron". This adds strength and rigidity and changes the appearance somewhat. A curved shape may be cut into the lower edges of the apron pieces to further alter the design, or, the plain edges of the table top may be made fancy with the addition of strips of molding. Further treatments can include the addition of a drawer, a lower shelf, or perhaps a drop leaf arrangement.

The same procedure may be applied to almost any project. Ordinary open shelving can be transformed into elaborate cabinetry with the addition of facia trim, some tastefully placed moldings, a couple of doors accented with molding borders or perhaps a few pieces of add-on carvings.

When you construct your own furniture or accessories you can expect to save at a rate of at least 10 to 1 over the cost of purchasing a similar manufactured item. The figure may even go as high as 15 or 20 to 1 so the value of making your own will pay off handsomely.

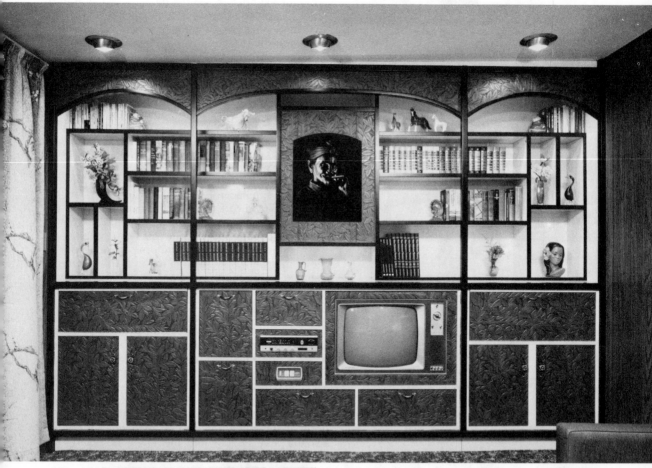

There is no limit to the creativity you can exercise when you do your own thing. Compare the before and after of this den treatment. Innovative use of exquisite wall paneling off-the-wall is most effective. This project was basically a plywood built-in surfaced throughout with specialty hardboard wall panels—constructed mainly with a table saw and several portable power tools.

2 Why Wood?

Come what may in this day of technological advances, nothing is ever likely to take the place of wood as the basic construction and decorative material. Among the many outstanding characteristics of this most versatile of our natural resources, several render it particularly suitable for workshop use: workability, durability, and beauty.

Readily available, relatively inexpensive and easily fabricated, wood is unexcelled as the basic construction material for use in the shop and around the home.

The rugged character of oak is well suited for this period cabinet. This tough and durable wood has been used for furniture through the centuries. (*Northeastern Lumber Mfgrs. Assn.*)

orkability

Wood may be cut and otherwise shaped with relative ease with even the simplest of hand tools. Any number of things can be constructed with wood using only a saw, hammer, and nails. With readily available power tools, wood can be quickly and easily worked into almost any imaginable shape and form. It can be joined and assembled with a variety of hardware fastenings or with excellent modern glues and adhesives.

The structural and decorative properties of plywood are effectively utilized in this handsome attic conversion. (*U. S. Plywood*)

Durability

The durability of wood is legendary. If properly protected from dampness and insects, it can last indefinitely. Antique furniture, still standing structures that are hundreds of years old, and well preserved wooden implements found in ancient tombs, attest to the endurance of wood.

Treated with modern chemicals, the durability of wood can be further improved. Preservative applications to wood render it resistant to decay under extreme conditions, such as direct contact with the ground or other severe moisture and exposure conditions, such as high humidity.

Both of these outdoor storage facilities were constructed with ordinary wood pre-treated with wood-preservative before assembly. They will hold up in "mint" condition for many years.

Advances in the chemistry of wood preservatives have extended the usefulness of ordinary species of wood so that it can better withstand the elements and the threat of wood-eating insects.

11

Beauty

Wood is distinctively attractive because of variations of grain, either subtle or bold, its depth of pattern, and its soft natural glow. The ability of wood to take fine finishes can enhance and preserve its beauty. The variations of color and figure within an individual board, as well as among the numerous species, render each piece of wood unique. This interesting individualism is one of the most appealing factors of genuine wood. No two pieces of wood can ever be alike. These are among the features that make wood so desirable for use in construction, furnishings, and decor.

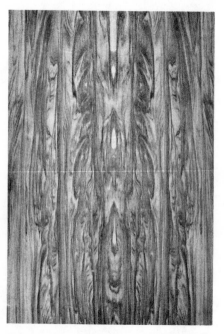

The beauty of wood lies in its grain pattern, color and texture (above, left). The variations in color and grain are infinite. Consider that there doesn't exist, nor will there ever, another piece of figured gum wood in grain pattern exactly like this one. (*Hardwood Plywood Mfgrs. Assn.*)

This interesting salt and pepper set (above, right) is chock full of beauty—the lathe turning blocks were made up by gluing thin sections of veneer. They contain 48 species of fine woods from all over the world.

Wood can take many distinctive finishes which will produce almost any desired effect. Improved materials result in factory quality with simple brush application.

Availability

Although industry is the prime user of wood, the home woodworker—craftsman and handyman—is buying and using wood at an unprecedented rate. This is an indication of the magnitude of the do-it-yourself trend. Fortunately, the timber in our forests is a natural resource that is self-replenishing. Through planned reforestation and timber crop management an ample supply of useful wood is assured.

Add zest and interest to your life by pursuing a hobby in woodworking. The pages that follow will provide you with related information and techniques. Words and pictures, however, will serve merely to guide you. You'll learn only by doing, for experience is the best teacher. So get to it and start the wood chips flying. You'll enrich your life with fun and relaxation while you make things of functional value and beauty.

Should you already be involved in the craft, perhaps you can brush up on techniques and pick up some new ideas that you can adapt to your own work.

If you're already into woodworking you may find in the following pages some new ideas, techniques and shortcuts which will help you to get more out of the craft.

Get to it and let the wood chips fly. There's nothing quite so satisfying as working with wood.

SECTION 2 FROM FOREST TO WORKBENCH

5 Wood Facts

Whatever your specific interests in the broad scope of woodworking—carving, furniture making, toy making, model making or home improvement—a basic familiarity with the structure and characteristics of wood is essential. You should know something about the materials you'll work with.

Forests comprise over one-third of the total land mass of the United States, providing a plentiful supply of wood, our greatest natural resource. After felling (cutting), the tree is trimmed of its limbs. The trunk is then cut into logs of manageable length which are skidded by tractor to either a train or truck for hauling to the saw mill. Logs wait their turn for processing into lumber at the saw mill's cold deck where they are continually sprayed to prevent the ends from drying out too rapidly.

Logs are hauled to the headrig bandsaw which cuts them into large planks, called cants. The cants are passed through edging and trimming saws for cutting into various widths and lengths. The rough green lumber is conveyed either to air drying stacks or to the drying ovens (kilns) where it is seasoned before further surfacing operations. A tremendous volume of lumber produced annually. Boards are shown being automatically sorted at a saw mill. (*Western Wood Products Assn.*)

ood Cells

Wood is not a solid material. Its basic structure consists of fibrous cells formed during the growth of the tree. Seen under magnification, wood appears as a honeycomb composed of the walls and cavities of the cells. The relative softness and hardness of wood depends on the thickness of these cell walls.

In hardwoods the cell walls are thick and the cavities relatively small. The opposite is true of softwoods which reveal thin cell walls and large cavities. The technical procedure for determining the actual hardness of wood is quite complex. For all practical purposes you can approximate the relative hardness or softness of a piece of wood by simply pressing it with your thumbnail.

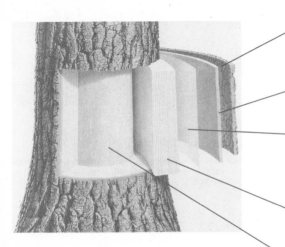

The outer bark is the tree's protection from the outside world. Continually renewed from within, it helps keep out moisture in the rain, and prevents the tree from losing moisture when the air is dry. It insulates against cold and heat, and wards off insect enemies.

The inner bark, or "phloem" is the pipeline through which the food is passed to the rest of the tree. It lives for only a short time, then dies and turns to cork, to become part of the protective outer bark.

The cambium cell layer is the growing part of the trunk. It annually produces new bark and new wood, in response to hormones that pass down through the phloem with the food from the leaves. These hormones, called "auxins," have the power to stimulate growth in cells. Auxins are produced by leaf buds at the ends of branches as soon as they start growing in spring.

Sapwood is the tree's pipeline for water moving up to the leaves. Sapwood is new wood; as newer rings of sapwood are laid down on top of it, its inner cells lose their vitality and turn to heartwood.

The growth of a tree trunk is a complex process. All of a tree trunk's growing is done in a thin layer of living cells that surrounds the wood. This layer, the cambium, creates new wood on the inside of itself, bark on the outside. It thus, in effect, moves outward, pushing the bark before it. (© *St. Regis Paper Company*)

Heartwood is the central, supporting pillar of the tree. Although dead, it will not decay or lose strength while the outer layers are intact. A composite of hollow, needlelike cellulose fibers bound together by a chemical glue called lignin, it is in many ways as strong as steel. A piece 12" long and 1" by 2" in cross section can support a weight of twenty tons.

Greatly magnified view shows the honeycomb cell structure of wood. Much of the volume of wood consists of hollow spaces within the individual fibers. Most cells run vertically along the length of the trunk while some, the rays, run horizontally to transport food towards the center of the tree. (© *St. Regis Paper Company*)

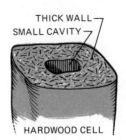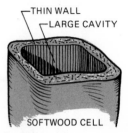

THICK WALL
SMALL CAVITY

THIN WALL
LARGE CAVITY

HARDWOOD CELL   SOFTWOOD CELL

The strength of a wood is dependent upon the volume or thickness of the individual cell wall rather than upon its overall size.

Growth Rings

A tree grows outwardly from the center. A layer of new wood is added each year to the outside of the previous year's growth. The cross section of many trees shows a distinct series of rings, alternately thin and thick, light and dark. These rings display the growth characteristics for each year. Spring growth, being more vigorous than summer's, is generally indicated by wider increments.

Some trees in the temperate zone and many tropical trees do not, however, display sharply defined annual growth rings. For tropical trees this is primarily due to the uninterrupted growing season.

The varied, intricate figure we see in wood is influenced by the collective distortions and irregularities in the arrangement and coloration of the cells, while the distinct grain patterns in some species are directly due to the annual growth rings.

Cross section of a log showing annual growth rings. Each light ring is springwood. The darker rings are summerwood. (*Forest Products Laboratory.*)

This angled block of wood illustrates how the individual annual rings form a distinct grain pattern on the surface.

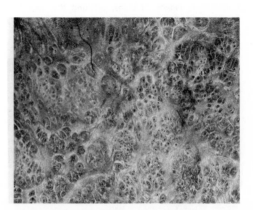

Strong figure variations such as this are the result of distortions in the arrangement of the wood cells.

16

SPRING AND SUMMER WOOD

That part of the growth ring that is formed early in the growing season is called springwood and the later growth, summerwood. Generally, the springwood has larger cell cavities and thinner walls rendering it lighter, softer, and weaker than summerwood.

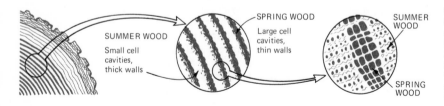

Growth rings consist of springwood and summerwood. The growth formed early in the season is called springwood and the later growth, summerwood. Springwood cell cavities are larger and the cell walls thinner than summerwood cells. The summerwood portion is tougher than springwood.

SAPWOOD AND HEARTWOOD

Another feature that can usually be observed in the cross section of a tree log is the darkness of the wood towards the center and the lighter color of the wood nearer the bark. The darker inner portion is the heartwood; the outer part is the sapwood.

Sapwood consists of living cells that are actively engaged in the growing processes of a tree. As the tree grows, the inner sapwood gradually converts to heartwood; the cells become inactive and "retire". In the process the cavities of these cells become plugged with gums and resins. This results in a denser, more durable wood. Thus heartwood is more resistant to decay than sapwood.

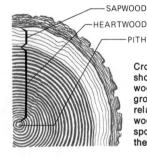

Cross section diagram of log shows the location of sapwood and heartwood. Fast growing trees usually have a relatively wider band of sapwood. The pith is a soft spongy section of tissue in the center of the tree.

A section of Ponderosa pine clearly showing the difference between sapwood and heartwood. In some species there is very little difference in appearance between the two. Heartwood is generally preferred because it is more durable.

The bases of these outdoor storage units are made of heartwood redwood which is very well suited for use in direct contact with the soil.

Hardwood and Softwood

Wood is commonly classified in general terms as being hardwood or softwood. This is purely a botanical reference that distinguishes not according to the relative hardness or softness of the wood, but rather by the type of tree from which it was cut.

Wood from broad-leaf deciduous trees, those that shed their leaves in the fall, is called hardwood. Wood from the needle-bearing trees, the conifers, is termed softwood. This sometimes leads to confusion because certain softwoods are actually harder than some of the hardwoods. Pine, fir, redwood, and cedar are examples of softwood. Some common hardwoods are birch, cherry, maple, poplar, and oak. Poplar is actually a *soft* hardwood.

Broad-leaf deciduous trees, those that shed their leaves once a year are botanically termed hardwood. A stand of hardwood trees consisting primarily of poplar, beech, maple and oak. The leaves have fallen; the trees will lie dormant until the next growing season. *(American Forest Institute)*

The softwoods are cut from the needle, or cone bearing trees, the conifers. These trees do not shed their needle-like leaves at summer's end. A sugar pine dominates the scene in this softwood evergreen forest. The botanical terms do not necessarily indicate the relative softness or hardness of the wood. *(Western Wood Products Assn.)*

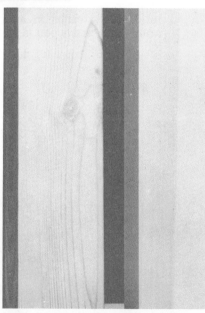

The piece of yellow pine on the left, a member of the "softwood" family, is actually much harder than the poplar sample, right, which is botanically termed "hardwood".

Surface Characteristics

The physical properties and appearance of wood are of prime importance to the woodworker. The choice of wood for a particular project depends on the end product. For general construction purposes the appearance of wood is usually not so important as the properties of workability, weight, strength, and durability. Wood intended for cabinetry and furniture-making must be strong, durable, and attractive. Important features that will influence the choice and selection of the finer woods include *grain, figure, texture,* and *color.*

GRAIN

Grain, in the stricter sense of the term, refers to the cell structure of the wood. The arrangement of the cells when the wood is cut longitudinally determines the type of grain. The size, orientation, and appearance of the cell fibers result in distinguishing characteristics. The main types of grain are *straight, curly, wavy,* and *irregular.*

Straight grain results when most of the cells run parallel to the trunk of the tree. Bird's eye maple is an example of wood with curly grain; the fibers of the cells are distorted in such a way as to appear curly. When the cell fibers collectively take the form of undulations or waves, the result is called wavy grain. Knots, burls, crotches, and stumps cause an unusual alignment of the cells, resulting in what is called irregular grain. Other deviations in cell orientation, such as occur when the cell fibers run a spiraling course around the trunk or when they grow in alternately twisting directions as they progress vertically up the tree, form what are termed spiral and interlocked grain. These, too, are frequently described as forms of irregular grain.

The choice of a wood for a particular project depends on the end product. Ordinary construction lumber, left, is quite suitable for general use. For fine cabinetry or furniture making, the attractively figured species, right, would be preferred.

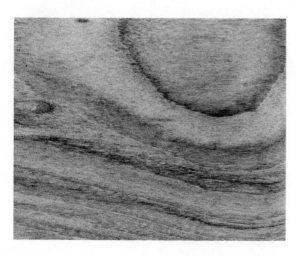

The physical property which is generally given most attention in the selection of the finer woods is the grain.

THE VARIOUS GRAINS AND THEIR RELATION TO WOOD CELLS

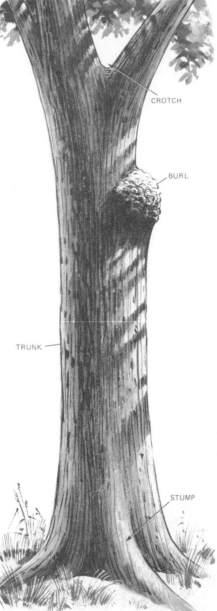

CROTCH

BURL

TRUNK

STUMP

This is a piece of straight grained wood, in this case pine. The cells run parallel to the trunk of the tree.

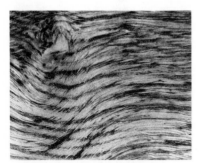

A distortion in the alignment of the wood cells in the area of a knot formed this grain pattern.

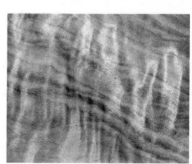

Birds-eye grain features a distinctive pattern of small curled spots which look somewhat like bird's eyes. It is not clearly understood what causes such curly grain. It is most commonly found in maple.

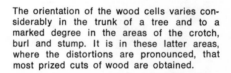

Gentle undulations caused by a waving growth pattern of the cells form what is called wavy grain.

The orientation of the wood cells varies considerably in the trunk of a tree and to a marked degree in the areas of the crotch, burl and stump. It is in these latter areas, where the distortions are pronounced, that most prized cuts of wood are obtained.

A sample of olive wood with dramatic figure. This was cut from the area of a burl. (Hardwood Plywood Mfgrs. Assn.)

FIGURE

Figure is the overall effect or pattern seen on the surface of the wood resulting from the combined features present. The size and contrast of growth rings, the type of grain, and variations in colors are factors that influence figure. Combined grain types and the varied distortions of grain in the area of knots, crotches, burls, and stumps contribute to make up very striking figures.

TEXTURE

Texture is another physical feature of wood. It pertains to the size and distribution of the pores or cell openings. Texture is described as being coarse or fine. Oak is an example of a coarse-textured wood, while maple is considered fine-textured. It is common practice to refer to coarse texture as open grain and fine texture as close grain. In finishing, the open grain woods require the application of a filler to close the pores, while close grain woods do not.

COLOR

Chemical substances in the cell walls impart the color to wood. Due to the larger amount of these materials in heartwood, it is usually the darker portion of the log. Wood color can vary considerably within a tree, aside from the normal heartwood/sapwood differences.

Texture differences are easily observed in this pair of hardwood samples. On the left is a piece of close grained maple. Its pores are not visible to the unaided eye. On the right is a piece of oak with its distinctive coarse grain. Note the large pores which are clearly visible.

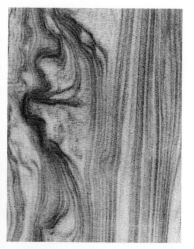

Attractive figure in a sample of quarter sawed gum wood. Deviation from normal grain structure forms a point of interest.

Color in wood is caused by the distribution of pigments in the cell walls. This Brazilian rosewood is deeply colored.

Logs are generally sawed into useable lumber by either of two methods: plain-sawed or quarter-sawed. Economy, appearance, and stability of the wood determine how it will be cut.

HOW THE LOG IS USED

Large circular saws as well as band saws are frequently used to cut logs into useable lumber. Sawmills make every effort to practice economy of timber by extracting the maximum amount of lumber from a log. This idealized picture shows how the entire log is utilized for lumber and by-products. *Photo above courtesy of Northeastern Lumber Mfrs. Assn.; illustration at right © St. Regis Paper Company.*

Debarking the log is essential to its full utilization because bark cannot be used for papermaking, and therefore any piece dropped in the chipper has to be free of bark. But the bark can be used for fuel and soil mulch.

The rounded sides of the log, called "slabs," are the first pieces sent to the chipper as the log goes through the sawmill. Actually, as cutting continues, other pieces go to the chipper, including edgings, trim ends, and other parts of the log not usable as lumber. Each log presents different problems and can be handled differently.

The outer portions of the log have the fewest knots. This "clear" lumber is usually made into boards or planks varying in thickness from one to three inches.

Toward the center of the log, knots increase and the wood is less suitable for boards. Heavier planks, and square or rectangular beams are normally sawed from this section. The center of the log is used primarily for structural beams strong enough so that they are not weakened by knots. Knots are most frequent here because this is the oldest section of the tree. Branches that were removed during the early years of the tree's life left knots that were covered over by new growth as the tree grew outward.

Cutting Methods

The simplest and most economical method of cutting is called *plain-sawed* when referring to hardwood, or *flat-grained* for softwood. This cut is made made tangent to the growth rings. After squaring, the log is sawed lengthwise to obtain the maximum number of pieces of varied dimensions with minimal waste. Lumber cut by this method displays the annual rings most conspicuously, spreading widely across the surface and appearing as ovals or U shapes. Wood cut this way is subject to warping, especially those pieces taken from the outer sections of the log. Since plain sawing results in less waste, such wood is less costly than wood cut by the alternate method.

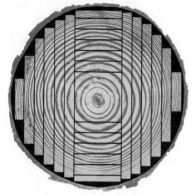

Plain sawed or flat grained method of cutting the log. Cuts are made tangent to the annual rings.

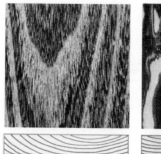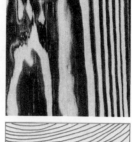

Hardwood (left), plain sawed. Softwood—flat grained cut, (right). Note how the annual rings appear as U shapes at the points of intersection.

The second method of cutting wood is called *quarter-sawed* for hardwood, or *edge-grained* for softwood. The term *quarter* is used because the log is first cut into quarters, then into boards. The cuts are made parallel to the radius, that is, from the bark towards the center of the log. Lumber cut in this manner is more wasteful of the log, thus more expensive. The advantages of quarter sawing are: less danger of warping, better wearing quality, and greater beauty of figure in some species. The annual rings appear more or less as straight lines in quarter sawed lumber.

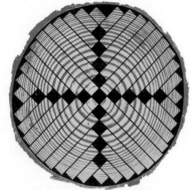

Typical sectioning of the log for quarter sawed or edge grained cutting. The cuts are made radially, in most cases toward the center of the log.

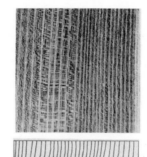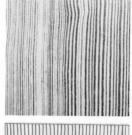

Hardwood (left), quarter sawed. Softwood (right) edge grained cut. Note how the annual rings appear as rather straight lines. Rays in the hardwood are clearly defined running across the grain.

Seasoning

New or green lumber contains an excessive amount of moisture; between 30 and 200 percent more than the oven-dried content is not uncommon. If serviceable lumber is to be obtained, this moisture must be evaporated. There are two commonly used methods of drying lumber: *air* and *kiln* drying.

Green or unseasoned lumber contains a large volume of water. Most of the moisture in the wood must be reduced by evaporation before it can be sent to market.

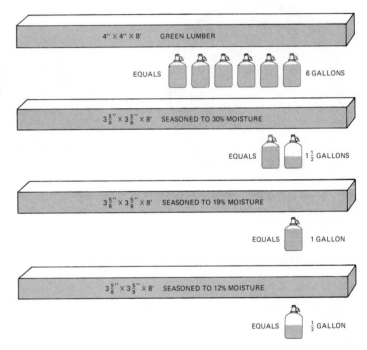

4″ × 4″ × 8′   GREEN LUMBER

EQUALS   6 GALLONS

$3\frac{5}{8}″ \times 3\frac{5}{8}″ \times 8′$ SEASONED TO 30% MOISTURE

EQUALS $1\frac{1}{2}$ GALLONS

$3\frac{5}{8}″ \times 3\frac{5}{8}″ \times 8′$ SEASONED TO 19% MOISTURE

EQUALS   1 GALLON

$3\frac{5}{8}″ \times 3\frac{5}{8}″ \times 8′$ SEASONED TO 12% MOISTURE

EQUALS $\frac{1}{2}$ GALLON

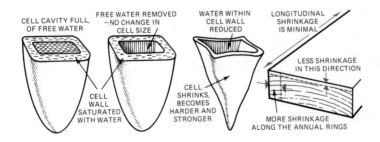

CELL CAVITY FULL OF FREE WATER

FREE WATER REMOVED —NO CHANGE IN CELL SIZE

WATER WITHIN CELL WALL REDUCED

LONGITUDINAL SHRINKAGE IS MINIMAL

CELL WALL SATURATED WITH WATER

CELL SHRINKS, BECOMES HARDER AND STRONGER

LESS SHRINKAGE IN THIS DIRECTION

MORE SHRINKAGE ALONG THE ANNUAL RINGS

When moisture content is reduced to below 30 percent wood shrinks appreciably. Most of the shrinkage occurs tangentially to the annual rings; this amounts to about twice as much as across the rings.

24

AIR DRYING

Air drying is done outdoors with the lumber stacked on stickers (cross pieces) with space between the boards so that air can circulate freely about them. Drying time varies from one to three months. The moisture content of air-seasoned wood ranges from 12 to 19 percent. Air-dried lumber is suitable for outdoor usage and general construction purposes, but lumber that is intended for cabinet or furniture work should contain no more than 6 to 8 percent moisture, or slightly less. Kiln drying is therefore required to satisfy this need.

Air seasoning. Lumber is carefully stacked with space between each board to allow free circulation of air. The amount of moisture removed and time required depend upon climatic conditions. (*Western Wood Products Assn.*)

KILN DRYING

In kiln drying the lumber is also stacked on stickers, then placed in an oven (kiln) in which climate is very carefully controlled. Steam is first applied to the wood together with low heat. The steam is gradually reduced, while the heat is steadily increased. Heat is applied until most of the moisture is removed from the wood. Any wood that has been seasoned should be carefully protected from the elements to prevent it from reverting back to its original moisture-laden condition.

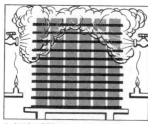
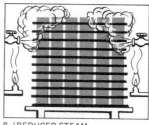
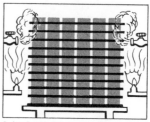

A. (HIGH STEAM - LOW HEAT) B. (REDUCED STEAM INCREASED HEAT) C. (HIGH HEAT - LOW STEAM)

Kiln drying. Piles of lumber, stacked similarly as for air drying, are placed into huge kilns where carefully controlled temperatures, humidity and air circulation reduce the moisture to any required percentage. (a) Green lumber is exposed to high steam with low heat. (b) Lumber begins to dry as steam is reduced and heat is increased. (c) Lumber is seasoned after being in high heat and low steam.

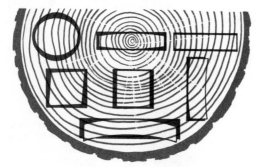

Wood shrinks and distorts as it dries. Diagram shows characteristic effects on flats, rounds, and squares in relation to the direction of the annual rings. Lumber is planed after drying in order to obtain trued surfaces. (*Forest Products Laboratory.*)

25

Lumber Defects

Defects in lumber are those flaws that can adversely affect its quality, either in appearance or strength. An awareness of the common faults and the ability to recognize them will enable you to select lumber more wisely. Some of the more common defects:

Knot. A dense, compact mass of fibers in a board that was sawed through a portion of a branch or limb of a tree. According to their size and number, knots can appreciably reduce the strength of a board.

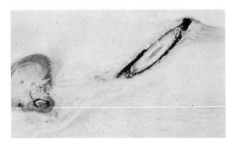

Check. A separation or split across the annual growth rings caused by stresses during the drying process.

Pitch. An accumulation of resin usually found in a concentrated cavity is called a pitch pocket. Pitch is objectionable if present in large amounts. It is extremely tacky and somewhat messy. Paints or finishes do not take well over pitch. Kiln drying minimizes the problem.

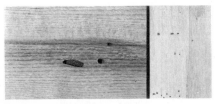

Worm Holes. Small holes caused by insects, usually occurring in the sapwood.

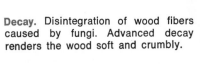

Decay. Disintegration of wood fibers caused by fungi. Advanced decay renders the wood soft and crumbly.

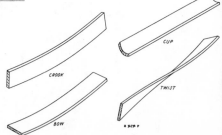

Warp. A deviation from the true plane surface. Crook, bow, cup, and twist describe specific types of warp, but a board may include any combination.

Kinds of Wood

There are hundreds of species of wood and thousands of varieties among them. Not all of them, of course, will be at your disposal. Availability varies regionally and local lumber dealers stock their bins accordingly. You will generally have a reasonable variety of species and sizes to choose from, however.

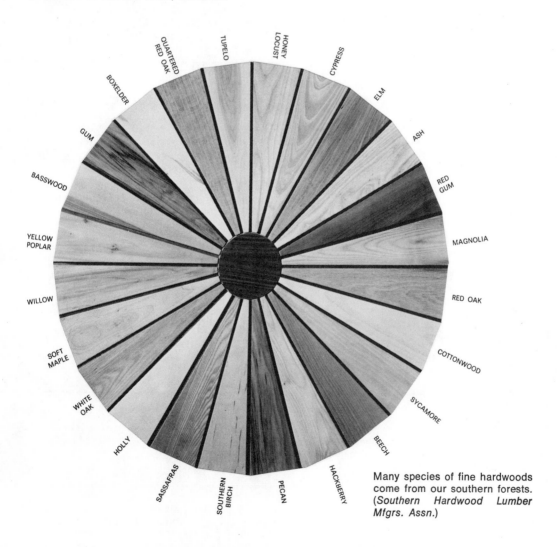

Many species of fine hardwoods come from our southern forests. (*Southern Hardwood Lumber Mfgrs. Assn.*)

Selection and Suitability

The decision about which wood you select for a project will necessarily be influenced by several factors. Determine first the specific requirements for the job at hand as they relate to the following considerations:

Hardness. The capacity of a wood to resist denting is of prime importance for items of furniture, cabinetry, and flooring.

Strength. Structural members for general construction, certain parts of large furniture pieces, and particularly chairs require wood that is strong.

Workability. Will you be using hand or power tools? Pine and poplar are easily worked with hand tools, but such woods as maple or oak are not. Also, some woods machine better than others.

Warp Resistance. Freedom from warping is desirable for all uses, but is especially important in furniture and cabinet work. Warp-prone wood can split or tear apart at joints.

When selecting a wood for the purpose of making furniture, hardness of the species is of prime importance. Oak, walnut, cherry, and maple are among some of the woods which possess this important quality.

Strength and hardness are qualities of wood which are frequently referred to as meaning the same thing. They are not. The Douglas fir used in this house framing is very strong but it is nowhere nearly as hard as oak or walnut.

Cherry was the choice for this furniture because it is both strong and hard. The slender arms of the chairs will stand up better than similar arms made of chestnut, which is also another type of hard wood but not quite as strong. (*Northeastern Lumber Mfgrs. Assn.*)

28

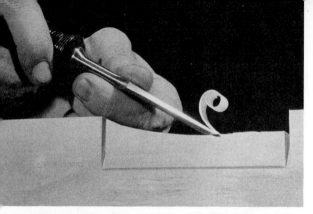

A certain amount of discretion must be exercised when selecting a wood on the basis of workability. Sugar pine handles nicely under a chisel or handsaw but will the finished product be inferior due to the softness of this wood? You must weigh the factors.

The way the wood was cut from the log, plus changes in atmospheric conditions and the nature of the species are factors which result in warp or freedom thereof. The use of wood with low decay resistance in outdoor construction is very wasteful of money and labor. This garage door wouldn't be in this condition if wood of the proper species had been used.

Decay Resistance. Prime factor for wood to be used in wet areas or on the ground. Not important for articles to be used indoors.

Appearance. Will beauty of figure and color show enough to warrant higher cost? Or will a less costly variety do as well?

Frequently, any one of several species can be used to satisfy the requirements for a specific project, while other kinds of wood will prove entirely unsuitable. It should also be noted that only rarely does one property dictate the choice of wood for a particular job. Usually a combination of two or more properties will be the deciding factor.

The following lists classify various common woods in three broad groups according to several important properties. Refer to these classifications to determine which woods will best suit your purpose. The data is adapted from material obtained through the courtesy of the Forest Products Laboratory, Forest Service, U. S. Department of Agriculture.

Low cost fir plywood was used in the construction of this valet chair. This wood is not particularly noted for fine figure but the choice was a wise one inasmuch as the piece was ultimately painted. More expensive cherry wood was selected for this piece because of its fine grain and color which show to advantage when treated with a clear finish. (*Northeastern Lumber Mfgrs. Assn.*)

Wood Suitability Tables

HARDNESS. Hardness is the property that makes a surface difficult to dent, scratch, or cut. The harder the wood, generally, the better it resists wear.

RELATIVE HARDNESS

High	Intermediate	Low
Ash	Chestnut	Basswood
Beech	Cypress	Butternut
Birch	Douglas fir	Cedar, northern white
Cedar, eastern red	Gum	Cedar, southern white
Cherry	Hemlock	Cedar, western red
Elm	Redwood	Cottonwood
Hackberry		Fir, balsam
Hickory		Fir, white
Larch		Pine, northern white
Locust		Pine, ponderosa
Maple		Pine, sugar
Oak		Pine, western white
Pine, southern yellow		Poplar, yellow
Sycamore		Spruce, eastern
Tupelo		Spruce, Engelmann
Walnut		Spruce, Sitka

BENDING STRENGTH. The capacity of wood to carry a load when it is used horizontally, resting on two or more supports, is measured by its comparative bending strength. This property is especially important for house framing members and also in certain modern furniture designs that feature slender structural parts.

COMPARATIVE BENDING STRENGTH

High	Intermediate	Low
Ash, white	Ash, black	Basswood
Beech	Cedar, eastern red	Cedar, northern white
Birch, yellow	Cypress, southern	Cedar, southern white
Cherry	Elm, soft	Cedar, western red
Douglas fir	Fir, white	Chestnut
Elm, rock	Gum, red	Cottonwood
Hickory, pecan	Hackberry	Fir, balsam
Hickory, true	Hemlock, eastern	Maple, soft
Larch, western	Hemlock, western	Pine, northern white
Locust, black	Pine, western white	Pine, ponderosa
Locust, honey	Poplar, yellow	Pine, sugar
Maple, hard	Redwood	Spruce, Engelmann
Oak, red	Spruce, eastern	
Oak, white	Spruce, Sitka	
Pine, southern yellow	Tupelo	
Walnut		

HAND TOOL WORKABILITY. Wood is usually easy to cut, shape, and fasten with ordinary tools. For some purposes the difference between woods in ease of working is negligible, but for others the smoothness and facility with which it can be worked have a decided influence on the quality of the finished job.

COMPARATIVE EASE OF WORKING WITH HAND TOOLS

High	Intermediate	Low
Basswood	Cedar, eastern red	Ash
Cedar, northern white	Chestnut	Beech
Cedar, southern white	Cottonwood	Birch
Cedar, western red	Cypress	Cherry
Pine, northern white	Fir, balsam	Douglas fir
Pine, ponderosa	Fir, white	Elm, rock
Pine, sugar	Gum	Elm, soft
Pine, western white	Hemlock	Hackberry
Poplar, yellow	Redwood	Hickory
	Spruce, eastern	Larch
	Spruce, Engelmann	Locust
	Spruce, Sitka	Maple
	Walnut	Oak
		Pine, southern yellow
		Sycamore
		Tupelo

NAIL HOLDING. As a rule, fastenings are the weakest link in all forms of construction and in all materials; therefore the resistance offered by the wood itself to the withdrawal of nails is important. Usually, the denser and harder the wood, the greater is its inherent nail-holding power.

COMPARATIVE NAIL-HOLDING POWER

High	Intermediate	Low
Ash	Chestnut	Basswood
Beech	Cypress	Cedar, northern white
Birch	Douglas fir	Cedar, western red
Elm, soft	Gum, red	Cottonwood
Hickory	Hemlock	Fir, white
Larch	Pine, northern white	Spruce, Engelmann
Locust	Pine, ponderosa	
Maple, hard	Pine, western white	
Maple, soft	Poplar, yellow	
Oak	Redwood	
Pine, southern yellow	Spruce, eastern	
Sycamore		
Tupelo		

SPLITTING IN NAILING. The splitting of wood by nails greatly reduces their holding power. Even if the wood is split only slightly around the nail, there is considerable loss in holding power. Heavy, dense woods split more than do lightweight woods. Woods not uniformly textured, like southern yellow pine, split more easily than the uniformly textured woods, like sugar pine.

COMPARATIVE SPLITTING IN NAILING		
High	**Intermediate**	**Low**
Beech	Ash	Buckeye
Birch, sweet	Basswood	Cottonwood
Hackberry	Chestnut	Elm, soft
Hickory	Gum	Poplar, yellow
Maple, hard	Magnolia	Sycamore
Maple, soft	Oak	Willow
Oak, chestnut	Tupelo	
Pecan		

SHAPING. Almost any wood makes a passable showing when shaped at a slight angle to the grain. It is in shaping across the end grain that the big differences between species show up. Smoothness of cut and absence of splintering or chipping is indicated for hardwoods.

COMPARATIVE DIFFICULTY OF SHAPING		
Least Difficult	**Intermediate**	**Most Difficult**
Birch	Ash	Basswood
Hickory	Beech	Buckeye
Maple, hard	Chestnut	Cottonwood
Oak	Elm, soft	Magnolia
Pecan	Gum	Tupelo
Sycamore	Hackberry	Willow
	Maple, soft	
	Poplar, yellow	

TURNING. In general, the heavier woods turn better than the lighter ones and heavier pieces turn better than light ones in the same wood. The percentages shown below rate the hardwoods according to the quality of turnings. Quality is measured by general smoothness, sharpness of detail, and occurrence of broken or chipped edges.

RELATIVE YIELD OF "SMOOTH" TURNINGS					
Percent		**Percent**		**Percent**	
Beech	93	Oak, red	84	Maple, soft	78
Pecan	89	Oak, white	82	Gum, black	75
Gum, red and sap	86	Ash	81	Elm, soft	70
Hickory	86	Hackberry	79	Basswood	70
Sycamore	85	Magnolia	79	Cottonwood	70
Poplar, yellow	84	Tupelo	79	Willow	60

WARPING. Warping is responsible for much waste in fabricating and for some unsatisfactory service. The table below shows the tendency of different woods to warp and twist during seasoning and after the wood is dry because of changes in atmospheric conditions.

COMPARATIVE FREEDOM FROM WARPING		
High	**Intermediate**	**Low**
Cedar, eastern red	Ash	Beech
Cedar, northern white	Basswood	Cottonwood
Cedar, southern white	Birch	Elm, soft
Cedar, western red	Cypress, southern	Gum
Cherry	Douglas fir	Sycamore
Chestnut	Elm, rock	Tupelo
Pine, northern white	Fir, balsam	
Pine, ponderosa	Fir, white	
Pine, sugar	Hackberry	
Pine, western white	Hemlock	
Poplar, yellow	Hickory	
Redwood	Larch	
Spruce, eastern	Locust	
Spruce, Engelmann	Maple	
Spruce, Sitka	Oak	
Walnut	Pine, southern yellow	

DECAY RESISTANCE. Wood will last indefinitely if kept continuously dry. Most wood is used in dry locations and is therefore not in danger of decay. It is only in certain parts of buildings that decay resistance is of importance, such as where the wood is damp or in contact with the ground. Use of heartwood of a decay-resistant species avoids the possibility of decay.

COMPARATIVE DECAY RESISTANCE OF HEARTWOOD		
High	**Intermediate**	**Low**
Cedar, eastern red	Douglas fir	Ash
Cedar, northern white	Elm, rock	Basswood
Cedar, southern white	Elm, soft	Beech
Cedar, western red	Gum, red	Birch, yellow
Chestnut	Larch, western	Cottonwood
Cypress	Locust, honey	Fir, balsam
Locust, black	Pine, southern yellow	Fir, white
Oak, white		Hemlock
Redwood		Hickory
Walnut		Maple, hard
		Maple, soft
		Oak, red
		Poplar, yellow
		Spruce
		Sycamore
		Tupelo

Wood Identification

The capability to identify wood is important in woodworking. Identification of some species is not too difficult as you can learn to recognize them by the general appearance of their pronounced grain characteristics. You will become familiar with other species as you gain experience in seeing and feeling the actual wood and working with it.

Some of the more common native species are illustrated in triplet form; each panel displays, from the top, end-grained, edge-grained (quarter sawed), and flat-grained (plain sawed) surfaces. This is done because certain identifying characteristics show up differently on each surface.

The manner in which it is sawed from the log will determine whether a piece of wood shows flat- or edge-grained patterns of annual growth rings on its wide surfaces. Lumber is manufactured in both forms.

The species shown are the ones most commonly found in retail lumber markets.

DOMESTIC SOFTWOODS

These wood samples show end grain, edge-grained, and flat-grained surfaces.

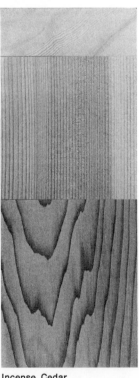

Bald Cypress   Incense Cedar   Western Red Cedar   White Fir

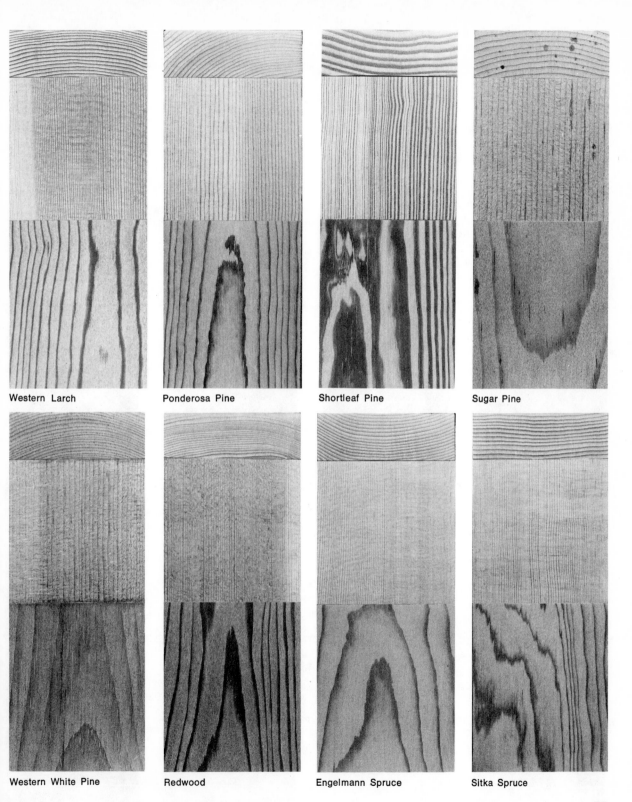

Western Larch

Ponderosa Pine

Shortleaf Pine

Sugar Pine

Western White Pine

Redwood

Engelmann Spruce

Sitka Spruce

33

DOMESTIC HARDWOODS

These wood samples show end grain, quarter-sawed, and plain-sawed surfaces.

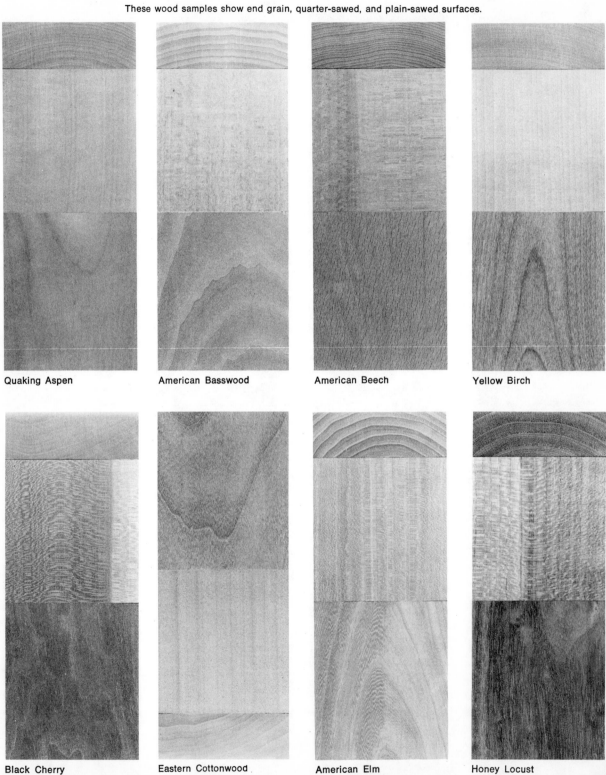

Quaking Aspen

American Basswood

American Beech

Yellow Birch

Black Cherry

Eastern Cottonwood

American Elm

Honey Locust

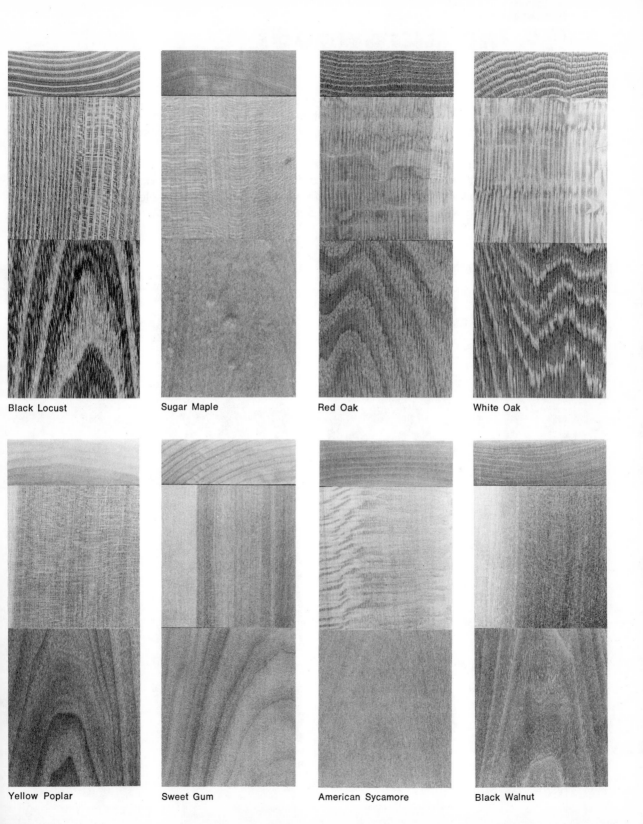

Black Locust

Sugar Maple

Red Oak

White Oak

Yellow Poplar

Sweet Gum

American Sycamore

Black Walnut

ine Hardwoods

The following are illustrations of other species of wood. Some are widely used varieties while others, including a small group generally referred to as the exotics, are less well-known. Among them are some of the most exciting woods imported from all parts of the world.

The exotics are rather costly and available only in limited supply. The reason is not a rarity of timber growth, but the difficulty in obtaining the logs. Some of the trees grow only deep in the world's wildest, most inaccessible jungles that are teeming with ferocious animals, deadly reptiles, and insects.

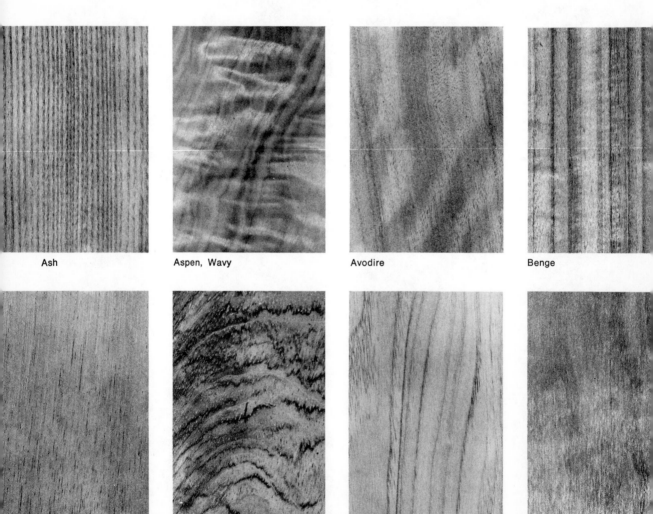

Ash

Aspen, Wavy

Avodire

Benge

Blackwood

Bubinga

Butternut

African Cherry

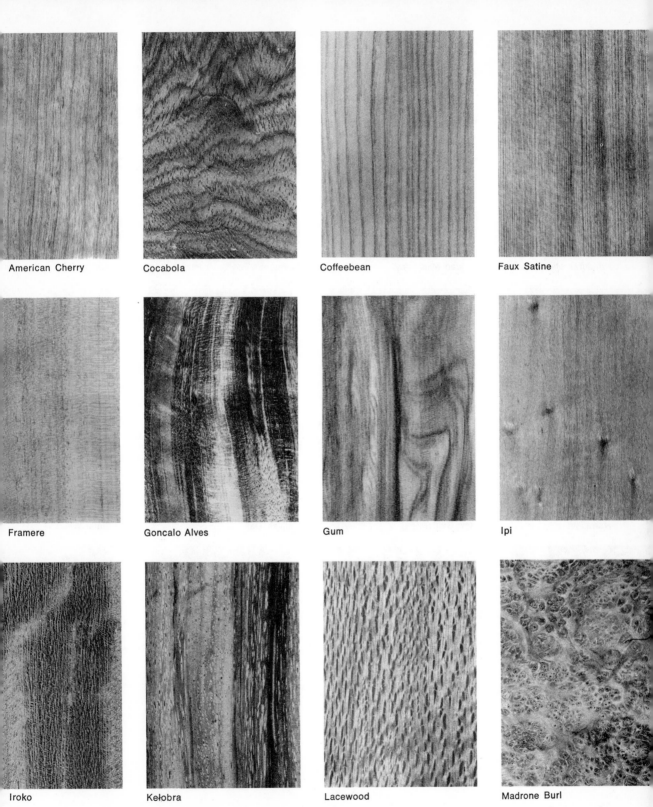

American Cherry

Cocabola

Coffeebean

Faux Satine

Framere

Goncalo Alves

Gum

Ipi

Iroko

Kełobra

Lacewood

Madrone Burl

37

Honduras Mahogany

African Mahogany

Marnut

Myrtle Burl

Narra

New Guinea

English Oak

Oriental Wood

Padouk

Paldao

Pecan

Peroba

38

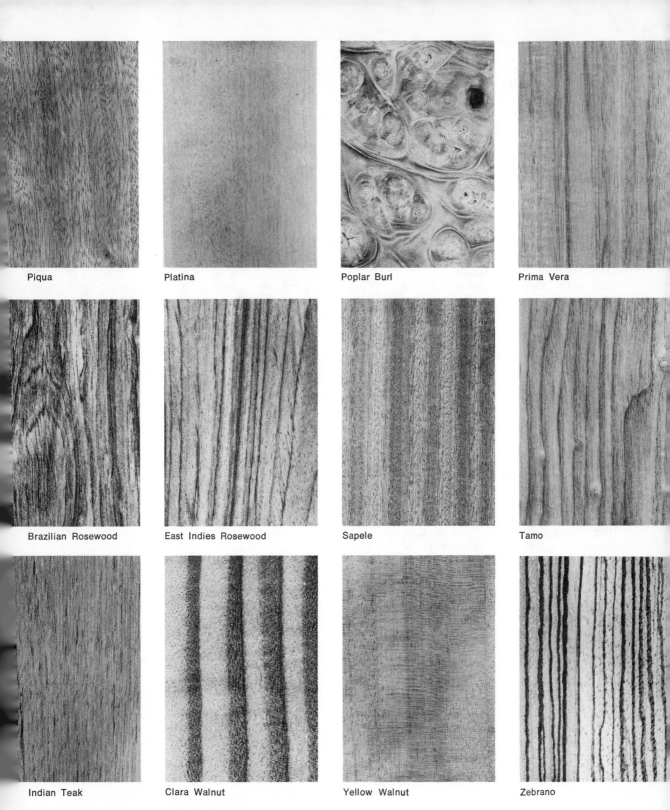

Piqua

Platina

Poplar Burl

Prima Vera

Brazilian Rosewood

East Indies Rosewood

Sapele

Tamo

Indian Teak

Clara Walnut

Yellow Walnut

Zebrano

39

5 Plywood

One of the most significant developments in wood technology was the "invention" of plywood. This is wood manufactured into one of its most useful and versatile forms. Plywood enables the woodworker to make sturdy and attractive constructions quickly and economically.

Solid wood, although relatively strong in the direction of the grain, is rather weak across the grain. Also, the width of serviceable solid lumber obtainable from a log is somewhat limited. These were two definite shortcomings until the advent of plywood.

Description. As its name implies, plywood is made up of plies, or veneers of wood bonded together with glue. One or more pairs of veneers are laminated with grain directions alternating at right angles over a center core. Odd numbers of plies are used: three, five, seven, nine, and sometimes more. The use of odd numbers of layers results in a "balanced" construction: equal stresses on each side of the core.

Thus, having grain that runs in both directions, a plywood panel has equal strength in length and width. Also, plywood possesses the quality of being less prone to warping, checking, and splitting and its dimensional stability rates quite high.

Since thin veneers of unusually large dimensions can successfully be cut from logs, their utilization in plywood makes many beautiful woods available in big panels, as well as ordinary ones, which formerly were available only as solid lumber in relatively narrow widths.

This unique piece of children's furniture is built entirely of softwood plywood. (*American Plywood Assn.*)

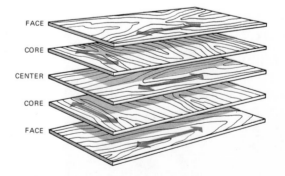

Plywood is termed a "balanced construction" because it is made of thin sheets of wood glued to each other with the grain running in alternate directions.

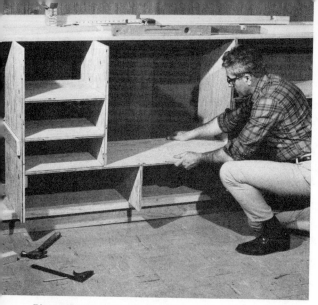

Plywood is the ideal material for use in the construction of built-in modules and similar projects in terms of economy in labor and costs.

Weatherproof exterior type plywood house siding has gained popularity as the basic material for attractive outdoor constructions.

This large construction was easily made with plywood. Such a project would prove to be an impractical and painstaking task using relatively narrow boards of solid lumber. Nor would it be nearly as strong.

The relative high strength of plywood permits the design of trim constructions without the need for built up framing. A single ½" panel becomes a pair of legs, main cross member and upper side of this chair, all cut out of one piece.

Unlike solid lumber, which is available in narrow widths, plywoods with face veneers of unusual beauty are available in 4 x 8-ft panels. (*U. S. Plywood*)

41

THE MANUFACTURE OF PLYWOOD

Top quality logs from evergreen forests are selected for use in plywood fabrication. At the mill they are sorted by quality and species. Logs move through a debarker to remove bark and other debris. They are then steamed to soften the wood before cutting. A huge lathe revolves the log against a long knife which peels a continuous thin ribbon of veneer at up to 600 lineal feet per minute.

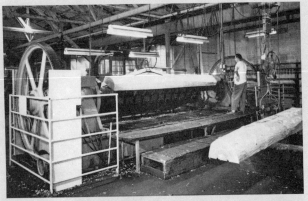

Another method of obtaining veneer is by slicing. This is used primarily to cut face veneers from hardwoods.

A clipper machine cuts the veneer into useable widths and defective sections are removed.

Veneer sheets emerge from dryers which reduce the moisture content to about 5 percent. After drying and patching, core veneer passes through glue spreader and is sandwiched at right angles between large sheets of face and back veneer. The veneer sandwiches go into a hot press where they are pressed together and bonded, under high heat and pressure, to become plywood panels. Rough plywood panels are sawed into 4 x 8-ft. sheets, sanded, graded, stamped and bundled for shipment. (*American Plywood Assn.*)

Kinds of Plywood

There are two principal kinds of plywood in common use—*veneer-core* and *lumber-core*. Veneer-core is made of layers of veneer throughout. Although the thicknesses of each pair of layers may vary, the core thickness is not appreciably greater than the crossband and face veneers.

Lumber-core differs in that the core material is much thicker in relation to the crossband and face veneers. The core is made of edge-laminated solid wood strips with low density and good workability. Lumber-core is especially suited for cabinetry work because the easy working core lends itself to edge-shaping, doweling, hinge installation, and other manipulations of the edge. In many applications the edge is quite suitable to be left exposed as a finished surface. The edges of veneer-core ply are generally too rough to serve as finished surfaces. There are methods of treating such edges, however. They will be detailed later.

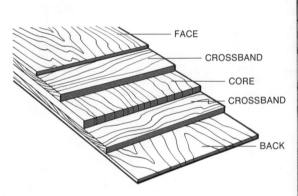

Veneer core plywood has a mid section consisting of an odd number of veneer sheets, usually 3, 5 or 7, sandwiched between a face and back veneer.

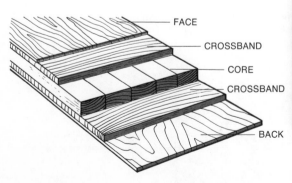

Lumber core plywood has thin veneers sandwiched over a thick core of solid wood. It is used for quality work.

A variety of plywoods. From top: mahogany faced veneer core, M. D. O. veneer core, birch faced lumber core, and Douglas fir veneer core.

43

ow Plywoods are Classified

There are two classes of plywood: *hardwood* and *softwood.* Most softwood plywood is made of Douglas fir, but western hemlock, white fir, ponderosa pine, redwood, and other species are also used. Nearly one hundred species of wood are used as veneer facing for hardwood plywood.

Softwood plywood is intended for all kinds of general use: building construction, furniture, closets, cabinets, built-ins, and countless other things. It is available in both interior and exterior types, depending on the kind of adhesive used in manufacture. The hardwood plywoods are also bonded according to the intended use, whether it will be interior and exterior. Details are given under Lumber Grading.

This attic built-in is made of softwood veneer core plywood. (*American Plywood Assn.*)

Hardwood plywood is available with many species of fine face veneers for use in interiors, furniture, and cabinetry. It also is a great pleasure to work with. (*Hardwood Plywood Mfgrs. Assn.*)

This collapsible hardwood table is made of matched oak face veneer core plywood.

Pre-finished plywood wall panels are economy priced to appeal to inflation conscious home owners. (*U. S. Plywood*)

44

Special Surfaces

In addition to the smooth-faced plywoods, there are a number of specially textured plywoods that are used for unusual interior and exterior wall treatments and unique decorative effects. Among the most popular are: relief grain, striated, embossed, and an infinite variety of grooved panels.

Another form of plywood is M. D. O. (medium density overlaid). This is an exterior softwood plywood with a surface of baked-on phenolic resin especially well suited for painting. Primarily a house siding panel, it is also widely used as a shop material because of its fine painting qualities. Its surface is smooth and needs no sanding. It is available with one or two sides surfaced. For use other than siding the two-sides-surfaced is the preferred choice because of the tendency of the other to warp.

Standard sizes of plywood panels are 4' x 8' x ⅛", ¼", ⅜", ½", ⅝" and ¾". Other sizes are available on special order.

Details of some of the varied specialty plywood sidings which are available. They are frequently used in interior applications for interesting accents. (*American Plywood Assn. & U. S. Plywood*)

7 Manufactured Wood

Another advance brought about through wood technology and research was the development of "manufactured" wood. This refers not to artificial wood by any means, but to real wood that has been reconstituted in another form. Through unique manufacturing processes, the versatility and usefulness of wood has been expanded, and in some ways, its properties improved.

Hardboard and particleboard are two such manmade wood panel products that are advantageous for use around the home and shop because of the many ways in which they can be used and their relatively low cost.

This textured wall has the look and feel of old barn wood. It's actually a tough, washable plastic finished hardboard panel. Tongue and grooved edges permit easy, precise installation. (*Marlite Division*)

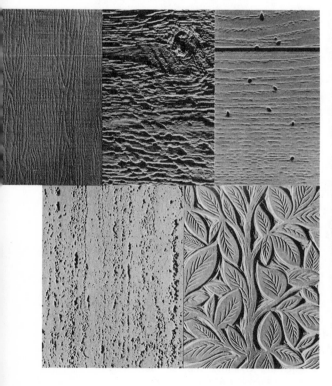

Hardboards

Hardboard is made by cutting selected logs into small chips. The chips are then subjected to an *explosion* process with superheated steam that further reduces the chips into individual fibers. The fibers are formed into a mat or thick blanket of wet, loose fibers. Compressed under tremendous pressure and heat, the fibers are bonded together with lignin, the natural binding substance of wood. The result is hardboard, a dense, uniform panel.

Hardboard is tough, durable, and highly resistant to moisture, abrasion, scuffing, and general hard use. Since it has no grain nor knots, it is equally strong in all directions. Like the wood from which it is made, hardboard can be worked with any of the woodworking tools. It can be sawed, planed, drilled, routed, and bent. The smooth hard surface offers an excellent base for painting.

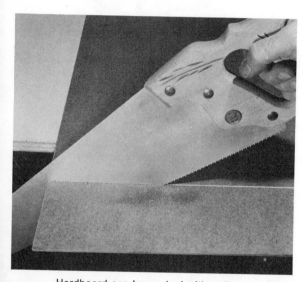

Hardboard can be worked with ordinary tools with ease. It can be sawed, planed, drilled, sanded and painted.

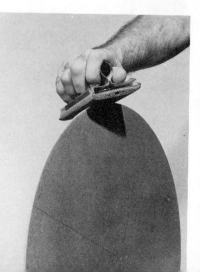

HOW HARDBOARD IS MADE

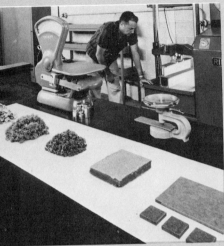

The hardboard industry helps to utilize the "whole tree" since wood in almost any form can be reduced to fibers to make hardboard. Logs on their way to the chippers, the first step in the manufacture of hardboard. Wood chewing machines reduce the logs into mountains of small chips, which are subsequently fed into defibering machines where steam and pressure reduce them into small individual fibers.

The fibers are formed into a wet mat, then pass through a series of rollers which compress the interlocking fibers. Huge hot presses squeeze water from the wetlap between a screened and glossy plate to form hardboard panels. Hardboard panels roll off the assembly line and are readied for shipment.

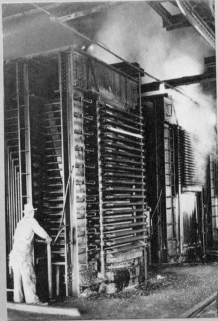

All photos Masonite Corp.

Types and Sizes

There are three types of hardboard: *standard, tempered* and *service*. Standard hardboard is the basic panel as it comes off the manufacturing press with no additional treatment. Tempered hardboard is essentially a standard board that has been further treated with chemicals and heat to produce a harder, more durable, and stronger panel that is highly resistant to weather extremes and rough treatment. Service hardboard is a lower density, lighter weight panel of somewhat less strength than the standard. It's less expensive, too.

Hardboard panels are available S1S and S2S (smooth one or two sides). The S1S panel has a light screen impression on the back side. Standard panel size is 4' x 8', but larger panels from 5' wide to 16' long are available. Thicknesses range from $\frac{1}{16}$" to $\frac{3}{4}$". The most commonly used are $\frac{1}{8}$", $\frac{3}{16}$" and $\frac{1}{4}$". Hardboard utility panels can be used for furniture, cabinet, workbench, and counter tops. They are also used in the construction of drawers, doors, toys, storage, and outdoor facilities of all kinds.

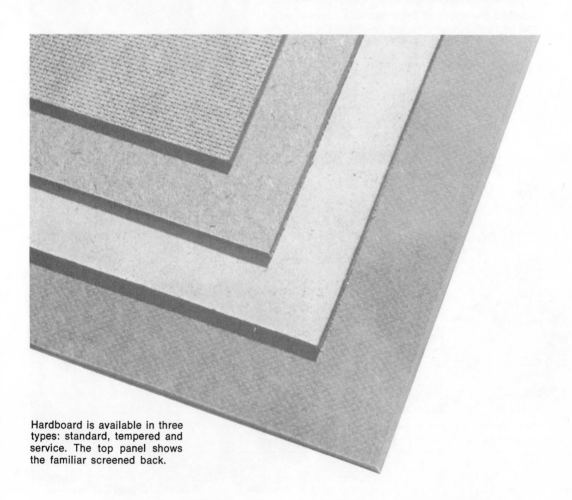

Hardboard is available in three types: standard, tempered and service. The top panel shows the familiar screened back.

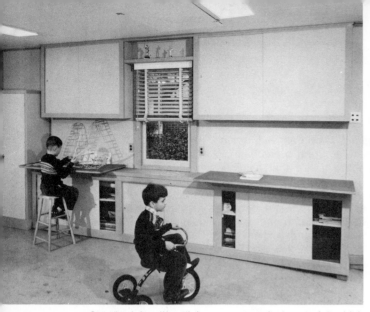

Standard hardboard is an economical material which can be used in countless applications in the home and shop. It was used quite effectively in this garage remodeling project.

Tempered hardboard panels are quite strong as evidenced in this use for a dome structure. The panels are unaffected by the elements.

The versatility of hardboard is illustrated in its use here as a form to make a curved concrete footing. The cost is low, and the results are excellent.

Self supporting hardboard panels of half-inch thickness can be used for easy construction of small shelters.

 pecialty Hardboard

In addition to the utility panels, hardboard is manufactured in varied forms, patterns, and colors. Most widely used are the wood-grained panels that simulate many fine woods, including oak, walnut, teak, pecan, cherry, and many more.

Other luxurious panels, some deeply embossed, *look* and *feel* like tapestry, leather, marble, and wood, to mention but a few. A system of interlocking edges and special moldings permits easy and accurate installations. Color-coordinated nails are available, as well as a wide choice of wood grained and textured moldings that are keyed to the basic color of the paneling. Although these panels are designed primarily for wall decor, they can also be used for varied and interesting off-wall projects.

Another kind of paneling is perforated hardboard. It has regularly spaced holes that accept accessory metal or plastic hanging fixtures of varied sizes and shapes that permit

Hardboard paneling in this Mediterranean room setting simulates hand carved wooden blocks. Each panel is actually 4 x 8-ft. (*Masonite Corp.*)

A few of the many specialty hardboard surfaces which are available for decorative and functional use.

unusual flexibility for storage. Standard sizes are ⅛" thick in 4' x 4' and 4' x 8' panels with ⅛" diameter holes. Heavy duty panels are ¼" thick in 4' x 8' with larger holes to accept ¼" accessories. They're available plain for painting or pre-finished in colors, woodgrains, and textured finishes.

Filigree hardboard is still another form that is used for special effects. This is a die-cut decorative panel with varied patterns: cloverleafs, diamond or star shapes, floral and rosette designs are the basic ones. These are used for room dividers, screens, doors, cabinet grilles, louvers, and accent panels. They are especially useful in places where semi-privacy is desired.

Hardboard is also extensively used for exterior house siding. It wears extremely well and is not affected by insects. Siding is available in a very wide range of textures and shapes and can be obtained unfinished, prime coated, or pre-finished.

This Carved Leaf hardboard panel is one of the most unusual and popular wall surfacing materials available. (*Marlite Division*)

This aromatic cedar chest is surfaced with hardboard wall paneling in oak and leaf design. Wall panels need not be restricted for use on walls alone. Left-overs from a wall paneling job find use in this wash basin cabinet.

Perforated board is ideal for use in tool storage as shown in this small combination woodworking and garden shop project. (*Masonite Corp.*)

Perforated board is probably one of the most widely used by homeowners of all the hardboard products.

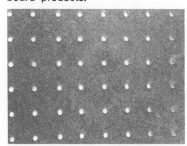

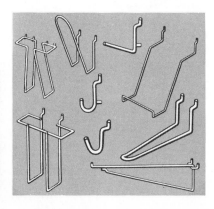

Some of the many special perforated board hooks which can be placed in holes for varied hanging chores.

Remodeling with hardboard paneling is not difficult and the results can be quite satisfying. Maintenance free walls and panels in refinished hallway (right) have a baked on plastic finish, never need painting. Note the effectiveness of the small areas of filigree in the archway and mirror set.

Filigree panels accent this room divider. It lets through light and air while providing semi privacy, an excellent application. (*Masonite Corp.*)

Decorative filigree hardboard is available in many patterns. These are a few. (*Masonite Corp.*)

Particleboard

Particleboard is a close relative of hardboard in that it is made of wood and is produced by a similar manufacturing process. There are basic differences between the two, however. Particleboard is made from large particles of wood instead of from individual wood fibers, as is the case with hardboard. Generally, materials that would otherwise be considered sawmill waste are utilized in its manufacture: sawdust, wood shavings, splinters, and chips.

The wood fragments are mixed with a resin-type adhesive, formed into a mat, then heated and pressed to produce a dense panel, smooth on both sides, much the color of oatmeal. Manufactured in varying densities for special purposes, the commonly available type is of medium density. Thicknesses vary from ⅛" to 2". Standard panel size is 4' x 8'.

Particleboard offers broad use potential around the home and shop. Among the advantages are low cost, strength, excellent paint and finish reception, and freedom from splintering during cutting and shaping operations.

Particleboard is grain-free and not prone to warping. Its smooth surface renders it especially well suited for surfacing with veneers and plastic laminates. Panels of ¾" thickness are suggested as the structural material for furniture, cabinets, built-ins, doors, and table tops. It doesn't hold screws or short nails as well as plywood or regular wood.

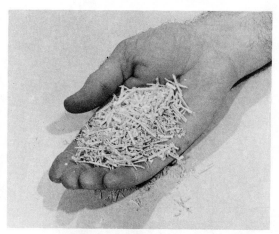

Natural wood in the form of chips, shavings and flakes are the main ingredients of particleboard.

Particleboard is widely used in the furniture industry in lieu of plywood because it has similar advantages while costing less. It can be utilized in the home workshop too. (*National Particleboard Assn.*)

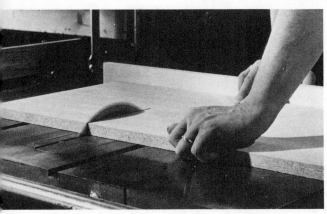

Particleboard saws easily with power tools but it can be worked with hand tools if necessary.

Since it has no grain, particleboard can be cut, shaped and drilled in any direction without splintering.

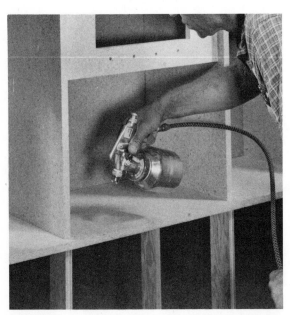

The smooth surface of particleboard needs no sanding and takes all types of finishing with good results. (*National Particleboard Assn.*)

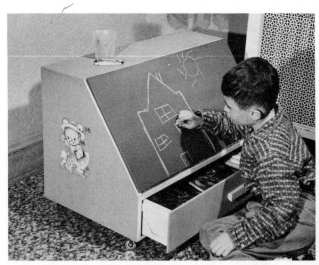

This sturdy toy chest is made of ⅜ and ¾-in. particleboard panels assembled with nails and glue.

Plastic Laminates

Even the experts could be fooled by this bold, exotic grain. Not real wood but plastic laminate in African teak woodgrain design. (*Formica Corp.*)

Much of the "wood" you see in furniture and varied interior applications is not wood at all, but plastic laminate surfacing.

Wood, with its many fine attributes, sometimes needs an assist when subjected to hard use, abuse, or constant exposure to moisture. A skin of plastic sheet material laminated to wooden table tops, kitchen counters, bar tops, bathroom vanities, and such will extend their serviceability to a remarkable degree. Highly resistant to water, stains, scratches, dents, and burns, plastic laminate is also unaffected by boiling water, household acids, alkalies, and alcohol.

More accurately defined as high-pressure melamine-phenolic plastic laminate, you undoubtedly know this material by common trade names of Formica, Micarta, Panelyte, and others. It is available in a wide selection of colors, modern decorator patterns, and woodgrain imitations. The latter have been developed to such a high degree of fidelity and exacting authenticity, they sometimes fool the experts. If you've been convinced by earlier statements that wood is supreme and "nothing can take its place", don't be disillusioned. Continue to hold this conviction. After all, the laminates are made with paper and versatile wood is used to make paper!

The surfaces of this desk, faced with a laminate skin, will withstand much abuse.

Plastic laminates are available in a variety of colors, patterns and surface textures in addition to the woodgrains. One of the more imaginative developments in plastic laminates is illustrated in this realistic three dimensional cane pattern.

onstruction

High-pressure laminates are made with layers of kraft paper that are impregnated with phenolic resins and variously saturated with melamine resins. A pattern sheet with image and color is also saturated with plastic, then topped with a translucent protective sheet. The multi-layered sandwich of built-up materials is fed into a large hydraulic press where it is subjected to extreme pressure and heat. The result is a hard-surfaced plastic laminate sheet of unusual strength and durability. The translucent top sheet becomes clear in the process, revealing the design and color below.

Diagram showing the various layers which make up a sheet of plastic laminate. The sandwich is fused together in a press under great pressure.

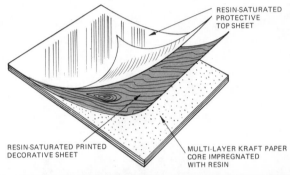

RESIN-SATURATED PROTECTIVE TOP SHEET

RESIN-SATURATED PRINTED DECORATIVE SHEET

MULTI-LAYER KRAFT PAPER CORE IMPREGNATED WITH RESIN

THE BASIC STEPS OF LAMINATING ARE EASY:

Very little special skill is required to successfully fabricate with laminates. There is nothing really difficult in this work, as you'll see later. Although power tools, primarily the router, speed up the work, fabrication can be accomplished with relatively few basic hand tools.

Vertical grade sheet can be cut through with a sharp knife. Contact cement is applied to both surfaces and allowed to set. Two sheets of wrapping paper are laid, overlapping, between laminate and wood (center photo). When the panel is aligned, the first sheet is slid out allowing the parts to make contact. The second sheet is then removed to permit full contact. Overhanging edges are trimmed flush with a router.

Sizes and Grades

Several differing surface finishes are generally available, including *gloss, satin,* and *textured.* The woodgrains, particularly in the textured finish, not only look like wood veneers, but feel like them, too.

Laminates are produced in a number of grades, including *standard, vertical, backing,* and *post-forming.* Only the first three would normally be of interest to the non-professional user. Standard grade is $1/16''$ thick and is used for a variety of top surface applications: sink, bar, table, desk, vanity, or wherever hard service will be encountered.

Vertical grade is half the thickness of standard, measuring $1/32''$. This is intended primarily, as the term implies, for vertical applications, such as walls, cabinet and furniture sides, fronts, and doors. The relative thinness of this grade has some desirable advantages: lower cost, ease of cutting and finishing of edges, and the ability to bend.

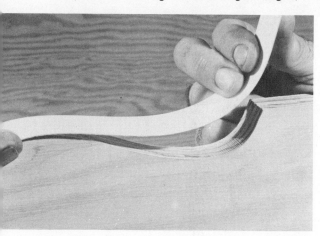

Extra thin laminates can easily be bent for application on curved surfaces.

Although the standard grade is best cut by sawing, the vertical grade sheet can be readily cut by scoring with a knife or scratch awl. This can effect quite a saving of time and effort on any job of sizeable proportions. Too frequently the heavier material is used when the thinner sheet would serve equally well.

Moderate curves can be easily handled with $1/32''$ sheet with little chance of breaking. Also, failure due to insufficient intimate contact throughout the curved lamination is less likely to occur with the more flexible sheet.

Backing sheets are regular laminates without a decorative side. They're relatively inexpensive and are used on the under or back side of large, free standing, and unsupported laminated work of four square feet or more. This effects a balanced construction and prevents warping that might otherwise develop. Backing sheets are available in thicknesses to match the face materials.

Sizes of laminates range in widths of 24", 30", 48", and 60". Actually, most manufacturers add at least $1/4''$ to the stated sizes to allow for edge trimming to assumed round figure sizes of construction core materials. Common lengths available are: 60", 72", 84", 96" 120", and 144". The square foot is the standard basis for pricing.

This crisply styled contemporary kitchen is surfaced entirely with plastic laminates. Maintenance free and remarkably durable. (*Formica Corp.*)

SHOPPING FOR MATERIALS

Lumber Sizes and Surface

A study of the descriptions and properties of the various woods listed earlier will serve to help you to decide which species best suit your needs for a particular project. But when you get down to the business of buying the wood, you'll need to know something about lumber dimensions and grading. These matters may seem to be a bit involved at first, but you'll soon catch on. In order to simplify ordering and to avoid confusion, it might be well for you to adopt the "language" of the lumber dealer.

Shopping for the raw materials is one of the important chores of your woodworking activities. If you talk the lumber dealer's language you'll avoid confusion and be assured of getting exactly what you want.

Lumber Dimensions

Lumber in the broad sense refers to wood that has been sawn from a log into a size and form suitable for use.

Softwoods are normally cut into standard thicknesses and widths in lengths of 8' to 20' in two-foot increments. Hardwood lumber, due to its higher cost, is generally cut in standard thicknesses, but in random widths and lengths (RW&L). This is done in the interest of economy —to minimize waste.

Lumber is classified by reference to the cross section dimensions of thickness and width:

Strip. Less than 2" thick and less than 8" wide

Board. Less than 2" thick and 8" or more in width

Dimension. Between 2" and 5" thick and from 4" to 12" wide

Timber. Smallest dimension is 6" or more.

These dimensions are based on the nominal (rough) size of lumber. There are three forms in which lumber can be purchased: rough, surfaced (or dressed), and milled.

STANDARD DRESSED LUMBER DIMENSIONS

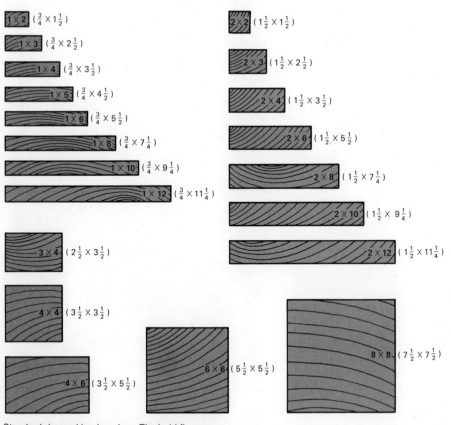

Standard dressed lumber sizes. The bold figure refers to the nominal dimension of the stock as it comes rough cut from the saw. After planing (surfacing four sides) the lumber is reduced to the actual sizes shown in brackets.

61

ROUGH LUMBER

Rough refers to the lumber that has not been smoothed and is just as it comes from the mill's saw. It is splintery and shows rough saw marks on all surfaces. The sizes of such lumber are approximately full dimensions as stated: 1" x 10", 2" x 3", 2" x 6", and so forth. A rough (RGH) 1" x 10" board measures just that — 1 inch thick by 10 inches wide.

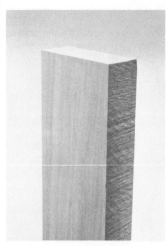

The blades used at the saw mills to cut logs into lumber are huge and coarse toothed. They leave the wood quite splintery and rough. The piece at left measures 4" x 4" (nominal size). Seasoning and surfacing will reduce it to $3\frac{1}{2}$" x $3\frac{1}{2}$" (actual size). The piece at right is surfaced on two sides (S2S). The faces have been planed smooth, the edges left rough.

SURFACED LUMBER

To be of value for common use, rough lumber must be planed to smooth its surfaces before it goes to market. This operation is called surfacing and it removes some stock. Surfaced lumber is consequently slightly reduced in size. A dry board that starts out in rough form as a 1" x 10" will actually measure $\frac{3}{4}$" x $9\frac{1}{4}$" after surfacing.

Although the final dimensions of dressed lumber are smaller than the original rough dimensions, the lumber is still referred to by its nominal or rough size. When you buy a "two by four" you ask for a 2" x 4" and you'll be charged for a 2" x 4", but what you get is a piece of lumber $\frac{1}{2}$" shy in both dimensions. The piece will measure $1\frac{1}{2}$" x $3\frac{1}{2}$".

Should you require a board that actually measures 1 inch by 10 inches, for example, you will have to specify clearly that you want a **full** 1" x 10". The dealer will then surface a board of larger dimensions in order to deliver the 1" x 10".

Softwood lumber stocked by most dealers is fully surfaced (S4S). This means that it is smooth or surfaced on four sides. Hardwood lumber can be purchased surfaced or rough. It is available surfaced one side (S1S), surfaced two sides (S2S), surfaced one edge (S1E), two edges (S2E), etc., in any combination. The abbreviated symbol is standard for identifying the surface condition of lumber. It should be noted that softwood is normally dressed down to a standard $\frac{3}{4}$" thickness, while hardwood is reduced to $^{13}/_{16}$".

MILLED LUMBER

Milled lumber refers to wood that has been worked by machine into any finished molded shape. This includes a wide variety of moldings, trim, flooring, and siding.

Knotty Idaho white pine is shaped into a wall paneling pattern at a lumber mill. You pay a bit more for milled lumber. (*Western Wood Products Assn.*)

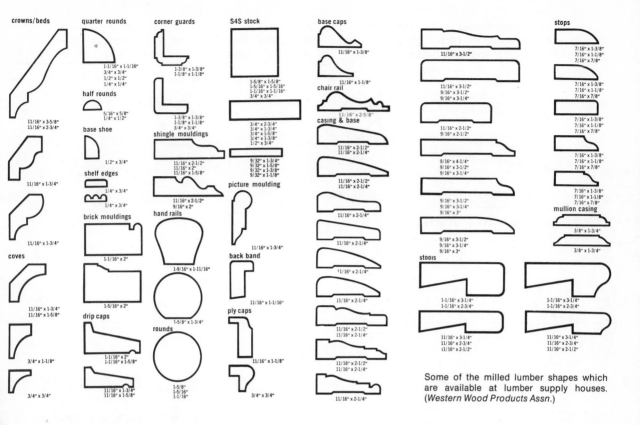

Some of the milled lumber shapes which are available at lumber supply houses. (*Western Wood Products Assn.*)

BOARD FOOT

Board Foot (bd. ft.) is the standard unit of measurement for solid lumber. It represents a piece of wood one foot square and one inch thick (nominal). Quantities and prices of most forms of lumber are designated in terms of board feet. A board 1″ thick, 12″ wide, and 10′ long would be considered 10 bd. ft. A strip measuring 1″ thick, 6″ wide by 20′ long would also contain a similar volume of lumber — 10 bd. ft.

There are several formulas for figuring bd. ft. The simplest is: thickness (in inches) x width (in inches) x length (in feet) divided by 12. Thus a piece 2″ x 3″ x 20′ would be calculated:

$$\frac{2 \times 3 \times 20}{12} = 10 \text{ bd. ft.}$$

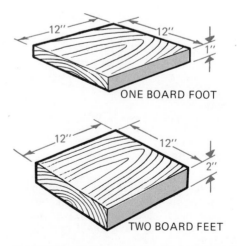

The board foot is the standard unit of measurement for solid lumber.

63

LINEAR FOOT

Linear Foot measure (lin. ft.) refers to the actual length of lumber. Quantity and pricing of certain items are based on length alone, regardless of thickness and width. Timbers, trim, molding, furring, and dowels are sold by the linear foot. Generally, lumber under ½" in thickness and 4" in width is also sold by the linear foot.

SIMPLE FORMULA FOR FIGURING BOARD FEET:

$$\frac{\text{THICKNESS (INCHES)} \times \text{WIDTH (INCHES)} \times \text{LENGTH (FEET)}}{12} = \text{BOARD FEET}$$

There are several formulas for figuring board feet. This is the simplest.

EXAMPLES

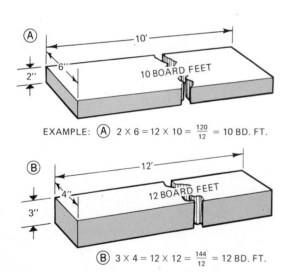

EXAMPLE: Ⓐ $2 \times 6 = 12 \times 10 = \frac{120}{12} = 10$ BD. FT.

Ⓑ $3 \times 4 = 12 \times 12 = \frac{144}{12} = 12$ BD. FT.

SQUARE FOOT

Square Foot measure (sq. ft.) is the basis for sizing and pricing plywood and other sheet materials, such as particleboard, hardboard, and wall paneling. The standard size of most sheet material is 4´ x 8´ or 32 sq. ft.

Dowels and moldings are priced by the linear foot (the length dimension). Sheet materials like plywood, hardboard and plastic laminates are sized and priced according to the square foot (the length x width).

64

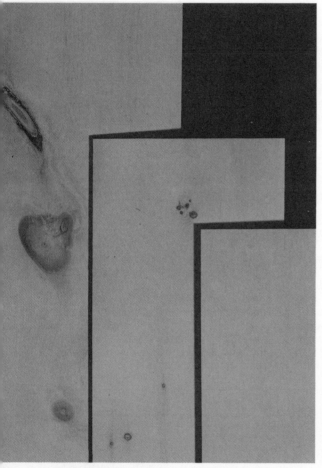

Lumber is graded according to quality and intended use by the degree of defects or freedom therefrom.

Softwoods and hardwoods are graded separately, each group being divided into several classifications. This allows some flexibility of choice that will enable you to buy lumber of a quality that best suits your needs. Lumber is priced according to grade, so refer to the accompanying charts and buy lumber according to your needs. Don't overspend on a better grade than will serve your purpose.

Softwood grade designations vary because different associations of lumber producers have their own rules for grading. However, they do establish their rules according to guidelines set forth by The National Bureau of Standards, called the *American Lumber Standards.* Consequently, while grading does result in rather uniform standards, nomenclature and specifications do differ. To list each one of the various associations' specific grading standards would be confusing. The following generalized specifications are representative.

Lumber is graded and priced according to the number of defects present.

Grading softwood lumber. This is generally done at the mill and sometimes at the railhead. (Western Wood Products Assn.)

oftwood Grading

Softwood lumber is generally divided into three basic grade classifications: *Select, Common,* and *Structural.* Select grade is further subdivided by letters into A, B, C, and D. Each letter from A to D represents diminishing quality in that order. Sometimes called *Clear,* A-Select is practically free of defects, while B-Select allows a few small ones. Wood in both of these grades is suitable for natural finishes. Grades C and D-Select have increasingly more defects but of a nature that can be concealed with paint.

Common grade lumber is generally subdivided by numbers into 1, 2, and 3. For some species numbers 4 and 5 are also included. Common lumber is suitable for all-around utility and construction work. Common 1 and 2 are fairly sound; grade 1 has tight knots and some blemishes, while grade 2 contains loose knots and other blemishes including checks at board ends and discoloration. Both of these grades can be fully utilized without waste. Grades 3, 4, and 5 involve a waste factor because they usually require cutting to eliminate flaws. Number 5 is the bottom of the heap, of course, and is practically waste lumber.

Structural lumber is graded mainly for strength. It is used where strength to support weight is required, such as in house framing. Grades in this category are: Construction, Standard, Utility, and Economy. Construction is the best quality and Economy is the poorest.

Hardwood Grading

Hardwood is graded according to rules established by the National Hardwood Lumber Association. Grading is based on the amount of clear or useable cuttings that can be obtained from the piece of lumber. The categories are as follows:

Firsts, Seconds and Firsts and Seconds (FAS). These are the top grades. Firsts are the best, but Firsts and Seconds are usually combined and sold as FAS. The criteria for this grade require that clear cuttings be not less than 6″ wide, nor less than 8′ long.

Selects is the next lower grade of hardwood. This grade allows pieces with defects on the back surface and clear cuttings of the face measuring no less than 4″ wide by 6′ long.

The third hardwood grade category includes the Commons: numbers 1 and 2. There are lower grades of hardwood, but they are substandard and lumber dealers usually cut out the defects and sell the pieces as Shorts (short lengths and narrow widths). No. 1 Common must yield 66⅔ percent, and No. 2 Common 50 percent clear cuttings. Such cuttings produce rather small pieces suitable for furniture parts.

Grade requirements vary with the project. Less expensive Select grade is suitable here because appearance of the wood need be good on one side only since the insides of the case will not be visible.

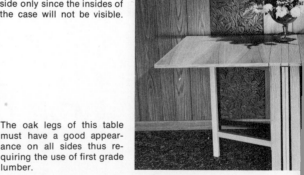

The oak legs of this table must have a good appearance on all sides thus requiring the use of first grade lumber.

WOOD GRADING CHARTS

The various lumber associations have developed their own official grading marks which are imprinted on each piece of lumber by the participating member mills.

SOFTWOOD LUMBER GRADES

Select

Grade A. Suitable for stains and natural finishes and practically flawless

Grade B. Also suitable for natural finishes, but contains a few small defects

Grade C. Contains defects that can be concealed with paint

Grade D. Slightly more defects than "C", but of a type that can be hidden with paint

Common

No. 1. Good, sound utility lumber with tight knots and limited blemishes, free of warp, splits, checks or decay

No. 2. Fairly sound, but with defects such as checks at ends, loose knots, blemishes and discolorations; no warp or splits

No. 3. Construction lumber of medium quality with defects of all types necessitating some waste removal in use

No. 4. Low quality construction lumber with numerous defects, including open knot holes

No. 5. Lowest quality; good only for use as a filler, including considerable waste

Structural

Construction. Best quality structural material

Standard. Similar quality to construction lumber with slight defects

Utility. Poor structural quality; requires added members for strength (closer stud spacing, for instance)

Economy. Lowest quality structural material

HARDWOOD LUMBER GRADES

Firsts. Lumber that is $91\frac{2}{3}$ percent clear on both sides; the best material available for cabinetwork

Seconds. Lumber that is $83\frac{1}{3}$ percent clear on both sides and quite suitable for most cabinetwork

Firsts & Seconds. A selection of lumber containing not less than 20 percent Firsts

Selects. Lumber that is 90 percent clear on one side only (other side is not graded); good for cabinetwork but with some waste

No. 1 Common. Lumber that is $66\frac{2}{3}$ percent clear on one side only; suitable for interior and less demanding cabinetwork

No. 2 Common. Lumber which is 50 percent clear on one side only; useable for painting, some paneling, and flooring

Reading the Lumber Mark

These marks are applicable to all western lumber species graded under the supervision of the Western Wood Products Association.

A WWPA grade stamp on a piece of lumber indicates its assigned grade, species or species combination, moisture condition at time of surfacing, the mill of origin and may also give other useful information. At buyers' request, mills authorized to use WWPA grade stamps will grademark the lumber they ship. Included are nearly a dozen commercially important western lumber species.

 This is the official Association certification mark. It denotes that the product was graded under WWPA supervision. The symbol is registered with the U. S. Patent Office and may be used only when authorized by the Western Wood Products Association.

12 Each mill is assigned a permanent number. Some mills are identified by mill name or abbreviation instead of by mill number.

2 COM This is an example of an official grade name abbreviation, in this case 2 Common Boards as described in the WWPA 1970 Grading Rules. Its appearance in a grade mark identifies the grade of a piece of lumber.

 This is a species mark identifying the tree species from which the lumber is sawn, in this case Douglas Fir.

S-DRY
MC 15
S-GRN
These marks denote the moisture content of the lumber when manufactured. "S-DRY" indicates a moisture content not exceeding 19 percent. "MC 15" indicates a moisture content not exceeding 15 percent. "S-GRN" indicates that the moisture content exceeded 19 percent.

 When an Inspection Certificate issued by the Western Wood Products Association is required on a shipment of lumber and specific grade marks are not used, the stock is identified by an imprint of the Association mark and the number of the shipping mill or inspector.

All of the above components may appear in various combinations in the official grade stamps.

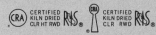

A sampling of some of the Western Wood Products Association grade marks.

Redwood Grade Marks

Standard grade marks include the grade designation and the symbol of an authorized grading agency. Grade marks may appear on either seasoned or unseasoned lumber on the face, edge, or end of a piece.

Lumber that has been kiln dried according to accepted standards includes the words "Certified Kiln Dried" in the grade mark.

Plywood Grading

Softwood and hardwood plywoods are graded differently, but as with solid lumber, it is the degree of imperfections that determines the grade. Grades indicate the quality of the face, back, and interior plies. In addition to the grade, plywood is also classified according to the type of adhesive bond relative to water resistance. There are three main types: waterproof, water resistant, and moisture resistant. These are respectively termed Type I, II, and III.

Type I is for exterior use and will withstand all kinds of weather. Type II is an interior plywood that will stand up through some wetting and drying. Type III is an interior plywood bonded with an adhesive that can withstand occasional exposure to moisture.

Plywood is graded according to the quality of the surface veneers. The combined quality of both the face and back veneers affect cost so be sure to determine your specific requirements and purchase accordingly. You have a choice.

The only difference between interior and exterior plywood is the type of glue used to bond the veneers in manufacture. Typical applications for exterior plywood include house sidings and outdoor furnishings. A project like the magazine rack below suggests the use of interior plywood A-B grade: the face is finish grade, back is solid and smooth.

HARDWOOD PLYWOOD GRADES

There are five grades of hardwood plywood:

Custom Grade (1) Has no defects; veneers may be made from more than one piece, but must be carefully color- and grain-matched.

Good Grade (2) This is similar to custom grade with the exception that the veneers need not be as carefully matched.

Sound Grade (3) Suitable for painting, but not for clear finishes due to stains and streaks which are allowable.

Utility Grade (4) Allows knot holes up to $3/4''$ in diameter, discoloration, and minor openings between joints.

Backing Grade (5) Permits knot holes up to $2''$ in diameter, splits up to $1''$ wide, and other defects that do not affect the strength of the panel.

The above grading may apply to one or both sides and it should be obvious that a panel requiring a No. 1 classification for both sides will be more expensive than one which has a back veneer of lesser quality.

SOFTWOOD PLYWOOD GRADES

The American Plywood Association has established the standards for grading the basic veneers used in softwood plywood. These are identified by letters as A, B, C, D, and N.

For most interior projects A-A or A-B interior-type plywood is chosen. The first letter indicates the grade of the face veneer, the second refers to the grade of the back.

Concerning lumber grading in general, bear in mind that although carried out in accordance to strict rules, grading is done by human beings and is therefore subject to some inconsistency due to errors or differences in judgment. Grading information or charts can help you to decide on a quality requirement, but the final selection of lumber should be a first-hand matter. Don't use the phone if you can go to the yard to make a purchase. There's nothing like a visual inspection.

SOFTWOOD PLYWOOD GRADES FOR EXTERIOR USES

GRADE (EXTERIOR)	FACE	BACK	INNER PLIES	USES
A-A	A	A	C	Outdoor, where appearance of both sides is important.
A-B	A	B	C	Alternate for A-A, where appearance of one side is less important. Face is finish grade.
A-C	A	C	C	Soffits, fences, base for coatings.
B-C	B	C	C	For utility uses such as farm buildings, some kinds of fences, etc., base for coatings.
303® Siding	C (or better)	C	C	Special surface treatment such as V-groove, channel groove, striated, brushed, rough sawn.
T 1-11®	C	C	C	Sanded or unsanded, with parallel grooves. For siding, soffits, screens, accent panels, etc.
C-C (Plugged)	C Plugged	C	C	Excellent base for tile and linoleum, backing for wall coverings, high-performance coatings.
C-C	C	C	C	Unsanded, for backing and rough construction exposed to weather.
B-B Plyform	B	B	C	Concrete forms. Re-use until wood literally wears out.
MDO	B	B or C	C or C-Plugged	Medium Density Overlay. Ideal base for paint; for siding, built-ins, signs, displays.
HDO	A or B	A or B	C-Plugged	High Density Overlay. Hard surface; no paint needed. For concrete forms, cabinets, counter tops, tanks.

SOFTWOOD PLYWOOD GRADES FOR INTERIOR USES

GRADE (INTERIOR)	FACE	BACK	INNER PLIES	USES
A-A	A	A	D	Cabinet doors, built-ins, furniture where both sides will show.
A-B	A	B	D	Alternate of A-A. Face is finish grade, back is solid and smooth.
A-D	A	D	D	Finish grade face for paneling, built-ins, backing.
B-D	B	D	D	Utility grade. One paintable side. For backing, cabinet sides, etc.
STANDARD	C	D	D	Sheathing and structural uses such as temporary enclosures, subfloor. Unsanded.
UNDERLAYMENT	C-Plugged	D	C and D	For underlayment or combination subfloor-underlayment under tile, carpeting.

VENEER DESCRIPTIONS

N Special order "natural finish" veneer. Selected all heartwood or all sapwood. Free of open defects. Allows some repairs.

A Smooth and paintable. Neatly made repairs permissible. Also used for natural finish in less demanding applications.

B Solid surface veneer. Circular repair plugs and tight knots permitted. Can be painted.

C Minimum veneer permitted in Exterior type plywood. Knotholes to 1". (Occasional knotholes 1/2" larger permitted providing total width of all knots and knotholes within a specified section does not exceed certain limits.) Limited splits permitted.

C plugged Improved C veneer with splits limited to 1/8" in width and knotholes and borer holes limited to 1/4" by 1/2".

D Used only in Interior type for inner plies and backs. Permits knots and knotholes to 2½" in maximum dimension and 1/2" larger under certain specified limits. Limited splits permitted.

The plywood grade stamps with symbols described. The grade stamp on the back or edge of plywood is your assurance of quality. Look for it and be wary of panels without it. (American Plywood Assn.)

TYPICAL BACK-STAMP

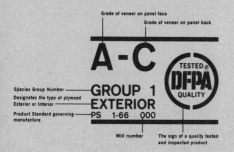

TYPICAL EDGE-MARK

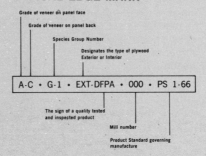

11 Buying Lumber

Buying wood for your projects is one of the important aspects of woodworking in which you will be frequently involved. You can save time and money, too, if you plan your purchase before you set foot in the lumber yard.

Determining Needs

The first thing to do is to determine your needs in terms of quantity. Sketch out the pieces you'll require with rough dimensions no matter how crude your drawing. This will enable you to visualize and group the pieces according to standard lumber sizes. Remember that most softwood lumber is available in lengths from 8′ to 20′ in 2-foot increments and in widths from 2″ to 12″ in multiples of 2 inches. Hardwood is more limited in size and much more expensive, therefore requiring even more careful consideration.

The following is a typical example of how you can waste (or save). Say, for example, you need a dozen 7′ lengths of 1″ x 10″ boards. You can buy a dozen 8′ pieces (nearest standard size), then cut off a foot of waste from each board. Or, more sensibly, you can buy six 14′ lengths and simply cut them in half to obtain the dozen boards with no waste! This is a simple example, but it illustrates the possibilities. Consider especially that pieces of varied sizes and odd shapes can sometimes be effectively grouped to avoid waste.

Form a habit of rough sketching the dimensions of lumber needed for a project. This will help you to purchase the best standard sized lumber for minimal waste.

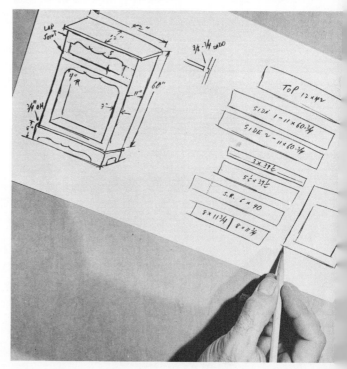

ECONOMIZING

Another thing to do before you lay down hard cash on the lumber dealer's counter—think out your quality requirements logically. Lumber shopping calls for more thought and advance planning than ever before, because of higher prices than in years past. When you can economize without sacrificing quality, by all means do so. Here are some ways:

• Buy the lowest grade and lowest-priced species that will do the job.

• Do not buy KD (kiln dry) lumber when AD (air dry) will do. Less expensive AD is quite suitable for most general construction work.

• Paint can hide many defects. Consider using No. 1 Common grade which has sound, firm knots for projects that will be painted.

• Hardwood veneer face plywood is priced lower than solid lumber of the same species; use it whenever possible.

• Buy the lower grades of lumber or plywood for projects that will be surfaced with laminates.

• Plywood prices are based on the quality of both sides in combination, so don't buy "good-two-sides" if the back won't be exposed.

• When you need small pieces of stock be mindful that you can get clear cuttings *between* the defects of Common grades.

• For some projects you can use thin wall paneling with built-up edges to obtain a "thick" look at lower cost.

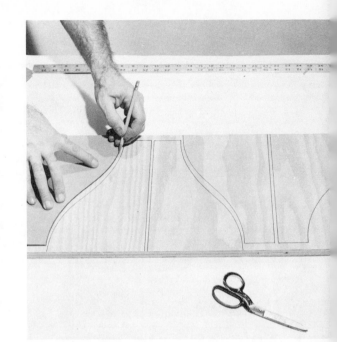

Group odd shaped pieces for cutting in close formation whenever possible.

Try your hand at designing "one piece" plywood projects. They're fun, challenging and economical, too. When all the pieces were cut as per this layout . . . they resulted in this functional piece. A handful of sawdust was the only waste!

Money Saving Tips

The use of kiln dry lumber (left) for outdoor construction is wasteful of money because the wood will revert to its air-dry state when exposed to the elements. Spackle and paint will readily disguise the fact that this project (center) was built with a low grade of lumber.

The less expensive oak veneer plywood, bottom, can serve as well or perhaps better than the costly solid oak at the top.

Utility grade plywood or lower priced particleboard (left) will serve quite satisfactorily as the core material for plastic laminates. Save on the cost of plywood by buying A-D grade (center) if the back won't show in the finished project.

This piece of low grade lumber will yield six pieces with perfect quality when the defects are cut away.

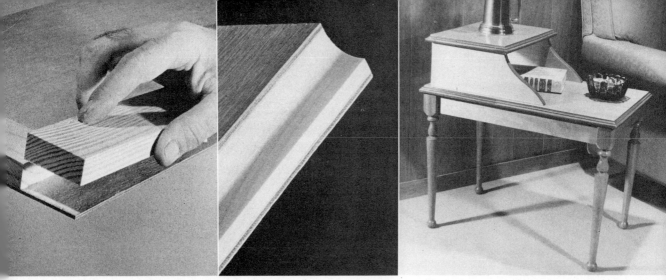

A thin hardwood panel can be built up around the perimeter with strips of solid wood to form a "thick" board (left). Edge shaping is possible with the built-up core. This trick is not new. Many commercially produced doors have hollow cores.

This step table was made with scraps of 1/8" wall paneling sandwiched over strips of 1" x 2" solid wood edging. Finished with clear varnish, the light-colored core stock creates an interesting accent. Such edges could be subdued, if desired, by applying a base coat of pigmented stain or ordinary latex or oil paint prior to the application of a final overall finish. For a close match, however, a core stock of a species similar to the panel can be used.

Lumber Terms

When your shopping list has been worked out, convert the information into a clear, concise lumber order. Use standard terms and be sure to include:

Thickness—State the thickness in nominal (rough) size: 1" or 2" or in fractions for 1" or more—$^4/_4$, $^5/_4$, $^6/_4$.

Width—Specify this in nominal dimensions also: 6", 8".

Length—Make reference to standard lengths: 10', 12'.

Seasoning—Indicate the type of drying: AD or KD.

Species—Specify the kind of wood by full name: *white* pine or *sugar* maple, etc.

Surface—Indicate the surface condition: S2S (smooth two sides) or S4S, etc.

Always order lumber by first stating the thickness, then width and length, in that order. Grade, species, surfacing and seasoning specifications follow. Thus, a typical order might read: 6 pcs. 1 x 6 x 10, A-Select, white pine, S4S, KD.

Write up your lumber order properly. It saves time, prevents errors.

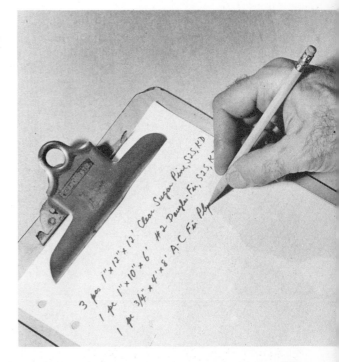

There are undoubtedly several sources of supply for lumber at your disposal. Where you buy will simply be a matter of personal preference, of course, but the following considerations may influence your choice.

THE LUMBER YARD

It may be to your advantage to buy from a local established dealer, the traditional lumber yard. Most of your lumber requirements can usually be obtained there. Although the bulk of their trade is with the professional user, these suppliers will welcome your business. There you will very likely find attendants who are knowledgeable and interested in you and your needs, personnel who are able and willing to help you to pick suitable grades and species and estimate quantities needed. The prices may be slightly higher than elsewhere, but you'll receive personal attention and enjoy the benefits of the dealer's integrity and dependability. Worthwhile considerations for perhaps a few pennies in price difference.

If you have the choice, be selective concerning the lumber supplier you deal with. Quality of material and service should be prime considerations. Bear in mind that "cheap" can sometimes prove expensive.

Personalized service is one of the advantages of dealing at the old fashioned lumber yards. It will be to your advantage to become familiar with the offerings of several dealers in your area.

HOME IMPROVEMENT CENTER

The major suppliers of lumber to the hobbyist woodworker and home improvement enthusiast, however, are the home improvement building supply centers. They cater almost exclusively to the non-professional. There, too, you will find a large and varied stock of lumber.

In dealing with some of the larger "centers" you'll probably find that the individualized personal contact is somewhat lacking. This is not necessarily intentional, but is due to the nature of the business. Big-volume selling dictates a production-line type of operation: you place an order with a counterman, who then dispatches it to a stock clerk, who makes the selection. Your material is then systematically forwarded to your car. Personal selection of the wood is generally out of the question.

If you've "done your homework" and learned something about the properties and grading of lumber, you'll be at a definite advantage here. The value of knowing what to order and the ability to recognize whether you receive what you pay for is quite evident. This is always true, but especially when you venture to buy wood at the next type of supplier.

Business at the home improvement centers is generally transacted at the sales counter (left). A clerk writes up the order then channels it to the warehouse. At the busy lumber centers (right), your lumber is selected for you. It will be up to you to check that it meets your specifications.

LUMBER SUPERMARKET

This is a colloquialism alluding to the cut-rate lumber supply houses. There are plenty of them around and they do a brisk business, but be advised that you must be on your toes when shopping in some of these places. Here you will generally experience impersonal service by sales clerks, who frequently are not at all knowledgeable about wood.

There are some bargain lumber dealers who will disclose the reasons for their low prices. They usually sell rejects and seconds, damaged railroad salvage, close-out stocks, and discontinued items. This is fine and so long as you're aware of why the prices are low, you may pick up some good buys.

Unfortunately, too many of these dealers deliberately withhold this information for obvious reasons. Thus it will be up to you to recognize bad stock when you see it.

SOME OF THE WAYS YOU CAN GET STUCK

The general appearance of lumber and panels is something that you can judge with your eye. But appearance will not always disclose whether a look-alike species has been substituted for a finer, more expensive one for which you are paying. Nor can you readily tell whether the lumber you get is, in fact, kiln dry if such is your requirement.

The purchase of bargain plywood will require special care. Be wary if the panel is not grade-marked. Plywood supplied by reputable lumber producers will be very clearly grade-marked, but substandard material will not. This means that you may get interior plywood instead of the exterior you need and pay for. Also, the inner plies may be of unusually poor quality. You can generally anticipate very poor inner-ply content by observing the edges of the panel. If they are thoroughly patched with wood putty, you can be sure that the core will have many voids and be composed of split and splintery waste wood veneers. Good construction is virtually impossible with such material. If you must shop for bargains, do so with your eyes wide open.

This veneer panel was no bargain at any price—it has become delaminated due to water damage. Some dealers specialize in insurance salvage lumber.

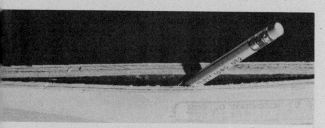

This plywood panel was purchased at a lumber supermarket during a special sale. It's actually a mill reject. Large portions of the veneers were missed by a faulty glue spreading machine. An unscrupulous dealer sold many like it.

Kiln dry lumber is generally, but not always, so marked. Lumber that has been resawn into shorter lengths by the dealer may not have the imprint thus you'll have to depend on his integrity.

Wood filler is sometimes used to plug up small spaces or knot holes which appear at the edge of a plywood panel. A reasonable amount may be tolerated but a major cover-up like this indicates quite clearly that this panel has a core of the worst quality. The audacity of the producer is reflected in the very sloppiness of the patch up!

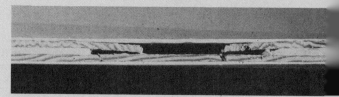

When cut into small pieces this plywood panel revealed an excess of oversize voids such as this. Nailing, screwing or gluing over such voids could prove very frustrating. A bargain panel?

HARDWOOD LUMBER YARDS

Many lumber dealers stock solid lumber hardwoods, but not a full line. If your requirement is not in stock, they can put in a special order to obtain it for you. In such situations you will be somewhat obligated to accept the lumber as is. At times this could prove disappointing if the appearance of the material doesn't suit you. You may have an alternative. Check your Yellow Pages; you may be fortunate enough to locate a hardwood lumber dealer in your area. Hardwood specialists are generally centrally located, since they are the ones who supply local dealers like your own with their hardwood stock. Some sell only wholesale, but the majority will sell retail as well.

At these yards you will find many species of solid lumber hardwood in a variety of sizes. You will very likely get exactly what you want. An important tip: If the dealer allows you to select the lumber on your own (most will), don't abuse the privilege by leaving boards strewn about in disorder. Such treatment can be quite damaging to the lumber and to your reputation, too. This, of course, holds true at any lumber yard.

MAIL ORDER

Rare, exotic woods with strange sounding names from far away jungles are also readily available to you through mail order. There are several wood mail order houses in the country and the "how-to" publications carry their ads. A list of mail order dealers will be found at the back of this book. Look them up and send for their well-illustrated catalogues.

Many of the items, such as unusual veneers, veneer plywood (of mailable sizes), lathe turning blocks, inlaid matched veneers for table tops, and inlaid wood border strips are but a few of the mail order house's offerings. Many of the materials will certainly be the basis for exciting projects.

A large selection of precision-made, colorful wood inlay borders and plaques will enable you to give your projects a professional touch.

This backgammon board project is embellished with easy-to-apply inlaid wood border strips. (A. Constantine & Sons.)

15 Specialty Items

The numerous short-cut, ready-made items available will enable you to turn out work of professional quality with little effort and few tools.

Lumber dealers' bins literally overflow with a great variety of legs, turned posts, spindles, carved plaques and trim, and filigree panels with mating frame members. These are but a few of the ready-made items that you can utilize to advantage. Look them over when you shop for wood; become familiar with the varied shapes, sizes and types. Some items, in combination, may inspire basic projects, while others can suggest important supportive applications.

A piece of paneling edged with carved trim and graced with a set of classic tapered legs becomes *instant furniture.* Easily assembled, prefabricated framing members can transform a filigree panel into a room divider, a valance, or decorative screen. Fancy turnings or embossed wood ornaments can add dimension and elegance to otherwise ordinary projects. The possibilities are unlimited.

Ready-made items of a more sophisticated nature are available through the woodworker's mail order supply houses. It may be beyond the scope of your ability or equipment, either as a beginner or advanced woodworker, to carve a set of Queen Anne legs for a piece of furniture that you'd like to construct. Resolve the problem as many professional cabinet makers do: buy them ready-made.

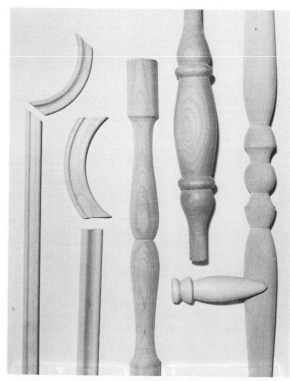

Mass produced wood turnings of fine quality and relatively low cost can be used to broaden your woodworking capabilities. Look over the many ready-made items available at the lumber supply houses. You'll learn to develop ideas for their use.

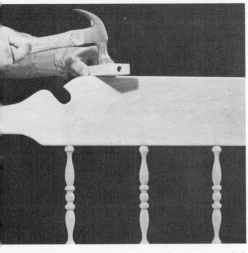

This is the back section of a colonial two seater chair under construction. A very effective use for spindles. Note block is used to hammer parts together.

This fiddle back stool is made with a scrap piece of construction lumber and a set of store-bought legs. A simple one evening project.

The system of screw together spindles offers many possibilities for interesting applications. Threaded dowels are used for assembly. These components are ideal for the woodworker with limited shop facilities. Cutting wood panels to size and drilling holes are the only operations involved. (Russ Stonier, Inc.)

A simply constructed cabinet acquires a fancy touch with the addition of a border of carved wood trim molding. These moldings are available in many varieties at most lumber or home-center outlets.

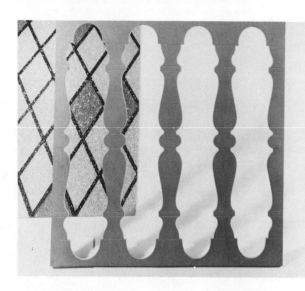

Softwood molding with embossed carved effect can be used for fine decorative accents.

Die-cut plywood strips and panels can be assembled in a variety of screens, dividers or backdrops as shown above and below.

Hardboard filigree panels and ready-made grooved and jointed framing components can be used for varied projects.

A special manufacturing process makes available these wood carved replicas at a fraction of the cost of hand carved counterparts.

A plain door takes on a dramatic dimension with the addition of these carved panel add-ons. (Russ Stonier, Inc.)

Picture frames are generally overpriced. This one was made with a combination of built-up stock moldings at relatively low cost.

The basic construction of this charming hanging shelf was quite easy. The louvered door and the turned spindle are ready-mades.

Grandfather clock kits are available with all major parts pre cut in fine cabinet woods. Assembly takes a reasonable amount of simple skills.

The cost of a comparable clock would be at least twice the price of the kit.

SECTION 4

YOUR WORKSHOP AND TOOLS

14 The Workshop

When first starting out in woodworking your collection of tools may be moderate, your activities scantling, and your workplace humble. As your skills and interests grow, so will your accumulation of tools and equipment. With this pleasant prospect will come the realization of the need for a workshop.

The *dream* shop is certainly something to aspire to, but it isn't an absolute necessity. You will do good work and get by very well with a practical, average shop. A place to store your tools within easy reach, a sturdy workbench, space for power tools, and lumber storage facilities are the essentials.

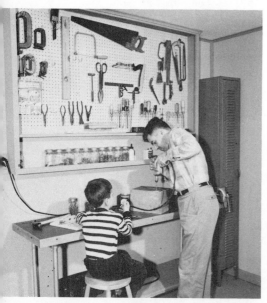

For some this may be the ideal workshop; for others it may be only the beginning of bigger and better things to come in woodworking.

Adequate working space, a variety of tools and pleasant surroundings like this can be the hub for productive and enjoyable activities. (Western Wood Products Assn.)

Shop Location

Where you set up shop depends on where you have available space. Basements, garages, spare rooms and attics, in that order, are the usual locations for the home workshop. If none, or only parts of these areas are available, you may have to settle for a portable shop. You can accomplish quite a bit with a few portable power tools, a pair of saw horses, and a plywood panel work surface that can be set up almost anywhere.

Basements are the most widely used for shops because heating, electric power, and lighting are so readily available. Also, noises are confined within the thick masonry walls and not apt to disturb the neighbors.

If yours is a dry basement with sufficient headroom, no matter how dark or dingy, don't hesitate for a moment to consider it for your shop. A bit of paint, perhaps some inexpensive wall paneling, and the installation of lighting fixtures can do wonders to convert it into a cheerful workplace.

Damp basements can play havoc with tools and wood alike; moisture rusts tools and is readily absorbed into wood. But a damp basement need not be discounted as a workshop location because there are a couple of simple ways to minimize or even eliminate the problem.

If yours is a damp basement, try painting the masonry walls and floor with a hydrostatic paint. This is a special paint which forms an effective barrier against moisture. If the condition is a severe one, a special cement-based material, which can be brushed on, may be required. Both types are available at masonry supply houses.

The second possibility for solving the moisture problem is through the use of a dehumidifier. This is a small electrical appliance which does a remarkable job of absorbing moisture from the air. It draws very little current and may be operated continuously. Either one or both of these methods may be necessary, depending on the degree of dampness prevailing.

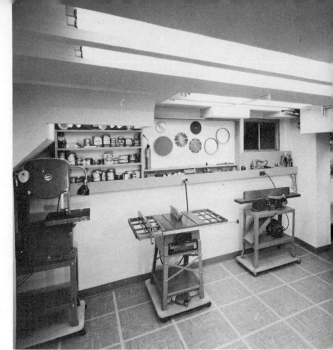

This shop is not large by the 'ideal' standards; it measures only 12' x 16', but it packs a lot of function. It houses all the basic stationary power tools (lathe and radial saw are out of view). All tools are on wheels for mobility. A sturdy workbench, ample tool and accessory storage, good illumination and plenty of power outlets render the shop a safe and efficient place to work.

Inexpensive plasterboard was installed over furring to convert an ordinary, seldom used basement into this cheerful, efficient workshop. The open joists overhead were also lined with board leaving bays for fluorescent lighting fixtures. Asphalt tiles on the floor are a worthwhile investment which make clean-up easy.

With a pair of saw horses and a few portable tools you can set up shop wherever you have space, even outdoors.

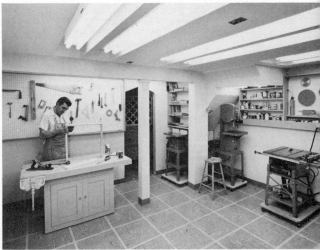

If you dare leave your car outdoors (they *are* weatherproof), the garage makes an excellent candidate for a workshop. Uninterrupted walls, ease of getting in and out with materials, and the possibility of ample storage on the overhead rafters, fresh air and daylight are the strong points. Also, during good weather shop work can be done outdoors. Heating the garage for winter is easily done with a gas space heater. The type that vents to the outside is very safe for use in a dusty shop atmosphere.

To suggest to you precisely what the size and shape your shop should be would be of no value. Your particular situation will decide that. Be strongly advised, though, to allot as much space as possible. A small, cozy shop may seem very appealing at first, but it can soon become sufficiently crowded to the point where it can cause frustrations. Consider the problems of working with a 4´ x 8´ plywood panel in, say, an 8´ x 12´ shop equipped with a workbench and several stationary power tools!

If you're pressed for workshop space, remember that your auto is quite mobile and weather resistant. With tools on wheels and portable work tables, your garage can serve a dual purpose.

A garage like this is nothing more than a very expensive warehouse for junk. With determination, elbow grease and some building materials you can convert wasted space like this into a fine workshop.

Once an eyesore, this appealing knotty pine workshop has been designed to take up minimal floor space along one wall. The cabinetry is dimensioned to allow sufficient space in the garage for two cars. A drop leaf work table hinged to the rear wall (below window) can be pressed into service when needed. (Western Wood Products Assn.)

An advantage of a garage workshop—during good weather you can easily move your activities outdoors to work in the fresh air.

If you have the choice, don't make your shop too small and cozy. Working on a typical 4 x 8-ft. plywood panel can crowd a small shop and be a constant cause of frustrations.

Installation of a space heater will enable you to work in a garage shop during severe cold weather. The gas heater below is designed to fit between wall studs for space economy. Vented to the outside and non exposed flame features are strong points of this type of heater.

For auxiliary heat in a small basement shop you may want to consider a portable or an in-wall electric heater. (Rockwell Mfg.)

Shop Planning

Plan your shop with care. Machines and free-standing workbenches can always be rearranged, but built-in cabinet workbenches and tool and lumber storage facilities will be permanent and not readily moved. For this reason it would be wise to do some pre-planning on paper.

Use graph paper with $\frac{1}{4}''$ squares and sketch to scale the floor and wall dimensions. Let 2 squares represent a foot ($\frac{1}{2}''$ scale). On this rough drawing indicate all physical features of the room: doors, windows, wall set-backs, electric outlets, pipes, furnace, and whatever.

Make templates, to the same scale of $\frac{1}{2}'' = 1'$, of all presently-owned or anticipated items of equipment and furniture. Cut one set of the top views and another set of the side views of the various items. The outline shapes of machines shown here are printed to $\frac{1}{2}''$ scale for your convenience. Simply trace them on thin cardboard and cut them out.

Lay the cutouts on your drawings, then arrange and rearrange them until you establish the most suitable layout. This graphic representation will help you decide where to locate built-ins and furniture, electric outlets, and lighting. It also will aid you to determine dimensions for the built-ins.

Unless your shop is of tremendous size, you'll find that very few power tools can be set in permanent locations if they are to be fully and properly utilized. Most power tools require access by the operator on two, three, and sometimes four sides. Similarly, clearance for the material is also required.

Make a scale drawing of your tentative shop area space to help you to determine the most suitable arrangement. A scale of $\frac{1}{2}''$ per foot produces an easy working size, not too confined.

These outlines of various stationary power tools are printed on a scale of $\frac{1}{2}$ inch to a foot. They represent the approximate floor space dimensions. You can use them to make templates for your shop layout planning.

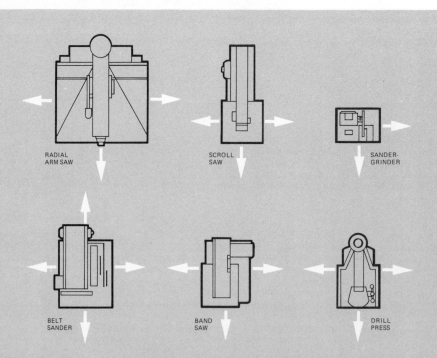

RADIAL ARM SAW

SCROLL SAW

SANDER-GRINDER

BELT SANDER

BAND SAW

DRILL PRESS

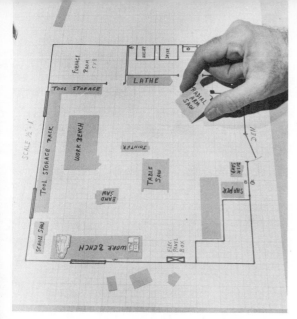

To make templates of the power tools simply trace on tracing paper the outlines out of the book, then retrace the drawings onto thin cardboard and cut them out. Arrange and rearrange the templates on your site plan to work out the bugs. It would be wise to consider future tool acquisitions to allow for growth.

Accessory casters are available for most power tool stands. They permit moving heavy machines with ease. (Sears Roebuck)

Power tools have differing access and working space requirements as indicated by the arrows. Actual distances are not given because they would vary according to the size of the workpiece. The advantage of rollable tools is obvious.

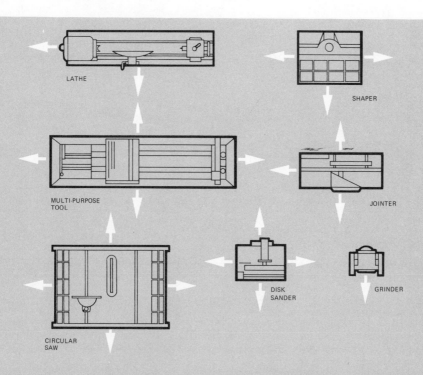

LATHE

SHAPER

MULTI-PURPOSE TOOL

JOINTER

CIRCULAR SAW

DISK SANDER

GRINDER

For small work the tools can be positioned in close proximity to each other, but large work pieces frequently will require movement of the tools to provide the necessary clearance. For this reason, consider equipping the heavier tools with plate or retractable casters. The latter are available as accessories with most pieces of equipment.

An added advantage of tools on wheels is that a relatively small shop can be more fully equipped, tools can be bunched in a group and each one rolled out as needed.

Power tools on wheels or casters enable you to work outdoors for pleasure, or more importantly, when handling oversize pieces.

This relatively small shop has most machines on wheels. They can be moved wherever the homeowner desires in the shop to best working locations with ease. (Sears Roebuck)

The Workbench

Many of your activities will take place at the workbench, so you'll want to have a good one. This means that it should be sturdy and equipped with a heavy-duty wood vise and preferably, a thick maple top. The length and width can vary considerably, but height should be about 32" for standing comfort.

There are many good benches available commercially, but costs can run quite high. Why not let one of your first practical woodworking projects be the construction of a workbench?

This homemade bench utilizes a ready-made hard maple top. Two dozen drawers provide ample storage for tools and hardware.

Plywood of ½-in. thickness is suitable for the four sides of the drawers. Hardboard panels set into dadoed grooves serve very well for the bottoms. Glue is used throughout.

View of the simple framing used to construct the 24 drawer bench. Note the use of the extra legs at the center for added rigidity.

BENCH TOPS

The construction of a basic workbench is not difficult, but the fabrication of a laminated hard maple bench top is. This is a job for the advanced woodworker or the professional. Maple bench tops can be purchased separately. If you plan to use a ready-made top, it would be advisable to acquire it, or at least its dimensions, before you begin construction of the base.

There are several alternates to the maple top. You can obtain a very sturdy top by laminating ordinary 2″ x 4″ construction lumber (which is a lot easier to handle than hard maple). You can use it as-is, but it will dent easily. Or, you can surface this softwood top with a piece of tempered hardboard for tough, lasting service.

Another possibility is to double or triple up some 3/4″ plywood and surface the top with tempered hardboard. To gain solidity, glue should be used between the layers of plywood.

Whether you buy or build the bench, it should have provision for storage below. Open

A good workbench must have a solid top and a sturdy wood vise. It should be heavy enough to stay in place when side pressures are applied. This bench features a solid maple top and storage cabinets below.

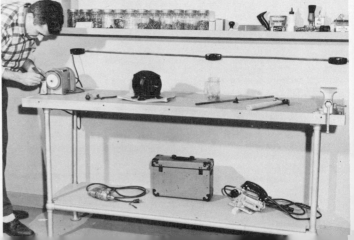

This novel light duty workbench is made with ordinary pipe, fittings and flanges with a top of plywood which is covered with hardboard.

shelving is fine for storing portable tools and various large items, but sliding drawers are great to hold the numerous miscellaneous small tools and hardware that are a part of every shop.

Where you locate the bench is a matter of personal preference, if you have the choice. It can be set up, as is most commonly done, against a wall or centrally placed for access from all sides. When locating against a wall, try to allow about 24" of clearance on both sides.

Regardless of how large your workbench or how many you may have, there will always be a need for a temporary auxiliary work surface. Keep a pair of saw horses and a plywood panel handy for use as an additional surface.

This easy to construct workbench is a good beginner's project. It's made of ordinary 2" x 4" construction lumber throughout. The tool rack can be added or omitted as desired.

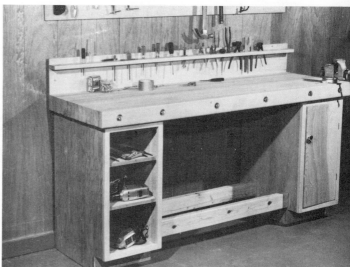

An alternate base for the workbench uses a pair of ³/₄" plywood cabinets in lieu of the legs. They give open or closed storage space.

Construction details for the 2" x 4" workbench.

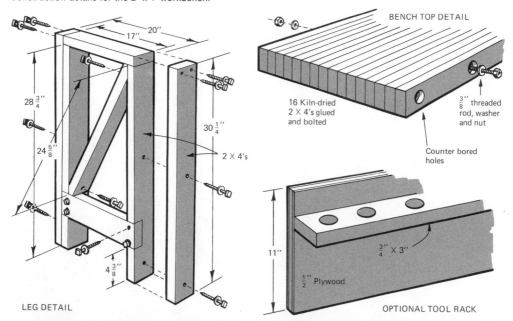

20''

17''

28 ³/₄''

24 ⁵/₈''

30 ¹/₄''

2 X 4's

4 ³/₈''

LEG DETAIL

BENCH TOP DETAIL

16 Kiln-dried
2 X 4's glued
and bolted

³/₈'' threaded
rod, washer
and nut

Counter bored
holes

11''

³/₄'' X 3''

¹/₂'' Plywood

OPTIONAL TOOL RACK

91

SHOP ACCESSORIES

These commercially available steel based work-benches have particleboard tops. They're especially useful as stands for power tools or can hold heavy objects. (Sears Roebuck)

Heavy duty retractable casters are available for use on heavy workbenches. A movable bench can frequently prove advantageous.

Ready made steel saw horse hardware permits quick assembly. Standard 2″ x 4″ lumber is merely inserted into an end and secured with nails. (Quality Steel Products)

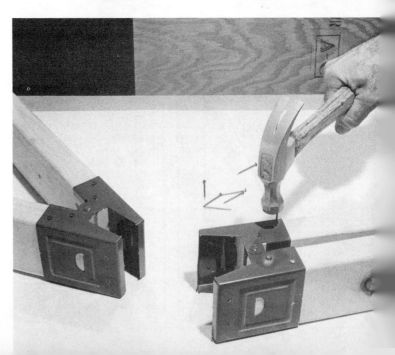

Tool Storage

Hand tool storage is most efficiently accomplished with perforated hardboard and accessory hooks. After you've established the final layout of your shop, you can proceed to install tool storage boards. The perforated hardboard panels are available in 4' x 4' and 4' x 8' sizes.

You can build the storage boards as separate cases with framing and install them as units or you can build them in place on the wall. In either case, a ³⁄₄" space must be provided between the perforated panel and the wall to allow clearance for the hooks. Ordinary 1" x 2" furring strip is used for a stand-off base. If you have open stud walls, you need not be concerned about clearance, of course.

Regular, perforated panels are a deep brown color, quite lacking in eye appeal. You will have to paint them to brighten up the scene. If you decide to paint, you'll get better results with a roller than a brush. In either case, do not overload with paint so as not to plug up the hook holes. Several light coats are better than one heavy application.

For a truly luxurious tool panel you may want to use colored, perforated board. These panels have a baked-on plastic finish available in several pastel shades or woodgrains. Dust won't cling to the surface as readily as it will to a painted version.

Perforated hardboard has proven to be one of the most practical systems for hanging tools. This shop may never want for a place to hang a tool. Such a saturation treatment has an interesting decorative effect as well. (Masonite Corp.)

This design may be of special interest to you if wall surface space is limited. The swing-out cabinet doors permit storage on three surfaces. (Masonite Corp.)

CONSTRUCTION OF A TYPICAL TOOL STORAGE BOARD

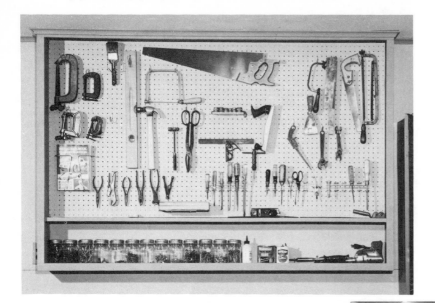

Box-like frame is pre assembled then nailed to wall. The perforated board is nailed to the perimeter and vertical cleats, one nail every 8 inches. At least ³/₄-inch of space is needed behind perforated board for tool hooks.

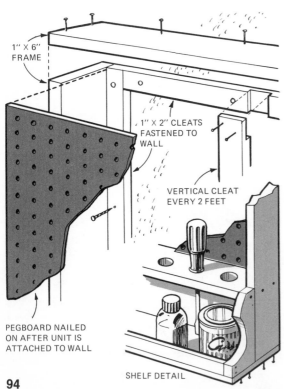

1" X 6" FRAME

1" X 2" CLEATS FASTENED TO WALL

VERTICAL CLEAT EVERY 2 FEET

PEGBOARD NAILED ON AFTER UNIT IS ATTACHED TO WALL

SHELF DETAIL

LUMBER STORAGE

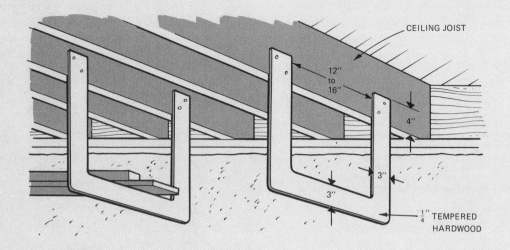

CEILING JOIST

12" to 16"

4"

3"

3"

¼" TEMPERED HARDWOOD

U shaped hardboard brackets nailed to the open framing of garage or basement workshop ceilings can provide handy storage for lumber.

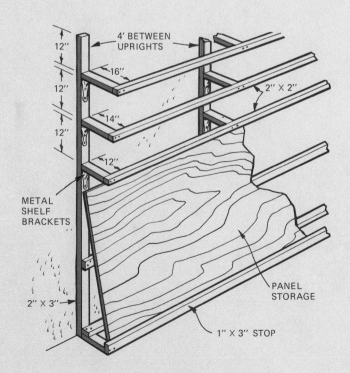

12"

4' BETWEEN UPRIGHTS

16"

12"

2" X 2"

14"

12"

12"

METAL SHELF BRACKETS

2" X 3"

PANEL STORAGE

1" X 3" STOP

This combination rack stores large panels and boards, provides easy access to them as well.

CONSTRUCTION OF HARDWARE FILE CABINET

Finding the right size nut, bolt, nail or screw and the countless other hardware items used in a home shop is easy if you build this large capacity cabinet. It features 13 slide out trays; 10 of which accommodate two dozen inexpensive 9-oz. plastic party cups. This provides a total of 240 small parts storage units. The three lower slides are shallow drawers used to store odd size miscellaneous items.

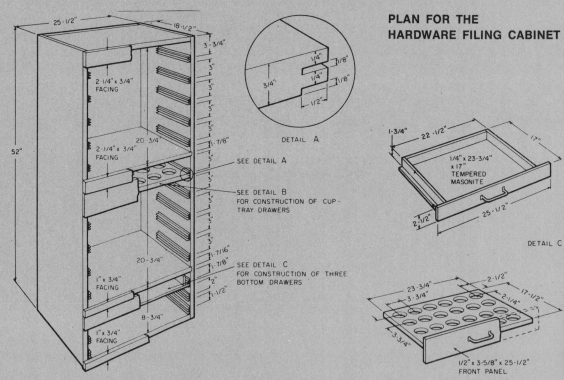

PLAN FOR THE HARDWARE FILING CABINET

25-1/2"
18-1/2"
3-3/4"
3"
3"
2-1/4" x 3/4" FACING
3"
3"
20-3/4"
2-1/4" x 3/4" FACING
1-7/8"
SEE DETAIL A
SEE DETAIL B FOR CONSTRUCTION OF CUP-TRAY DRAWERS
52"
1-7/16"
1-7/8"
20-3/4"
SEE DETAIL C FOR CONSTRUCTION OF THREE BOTTOM DRAWERS
1" x 3/4" FACING
2"
1-1/2"
8-3/4"
1" x 3/4" FACING

1/4"
1/8"
1/4"
1/8"
3/4"
1/2"

DETAIL A

1-3/4"
22-1/2"
17"
1/4" x 23-3/4" x 17" TEMPERED MASONITE
2-1/2"
25-1/2"

DETAIL C

23-3/4"
3-3/4"
2-1/2"
17-1/2"
2-1/4"
3-3/4"
1/2" x 3-5/8" x 25-1/2" FRONT PANEL

The trays ride on sections of aluminum sliding door track. Drill holes in the track flanges and secure with small screws.

The cabinet can be assembled after the tracks have been installed. Use ³/₄" plywood, butt joined, nailed and glued.

Use an adjustable circle cutter to bore the holes for the cups. Clamp the board to the table and keep the hands at a safe distance from the cutter.

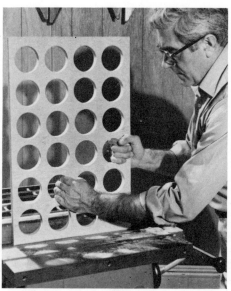

Make two passes on the table saw to groove the edges of the trays so that they conform to the shape of the aluminum track cross section.

Trays should fit snug with minimal side play. Lubricate the edges with silicone spray to make them slide easily.

Three inch diameter holes are just right to hold the plastic cups. Each tray holds 24 cups.

ighting and Power

For safety and efficiency in your work, your shop must be properly illuminated. This is one area where you definitely should not skimp; it's much too easy to make mistakes or to get hurt working around power tools under poor lighting conditions.

Ideally, the installation of at least six double or twelve single 8' fluorescent light fixtures in a shop of average size (16' x 20') is suggested. Strategically spaced throughout the shop ceiling, such a battery of lamps will provide bright, evenly distributed shadowless lighting over the entire work area. Discard any fears that such illumination might be "too bright" for comfort. At table height, with lamps on an 8' ceiling, the brightness would be less than a quarter that of natural daylight on an overcast day!

If your preference lies toward incandescent lighting, then one 150 watt lamp over each machine and workbench should be a minimum consideration. In either case, each light fixture should have its own switch to save electricity. Obviously it won't be necessary to have all lamps operating at all times.

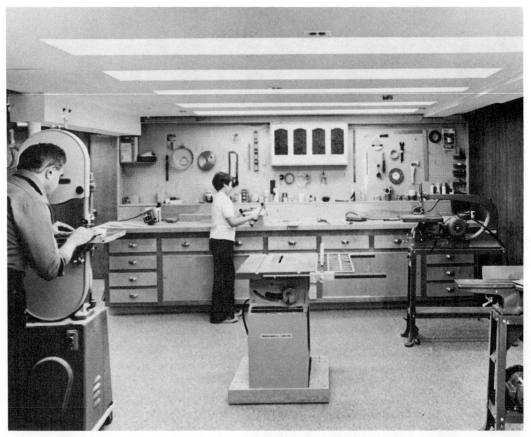

For safety and efficiency the workshop must be well illuminated. A series of fluorescent fixtures, properly spaced, will provide even illumination throughout the work area. The lighting in this shop is practically shadowless and non-tiring. The fixtures are recessed between the joists. The lamp fixtures should ideally be located approximately four feet from each other. The lamps indicated are double tube 8-ft. units.

iring

Adequate wiring for your shop will necessitate a minimum of two separate circuits, each with a capacity of 20 amps. One line is to feed the lights, the other to supply current for the power tools. All electrical outlets in the shop should be of the standard grounded-type and all circuits properly grounded, of course.

Provide a sufficient number of outlets throughout the entire shop to permit plugging in each tool without the need for hazardous extension cords strewn about. If young children have access to the shop, it would be advisable to install a master power cut-off switch so that tools can be rendered inoperative when you are absent from the shop.

If you have the know-how and your local electrical code permits, you can do your own wiring. Otherwise, hire an electrician. Aside from the possibility of personal injury due to faulty wiring, insurance claims for fire damage so caused would be difficult to collect.

Take your time in planning and building your shop. Make it plain or fancy, as you like, but do it right. With a good shop you'll do better work, faster, and with less effort.

WORKSHOP CLEANUP TIPS

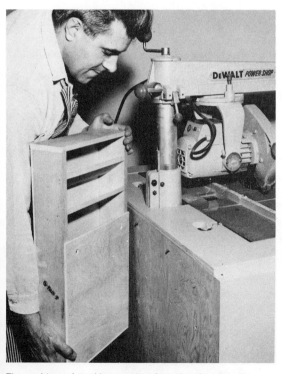

Metal filings tracked on the shoes from the shop floor to the house are not merely messy but also dangerous to children and pets. You can solve the problem by inserting a removable filing catcher tray like this one on the edge of your workbench.

The problem of tracking sawdust from the shop into the house can be minimized if you install a sawdust collector on your radial arm saw. A simple box like this with two angled deflectors which line up with the rear of the saw blade will do the trick. The box hangs on a pair of round head screws which project from the back of the saw cabinet. Note that the deflectors stop short about one inch from the back panel to allow dust to drop down.

15 Tools for your Shop

Tools are required in order to transform the raw material of wood into a finished product. As your plans for setting up shop begin to materialize you'll be confronted with making decisions concerning which tools to buy (unless you already have them). The degree of success you achieve in woodworking will depend upon the tools at your disposal as well as the skills you develop in using them.

THOUGHTS ABOUT SELECTION

There is an infinite variety of tools available on the market, so you'll have a wide range to choose from. While some of the hand tools will always be essential for shopwork, certain ones have been relegated to the sidelines because they just cannot compete with their power tool counterparts.

By all means you should own and endeavour to become proficient in the use of hand tools inasmuch as there will always be situations when they must be relied upon. But don't be old fashioned—get with power tools as quickly as you can, especially the portables, for a start. Power tools will enable you to do good work, more of it, and with minimal effort. You certainly won't need a completely equipped shop in order to turn out good work, but it stands to reason: the more tools you own, the greater will be your capabilities and versatility.

A well-rounded tool collection will include hand tools, portables, and stationary machines. There are similarities as well as differences between portable and stationary tools.

Hand tools may never become obsolete but they can't compete with their power driven counterparts. The saw and drill are probably the most widely used of the portables by amateur and professional alike.

There are many situations where an "old-fashioned" hand tool will serve best. The spokeshave is an ideal tool to use for smoothing out curve sawed edges.

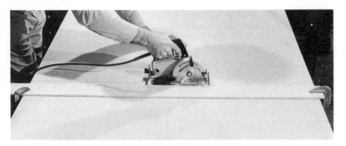

Paradoxically, large oversize panels are easily cut down to manageable working size with a small portable circular saw while a large stationary table saw proves its worth for further precision cutting of smaller parts. The table saw will, of course, handle large work too.

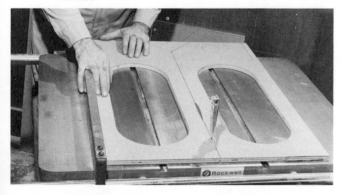

Another typical example of portable/stationary power tool teamwork: component parts of a project are surfaced on a stationary belt sander for quick, accurate results. Further sanding to shape the corners of this large furniture piece after assembly dictates that a portable sander be brought *to* the work.

Stationary tools are more precise and powerful than portables, but they necessitate taking the work to the tool. Portables, on the other hand, are taken to the work. Many situations arise where two tools of any kind may have to be utilized for a project. For instance, you may frequently find it more convenient or perhaps necessary to use a portable saw to cut a large plywood panel down to manageable size before you can take it to a table saw for further cutting. Or you may use a stationary sander to shape individual components for a large project. After the piece is assembled, it undoubtedly will require a final overall sanding. For this you'll want a portable sander. Hand tools, too, will often be required and called upon to serve a supporting role.

WHICH TOOLS FIRST?

The nature of your interests in woodworking, the size of your workplace, and the amount of money you can afford to spend are factors that will influence the kind and quantity of tools you acquire.

Lack of adequate work space and storage facilities may dictate a tool collection comprised of some basic hand tools and a few portable electrics. For example: a saw, hammer, plane, drill, combination square, steel tape measure, and several screwdrivers. Also, a nail set, awl, multi-bladed Surform tool, several wood chisels, a portable woodworking vise, and a few clamps would do for hand tools. Add to this a versatile portable electric drill with its numerous accessories, a saber saw, and a portable circular saw and you will have a compact kit capable of handling many types of projects.

Shortage of ready cash will hopefully impose only temporary restrictions, in which case you'll want to give thought to priorities: which tools first? The basic hand tools listed above must be considered a minimal kit with which to start. As your funds permit, you can acquire the basic portables—drill, saber and circular saws, then possibly expand on them with a sander and router to complete the set. By installments you can gradually add to your hand tool collection. After that you may want to get some stationary tools.

A radial arm saw is highly recommended as a "starter" machine. Besides its capability to make all sorts of unusual cuts, this saw can serve as a multi-purpose tool. Various accessories and cutters attached to the motor shaft enable this versatile tool to perform many functions.

Another tool worthy of consideration on the basis of relative economy of cost, as well as space requirement, is the multi-purpose tool. This is a combination of several basic machines built into one unit. Quick changes convert it into a table saw, sander, drill, and lathe. Separate tools, such as a jig and band saw, can also be attached to the single motor to further increase the machine's capabilities.

As your activities broaden and your finances permit, you may want to go all out towards a complete line of individual stationary tools. Acquisition of a table saw, jointer, drill press, band saw, jig saw, sander, shaper, and lathe will put you in the big leagues.

The area of major interest to you will, of course, have much to do with your choice of tools. An occasional handyman task around the house certainly won't warrant an arsenal bristling with tools. Nor will you need much more than perhaps a table saw in the way of stationary tools if your tastes lean towards the smaller type of projects.

Major home improvements, remodeling work, built-ins, and the like will require a well-rounded collection of hand tools and portables, such as a drill, saws, sander, possibly a router, a table saw, and a jointer. A serious interest in furniture production and cabinetmaking definitely suggests as complete a set up of hand tools, portable, and stationary power tools as space and money will permit.

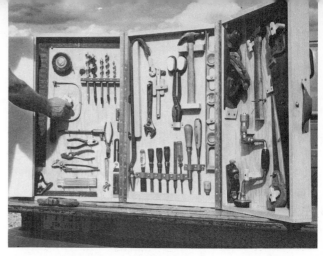

The owner of this tool kit, a skilled professional carpenter of the old school, has built many fine houses with only these basic hand tools. With power tools you too can turn out good work probably equal to his, without the prerequisite of many years of experience. (American Plywood Assn.)

The radial arm saw is a tool of many uses. If space and finances are limited, this is the stationary tool to consider as a first acquisition. (Black & Decker)

This is a small, table-top version of the multi purpose tool. The single centrally located motor supplies power to the various functions. A larger floor mounted type has greater capacity, more power and additional operating units.

16 Buying Tools

Cheap tools, like other cheap items, are a snare and a delusion. Once in a while a fine piece of work may be turned out by a craftsman using inferior tools, but it is a rare occurrence and proves only that an unusual craftsman with remarkable talent is at work.

Do not be caught in the snare. Start off right by working with good tools. Buy only tools of high quality. Better tools may cost a bit more than those of inferior quality, but it will prove decidedly more economical to invest the small difference in price. Not only will you turn out better work, but good tools wear well and with proper care can last a lifetime.

TOOL QUALITY

You can't determine the temper in a piece of steel merely by looking at it. Nor can you always judge the apparent overall quality of a tool by visual inspection. The results of good or poor manufacture can sometimes be seen or felt, sometimes not. Thus your best assurance for quality is to buy the product of reputable manufacturers. A reliable tool or hardware dealer will tell you which are the quality brands. When in doubt, however, examine the finish, design, construction and safety, all of which may influence your choice.

Sometimes you can't "see" quality so you must depend on the reputation of the product or the integrity of the dealer. Both of these saw blades are of similar design but not of similar quality. Which is better?

Cheap is expensive, not only in money but also in time. The drill bit on the left proved to be no bargain at any price. Note how the lip has worn down and how the cutting edge has actually melted into a rough burr. Both of these bits have been used for an equal length of time. Dull cutting tools can bind in the work causing motor overheating or even physical injury.

FINISH

When selecting a tool, begin by observing the finish. A nicely machined, clean-cut surface usually indicates care and good workmanship have gone into its manufacture. If a tool has a handle, this too should be well-finished, properly fitted, and shaped for a comfortable grip. Check castings in particular. Ill-formed, rough castings more often than not are indicative of poor workmanship throughout.

The finish of a tool is usually a good indicator of its quality. Good workmanship is generally not practiced on inferior tools. There are probably as many poor tools on the market as there are good ones. Compare the varied offerings: you'll soon learn how to spot the differences. Be especially careful of the 88 cent specials. (Stanley Tools)

DESIGN

Be observant of basic design features, especially concerning power tools. Switches, controls and adjustments should be conveniently located for easy access. Look for built-in adjustable stops at most commonly used operating positions to allow for quick and accurate tool set up. Clear visibility of the cutting edge(s) is a most important factor. Provision to shield dust and chips from the motor and moving parts is another feature of good design.

Check out the location of the on/off switch of power tools. The power switch on portables should be within easy reach of the operating hand so that it may be manipulated without changing the grip. The thumb controlled switch in the handle of this saber saw reflects good design.

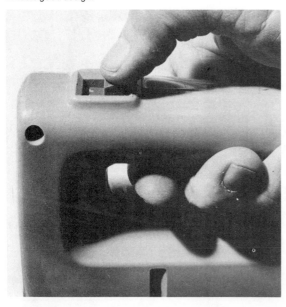

The conveniently located up-front controls on this saw facilitate and assure fast, simple operation. The large crank-wheels provide good leverage for easy turning and fine adjustments.

CONSTRUCTION

Check carefully the table surfaces of stationary power tools. Accuracy and good performance depend upon the precision with which they are ground. The eye can spot defects by sighting close to and across the surface.

Surprising as it may be to you, warping is not peculiar only to wood; cast iron can also warp. A quality machine table will be massive and adequately ribbed on the underside to prevent warping. Solid under-table construction is also important. Heavy trunnions, frames, and supports result in greater stability throughout. Lubricated-for-life bearings and built-in provisions for adjustment and alignment of moving parts that allow maintaining *like-new* performance are additional features worthy of consideration.

Look for sturdy bevel supports and an easy to read graduated angle scale on portable circular saws (left). Set the blade for a bevel cut and press down on the handle. There should be no "give" or springiness between the saw housing and the base in a properly designed tool. Clear visibility of the cutting edge (right) is of utmost importance, not only for accuracy in working, but for safety as well.

Built-in adjustable stops at most-used operating positions allow for quick, accurate tool set up. This is an important and desirable feature to look for.

Precision ground surfaces of machines are essential for accurate performance. The fineness of the machining of the work surfaces on this planer is evident. Coarse grinder marks and pitted surfaces would cause concern.

 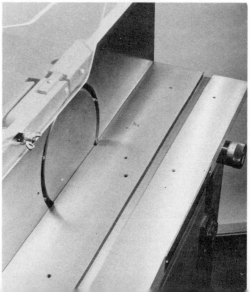

Solid under-table construction with heavy trunnions, frames and supports assure greater stability throughout. Check the specs for lubricated-for-life bearings which mean longer, trouble-free operation. *(Rockwell Mfg. Co)*

A high quality power tool table should be as impressive on the bottom side as it is top side. Massive cast iron tables should be amply ribbed to prevent warping. Note the fine quality of this casting which is indicative of good workmanship and design.

Check for built-in provisions for adjustment and alignment of all moving parts to permit maintaining like-new performance.

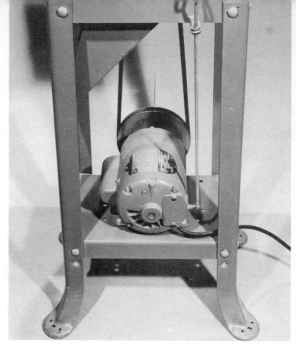

The moving parts and motor of this shaper are well shielded against dust and wood chips. This chunky machine has been in use for 20 years, will probably last a lifetime.

Sturdy machine stands are all-important. Don't settle for a lightweight sheet metal one if a table of heavy gage construction is available. Vibrations in a flimsy stand can cause it to creep along the floor.

SAFETY

Many of the portable power tools available to you are of the double-insulated, shock-proof type. Such a tool is one in which there are two independent insulating systems that separate all electrical components from the housing and handle, thus protecting against electrical shock hazards.

If the tool that interests you is of the non-insulated type, consider it only if it is equipped with a *three-wire* conductor and a three-blade grounding-type plug. This will protect against electrical shock, provided that your wiring circuits are properly grounded, of course. The same applies to all stationary tools; three-wire conductors and grounded plugs are of utmost importance.

There is often a choice of obtaining stationary power tools equipped with burn-out-protected motors. Such a motor automatically shuts off when it is subjected to an overload, thereby preventing a costly and possibly dangerous burn-out.

In addition, check for safety guards, shields, and other protective devices for maximum operating safety.

The housing as well as certain internal components of various portable power tools are constructed of high impact non-conductive plastic to protect against electrical shock.

Burn-out protected motors automatically shut off when they're overloaded. The push of a reset button after a short wait restarts the motor. This feature is sometimes optional.

This circular-saw blade guard lets you see the line of cut and blade without lifting the guard. It also features a built-in splitter and anti-kickback fingers.

17 Hand Tools

The number of hand tools available for woodworking runs well into the hundreds. One major manufacturer's catalogue lists 1500 tools! But take heart; your tool kit needn't bulge with all of them.

The reason for the thick tool catalogues is that there are many tools of a kind available in a multiplicity of sizes and shapes. Some are designed to serve specific purposes, while others are merely duplicates which vary sometimes only slightly in terms of size and weight.

Shown here are those tools that would comprise a reasonably complete set for the average shop. They are classified according to their functions: layout and measuring, cutting, boring, fastening and holding.

MEASURING AND LAYOUT TOOLS

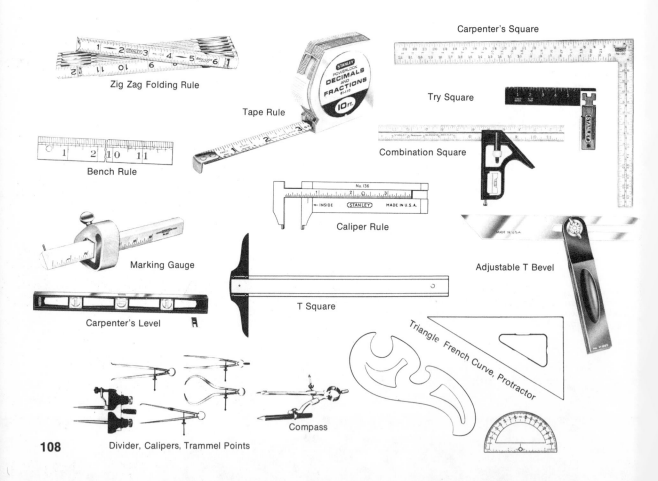

Zig Zag Folding Rule

Tape Rule

Carpenter's Square

Try Square

Combination Square

Bench Rule

Caliper Rule

Marking Gauge

Adjustable T Bevel

Carpenter's Level

T Square

Triangle, French Curve, Protractor

Compass

Divider, Calipers, Trammel Points

CUTTING TOOLS

Cross Cut Saw

Rip Saw

Back Saw

Dovetail Saw

Miter Box

Hack Saw

Mini Hack Saw

Keyhole Saw

Keyhole Saw (above), Coping Saw

Smooth Plane

Compass Saw

Spokeshave

Wood Chisel, all steel

Block Plane

Wood Chisel, plastic handle

Wood Chisel, one piece blade and shank

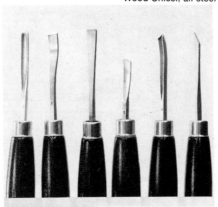
Carving Chisels

Rabbet Plane

109

VARIOUS SHAPING TOOLS

SURFORM TOOLS

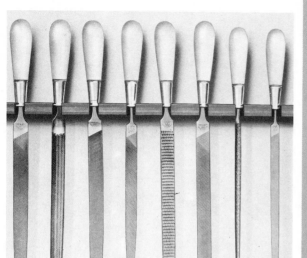

Files and Rasps

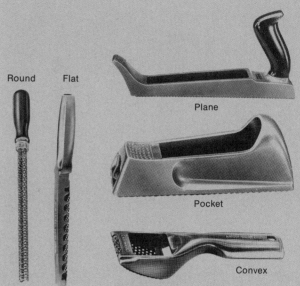

Round   Flat

Plane

Pocket

Convex

Combination Wood Rasp

Heavy Duty Utility Knife

Slim Blade Knife

HOLE BORING TOOLS

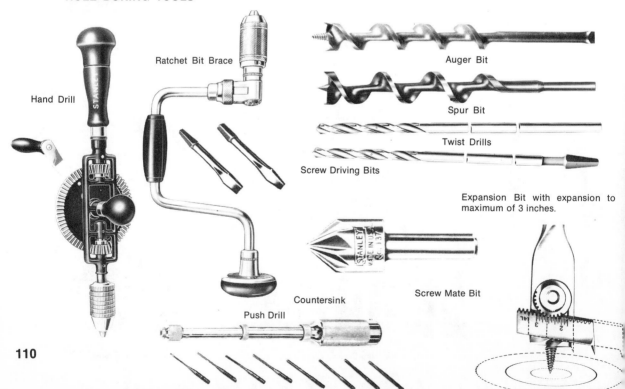

Hand Drill

Ratchet Bit Brace

Auger Bit

Spur Bit

Twist Drills

Screw Driving Bits

Expansion Bit with expansion to maximum of 3 inches.

Countersink

Screw Mate Bit

Push Drill

FASTENING TOOLS

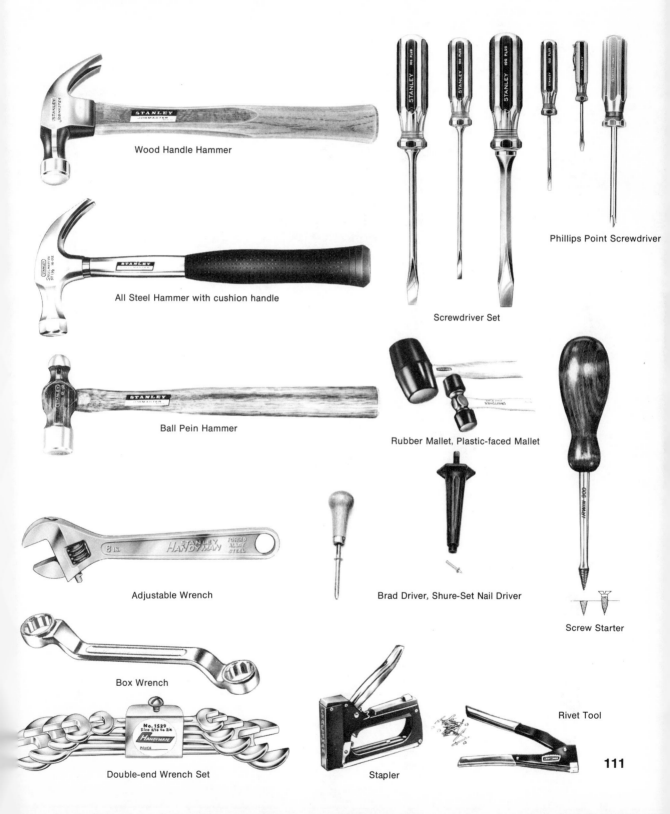

Wood Handle Hammer

Phillips Point Screwdriver

All Steel Hammer with cushion handle

Screwdriver Set

Ball Pein Hammer

Rubber Mallet, Plastic-faced Mallet

Adjustable Wrench

Brad Driver, Shure-Set Nail Driver

Screw Starter

Box Wrench

Rivet Tool

Double-end Wrench Set

Stapler

111

HOLDING TOOLS

Various Woodworking Clamps (Adjustable Clamp Co.)

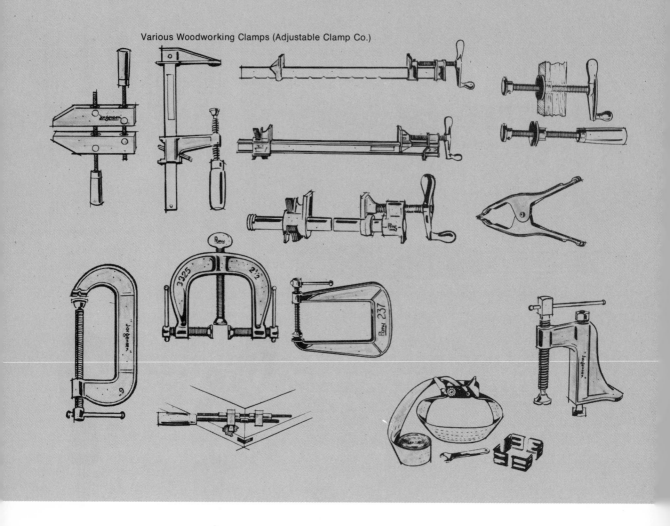

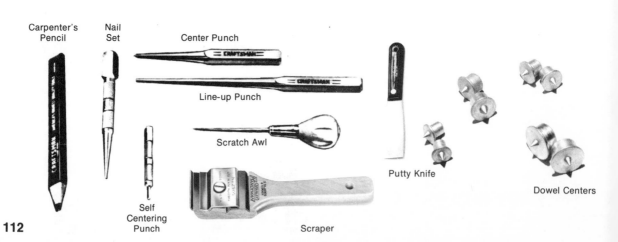

Carpenter's Pencil

Nail Set

Center Punch

Line-up Punch

Scratch Awl

Self Centering Punch

Scraper

Putty Knife

Dowel Centers

VISES

PLIERS

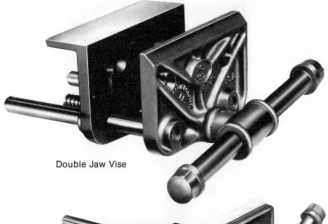

Double Jaw Vise

Slip Joint Pliers

Single Jaw Vise

Adjustable Pump Pliers

End Cutting Nipper

Needle Nose

Metal Vise with adjustable swivel base (Littlestown Hardware & Foundry Co.)

Bent Needle Nose

Diagonal Cutter

Vise Grip Plier-Wrench

Adjustable Clamp-on Vise with jaws for top and side use

Saber Saws

Sometimes called a jig or bayonet saw, this tool could very well be called the "jack-of-all-trades" saw. Designed primarily to cut irregular shapes, the saber saw can be effectively utilized to perform the duties of any of the others in the family of saws—handsaw, keyhole, coping, hack saw, band, jig, and circular saw.

Though it excels for making intricate and decorative curved cuts, this little bundle of energy can be used to do heavy-duty cutting with no strain whatsoever. Equipped with a coarse-tooth blade, the average saber saw can cut through 2½" thick lumber in reasonably quick time.

The blade action of the saw is basically up and down with upward facing teeth cutting the material on the up stroke. On some saws this action is straight up and down, so that the teeth are in contact with the work during both the up and down

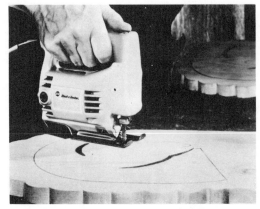

The saber saw excels for cutting irregular shapes in wood, plastic or composition. Most saws will cut through wood up to 2½" thick. (Black & Decker)

A special base insert which hugs the blade of this saw helps to prevent splintering of plywood paneling and plastic laminates. (Rockwell)

This saw features variable speed which is selected by the turning of a dial. Others have dual-speed triggers for high and low speeds, some have one speed. (Stanley)

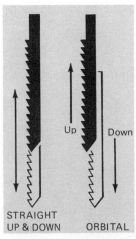

STRAIGHT UP & DOWN   ORBITAL

Diagram shows difference in blade travel between straight and orbital motion saws.

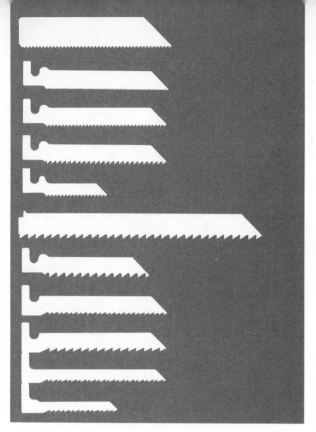

Profiles of some of the numerous saber saw blades used for cutting different materials. They range from a coarse 6 teeth per inch for fast cutting of wood to 32 teeth for cutting metal.

A hollow ground blade such as this one has teeth with no set (they don't protrude to the sides), makes a very smooth cut. This blade won't bind in the wood because it is ground with a taper toward its back which provides the necessary clearance.

strokes. This causes blade drag, overheating, and premature wearing of the teeth.

The better saws feature an orbital blade motion whereby the teeth of the blade make contact with the work only on the cutting or upward stroke and back away from it on the return stroke. This reduces heat and blade-wearing friction, while providing faster cutting and longer blade life.

The speed-of-cutting capability of the saw is dependent on strokes per minute (spm). This varies among saws, ranging from 2500 to 4500 spm. Obviously, the greater the number of strokes, the faster the cut. For average cutting tasks in wood of moderate density, speed of cut is a desirable factor. But a blade moving too rapidly through a thick plank, hardwood, or metal will soon become overheated and lose its temper. In the interest of blade longevity, saber saws are made with several modes of speed selection control in addition to the standard single speed models.

Some saws have dual speeds: high and low, while others offer a choice of high, medium, and low speed selection. The third and probably most popular type is the one with variable speed control of-

The saber saw is useful in home remodeling projects. Here it is used to make an internal cut in wall paneling.

fering a choice of speeds from zero start to maximum spm. This is usually accomplished with a sliding switch that is simply stopped when the desired speed is reached.

Many blades are available for use with the saber saw. They vary in type depending upon the kind of material to be cut and the degree of smoothness desired. For fast cutting of wood, a coarse six-pointed blade with "set" teeth is used. This leaves a somewhat rough edge. To obtain a cut that produces a smooth-finished cut, a slower cutting, hollow ground blade is available. Narrow blades of ¼" width and ten teeth per inch are used for doing scroll work.

Among the numerous types of blades (there are over 20) there is certainly one that will handle any job at hand, be it wood, plastic, metal, mineral, or composition material. Tungsten carbide blades are available for cutting tiles, ceramics and other hard materials.

The versatile saber saw can be used for cross-cutting, ripping, plunge cutting, rafter notching, and many other chores, in addition to its typical use in cutting irregular shapes. Many models have adjustable tilting bases that enable them to be used for cutting bevels and compound angles. This is a desirable feature.

Many woodworkers are not aware of the potential of the saber saw for doing highly precise cutting. It definitely can be done with the aid of simple jigs clamped on straight edges, and the selection of the proper blade. More on this later.

A saber saw makes easy work of cutting through thick boards. This one's making a compound cut; a miter and bevel angle at the same time. It is wise to use a clamped-on straightedge guide when making a cut like this.

Equipped with the proper blade, a saber saw can tackle this otherwise laborious task with ease and speed. The material is heavy gauge sheet metal.

A curved bevel cut, precision ripping and heavy duty metal cutting illustrate the capabilities of this handy tool. A fine tooth blade and low speed are the essentials for cutting ferrous metals.

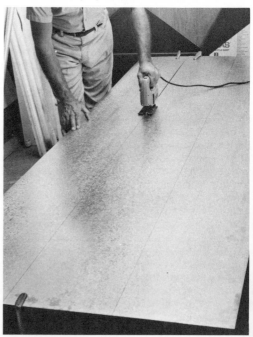

Portable Circular Saws

This saw can be used to do varied cutting jobs, such as building construction, cabinetry, paneling and others, with ease, speed, and accuracy.

Often called a cut-off saw, this tool can do many things that a table or radial arm saw can do. In some situations it is more versatile. But don't get it wrong; the radial arm and table saw are here to stay because they have their own important advantages. The major advantage of the cut-off saw over the stationary saws is its portability—an important factor when the work is being done outdoors, say, on a roof, from a ladder, or in a room other than the shop. In addition, it can be used for certain cutting tasks that would be extremely difficult and cumbersome with stationary saws.

Consider crosscutting through the center of a 4' x 8' plywood panel, which is a common requirement. A big capacity, professional-sized radial arm saw will just about cut through 24" in one pass. To complete the cut requires flipping the panel over, realigning it, and hoping the second cut from the opposite side meets the first one.

The ordinary bench saw has insufficient table area to support a large 4' x 8' panel during and after the cut-off, so it's usually necessary to round up some extra hands for the operation (after a method of guiding the panel has been figured out, since the miter gauge or rip fence are unusable with oversize work pieces).

The portable power saw can be used for many types of cutting, especially on large panels.

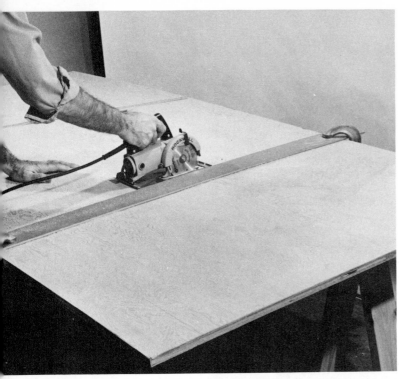

Large plywood panels are difficult to handle on stationary saws but easy to cut with a portable. For straight cuts a clamped-on straightedge guide is essential to saw in a straight line.

Guided repetitive cuts with an ordinary saw blade can be used to make accurate dadoes.

The depth of cut adjustment is made by loosening a knob which allows the saw housing to be raised or lowered in relation to its base. (Black & Decker)

A medium-sized 6½″ saw is more than adequate for most jobs. Note how the blade projects below the 2 x 4 stock which indicates it can handle even thicker material.

But such a cut is not difficult with the portable saw. To cut a truly straight line, however, it is necessary to set up a guide for the saw. With the panel set on a pair of saw horses and a straight-edged board clamped on as a guide, the cut is made quick and easy. In addition to straight cut-off sawing, the portable can be used to make dadoes, rabbets, and several other simple joints. Again, however, for intricate precision joints the stationary saws do excel.

The portable can be used to make pocket cuts in wall paneling projects where an opening for a door or window is needed inside a whole panel. Beveled miter cuts (compound angles) are easy even on large 4′ x 8′ panels. This job would constitute an engineering feat with a stationary saw, but requires only a bevel angle adjustment and a guide board clamped to the work at the desired angle to accomplish the cut with the portable.

All power saws are basically similar in design, consisting of a motor housing which extends over and around the upper part of the blade to protect the operator. A lower blade guard is retracted by the pushing action as the stock is being cut, so that for safety during operation only a small portion of the blade is exposed.

Two adjustments are possible to control the depth and angle of cut. Depth of cut can be varied according to the thickness of the material being cut. This is accomplished by raising or lowering the saw which pivots near the front end of the base. Angle cuts can be made from 0 to 45 degrees by loosening the bevel-adjusting wing nut and tilting the base to the desired angle indicated on a quadrant.

Cross and rip cuts can be made with the combination blade which is generally supplied with the saw. For rough work these cuts may be made freehand and sighted by eye on a pencil line. A large variety of blades are available for the saw, including planer or miter blades for smooth finish cuts, plywood blades, cross cut, rip, and flooring blades. Also available are a variety of cut-off wheels for cutting metals or masonry. (Various blades are described in Chapter 19.)

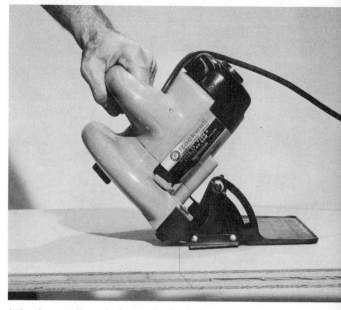

A thumbscrew allows the base to be tilted to any angle between 0 and 45 degrees for cutting a bevel.

Free-hand use of the saw makes jobs go fast. Although this saw is large, it isn't heavy because the housing is made of lightweight high-impact plastic. (Rockwell)

Many saws have exclusive features. This one has an easy to reach handle on the retractable blade guard. It is handy for shifting the guard out of the way when making pocket cuts. (Black & Decker)

Blades are similar to those for circular and radial arm saws. Blades at top are: combination, miter and hollow ground plywood. Cut-off wheel for sawing through masonry and a hardtooth blade are below. The latter can slash through an occasional nail. (See blade descriptions later.)

Power saws are available in light and heavy duty models in sizes ranging from 4″ to 10¼″. The dimension refers to blade diameter, the factor that determines the maximum thickness of stock that can be cut. Usually, a 5½″ saw will cut through 2″ dressed lumber; the 10¼″ will cut through 3⅞″. As for power, this will vary among models and brands. Usually the range is between ¾ and 2 horsepower. The smaller saws run around 1 hp, while the larger tools, sometimes referred to as builder's saws, deliver about 2 hp. The average home craftsman need consider nothing larger than an 8¼″ saw; the 10¼″ is a monster used by professionals in heavy construction work. For general use an easily handled and controlled 6½″ or 7½″ saw will prove satisfactory.

Without doubt, the portable circular saw is an indispensable time- and labor-saving tool which has a place in any shop.

A tough job made easy: cutting slabs with a cut-off wheel.

Odd angled cuts are readily made with the portable saw. It's best to use a guide with this tool.

The only practical way to cut configurated fiberglass panels is with the portable circular saw. Acrylic plastic is also easily cut using a plywood blade.

This homemade table of 2 x 4's and ¾" plywood converts an 8¼" saw into a bench saw. Note the simple but positive rip fence which is secured with C clamps. The miter guide also is homemade. It rides in a groove cut in the top.

Saw is left intact and attaches to bottom of table with four screws through the base. It can be quickly removed for portable use. Here ¾-inch plywood top is marked to take saw.

Saw is plugged into a power cord which has a switch. A block of wood wedged into the pistol grip keeps the trigger switch in the "on" position. In use the power is turned on and off at the remote switch.

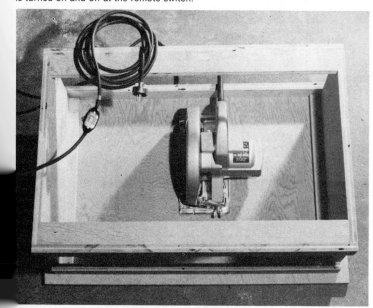

Some manufacturers make auxiliary tables which can be used to convert a portable saw into a stationary tool. The saw mounts up side-down from the bottom. (Skil)

121

Portable Drills

One of the most frequently used tools in the workshop or around the home is the portable electric drill. Due to its low cost and efficiency, this tool has all but made obsolete the manual drills. It does everything the old-fashioned brace-and-bit or eggbeater type could do, but better and faster.

With various attachments the portable drill can be used for sanding, buffing, grinding, and driving screws. With the insertion of a rotary rasp or cylindrical forming tool, the drill can also be used to do contour shaping.

Drills vary in size and are described according to the capacity of the chuck—the maximum diameter of the bit shank or accessory that it will accept. Three sizes are available: $1/4''$, $3/8''$, and $1/2''$. As a rule, there is a direct relationship between size, speed, and power. The $1/4''$ drill rates higher than the $1/2''$ in rpm, but the latter takes the lead when it comes to power. This is the result of down-gearing, whereby speed is sacrificed for increased power. The in-between $3/8''$ drill is the compromiser; it typically is more powerful than the $1/4''$ drill and is proportionately faster than the $1/2''$, and thus is the most widely used.

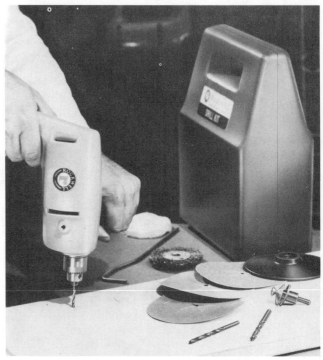

The drill is one of the most frequently used portable tools because of its versatility of function. (Rockwell)

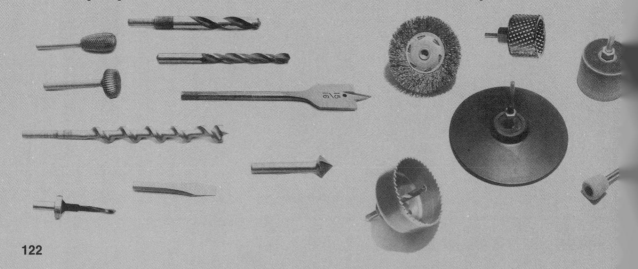

Some of the varied bits which can be used with the drill: drill bits, countersink, rotary files and rasps, screw driving bit, and screw-mate combination bit. Additional drill accessories include wire brush, sanding drum and disc, hole saw and grinding stone. Drum Surform tool can be used in electric drill for contour, circular, or straight cuts.

A set of ¼" shank wood bits. They're available up to 1½" size. (Irwin)

Large size holes can be bored with oversize spade type bits. They cut fast and clean.

The bell type hole saw is efficient, puts little strain on the motor.

When drilling into steel the maximum size of the bit which the chuck will take should be the limit. The use of a reduced shank bit of larger size may put a strain on the motor and shorten its life.

Right angle attachment is another accessory which permits drilling in tight quarters.

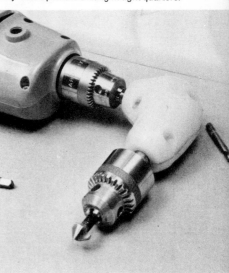

Drills are designed to function at the stated size relative to boring into steel, that is: a ¼" drill for holes up to ¼" in diameter, and ⅜" and ½" drills respectively for those sizes. When working with wood, however, these bounds can be overstepped. Drill bits with over-size cutters are available. They have reduced shanks of ¼" diameter thus permitting their use with ¼" tools. Holes up to 1¼" diameter can be bored in softwood with a ¼" drill equipped with a spade or speed bit, as it is commonly called. With hardwood the limit is about 1" with a ¼" drill and 1½" with a ½" drill. A hole saw will permit cutting large holes up to 2½" diameter. For all-around use the ⅜" drill will probably serve best.

Drills have come a long way in recent years with innovations that have further increased the versatility of the tool. Variable speed and reverse rotation features have proven so popular that they have more or less become the standard. Shock-proof insulated housings that protect against electrical shock hazards and compact heavy-duty ½" drills weighing only ounces more than ¼" and ⅜" drills are also noteworthy developments.

The variable speed drills permit complete control of rpm from zero starting to maximum speed by a pull on a trigger switch. This is most advantageous when starting a hole; a slow start prevents the bit from skipping around and possibly starting the hole in the wrong spot. This is a common occurrence with single speed, high rpm drills. Also, harder materials require operating at lower rpm and this can be satisfied with the variable speed control.

Reversing switch changes the direction of rotation. This helps to ease removal of drill from deep holes. Reverse is also useful for withdrawing screws when drill is used as a screwdriver or nut driver.

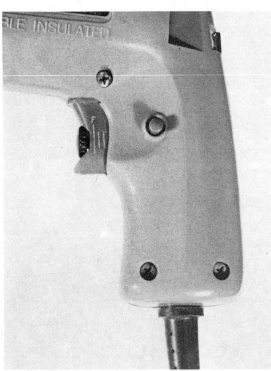

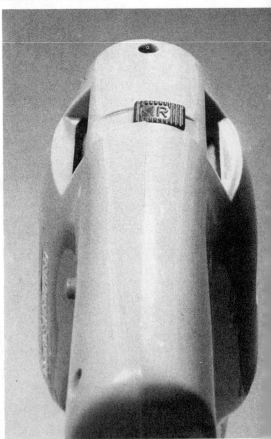

This trigger switch is adjustable from 0 to maximum rpm. Desired speed limit can be pre-set by turning the adjusting screw.

The masonry bit makes easy work of drilling into concrete. Variable speed drill of 3/8" or 1/2" capacity is the tool for this job.

Driving screws with a variable-speed drill at low rpm. A special screw driving sleeve attachment which fits over the screw head helps to keep the tip in place over the screw head to prevent slip-offs. (Rockwell)

A beading cutter used with an electric drill makes a smooth decorative molding cut. Several shapes are available. (Black & Decker)

Some of the extra chores which are effectively handled with the power drill includes sanding (left), wire brushing (center), and grinding. (Rockwell)

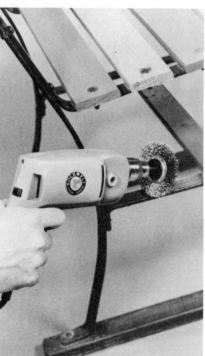

Many models have pre-set speed adjustments so that a full pull on the trigger will deliver the pre-selected speed.

The variable speed function also permits driving screws at low speed without the need for a special reduced speed adapter. The reverse rotation feature is especially useful for withdrawing screws.

The effective power of a drill, as is true with any portable power tool, is based on a somewhat complicated relationship between amperage and horsepower rating. As a rule of thumb, the greater the horsepower rating, the more powerful the tool. The ampere rating refers to the amount of current the motor uses when working at normal capacity. An overworked tool will draw more amperage, develop excessive heat and consequently head for early retirement if such abuse is continued.

Besides its main function of drilling holes, the drill is widely used for disc and drum sanding. The disc sanding accessory consists of a rubber pad onto which a circular sheet of abrasive is attached, through the center, by means of a depressed screw and washer. This accessory is useful for rough work, contouring and paint removal, but definitely not suitable for smooth finishing of flat surfaces.

Reasonably smooth finished work can be done with the drum sanding attachment, however. This is a rubber drum with a spindle on one end that fits into the chuck of the drill. Available in several diameters with matching cylindrical abrasive sleeves, the drum sander is very useful for smoothing the edges of contoured work pieces.

Battery powered cordless drill offers the freedom and convenience of working without a nearby electrical supply. Battery is rechargeable. (Black & Decker)

A useful accessory for any shop, this drill bit sharpener makes quick work of an otherwise difficult task. It only takes seconds to grind new points. (Black & Decker)

Portable Sanders

Regardless of how good the workmanship performed in the various steps of construction of a project, the quality of the end product quite naturally will be judged by its finish. Quite frequently an otherwise fine piece of work will fall short of perfection because of a poor finish which, more often than not, is the result of insufficient sanding.

Modern wood finishes are easy to apply with excellent results assured, provided the wood is properly prepared. But no finish will mask a poorly-sanded surface!

Hand sanding can be a boring and tiring chore, accounting for an occasional tendency by craftsmen to cut corners during this very important phase of woodworking. But sanding need not be a tough task if a power sander is used. It will save much time and effort and produce smooth-as-silk surfaces so necessary for fine finishing.

There are two types of portable sanders commonly used in the workshop: the belt and the finishing sander. The belt sander, although capable of imparting a reasonably fine surface, is primarily used for preliminary rough work. The finishing sander is used for final smoothing of the wood and for sanding between finishing coats.

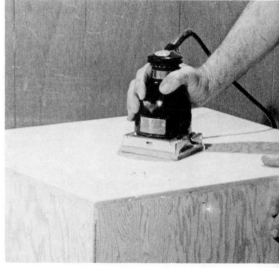

Final sanding is one of the most important operations in any woodworking project. Hand sanding can be tiring and time consuming. This job could take hours if done by hand, but only minutes with this high speed finishing sander.

The belt type is the workhorse among sanders. This one has a 3" x 21" belt which travels at a rate of 850 sfpm (surface feet per minute). That's about 10 miles worth in an hour! It excels with heavy stock removal. (Stanley)

The finishing sander is the tool used for the final smoothing of the wood. No skill whatsoever is required to use this sander; it needs only to be applied to the work and slowly moved over the surface. (Black & Decker)

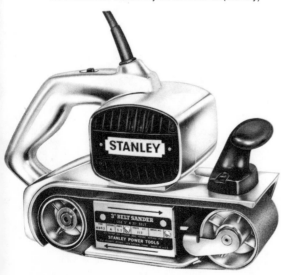

BELT SANDERS

The belt sander utilizes a continuous abrasive belt that travels over two drums in a straight-line front to rear motion. Belts are readily changed by retracting the front drum which allows the belt to slip off. A single adjustment, usually a thumbscrew, controls the belt tracking to keep it centered over the drums.

Loaded with a coarse grit belt, this sander is very useful for fast stock removal and shaping work. It can also be utilized for removing finishing materials.

The size of the tool is determined by the width and length of the belt. Sizes range from 2" x 21" to 4½" x 26". The most popular sizes for general use are the 3" x 21" and the 3" x 24" machines. Some models are available with dust bags that effectively draw up the sanding dust.

The belt sander removes stock quite rapidly. It is useful for trueing up surfaces, to shape wood and to remove old finishes. This one has a dust-collecting bag, standard equipment on some sanders, optional as an accessory on others, and well worth the extra cost.

Belt is removed by pushing in on the front idler drum to release the spring tension. Drum is snapped out after new belt has been inserted. Abrasive belts are available in several grit sizes from very fine to extra coarse.

THE TWO TYPES OF FINISHING SANDERS

Finishing sanders vary not only in size, but also according to the type of motion, which can be either orbital or oscillating. Some models feature a dual motion capability that allows a choice between orbital and reciprocating action.

The pad of the orbital sander moves in a tiny circular motion so that the abrasive actually cuts in all directions. Since the smoothest sanding possible is obtained when the abrasive is moved in the direction of the grain, the reciprocating sander that has a straight back-and-forth motion produces the smoothest surface.

The orbital sander removes wood somewhat faster than the reciprocating type, so it is generally more widely preferred. The cross grain scratches that it imparts in the wood are so minute they are hardly discernible. The dual action sander can be used in the orbital mode for preliminary sanding, then switched to reciprocating-straight-line motion for the final touch. An additional feature of straight-line sanders is that they allow working right up to the corners of vertical surfaces, an important consideration.

A dual action finishing sander. It has a selector switch which allows a choice of motion, straight-line or orbital. Straight-line sanding removes wood at a slower rate than orbital but the result is smoother. With this type you can use the orbital action for the initial sanding then switch to straight for the finishing touch. (Skil)

A tungsten carbide pad is used to remove thick layers of paint down to the raw wood in short order. The pad is composed of chips of the hard metal welded to a thin flexible sheet of steel. It cuts quickly with minimal clogging.

This heavy duty finishing sander is designed for one-hand use. The edges of the pad may be used to advantage for smoothing inside curves, or for forming soft curves on sharp corners, like this.

Materials other than wood can be finish-sanded with the power sander. This is Corian, a tough, increasingly popular, marble-like synthetic.

Routers

For the final touch that often says "done by a pro," the router has no equal. It is a tool with many uses, most of which can be carried out to perfection on the first attempt by a novice woodworker. It's that easy to use!

The router is a precision-built tool of rather simple construction. It consists of a high speed motor with a built-in chuck that holds any one of a large variety of shaped cutting bits. The motor is supported vertically, with the business end down, in a frame that is an integral part of the base.

In use the base rests on the work surface with the bit projecting beyond the base. The depth of cut made by the bit is controlled by raising or lowering the motor in the frame. The lower portion of the motor housing is threaded, as is the inside of the frame. Fine adjustments for bit projection are made

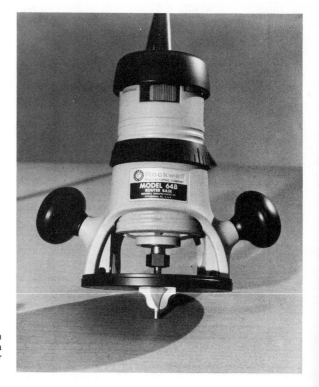

The router is one of the easiest tools to master. You can learn to use it in minutes. It is a simple tool, consisting of a motor with collet chuck, an adjusting ring, a cantilever base and a plastic, non-scratching sub base. (Rockwell)

The depth of cut adjustment of the router is made by raising or lowering the motor in the base by turning the adjusting ring (A) after loosening the locking screw (B). The graduations on the ring are aligned with index (C) for precise settings to control depth of cut. (Rockwell)

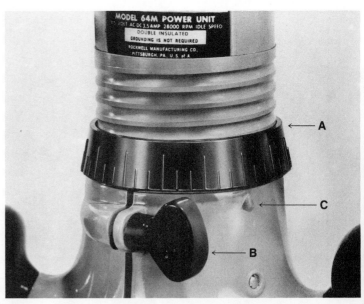

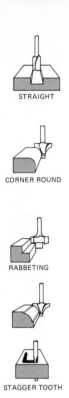
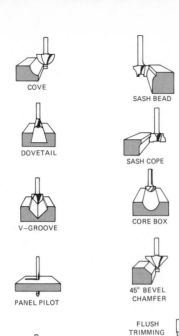

STRAIGHT

COVE

SASH BEAD

CORNER ROUND

DOVETAIL

SASH COPE

RABBETING

V–GROOVE

CORE BOX

STAGGER TOOTH

PANEL PILOT

45° BEVEL CHAMFER

MORTISE

FLUSH TRIMMING BITS

25° BEVEL TRIMMER KIT

Some of the more commonly used router bits. Many other shapes are available to meet any need.

by turning an adjustment ring. A thumbscrew clamp arrangement locks the parts.

The router makes remarkably smooth cuts as a result of the high speed at which the cutting bit revolves. Operating speeds vary with machines ranging from 20,000 to 30,000 rpm. The power of the router is measured by the horsepower rating of the motor. This varies from ¼ to 3 hp. A router of ½ or ¾ hp is adequate for most home work-shop use. The heavy duty models are for industrial purposes.

The varied sizes and shapes of router bits permit almost any cut imaginable. All kinds of wood joints, such as rabbets, tongue and groove, laps, dadoes, and grooves, are easily and accurately cut with this tool. Concave-convex drop leaf table joints can be shaped with a pair of matched cutters.

Rabbets (left) are quickly cut with the router. A guide is not necessary because the bit is self piloting. Cutting a molded edge (right) on a table top is a routine chore for the router.

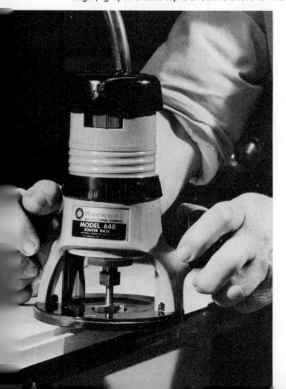

JOBS THE ROUTER CAN DO

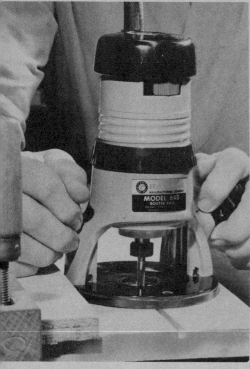

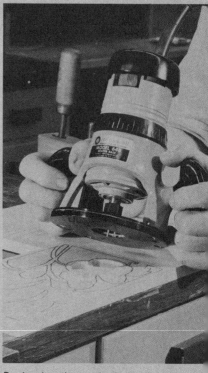

A clamped strip guides the router with a straight bit to cut a groove.

A pair of straight edged strips guide the router to cut big dadoes.

Freehand routing can be done to form a recessed background for raised designs.

An accessory dovetail jig permits cutting perfect fitting dovetail joints with ease.

Special laminated trimming bit is used to trim plastic laminate sheet flush to the wood edge for perfect joiner.

The router is easy to handle even on location. It's being used here to trim plastic laminate on a built-in wall valance.

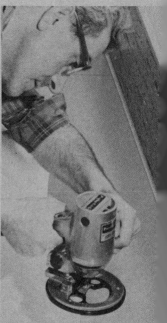

Decorative molded edges for cabinet doors, furniture edges, and table tops are run-of-the-mill tasks for the router. With simple jigs or guides, this tool can be used to cut inlay recesses, hinge butt mortises, and make perfect circles. A special dovetail jig can be used to cut perfectly matched, snug-fitting dovetail joints. Freehand, the router can be used to do carving and lettering.

Plastic laminate work is dependent entirely on the router for quick, perfect fitting and finishing of joints. Cutters with special ball bearing pilot guides are available for this work. A pair of these bits, one for flush trimming and one for finish beveling, can be used to do the most complex laminating work.

The versatility of the router can be further increased by using it in an overarm mount. This is a special bracket that can be clamped to a standard drill press column so that it becomes, in effect, a stationary tool somewhat like a shaper in reverse, but with far more flexibility and control.

The overarm is designed to clamp around a 2¾" diameter column, but if your column is off-size or if you don't own a drill press, there is available a special column and base that can be purchased with the overarm as a complete, ready-to-use unit.

The most important feature of this kind of set up is that it allows pin routing: A metal pin sized to match the router bit being used is inserted into the table top, perfectly centered under the bit and projecting slightly above the surface. The lower edge of the workpiece is simply moved against the guide pin to allow the upper edge to be shaped by the bit. For intricate surface work a template is tacked to the bottom of the workpiece. The template edges are moved against the pin to duplicate the shaped cut on the top surface of the work.

By tilting the table and using simple jigs or fences, all sorts of special mortising can be done with ease and to perfection. Clear visibility of the cutting edge and accurate depth control allow work to be done to precise tolerances.

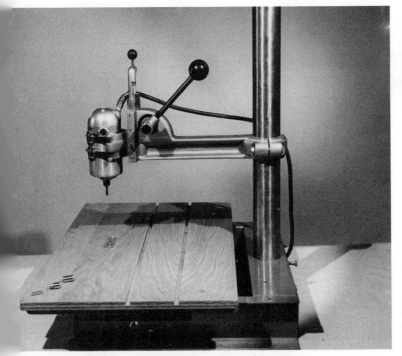

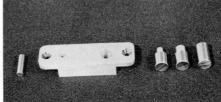

The block holds pins of varied end diameters. A pin of the same size as the router bit is used to obtain template guided cuts. (Bryden Overarm)

Cutting a decorative recess in a cabinet door using the template and pin method. (Bryden Overarm)

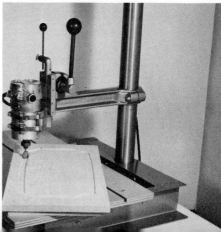

A router overarm mount such as this can be attached to a drill press column. The lever is used to raise and lower the router. A depth stop rod adjusts for depth of cut. The router is clamped firmly on the mount with a pair of adjustable bands. An auxiliary wood sub table with grooves and an aluminum pin recessing block are the only extras required. Rig offers unlimited possibilities. (Bryden Overarm)

Power Block Plane

The power block plane can be considered a luxury tool in the average shop equipped with a jointer, which will do an excellent planing job. But for some large workpieces or out-of-shop projects requiring edge planing or surfacing, this handy tool can't be beat. It takes the drudgery out of laborious planing tasks.

The plane is rather light, usually about five pounds, and is designed to fit in the palm of the hand for easy manipulation. A right angle fence supplied with the tool assures the cutting of perfectly true edges. Accurate bevel cuts from 0 to 45 degrees are easy to make with an accessory bevel planing fence. With the fence removed, it is easy (and fun) to do freehand contour shaping.

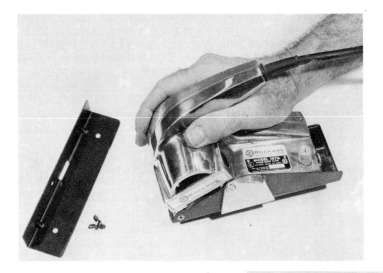

This power block plane is lightweight and designed to be held comfortably with one hand. A removable right angle fence (left) attaches quickly with a thumbscrew. An adjustable bevel fence is also available.

Bottom view shows the two lip spiral cutter which has a cutting width of 1$^{13}/_{16}$". It turns at 21,000 rpm.

The fence assures perfectly square edge planing. The maximum depth of cut is 1/64″.

The tool is especially handy for surface planing of large boards, trimming doors or windows.

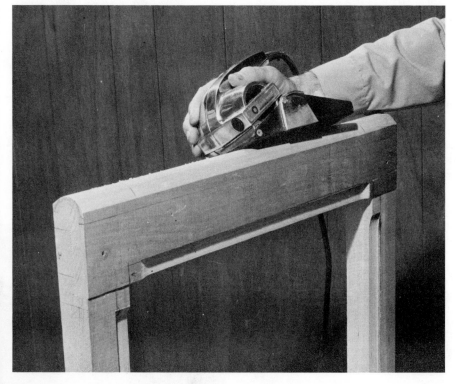

Rough rounding a hardwood chair frame section with the block plane is quick and easy. Bevels also can be cut easily with accessory guide.

The Impact Tool

The impact tool has been widely used in industry for many years, but has only recently been discovered as a useful tool to have around the home and shop. It is actually a combination drill and percussion tool.

It looks very much like a conventional drill except for an extra ringed bulge between the chuck and housing. This is a selector ring that controls the modes of operation obtainable: drill-drive, hammer-drill, and hammer-chisel.

As a basic ⅜″ drill the tool has good features, such as double insulation, variable speed control, forward and reverse rotation, and a locking switch for continuous operation. It handles the usual drilling chores quite well, although somewhat slowly in some uses because top speed is 850 rpm.

By shifting the selector ring to the hammer-drill function the action is converted to a combination revolving/percussion motion; the chuck moves repeatedly up and down while turning. This is quite effective for drilling into masonry materials. The tool is a time and labor saver and worth consideration if you anticipate doing a reasonable amount of home improvement type projects that require boring into masonry.

The third function, hammer/chisel, delivers a straight back and forth motion used for chiseling, chipping and scraping operations. Accessory tools include flat chisels, gouges, and flexible scrapers. The tool is not intended for precision chiseling work on wood, but it serves reasonably well for fast stock removal. This mode is also useful for the numerous handyman scraping chores around the home and shop.

Hammer-drill mode makes drilling through tough materials an easy task. The setting for this operation delivers 33 blows per minute while the bit rotates continually.

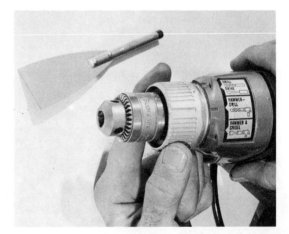

Selector ring clicks into any of three modes with a twist. Safety rules dictate that changes be made with tools removed.

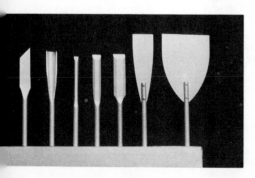

Accessory tools include chisels and scrapers which are made of tough steel. A carbide-tipped masonry drill bit (shown in earlier picture) is required for boring into masonry or cement.

Healthy bites can be taken in wood for fast stock removal. The tool is set at "hammer-chisel" for this work.

The Circular Saw

The circular saw, sometimes called a table or bench saw, is the basic machine used to perform the fundamental operations of straight-line sawing. It is estimated that 80 percent of all woodworking involves sawing, so the value of a clean-cutting precision tool for the purpose is apparent.

Designed primarily for crosscutting (across the short dimension of stock which is usually at right angles to the grain) and ripping (cutting along the length of a board in the direction of the grain), this saw is also especially useful for making miter and bevel cuts. A limitless variety of joints may be made with this machine, and by substituting a dado head or molding cutter head for the saw blade, its versatility can be fully appreciated.

The table saw is unsurpassed for straight line sawing. It cuts fast and has built-in accuracy.

The saw consists of a sturdy frame that supports a table, arbor and motor. The blade is secured to the arbor, which is driven by the motor with belts and pulleys. In some models the arbor is simply an extension of the motor shaft, making the drive direct.

Earlier models and some multi-purpose saws utilize a tilting table in which the blade remains in a fixed position; the table must be tilted in order to achieve beveled cuts.

Most of the commonly available saws feature a tilting arbor; the table remains fixed and the arbor is adjustable to tilt to any angle from 0 to 45 degrees. Thus the term tilting arbor circular saw.

Saw size is determined by the diameter of its blade, ranging from 8″ to 9″ and 10″ for general

This 12″ table saw has the capacity to cut wood up to 3⁹/₁₆″ thick. Table extends to 57″. (Sears)

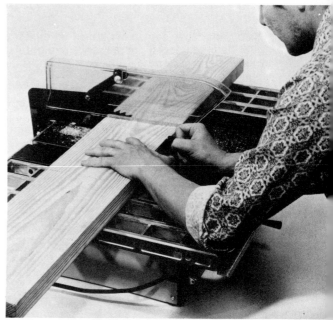

Crosscutting (above) and ripping operations are the basic functions of the circular saw. (Rockwell)

A bench type table saw with 9″ blade capacity. (Toolkraft)

shop use. The blade can be raised or lowered by means of a handwheel crank to adjust for the thickness of the material to be cut. The advantage of the larger blade is apparent— it'll cut through thicker stock. The tilt angle of the blade for bevel cutting is also controlled by a crank.

Two means of guiding the work accurately past the blade are provided: a rip fence and a miter gage. The rip fence is a metal guide supported at the front and rear of the table. It can be shifted from side to side, always remaining parallel to the saw blade. After adjustment for the width of cut desired, a locking lever secures it firmly in place. Rip sawing wood accurately to dimension simply entails feeding it into the blade with one edge held firmly against the fence.

The miter gage guides the wood for all crosscutting operations. It, also, is essentially a fence that is connected to a bar that rides in either of two grooves which are milled in

A molding head converts the saw for fancy shaping operations. A large variety of cutter shapes is available.

The circular saw is especially well suited for cutting complex shapes such as these with speed and accuracy.

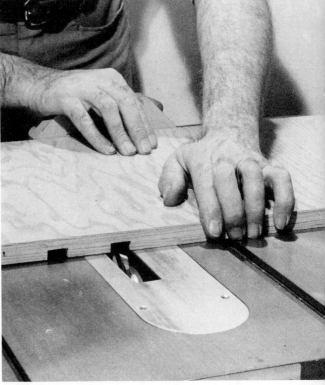

A dado head is used to cut dadoes across the grain and grooves parallel to the grain.

the table top. The wood is held against the gage which is normally locked in its zero position and pushed past the blade to obtain a perfect right angle cut. The gage can be adjusted to any position from 0 to 60 degrees, left or right, to guide the work past the blade at an angle for miter cuts. Compound angle cuts are easily accomplished by tilting the blade and setting the miter gage at an angle.

Three protective devices are standard on most saws: the blade guard, anti-kickback fingers, and a splitter. The blade guard serves primarily to keep fingers away from the moving blade, but it also helps to deflect flying chips which can otherwise be a threat to the eyes. Loose knots sometimes splinter and can be thrown with considerable force toward the operator if the guard is not used.

The blade of the tilting arbor saw tilts for angled cuts while the table remains stationary and level.

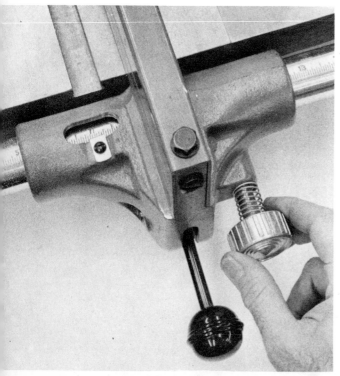

The rip fence rides parallel to the blade to guide the wood for accurate ripping. This sturdy fence has a micro adjusting knob which is pushed in and turned to move the fence for extra fine settings.

The miter gage is used for all crosscutting operations. It can be adjusted to cut accurate miters up to 60 degrees left or right as well as for straight right angle work.

For some operations the guard must be removed, in which event extra care must be exercised to avoid accidents. Many illustrations in this book (and others of the kind) show the saw in use with the guard removed. This is done only in the interest of the clarity of the pictures and should not be construed as a normal working procedure.

The splitter is a piece of metal that projects above the table directly behind the blade. Its purpose is to keep the saw kerf (the cut) open, thus preventing the wood from binding against the blade. The anti-kickback fingers prevent the wood from being thrust back toward the operator in situations in which the stock binds or a dull blade meets a tough section of wood,

A combined splitter bar with anti-kickback fingers. The splitter keeps the kerf open while the fingers prevent the wood from being thrust back. The unit can be depressed out of the way when necessary while dadoing or shaping.

The table saw can be utilized for sanding convex corners and ends with an accessory disc.

Compound angle cuts are made by tilting the blade and setting the miter gage at an angle.

such as a knot. For certain operations, such as grooving or dadoing, the splitter and blade guard must be removed or retracted.

Other than the special blades mentioned, accessories include a sanding disc, a miter gage clamp attachment and, probably most important, a tenoner. The tenoner is basically a specialized clamp that is used to hold small pieces and to simplify the operation of cutting tenons for mortise and tenon joints. This is not an inexpensive accessory, however, so simple jigs are frequently utilized to serve the purpose.

The table saw adjustments and set ups are quickly learned and easily made. No special skills are required to obtain consistently good results with this useful machine.

Using a miter gage clamp attachment to hold small work while crosscutting. This is a safety factor in keeping fingers away from the blade.

The tenoning jig holds small pieces to allow safe and accurate cutting. It slides in the miter gage groove in the table top. The side sliding fixture can be adjusted to fine tolerances.

CIRCULAR SAW BLADES

Sawing wood properly and efficiently requires the use of the right blade for each type of cutting operation. As you may have learned through experience with hand saws, a blade designed for ripping, cutting *with* the grain, will not perform with equal efficiency in *cross* grain work. The same is true with power circular saw blades—they're designed to do specific-purpose cutting.

There are but a few basic blade designs and these are made in varying sizes to fit the portable as well as the bench and radial arm saws. The common ones include:

• **Crosscut.** This blade is used for cutting straight or diagonally *across* the grain of the wood. It has many small, fine teeth which are set, that is, alternately bent left and right (to cut clearance). These teeth shear the wood fibers leaving a smooth cut across the grain.

• **Ripsaw.** This blade is for cutting *with the grain* or along the length of the wood. It has a relatively small number of large teeth which are long and claw-like in shape. Deep gullets between the teeth remove the sawdust, so the following tooth has a free path to cut the wood.

• **Combination.** A general purpose blade designed for ripping *and* crosscut work. It is a good all-around blade and is usually the one that is supplied with new equipment. This blade has more teeth than the standard rip blade and the gullets are usually shallower.

• **Hollow Ground Combination.** This blade is also used for ripping and crosscutting, but with an important difference. It makes an exceptionally smooth cut that can be glued without sanding. This blade is thicker at the teeth than it is toward the hub (hollow ground), thus eliminating the need for any *set* in the teeth. The groups of four cutting teeth are separated by a deep gullet and a raker tooth to carry out the sawdust. An excellent blade for finish work.

a. Crosscut blade is for cutting across the grain.
b. Ripsaw blade is designed to cut with the grain.
c. Combination blade is used to cut wood in varied directions, with or across the grain.

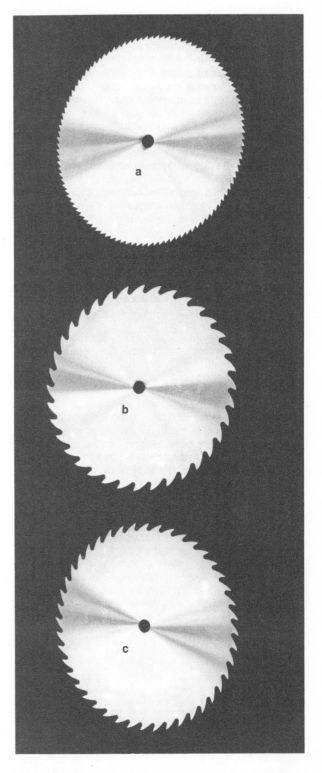

• **Plywood.** As its name implies, this blade is designed exclusively for cutting plywood, veneers, and veneer-faced products. It is a fine-tooth blade that eliminates the objectionable chipping and splintering of veneer faces usually encountered with other blades. It makes a fine, smooth cut.

• **Carbide Tipped.** Carbide is a tough alloy almost as hard as diamond. Saw blades of various standard designs are available with carbide tipped teeth. Such blades have an unusually long life. They cost considerably more, but they maintain a sharp cutting edge at least 25 times longer than a conventional blade before resharpening is necessary.

• **Dado Head.** A dado head is one of the most useful accessories for both the radial arm and bench saw. It is used for cutting grooves wider than the normal saw-blade kerf. There are two kinds of dado heads in common use: the single unit adjustable type and the multiple-blade dado head set.

The adjustable head is by far the most popular for home workshop use because of the ease with which it can be adjusted to vary the width of cut simply by setting a dial. This type usually has a range from ¼" to $^{13}/_{16}$" wide and a depth limit of ¾".

A typical dado head set consists of two outside cutters, each ⅛" thick, and several inside chipper blades that can be installed between the two outside blades to increase the kerf width from ⅛" to $^{13}/_{16}$" by $^{1}/_{16}$" increments. Paper shims inserted between the chippers will permit cutting grooves up to 1" wide.

• **Molding Head.** Another useful accessory for the radial arm and bench saw is the molding head. This consists of a cutter head in which steel knives of various shapes can be mounted for cutting many kinds of fancy moldings. Inasmuch as both the radial arm and bench saws have tiltable arbors, the variety of cuts possible with these tools is greater than that of the standard shaper.

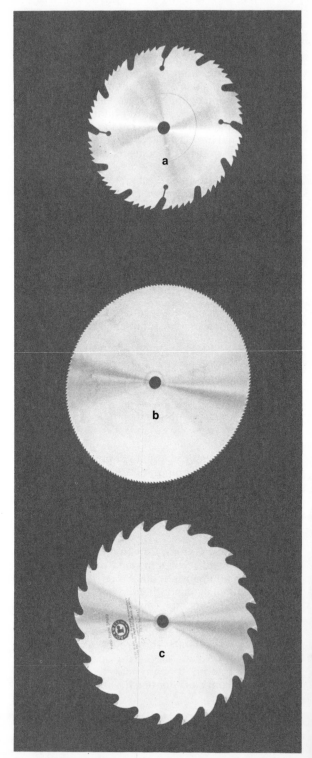

a. Hollow ground combination blade cuts very smooth. Can be used for ripping and crosscutting.
b. Plywood blade cuts plywood smoothly with minimal splintering of the surface fibers.
c. Carbide tipped blade has tips of extremely hard tungsten carbide. Cuts tough materials with ease and stays sharp longer than all other blades.

144

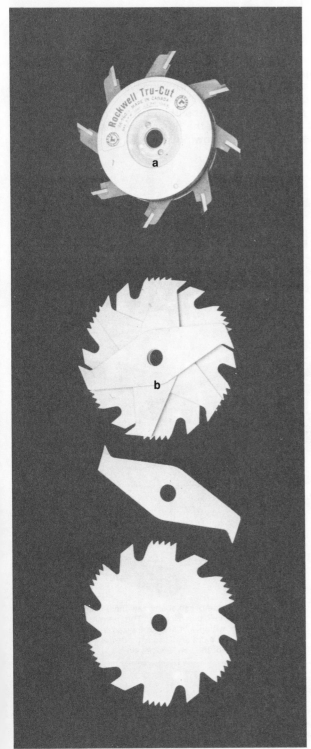

a. Adjustable one piece dado head can be set to cut varying widths by turning the rims.
b. The standard dado set consists of two outside blades and several inside chippers of different thicknesses. Minute variations can be made by inserting paper shims or washers between chippers.

1/2" COVE, 5/16" QR. RD.	5/16" COVE, 3/8" BEAD	1/8" & 3/8" QR. RD., 1/4" BEAD	1/4" & 1/2" QR. RD.	
90° FLUTE	1/4" FLUTE	DRAWER JOINT	OGEE	FEMALE SASH
CAB. R.H. MALE	CAB. L.H. FEMALE	CAB. L.H. MALE	CAB. R.H. FEMALE	MALE SASH
GLUE JOINT	COVE & BEAD MLDG. L.H.	COVE & BEAD MLDG. R.H.	COVE & BEAD COPE R.H.	
COVE & BEAD COPE L.H.	3-BEAD (3/16" BEAD)	5-BEAD (1/8" BEAD)	WEDGE TONGUE	WEDGE GROOVE
OGEE & BEAD TABLE EDGE	1" CONVEX EDGE	1/2" FLUTE	1/2" BEAD	1/4" BEAD
3/4" FLUTE	1" FLUTE	3/8" BEAD	PANEL RAISING	1" BEAD
9/16" QR. RD	3/8" FLUTE	3/4" BEAD	DOOR LIP	1/2" & 1/4" RADII R H

Some of the common shapes of molding cutter knives.

Radial Arm Saws

The radial arm saw is a remarkable machine capable of performing many operations in addition to the basic functions of crosscutting, ripping, mitering, and beveling. It is especially advantageous for crosscutting long pieces because the stock need not be moved; it remains stationary while the saw blade is moved over the wood.

Originally developed for use by industry in production shops, building construction and lumber yards, the radial arm saw was eventually recognized by the home craftsman for its versatility and ease of operation. Manufacturers observed the growing interest in this saw by

The radial arm saw is one of the most versatile of the stationary power tools. It can perform many functions.

On this type of radial arm saw there is an extra track below the overarm. This permits angle cutting within a more centralized area of the table. The extra arm also extends the cross cut capacity of the saw. (*Rockwell*)

On this machine the saw unit moves directly back and forth under the overarm, the ideal method of crosscutting. (*Black & Decker*)

by amateur woodworkers and soon began redesigning smaller versions of the heavy-duty machines to satisfy a new and appreciative market.

They went a step further and developed a number of accessories which could be used with the saw, thus widening its versatility to the point where it is now considered a multi-purpose tool. With the various accessories available the radial arm saw can be used to do dadoing, surfacing, molding, shaping, routing, drilling, sanding, grinding, and even faceplate turning operations.

Basically, the radial saw consists of a yoke-mounted motor suspended from a horizontal arm which, in turn, is mounted on a sturdy column at the rear. The arm can be raised or lowered by means of an elevating crank. This controls the depth of cut. The motor, yoke,

The arm in position for basic cross cutting.

The motor tilted for a 45 degree bevel cut. A spring loaded locating pin automatically stops at 0, 45 and 90 degrees.

Radial arm positioned for a miter cut. The arm can swing the same amount left and right. There are click stops at the most used positions.

and horizontal arm can be adjusted to any desired angle, making possible unlimited universal movements of the saw or other cutting tools that adapt directly to the motor shaft. It is this flexibility of movement and positioning of the cutting tools that enable this machine to perform an almost unlimited variety of functions.

One of the most important features of this saw is that the cutting is done from above the work so that layout lines are always visible and easily lined-up with the cutting edge.

For all crosscutting operations, including bevel, miter and dado work, the blade moves

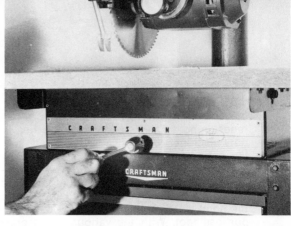

Depth of cut adjustment is made by turning a hand crank to elevate or depress the arm.

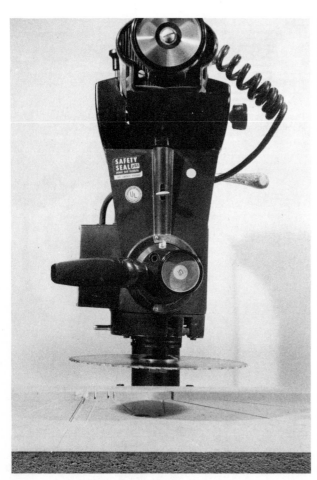

The blade set for horizontal cutting.

Yoke is rotated 90 degrees for ripping operations.

An advantage of the radial arm saw is that it allows clear visibility of the blade and the line of cut during any operation.

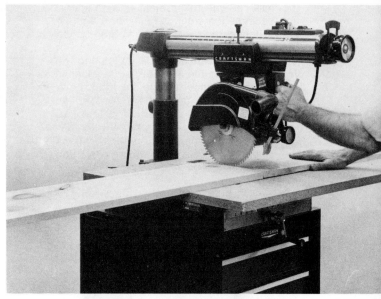

Crosscutting long boards is easy because the bulky workpiece remains stationary while the saw blade is pulled through it.

Motor adjustment for making bevel rip cuts. The blade guard has been removed for these views for clarity. The guard should always be used when the saw is in operation.

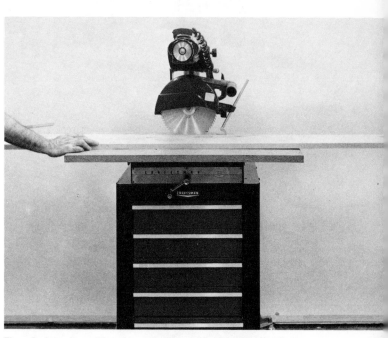

The yoke is easily positioned to make rip cuts. For this operation the stock is pushed past the blade which remains in a fixed position.

149

in the same direction in which it rotates. Thus the blade's thrust is downward and toward the rear. This results in relatively safe operation because the stock is held firmly against the rip fence and table by the cutting action of the tool.

Ripping cuts can be made by locking the yoke carriage on the arm so that the blade is parallel to the fence. In this situation, however, the thrust is upward and toward the operator. To prevent dangers of kickback of stock, all radial saws are equipped with anti-kickback finger clamps. In ripping operations the blade remains in a stationary position while the wood is pushed past it.

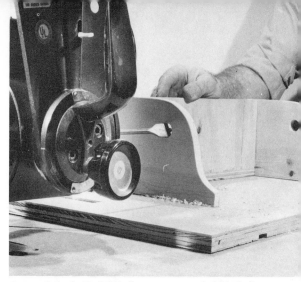

A geared chuck attached to the accessory end of the shaft enables the saw to take drilling bits for horizontal boring jobs. This method insures accuracy.

The sanding disc in use for end finishing. It can be set to make precise angle cuts.

Straight or angled dadoes are readily cut with this saw. Again, clear visibility of the tool and the piece being cut means better results.

The rotary planer converts the radial arm saw for precision planing. The head is adjusted to the required height and locked into place. The wood is simply pushed past the rotating cutter. Useful for dressing, trueing up and sizing stock, it cuts a 2½" width and presents no kickback problem.

Saw sizes are determined by the diameter of the largest blade accommodated. The length of the arm and the table width determine both the maximum crosscut and ripping capacity. Saw sizes for home workshop use range from 8″ to 12″ with motor ratings from ³⁄₄ to 2 horsepower. For average use a 9″ or 10″ saw will generally prove quite adequate.

The speed of most saw motors is usually 3,450 rpm, but some newer models feature variable speed motors that can be adapted to the needs of particular jobs, such as routing and shaping operations that are better done with high cutter speeds.

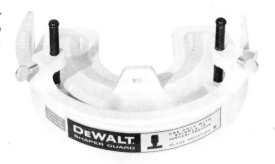

An adjustable tool guard is a must for all horizontal shaping, dadoing, and sawing operations.

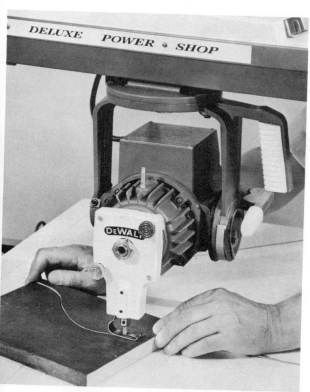

A saber saw accessory attachment converts the radial saw into a saber saw for irregular and curved cutting. The unit also may be tilted. (*Black & Decker*)

Installing molding head blades is easy with two wrenches. One fits over flats on the arbor to hold it while a hex wrench is used to turn the arbor nut.

Band Saws

The band saw is a very useful tool, an asset in any shop. It can be used for many cutting chores that other saws cannot do. Primarily used for cutting irregular shapes, the band saw does equally well on straight work. Re-sawing wide boards into narrow ones is a simple task for this saw, as is gang sawing — cutting a number of identical pieces at one time. Bevel cuts with angles up to 45 degrees, either straight or curved, are routine with this tool. Compound cutting, pattern sawing, and thin kerfing are a few more of the special jobs for which this saw excels.

Most band sawing is done freehand, but the table is usually slotted to accept a miter gage that can be used for accurate crosscutting. With the aid of numerous simple jigs and fences that can easily be made as needed, the band saw can be utilized to turn out highly precise work.

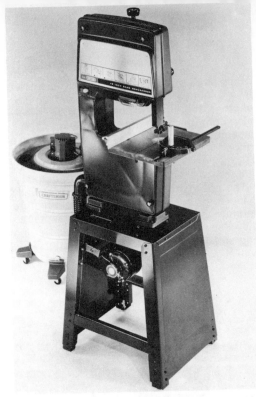

This saw has a larger capacity. It'll handle wood 12″ wide on the inboard side and up to 6″ thick. (*Sears Roebuck*)

The band saw is primarily a tool used for cutting curved and irregular shapes quickly and accurately.

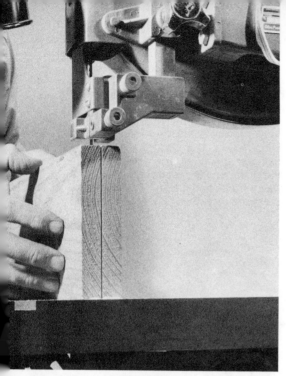

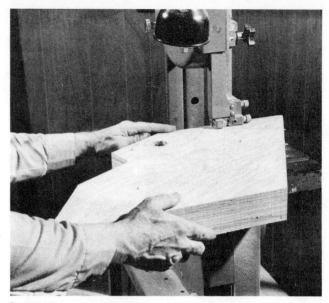

Several pieces of stock can be ganged and cut simultaneously to save time and assure identical sizes.

The band saw affords the easiest way to resaw stock into thinner pieces. Fingers should never get closer to the blade. A pusher jig will be used when nearing end of cut for safety.

Deep curved cuts are one of the band saw's specialties. Stock twice the height of this can be handled on this saw.

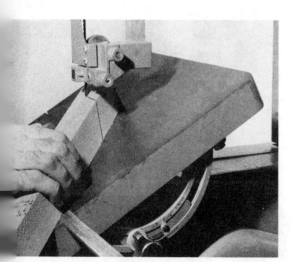

Accurate compound angles can be cut by tilting the table and the use of a miter gage.

Compound sculptured cuts can be made with narrow blade on the band saw. (*Sears Roebuck*)

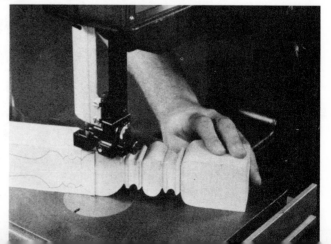

The band saw is so named because its blade, made of thin flexible steel with its ends welded together, forms a continuous band. The blade rides over two large wheels, one above and one below the table level. The lower wheel, powered by a belt from an externally-mounted motor, drives the blade. The upper wheel, which is adjustable to provide blade tension and proper tracking, is an idler.

The size of a band saw is measured by the wheel diameter which, in turn, determines the "depth of throat": the horizontal dimension between the blade and the frame. This limits the width of stock that can be cut on the inboard side (between frame and blade) but imposes no restrictions on the size of stock that can be fed on the outboard side. Band saws for workshop use range from 10″ to 18″.

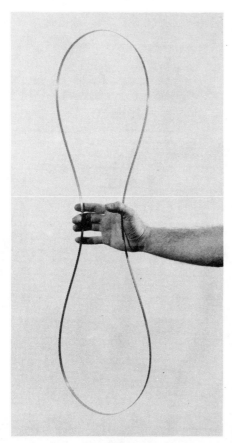

The band saw uses a flexible steel blade which is welded together at the ends to form a continuous band. Available in widths from ⅛″ and up.

Blade guards are removed to reveal the inside view of the saw. The wheels are covered with a thin rubber tire to protect the teeth. The lower wheel is the driver, the upper is free running. Blade tension is adjusted by raising or lowering the upper wheel. Upper and lower blade guides hold the blade in line and prevent twisting.

The maximum thickness of stock that can be cut depends on the distance between the table top and the upper limit of the adjustable blade guide assembly. This is usually a generous 6″ on a 10″ or 12″ saw and up to 12″ on the larger models.

Band saw blades come in varying widths from $1/8$″ to $3/4$″ with a choice of tooth number per inch of blade. A wide, coarse-toothed blade does fast rough cutting, while a narrow, fine-toothed one is chosen for intricate pattern work. The turning radius capability is directly related to the width of the blade. A minimum turn of $1/4$″ radius is possible with a $1/8$″ blade, while a $3/4$″ blade is limited to a $1^3/4$″ radius. Metal cutting blades can also be used on the band saw, but RPM should be reduced.

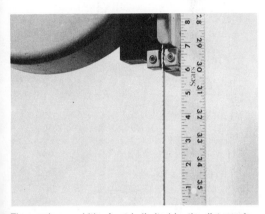

The maximum width of cut is limited by the distance between the frame and the blade. Maximum height this saw will accommodate is 6″. Some saws will handle 12″.

Width	Minimum Radius of Circle That Can Be Cut
$1/8$″	$1/4$″
$3/16$″	$1/2$″
$1/4$″	$3/4$″
$3/8$″	1″
$1/2$″	$1^1/4$″
$5/8$″	$1^3/4$″
$3/4$″	$2^1/2$″

Minimum Radius Chart

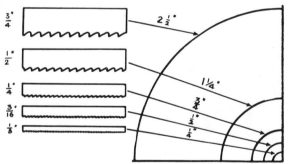

Chart shows the minimum radius cutting capabilities of various sized blades. Small blade will permit fine scroll work.

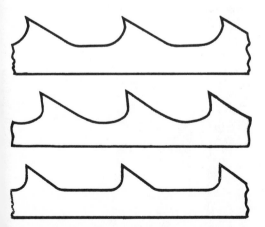

Typical band saw blade designs. The sabre tooth, top, has a 10 degree hook on the face or cutting edge which lets it feed easy and cut fast. The F-34 tooth, center, is a recently developed tooth design. It also has a 10 degree hook but it extends further down the tooth and blends into a larger, rounded gullet. Consequently it cuts faster and freer, feeds easier, too. Skip tooth blade, bottom, is widely used. It cuts fast and smooth and has ample gullet capacity for chips. All wood cutting blades have teeth alternately set in opposite directions. (Simonds)

Sanding belts can be substituted for the saw blade to allow precise sanding of intricate shapes. A special sanding attachment with flat and curved platens must be used for this purpose. (Rockwell)

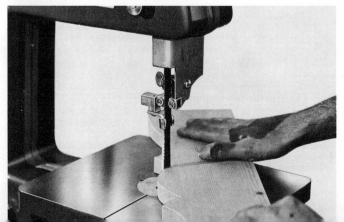

ig Saws

The jig saw is basically a motor-driven coping or scroll saw. It is closely related to the band saw and saber saws in that its main function is the cutting of curved or irregular shapes, but it surpasses both in the fineness of work it can do. With a thin jeweler's-type blade inserted, there is practically no limit to the intricacies of the designs and patterns that can be made with this saw.

This machine uses a small, thin blade held between two chucks, one below the work table

The jig or scroll saw is used for cutting curves and irregular shapes. It has an advantage over the band saw in that it can be used to make internal cuts. Note the inside cuts made on these novel bookends.

This jig saw is capable of handling almost any home shop projects. It has a tilting table, a 16" capacity from blade to arm and a 2" thickness of cut limit. (*Rockwell*)

Large work is no problem for a jig saw using a wide blade. Rotatable blade feature allows extra long cutting capability. Helpers must be used for a job like this.

and one above. The lower chuck, connected to a rod, travels straight up and down in short strokes by the action of a cam mechanism. The upper chuck is spring loaded to maintain tension on the blade, which passes through a hole in the table. The upper and lower sections are joined by a curved overarm.

The size of a jig saw is determined by the distance from the blade to the back of the overarm (throat size). This may vary from 16″ to 24″. The former has the capacity to cut to the center of a circle 32″ in diameter, the latter, 48″. Some saws are designed with a removable overarm to permit working on oversize pieces. Stiff saber saw blades, held only by the lower chuck, are used for this purpose. The maximum thickness of stock that the average saw will handle is usually 2″. Practically all jig saws feature tilting tables to

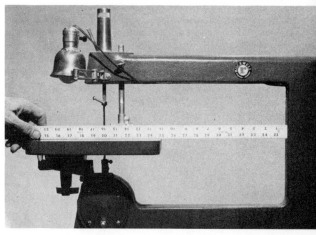

The size of the saw refers to the distance between the blade and the upright of the overarm.

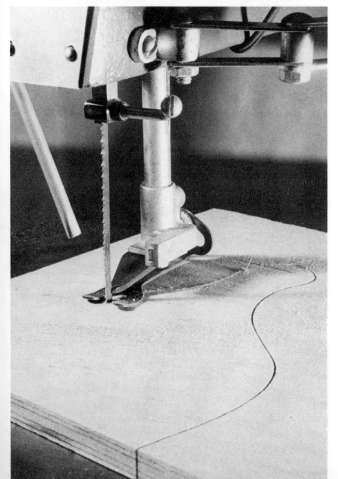

The table can be tilted 30 degrees left or 45 degrees right for angle cutting. When an extreme tilt is used the maximum depth of cut is reduced due to the bulk of the blade guide.

The blade guide assembly includes a spring hold down foot which steadies the work and prevents it from pulling away from the table on the blade's upstroke. The metal tube to the left of the blade blows air to the cutting area to remove sawdust.

157

allow bevel cutting, but it should be noted that a full tilt, the maximum thickness of cut is slightly reduced due to the bulk of the blade guide assembly.

Jig saws are generally equipped with a four-step cone pulley arrangement with V belt drive. This makes possible four speeds from approximately 600 to 1700 cutting strokes per minute (csm). Some models feature variable speed mechanisms that permit a wider selection of speeds.

A large variety of blades is available for the saw to make possible all sorts of cuts in practically any material from steel to dozens of others, including extremely thin wood veneers. Teeth per blade inch (tpi) range from 7 tpi for fast wood cutting to 20 tpi for intricate work in veneers and plastics.

The ease with which a blade can be inserted through a hole in a board, then chucked onto the machine is undoubtedly one of the most important features, the saw's ability to make internal cuts that begin and end within a board without requiring a lead-in cut from the outside. This is a great convenience for the user.

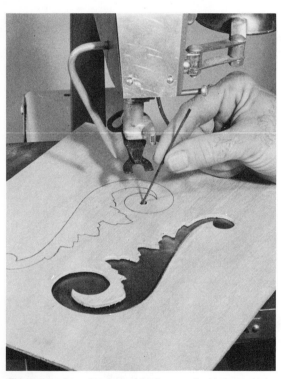

This is the prime advantage of the jig saw—the blade can be inserted through the work for making internal cuts.

Most jig saws are equipped with a four-step cone pulley on the motor and saw with a V belt drive. Speeds are varied by shifting the belt position. The belt and pulley guard has been removed.

An accessory sanding attachment is very useful for smoothing scrolled designs. It can handle with ease concave, convex or flat surfaces.

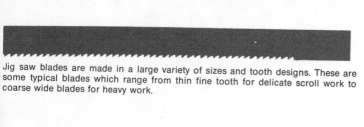

Jig saw blades are made in a large variety of sizes and tooth designs. These are some typical blades which range from thin fine tooth for delicate scroll work to coarse wide blades for heavy work.

Another type of jig saw of smaller capacity is geared for smaller, craft type projects. This saw is relatively safe to use, a good power tool with which to get the small fry started in shop work.

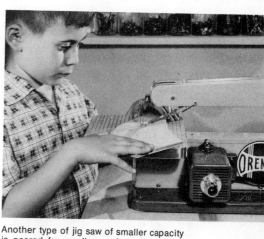

An auxiliary power take-off supplies power for a flexible shaft which operates accessory tools. It can be used for grinding, drilling, carving, routing and for other purposes in wood, plastic and metal.

The Drill Press

The drill press is a practical power tool, one of the easiest of all to use, and quite versatile in its scope of operations.

Its prime function is to make holes, of course, and it does this quickly and with precision for a tiny pin-sized hole or an oversized one up to 8" in diameter.

It is the precision factor, more than the speed and simplicity with which the drill press can bore holes, that renders this machine so advantageous. Many facets of serious woodworking

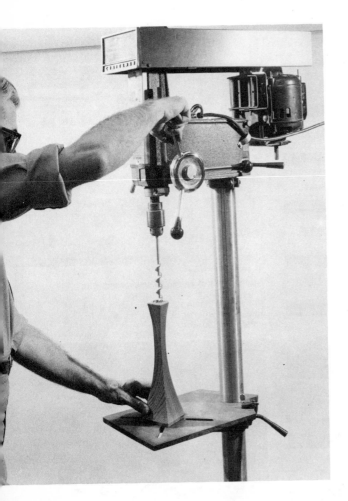

It can make tiny holes the size of a pin (above), or giant ones up to 8" in diameter with a circle-cutter attachment.

The drill press is considered one of the essential tools in the home workshop. It can drill holes with absolute accuracy, to pre-set depth and at any angle.

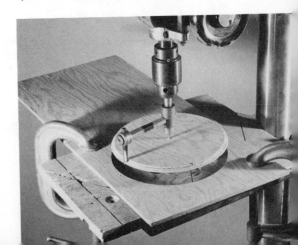

involve precision boring operations that can best be done only with the drill press. Blind dowel joints, straight or compound angle holes for table and chair leg joinery, round and square mortises, holes in circular work, and series drilling are but a few of the jobs that must be done to exacting standards. There are many more.

The drill press can also be used for a variety of operations other than to bore holes. Drum sanding, routing, shaping, surface planing, grinding, and buffing are among some of its secondary possibilities.

The machine consists of four basic parts: base, column, table, and head. The head, which attaches to the upper end of the col-

Using a plug cutter to make perfect fitting plugs to use for concealing counterbored screws in a project.

A drum sanding attachment can be used in this way on the drill press to obtain perfectly perpendicular edges.

Drilling holes at precise angles is a routine task for the press. An adjustable angle vise is used to hold small work.

161

Using a router bit to cut grooves. A clamped backup strip guides the workpiece for accuracy.

umn, contains all of the working mechanism. The table can be moved up and down on the column to accommodate work of varied sizes and it can be swung from side to side or tilted for angle work as required. Bench and floor types are available, differing only in the length of the column. Floor models are decidedly more advantageous because of the larger workpieces they handle.

A geared chuck holds the revolving cutting tool which is moved downward into the work by means of a feed lever. A four-step cone pulley arrangement usually allows a selection

Recessing a panel with a router bit. The quill is locked at the required depth to clean out the waste material after a series of preliminary holes have been bored.

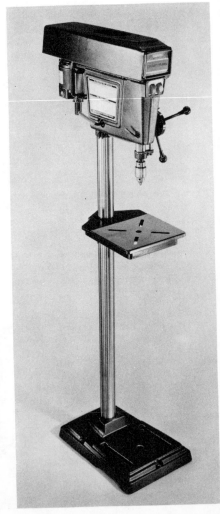

A 15" floor stand drill press. This type is most versatile because of the big workpiece capacity. (Sears Roebuck)

of speeds ranging from 650 to 5000 rpm. The higher speeds are necessary for operations such as routing and shaping. Medium speeds are used for drilling in wood and low speeds for metal work.

The size of a drill press is determined by the distance from the center of the chuck to the front of the vertical column. The machine is rated at twice this dimension. Thus a 16" drill press will measure 8" from chuck to column and will permit drilling to the center of a 16" board or a disc 16" in diameter. Drill press sizes range from 12" to 20".

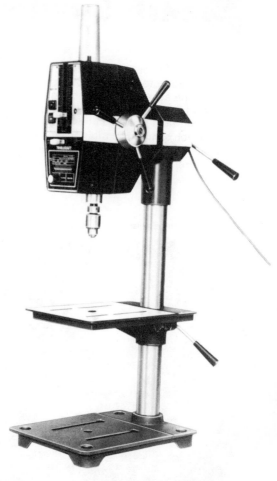

Chuck speeds are varied by shifting the drive belt to any one of four positions on the step pulleys.

A bench type drill press. This one features a variable speed control, eliminates the need for shifting the belt for speed adjustments. The only difference between floor and bench types is the length of the column.

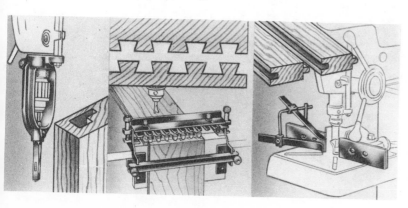

Some of the accessories which can be used on the drill press. A mortising bit (far left) permits drilling square holes. A dovetail cutting jig (center) and a shaping fence near left for use with molding cutters.

163

ench Sanders

What was said about portable sanders is also true of stationary sanders—electrical power is a great substitute for muscle power. Faster sanding without fatigue and better, more uniform work are the advantages over hand sanding.

The portable sanders are the only practical tools to use for sanding large work pieces, but small, hand held work is better done on the heavier, stationary bench sanders.

The bench sander is a tool that can be used to do rough sanding to shape, to fit pieces, and to finish sand almost any shape of work piece with great precision.

There are several types available: disc and disc/drum combinations and belt or belt/disc

The combination disc/drum sander is a simple machine which can be used for shaping and end grain sanding.

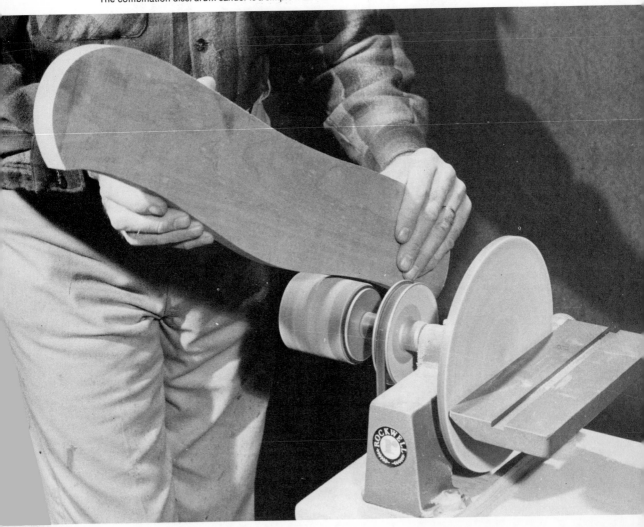

A tilting table used in combination with a miter gage will produce precise compound bevels.

combinations. The latter is by far the most versatile.

The disc sander consists of a metal disc to which a circular sheet of abrasive is attached with a non-hardening adhesive. A small tiltable table with a miter gage groove supports the work in front of the disc. This tool serves very well for quick roughing to shape and for contour sanding of outside curves as well as for smoothing the end grain of small pieces.

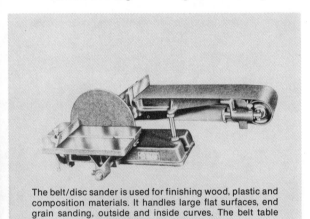

The belt/disc sander is used for finishing wood, plastic and composition materials. It handles large flat surfaces, end grain sanding, outside and inside curves. The belt table adjusts from horizontal to vertical. (*Toolkraft*)

Sanding the inside of a hole with the drum sander. Drums of several diameters are available.

The disc sander is not suitable for working large flat surfaces, but it is quite useful for shaping and finishing the edge of a curved piece.

Although the disc may measure 8″ or 9″ in diameter, the useable area is confined to the "down" side of the rotating disc or half the diameter. Additionally, the disc sands faster at the outer edge than at its center, making it difficult to sand a true straightedge longer than a few inches.

The belt sander, unlike the disc, features a continuous belt that provides uniform motion throughout. It is excellent for accurate straightedge sanding, surface sanding, and contour sanding of inside curves that will fit the radius of the belt drum ends. A tilting table makes it possible to hold the work at a precise angle to the abrasive, while a belt fence permits sliding the work accurately across the surface. The entire belt unit can be adjusted from horizontal to vertical to provide the most convenient working position.

Disc sanders are available in 8″ and 9″ diameters and belt sanders in 4″ and 6″ sizes (width of belt). Drum sanding accessories up to 3″ in diameter are available for use with the disc sander. Attached to the opposite end of the disc arbor, the drum works very well for sanding curved inside edges and is especially well-suited for doing freehand sanding of irregular shapes.

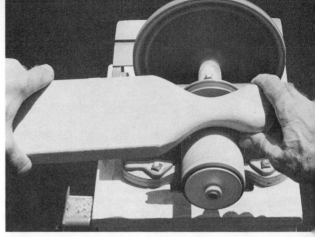

Wood can be sculpted to smooth contours on the drum sander after rough cutting with a saw.

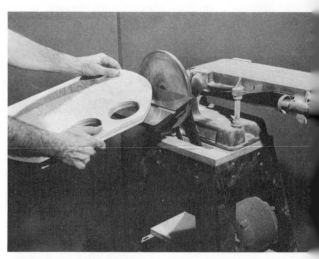

The disc sander here is used free-hand to smooth out band saw ripples of a beveled curve.

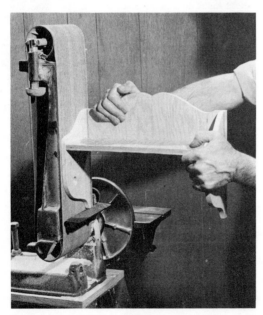

Several fence positions may be utilized with the belt sander. The large tilting table may be relocated from the disc position to the belt unit when the need arises.

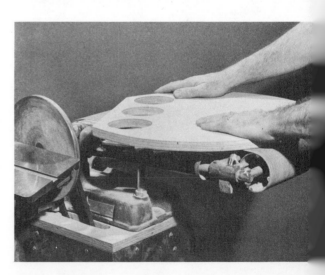

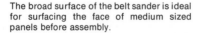

The broad surface of the belt sander is ideal for surfacing the face of medium sized panels before assembly.

Sander/Grinder

Primarily a metalworking machine, the Sander/Grinder is nevertheless quite at home and very useful in the wood shop. As its name implies, this is a dual purpose tool that can be used for both sanding and grinding.

A 1" wide abrasive belt travels over four wheels and through a slot in the table at a speed of 4000 surface feet per minute. This permits it to sand wood or grind metal at relatively high speed while building up very little heat at the point of contact.

A metal platen, which backs up the belt behind the table, provides the solid surface necessary for precision metal grinding or wood sanding. The important feature of the machine, however, is that the platen may be removed so that the flexible belt can be used to sand irregular shapes. By manipulating the two rear guide wheels the belt can be positioned to run through an opening in the work to permit flexible internal sanding. This is a very desirable feature for some special jobs.

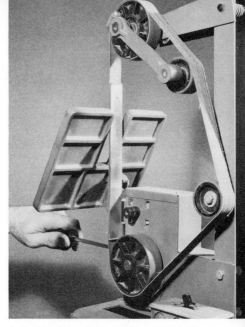

A steel back up platen can be removed when the work requires a flexing belt to follow curved shapes. Note how the table can be tilted.

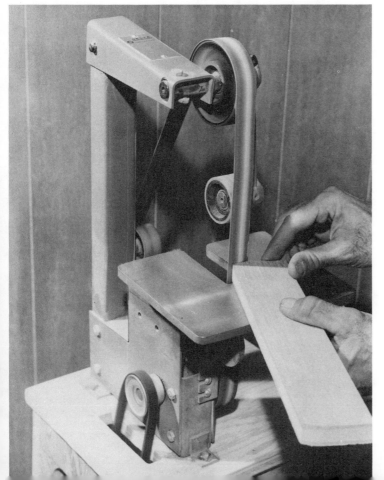

Internal sanding is done by passing the belt through the opening in the work. The procedure is somewhat similar to the one used on the jig saw for internal cutting.

This tool is quite versatile. It can be used to sand wood, grind and polish plastics and metal.

ᴊointers

The jointer is essentially a heavy-duty stationary power plane. It is used primarily to smooth the edges and surfaces of boards that have been cut on a saw. Further, it can be used to cut rabbets, bevels, chamfers, recesses, tapers and other cuts, including freehand preliminary rounding.

The size of a jointer is based on the length of the cutting knives which determines the maximum width of the stock it can surface. Jointers range in size from 4″ and up by increments of 2″. Anything above 6″ is strictly for commercial duty; 4″ and 6″ jointers are quite satisfactory for home workshop use.

This machine is one of the least complex of

The jointer planes the edges and surfaces of lumber, cuts rabbets, tapers, chamfers and bevels without added accessories. Machine is one of safest to use.

Glued up stock is trued up with a few passes on the jointer.

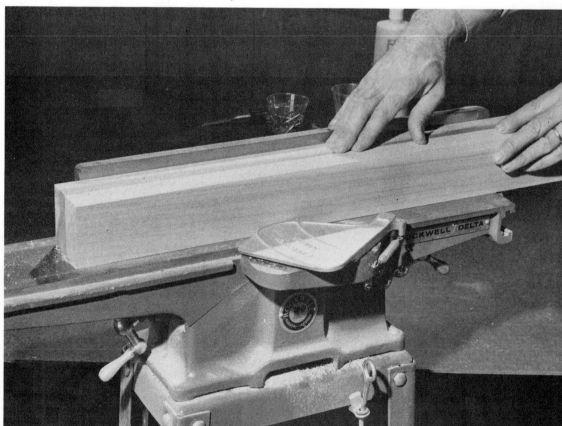

all the power tools in terms of both construction and operation. The principal parts consist of a base, a two-part table, an adjustable fence, and a solid steel cutterhead, which usually contains three cutting knives. The cutterhead revolves at high speed, driven by a belt.

The way the jointer works is quite simple. The rear table is set in a fixed position on a horizontal plane tangent to the cutting arc of the knives. This is termed the outfeed table. The front, or infeed table, is adjustable so that it may be changed for various depths of cut. Both tables are perfectly parallel in relation to each other and the offset or difference in height between the two determines the depth

A three-knife cutterhead revolves at high speed of 4200 rpm delivering 12,600 knife cuts per minute. This adds up to speedy stock removal.

A 6″ jointer is about as big a machine ever needed in the home workshop. The 4″ size is generally quite adequate to tackle most jobs. (Toolkraft)

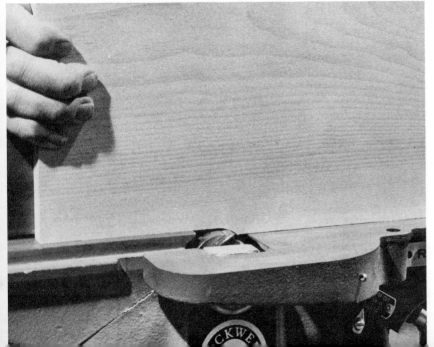

Planning an edge. The amount of wood shaved off is equal to the offset between the front and rear table. End grain can be planed without splintering if the work is reversed after a short cut is made at the opposite end.

169

of cut. The adjustment is made by means of a wheel or crank that raises or lowers the table for as fine an adjustment as is desired. The depth of cut is indicated on a sliding scale.

When a board is passed over the lowered front table its leading end makes contact with the knives that shave off an amount of wood equal to the offset. As the board advances onto the rear table its new surface makes flush contact with the rear table, so both the old and new surfaces are constantly resting on the respective tables. The action is simple and straightforward with little chance for error.

The fence has two movements. It can be tilted from 90 to 45 degrees left or right for bevel cutting and it can be moved from the front to the back of the machine for setting up rabbet cuts of various widths.

For safety in operation a side-swinging blade guard is constantly held in position over the cutterhead by spring tension. It is retracted by the leading end of the work piece. For rabbeting work the guard is easily removed to allow the necessary clearance.

Rabbet cuts are made by passing the work over the outside edge of the table. The width of the rabbet is limited only by the length of the cutterhead.

The fence can be tilted and locked at any angle up to 45 degrees left and right to plane bevels.

170

Uniplane

The Uniplane is a relative newcomer in the field of woodworking machines. It is actually a jointer that offers a unique and superior method for jointing and surfacing material as small as a matchstick up to 6″ in width or thickness with complete safety.

The cutter head is an entirely new concept consisting of a rotary disc with two sets of cutters—four cutters that score and four that shear the wood. This cutting action produces exceptionally fine surfaces.

A side benefit results from this unusual type of cutting action: there is absolutely no pos-

The Uniplane is a unique jointing and surfacing machine. It can be used for beveling, chamfering, trimming, tapering and other operations.

Flywheel type cutterhead has eight cutters which rotate at 4000 rpm. They project only slightly in a path ⅜″ wide thus rendering the machine quite safe to operate. The tool will surface-plane lumber up to 6″ thick with ease.

sibility of material kickback. Therefore, many kinds of cuts that would be difficult or impractical to perform with a conventional jointer are easily accomplished with this machine. It can be used to plane very thin stock, trim compound miters, square the ends of small blocks, and chamfer or surface extremely small pieces.

The table tilts to 45 degrees for bevel cutting and is grooved to accept a miter gage. With this combination it is indeed a very simple task to cut compound miters without the need for special jigs.

A graduated collar calibrated in 64ths of an inch permits exceptionally accurate depth-of-cut settings. The maximum depth of cut is $1/8''$ which seems like a trifling amount, but when you consider that the rpm is 4000 and 8 cutters are involved, this adds up to 32,000 cuts per minute! It takes very little time to shave $1/8''$ of stock from even a 6" thick timber.

If space and finances permit, this is certainly a useful tool to have around.

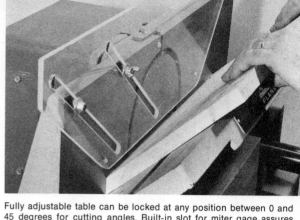

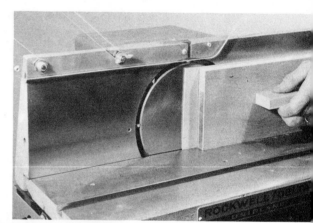

Fully adjustable table can be locked at any position between 0 and 45 degrees for cutting angles. Built-in slot for miter gage assures accuracy for trimming operations.

Thin stock supported by a pusher block can be trimmed to fine tolerances. Micro type cut control permits exceptionally accurate depth of cut settings. Graduated depth control collar is calibrated in 64ths of an inch.

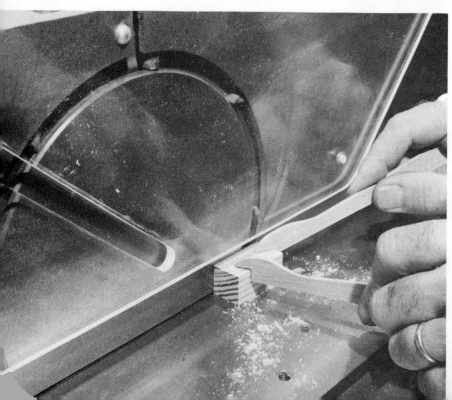

At the other extreme, tiny pieces too small to hold can be pushed past the cutters with complete safety. The rotary action eliminates kickback dangers.

hapers

The shaper is a machine that offers unlimited possibilities for making molding and cutting decorative shapes on straight, internal and external, curved and irregular edge surfaces. It can turn out superior work quickly and accurately and is relatively easy to operate.

The machine consists of a base and a solid cast iron table with a removable fence and a milled groove to accommodate a sliding miter gage. It has a vertical spindle that projects through an opening in the table. The spindle holds variously shaped cutters which rotate at very high speed to produce extremely smooth finished surfaces.

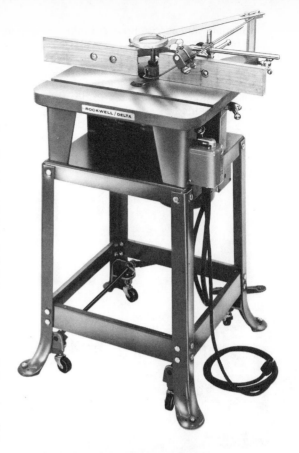

A home shop shaper with ½" spindle which rotates at 9000 rpm. It has a reversing switch which permits wide utilization of cutter shapes. (Rockwell)

The shaper is used to make a variety of molding and joint cuts on straight, internal and external, curved and irregular surfaces. Rabbet cut is shown here.

Shapers vary according to spindle diameter and rpm. Medium-sized shapers with ½″ spindles are the most practical for the average workshop. Motors range from ½ and 1 horsepower and with various pulley combinations deliver 9,000 to 18,000 rpm. Higher speeds produce smoother work.

A single adjustment raises or lowers the spindle to permit cuts of different thicknesses. Although cutters are available in dozens of shapes, hundreds of different ornamental designs can be obtained by simply passing the same edge of a work piece through a number of variously shaped cutters. This procedure requires spindle height and fence position adjustments which are easily accomplished.

A large assortment of three-lip shaper cutters. Many more are available.

The table of the shaper can be moved up and down to vary the relationship of the cutter to the edge of the work. On some models it is the spindle rather than the table which is moved. A three-lip one piece cutter is shown. This is the safest kind to use. Two-knife clamp type cutters can be dangerous and should be avoided.

Making a fence-guided cut. Accessory spring hold-downs help to keep the stock in place. Depth of cut is controlled by the distance between the spindle and fence.

Most shapers are equipped with a reversing switch that permits feeding the work from either direction. This can prove advantageous because on some shapes the cut may only be made by feeding the work from one side and not the other.

Shaping work can be done by any one of four basic methods: with the fence, depth collars, patterns, or forms. The nature of the work determines the method used. With custom made jigs and fixtures to guide the work for special applications, the capabilities of this machine can really be appreciated.

The shaper fence consists of two independently adjustable sections. Operations in which some part of the original wood edge remains uncut requires an in-line adjustment. When an entire edge is to be shaped the rear fence is offset to meet the new edge. The ring guard is especially recommended when working with the fence removed.

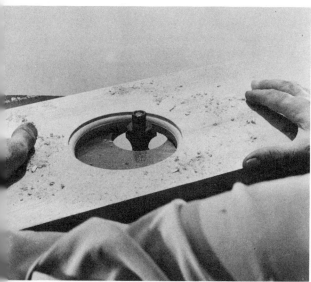

Using a depth collar to shape a curved edge. The uncut portion of the inside edge rides against the collar which controls the depth of cut. Top shape was cut first. A second pass is being made to shape the other side.

Shaping with a pattern. A pre-cut plywood pattern attached to the bottom of the workpiece rides against the depth collar. The molded edge matches the shape of the pattern to perfection.

Shaping with a form. In this case the form is a tenoning jig. A form is simply a device which is used to hold the work. Forms are made for special cuts.

Wood Lathes

The lathe is a unique power tool in that its only function is to spin a block or length of wood at varying degrees of speed. That's all it really does!

The beautiful wood turnings with graceful curves and intricate forms that can be produced on the lathe are the result of hand work done with chisels. In a broad sense, turning can be described as a form of carving. It is a fascinating craft that provides an excellent opportunity for artful achievement, yet it requires no special talents. With only a little practice any beginner can turn out reasonably acceptable work. With added experience and the application of special techniques and short-cuts, turning can be mastered by anyone with the desire.

The lathe can be used to turn out any number of finished items, such as bowls, vases, lamp bases, chandeliers, decorative display pieces, baseball bats, and the like. Or it may be used to make components for other projects, like table and chair legs and spindles, finials, posts, balusters, rings and wheels, to mention but a few.

The variety of items which can be turned on the lathe is unlimited. Some of the turning chisels used on this project were made by grinding the ends of small screwdrivers.

Lathe work is actually a form of sculpture as is evidenced by this graceful hanging lamp.

As a shop tool the lathe is in a class all its own. It can be used to turn out finished products with little or no dependence on other tools or machines. Lathe work is fascinating and relatively easy to do.

The basic parts of the lathe are the bed, headstock, tailstock, and the tool rest. The headstock is a fixed part of the left end of the bed. It houses a four-step pulley and the spindle, which is hollow and threaded at both ends. A spur or live center is inserted in the spindle.

The tailstock is movable along the lathe bed and can be clamped at any position by means of a clamp lever. It also has a hollow spindle which accepts a cup or dead center (so called because it doesn't turn). This spindle can be projected or retracted to secure or remove the workpiece by turning a feed crank.

Power is transferred to the headstock spindle by a V belt attached to a four-step motor pulley that is mounted directly below

The lathe is basically a very simple machine. It has a fixed headstock, a bed, a movable tailstock and a tool rest. A motor with V-belt drives the spindle which turns the wood.

An indexing pin is a valuable feature on a lathe. It is used for dividing faceplate work and for spacing cuts for fluting and reeding.

The drive system of the lathe. An extra accessory, the jack shaft, has been installed between the motor and spindle pulleys. This is a system of extra pulleys which increases the range of speeds obtainable at the spindle. Speeds are changed by choosing various pulley and belt combinations.

177

A crankwheel in the tailstock is used to drive the tailstock ram which presses the dead center into the wood.

Turning which cannot be worked between centers must be mounted on a faceplate. Screws pass through the faceplate into the waste part of the work.

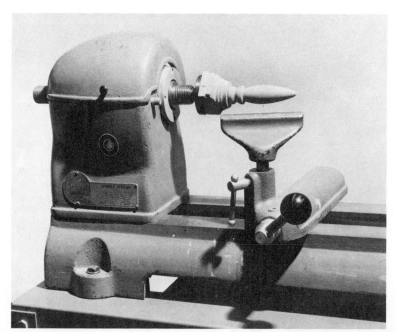

Work which is too small to do on a faceplate can be secured to a screw center.

the headstock. Lathe speeds vary between makes but generally range from approximately 600 to 4800 rpm. Speeds are changed by shifting the belt through the various pulley combinations. Lower speeds are used for large diameter turning and preliminary roughing work; the higher speeds are for small diameter and finishing work.

Stock can be mounted on the lathe in either of two ways: between centers supporting the piece on both ends, or on a face plate for those jobs requiring access on the end as well as on the circumference. Between-centers work is called spindle turning, while work done on stock that is secured to a face plate is called faceplate turning.

The maximum length of a spindle that can be turned on a lathe is limited by the space between centers. The maximum diameter of

Work which is too large to be turned over the bed can be worked on the outboard end of the lathe. A free standing accessory tool rest must be used with this method.

The lathe capacity is limited by the distance from the bed to the spindle center.

Horizontal drilling on the lathe is possible with a geared chuck inserted into the head or tailstock.

work that can be handled depends on the clearance between the spindle and the bed. The size of a lathe relates to these capacities. Thus a 12″ lathe with 42″ centers has the capacity to handle work within those dimensions.

Some lathes have a gap bed that is depressed in the area of the headstock. This results in a greater capacity in diameter for faceplate work. For extra large turnings the faceplate can be attached to the outboard side of the spindle which has a left-hand thread. The faceplate for this application must also have a left-hand thread.

The tools used for turning consist of variously shaped chisels, five of which comprise a basic set: gouge, skew, round nose, spear

The standard set of tools used in wood turning comprises five different shapes. This set has eight; the three at right are extra gouges of different sizes. (Sears Roebuck)

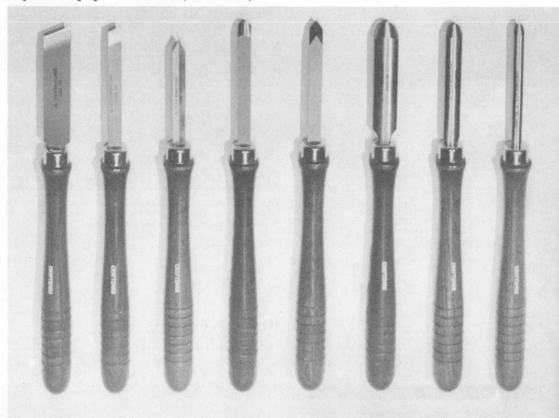

point, and parting tool. Skews and gouges come in several sizes, so a more complete set may include eight chisels. They're also available with carbide tips which keep their edges much longer than ordinary steel chisels.

Accessories include dividers and calipers for measuring, screw centers for small work, chuck arbors for drilling, and screw-on arbors that can hold buffing wheels, grinders, and wire wheels. A steady rest is an accessory that can be bought or easily made out of wood. This is used to steady long, slender spindle turnings to prevent them from flexing.

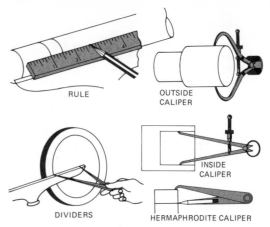

RULE   OUTSIDE CALIPER

DIVIDERS   INSIDE CALIPER

HERMAPHRODITE CALIPER

The measuring tools for lathe work. (Rockwell)

The caliper is the most used measuring tool for lathe work.

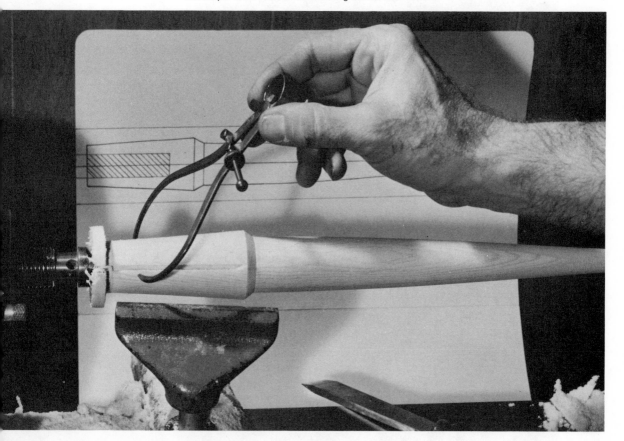

Bench Grinder

The grinder is a top priority tool for any shop, large or small. An occasional honing by hand will sharpen the cutting edge of a slightly dull tool, but a power grinder is necessary to remove nicks or to put a new bevel on a tool. Good shop work can only be done with sharp tools.

   Grinders are available in several sizes, rated by the diameter of the abrasive wheel. A 5″ or 6″ double wheel grinder equipped with a fine and medium grit wheel will be perfectly satisfactory for the home shop.

The fine stone is used to put a new edge on cutting tools. The coarse wheel is used for general stock removal.

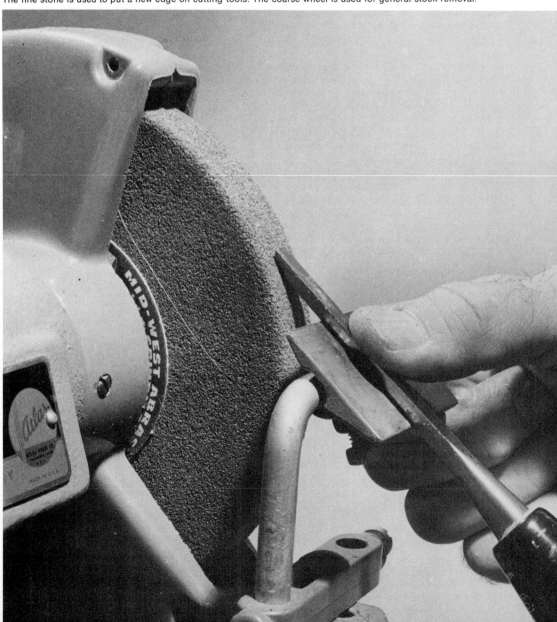

Motor speeds vary with different models ranging from 1425 rpm to 3450 rpm. The higher speed grinders will remove stock more quickly than the slower models, but more care is required to avoid burning the temper out of the tool's cutting edge.

Important features include lubricated-for-life bearings, precision balanced wheels, sturdy tool rests, adjustable spark deflectors, wheel guards, and unbreakable eye shields. Several accessories for the grinder are tool-grinding guides, wire brushes, buffing wheels, and a diamond-pointed wheel dresser.

A coarse wheel makes quick work of sharpening garden tools and the like. (Black & Decker)

A 5″ two wheel bench grinder equipped with a coarse and fine wheel. (Black & Decker)

A slow turning fine grit wheel is used to give a tool edge the finishing touch.

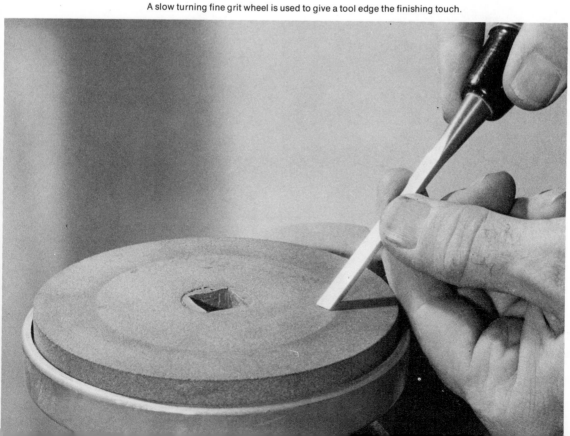

The Multipurpose Tool

If limited space prevents you from equipping your workshop with the various single purpose stationary tools, consider the acquisition of a multi-purpose tool. This is a single unit that readily converts for use as a circular saw, a drill press and horizontal drill, a disc sander and a lathe, all powered by one motor.

Accessory add-on tools, such as a jointer, belt sander, a bandsaw, and a jig saw, extend the capabilities of the basic machine to perform all of the essential workshop functions. These, too, are driven by the same heavy-duty motor.

By eliminating the necessity for individual stands and motors, an impressive economy in cost and space is realized. The unit illustrated requires a floor space measuring less than 2′ x

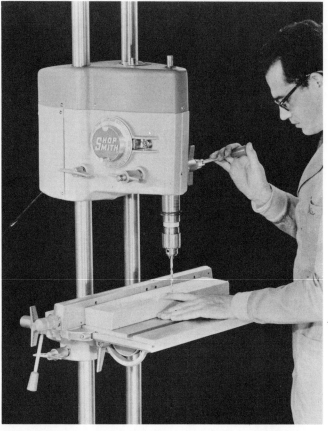

This multipurpose tool combines five machines in one space saving unit. Here the well-known author and craftsman R. J. DeCristoforo demonstrates use of the tool as a drill press.

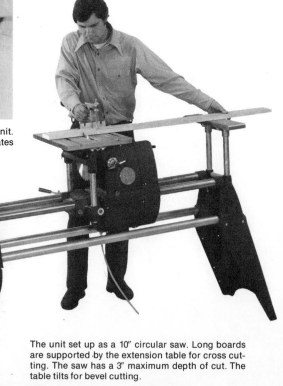

The unit set up as a 10″ circular saw. Long boards are supported by the extension table for cross cutting. The saw has a 3″ maximum depth of cut. The table tilts for bevel cutting.

6. The frame is equipped with retractable casters for easy mobility, so that it is conceivable to set up shop, for instance, in an occupied garage. By backing out the car and wheeling this machine into the open space you can enjoy the advantages of a well-equipped precision power tool shop.

Although there is a changeover time factor involved in shifting from one function to another, this is by no means a serious drawback. The multipurpose tool shown here has been engineered to a high degree of efficiency, not only in terms of working precision of the various components, but also to effect minimal changeover time. Some shifts, such as from disc sander to horizontal drill, may take as little as ten seconds. Others take longer, but with practice the steps become almost automatic and quickly carried out.

Molding cutter head accessory is used in place of the saw blade to cut fancy molded shapes in wood.

All of the specialty cuts which can be made with a conventional table saw can also be done with this tool. Here a cove is being cut.

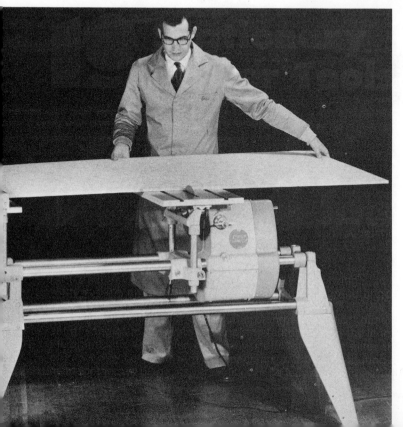

The extension table with rip fence permits easy cutting of oversize panels. The tool has the unusual capacity of cutting through the center of an 8' panel.

185

In one of its basic functions as a saw, the tool cannot boast of a tilting arbor; instead, the table must be tilted for making beveled cuts. This may prove to be a bit awkward when handling large work pieces. The saw is unique, however, in capacity. With the rip fence mounted on the extended table, the blade-to-fence distance is greater than 48″. This makes possible the cutting of large panels with relative ease, a feat not so easily accomplished with conventional table saws. The depth-of-cut capability is better than 3″ thus permitting ripping or crosscutting through thick stock.

The various other operations, such as sanding and drilling, can be carried out to exacting tolerances because of the quill feed and depth control features that are built into the spindle.

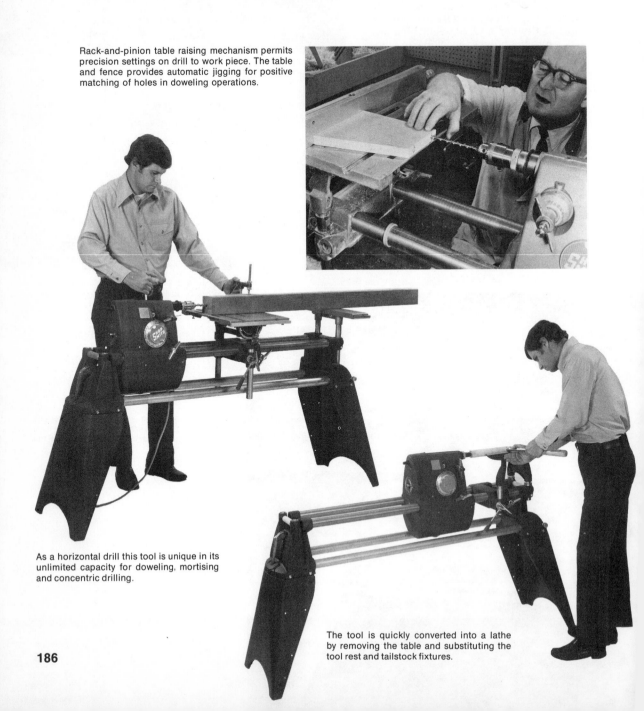

Rack-and-pinion table raising mechanism permits precision settings on drill to work piece. The table and fence provides automatic jigging for positive matching of holes in doweling operations.

As a horizontal drill this tool is unique in its unlimited capacity for doweling, mortising and concentric drilling.

The tool is quickly converted into a lathe by removing the table and substituting the tool rest and tailstock fixtures.

The manipulation of the table, fence, and miter gage adds up to automatic jigging that assures hairline accuracy. Precise duplication of work pieces, matching dowel holes, mortises, routing and shaping operations are easy and routine with this versatile tool.

As a lathe the machine offers an exceptional capacity of 16½″ for faceplate turning. For turnings of larger diameter the headstock is simply moved to the end of the ways to allow the faceplate to extend beyond the frame. The tool rest slides parallel to the work piece and this is a big plus feature. By clamping a cutting tool to the tool rest the turning of absolutely perfect cylinders is easily accom-

An excellent example of the versatility of performance of this tool. The table and fence serve as a cradle for this tricky drilling chore.

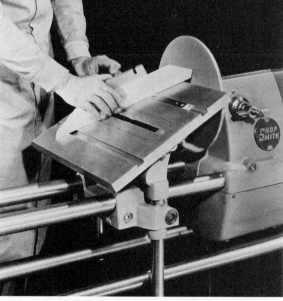

As a 12″ disc sander the tool gives a capacity in excess of that offered by many industrial sanders. Miter gage and tilted table permit sanding precise compound angles.

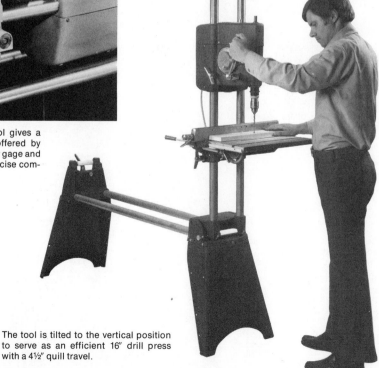

The tool is tilted to the vertical position to serve as an efficient 16″ drill press with a 4½″ quill travel.

187

plished by sliding the tool along the work. The action is automatically controlled. Also, an eccentric cup center mount is built into the tailstock permitting controlled offset for turning tapers.

Various materials and operations require differing spindle speeds. This machine is equipped with a variable speed control that provides a range of spindle speeds from 700 to 5200 rpm at the mere turning of a dial.

A small sampling of the capabilities of this machine are shown here; the possibilities are practically unlimited.

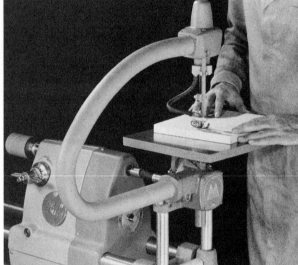

Add-on jig saw has an 18″ capacity, tilting table and a tubular arm which can be pivoted out of the way for saber sawing large panels.

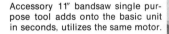

A 16½″ swing offers exceptional capacity for faceplate turning.

Accessory 11″ bandsaw single purpose tool adds onto the basic unit in seconds, utilizes the same motor.

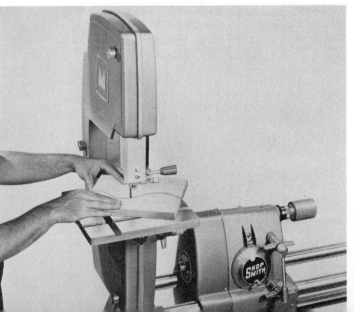

A 6″ belt sander accessory rounds out the sanding capabilities of the tool.

A heavy duty 4″ jointer add-on makes a good team mate for the circular saw.

A diaphragm type compressor sprayer with a one quart spray gun completes the total shop multipurpose tool concept. Air delivery is 2.4 cubic feet with a working pressure of 30 pounds.

5 TECHNIQUES WITH TOOLS

20 Measure and Layout

The first practical task in any woodworking project involves the making of measurements. After you have decided what to build and the kind of wood to use, it will be necessary to mark up the stock in order to guide yourself in cutting it to the required size and shape.

Accuracy of measurement is essential for good work and to avoid the waste of time and material. You can achieve extreme accuracy at little or no extra cost or effort if you use the tools properly.

There are a number of tools used for measuring, marking, and for checking the work. Some are specialized, while others serve overlapping functions.

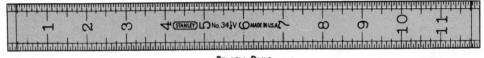

BENCH RULE

INSIDE AND OUTSIDE CALIPER RULE

ZIG ZAG RULE

OUTSIDE READ HERE

INSIDE READ HERE

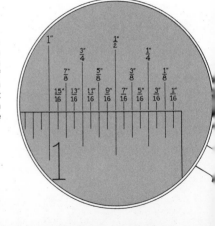

Rules. These are the most commonly used rules. The bench rule is made in 1 and 2 ft. lengths, graduated into eighths on one side, sixteenths on the other. It is used for measuring small work. The flexible "push-pull" steel tape and the folding zig zag wood rules are used for measuring and marking off large pieces of stock.

The caliper rule is used for taking accurate measurements of the thickness of stock or the dimensions of holes or openings, either straight or curved. *(Stanley Tools)*

Rules are divided into fractional parts of an inch. The number of divisions per inch denotes the denominator of the fraction. Sixteenth-inch graduations are the most common but 32-nd and 64-th inch rules are used for fine cabinetry work.

The Rules

The rule is the basic measuring tool. The one- or two-foot bench rule is used for average shop work, while the steel tape measure or the folding rule is used to measure and mark off large pieces of stock or areas of work. In any measuring or marking operation it is important to work with a sharply pointed pencil and to hold the rule on edge in order to bring the scale in close contact to the surface of the work. Whenever possible, a sharp knife or the point of a scratch awl should be used to scribe lines, to obtain the greatest accuracy.

Hold the pencil at an angle when striking a line against a rule to insure accuracy. To do otherwise may result in an erratic line. The same procedure is followed with a knife or awl but with less severe angle. Always make sure the end of the rule is even with the edge of the work to assure accurate measurement.

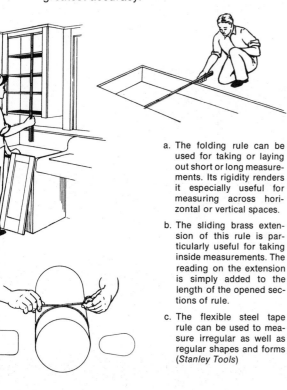

a. The folding rule can be used for taking or laying out short or long measurements. Its rigidity renders it especially useful for measuring across horizontal or vertical spaces.

b. The sliding brass extension of this rule is particularly useful for taking inside measurements. The reading on the extension is simply added to the length of the opened sections of rule.

c. The flexible steel tape rule can be used to measure irregular as well as regular shapes and forms (*Stanley Tools*)

A simple procedure used to divide a board of odd width into several equal parts: Place the rule at an angle across the board so that the number of increments desired span the outer edges of the stock. In this example four equal parts are required. The rule is positioned at the 8″ mark on one edge and the 16″ mark over the other edge. A mark is then placed at 2″ points along the rule to result in four equal divisions. Any number of divisions can be made in this way. The inner parts of the rule are used for greater accuracy in line up.

Using the steel tape for an outside measurement. The hook on the end slides the amount of its own thickness to adjust for accurate zero between inside and outside measurements. Accurate inside measurements also can be made with this rule. Be sure to add two inches to the measurement indicated on the blade to compensate for the width of the case.

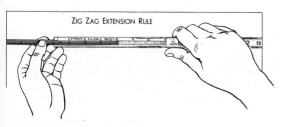

ZIG ZAG EXTENSION RULE

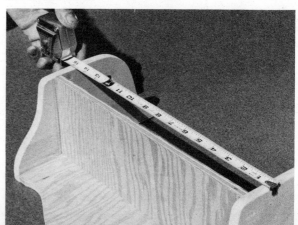

The Squares

The function of the square is to lay out lines perpendicular to an edge and to check adjoining surfaces for squareness. The try square was for many years the basic tool for this purpose, and while it is still widely used, the more versatile combination square has gained greater acceptance for general shop use.

The combination square is actually a try square and miter square and more. It can be used as a level and plumb, a marking gage, or a depth gage. The handle of this tool slides along a groove in the blade allowing it to be adjusted and locked at any position.

A. Parts of the try square. B. To mark an accurate line: Place the pencil or knife on the desired point, then slide the square against the marking tool and draw the line. C. Using the blade of the try square to test the face of stock for trueness. D. Hold the handle firmly against the work face and look towards the light. No light will show under the blade if the edge is square. E. Using the square to test the end in relation to the work edge. F. Using the square to test an inside corner. G. Scribing guidelines across the face of stock. H. When squaring lines across the edge, be sure to start exactly from the end of the line on the face. (*Stanley Tools*)

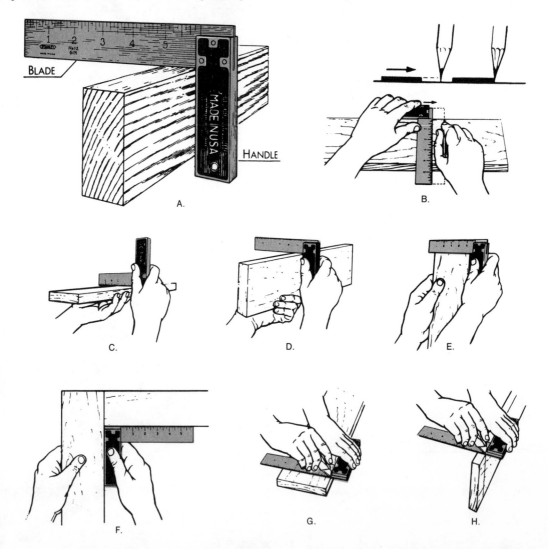

A. B. C. D. E. F. G. H.

TRY SQUARE

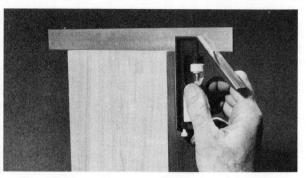

Using the combination square as a try square to check the end of a board for squareness.

The bubble vial in the handle permits use of the tool as a level. To check the plumb of a vertical surface you need only to hold the blade section up against the work.

The square can be used as a marking gage by adjusting and locking the blade to the desired projection.

Using the adjustable blade as a depth gage. Loosen the blade, let it touch bottom, then tighten and read the measurement. The depth capacity of over 10 inches is quite handy.

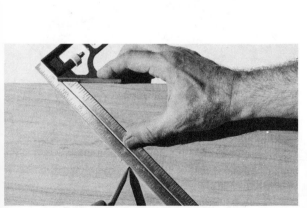

Using the combination square to mark off a 45 degree miter angle on a board.

THE FRAMING OR STEEL SQUARE

The framing or steel square is primarily a carpenter's tool calibrated with a special scale that is used to calculate rafter angles in house framing construction, but it is useful in the home workshop because of its large size. The 16″ x 24″ length of the body and tongue of this tool permits testing and marking larger workpieces with increased accuracy.

The sliding T bevel is the tool used to check or lay out any angle from 0 to 180 degrees. The blade slides along the handle and is locked in the required position with a small thumbscrew.

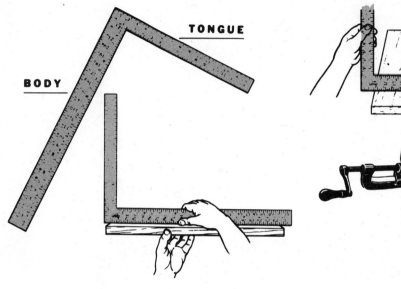

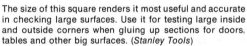

The size of this square renders it most useful and accurate in checking large surfaces. Use it for testing large inside and outside corners when gluing up sections for doors, tables and other big surfaces. (*Stanley Tools*)

SLIDING T BEVEL

a. Sliding T bevel
b. This tool is used to check beveled or chamfered edges.
c. Hold the bevel firmly on the handle and blade when laying off a miter.
d. The T bevel is useful for marking repeat angles when laying out special joints. (*Stanley Tools*)

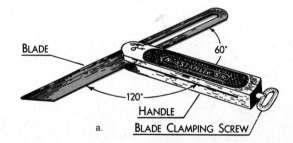

BLADE · 60° · 120° · HANDLE · BLADE CLAMPING SCREW

a.

b.   c.   d.

Other Tools

THE MARKING GAGE

Additional tools used for measuring and marking include the marking gage, scratch awl, dividers, trammel points, and protractor. The calipers, level, and plumb line are tools required for checking the work. All are easy to use.

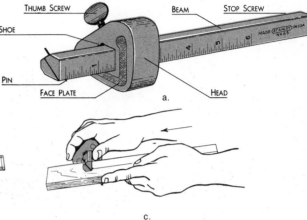

a.

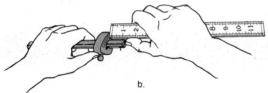

b.

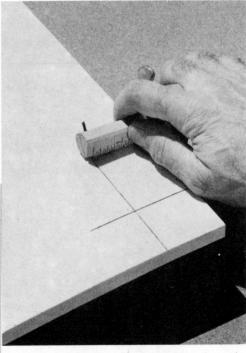

Cross-grain lines can be scribed but a light touch must be used because the pin tears those fibers.

a. **Marking Gage.**
b. This tool is used to scribe a line parallel to the grain of the wood. The gage is set by measurement from the head to the pinpoint.
c. Hold the gage as you would hold a ball. Then advance the thumb toward the pin to equalize the pressure between the pin and the head. The gage is pushed forward with the head held firmly against the work edge of the wood. Apply pressure in the direction of the arrows. The pin should project about ¹/₁₆″ from the beam. (*Stanley Tools*)

If the required degree of an angle is known, the T bevel may be set with the aid of a 180-degree protractor.

The bevel is frequently adjusted to a constructed angle then used to transfer the angle to new work.

HANDLE

FERRULE

BLADE

THE SCRATCH AWL

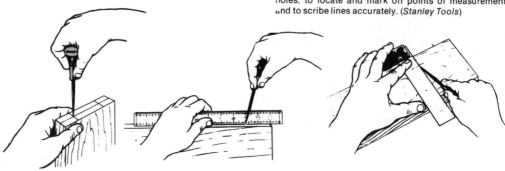

Scratch Awl
The scratch awl is used to mark centers for boring holes, to locate and mark off points of measurement and to scribe lines accurately. (*Stanley Tools*)

DIVIDERS

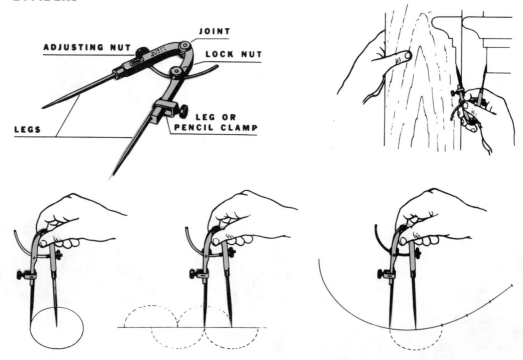

JOINT

ADJUSTING NUT

LOCK NUT

LEGS

LEG OR PENCIL CLAMP

Dividers
Dividers can be used to transfer an irregular profile to a flat surface. The points must be held horizontally throughout the procedure.

The divider is a tool with two pointed legs, one of which can be removed and replaced with a pencil point. It is used to scribe circles and arcs and to lay out equal spaces along a straight or curved line. (*Stanley Tools*)

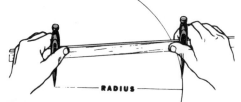

TRAMMEL POINTS

Trammel Points

Trammel points are a pair of matching metal pointers which can be clamped to a strip of wood or other beam of convenient length. It is used to draw large circles or arcs or to lay out measurements which are too long for the dividers. When required, a pencil may be held in the pencil clamp. (*Stanley Tools*)

The protractor is a simple drawing tool used for setting off angles. The center of the hole in the base is used as the index point. Here a protractor is used to divide a circle into equal parts. Set the 0 and 180 degree graduations on the base line (which runs through the center) then strike off the desired equal distances.

Outside calipers are set by butting one leg against the end of a rule. Inside calipers are set with one leg in line with the end of the rule. Dividers are set by holding both points on a pair of graduating lines.

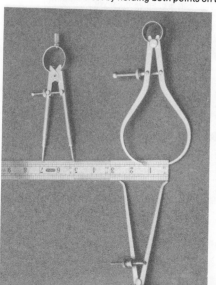

The plumb bob, a pointed weight on a string, is used to set a framing member to true vertical.

A carpenter's level can be used to check for plumb when assembling certain furniture projects. The work surface must first be leveled in the horizontal plane.

197

Drawing Various Shapes

It is frequently necessary to draw irregular shapes for parts of a woodworking project. The cutting lines can be drawn directly on the wood or they may first be drawn on paper and then transferred to the work. Templates and patterns are sometimes useful for checking the work, to help in planning the best way to cut sections out of a large panel with minimal waste, or simply to assure accuracy when laying out a number of identical pieces. Some useful hints on how to draw irregular shapes follow.

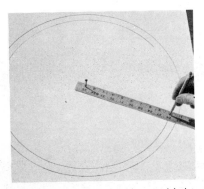

An aluminum yardstick with several holes drilled at the desired distances serves as a beam compass for drawing large circles.

When a project calls for drawing a number of arcs of several repeated sizes, a stick with pivot holes for a nail will insure absolute accuracy. The pivot is set at the intersection lines of the arc's radius.

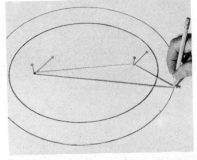

An ellipse (a flattened circle) can be drawn with the pin and string method: Tie a loop in a piece of string, place it over two pivot points and hold the pencil firmly against the string to draw the ellipse. Variations may be obtained by changing the size of the loop and the distance between pins.

The hexagon, a six-sided shape, is frequently used in woodworking. Drawing it is quite easy: Draw a circle with a radius equal to the length of one side of the hexagon. Place the pivot at any point on the circle and draw an arc. Move the pivot point of the compass to the arc and strike another arc. Repeat to divide the circle into six equal parts. Connect these points to form six equal sides. Note that a white pencil is used for clarity on the dark hardboard panels.

Enlarging an irregular scale drawing: Many project designs are drawn in reduced size on grid squares. Instructions on the drawing will note the degree of enlargement required to produce a full size drawing of the pattern. For example, the drawing shown calls for enlarging the squares to ½". Lay out the same number of ½" squares on a piece of large paper as are shown on the small drawing. Number the vertical and horizontal lines on both grids to match. Refer to the small drawing, locate a point, and transfer this point to its respective position on the large drawing. Repeat this procedure of transferring points, then connect the points to produce the outline.

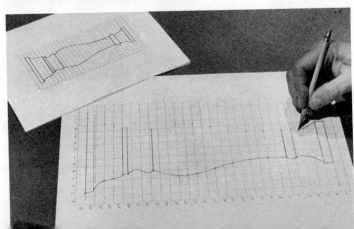

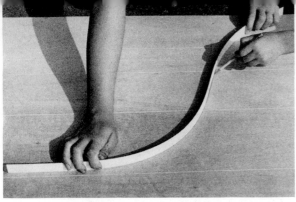

A strip of plastic laminate may be used to draw graceful irregular curves. Three hands are required for this operation, two to hold, one to draw.

Three nails and a flexible strip of wood are used in this manner to draw a simple curve. The center nail position sets the degree of curvature.

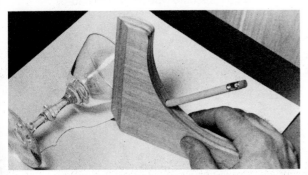

A handy jig for tracing a three dimensional pattern. Point the lead edge of the block and drill a hole at exactly 45 degrees, sized to hold a pencil snugly. The corner is mitered to allow the pencil point to project. The jig can be made in any size.

Time can be saved and accuracy assured if you use a cardboard template to lay out the cutting pattern on projects which have a number of identical parts. This technique also helps determine the most economical cutting arrangement on a large sheet of plywood.

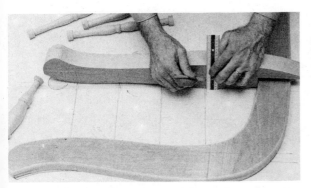

Full size drawings are especially helpful when working on projects with unusual shapes. Work directly on the drawings to spot difficult measurements.

The layout of hole drilling centers can be speeded up and accuracy assured with the use of a simple jig such as this when numerous identical parts are required.

When a design has a symmetrical shape on both sides, you can get by with a half pattern. Trace the outline on one side of the center line, then flip the pattern over and repeat it on the other side.

A handy trick for tracing the cutting outline of a wavy floor to a panel which must be accurately fitted. The same procedure can be used in the same way when working with baseboard molding.

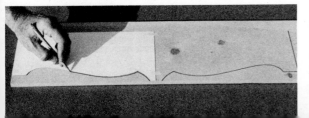

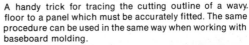

21 Sawing

Cutting wood to size and shape is usually the first step involved in any woodworking activity after the layout details have been worked out.

It could be said that any saw will cut any wood. This is quite true perhaps, but the statement doesn't hold a particle of sawdust from a practical standpoint. There are a number of hand-saws and six different kinds of power saws, all designed to do a specific type of cutting chore. As with most tools, there definitely is an overlap of function among some saws, but the selection of the right saw for the job is important. The techniques and shortcuts illustrated in this section will guide you to utilize the tools properly and most effectively.

Handsaw

Until that time when your shop is equipped with efficient power saws, you will be dependent upon the old fashioned, but quite reliable handsaws to do your wood cutting. Even if you do have power saws at your disposal, situations will always arise when you'll want to use a handsaw, due either to necessity or preference.

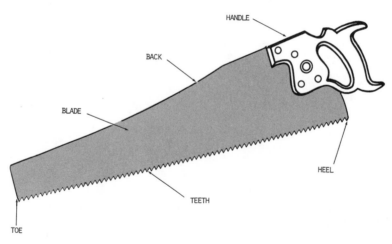

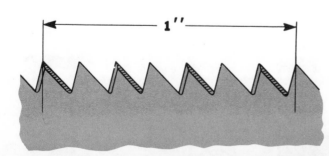

Points per inch are counted from point to point. This is an example of an 8 point blade. (*Stanley Tools*)

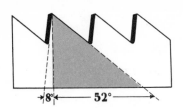

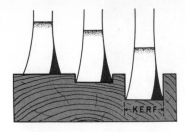

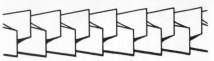

Top View of Rip Saw Teeth. When viewed from above, the teeth of a rip saw appear to form rows of chisel edges set to the right and left. (*Disston Saw*)

Rip saw teeth. The rip saw is designed for cutting with the grain and cuts on the push stroke. The front face of rip teeth has an angle of 8 degrees, the back angle is 52 degrees. Rip teeth are filed straight across the face and give the appearance of chisel edges. (*Disston Saw*)

Cross Section of Rip Teeth. A close look at the kerf of a rip saw in action illustrates the chisel-like action with which the rip saw cuts. Note first how the rip saw cuts into the board. Width of the kerf is determined by the set of the teeth which are bent alternately right and left approximately ⅓ of their thickness.

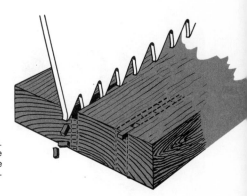

How a Rip Saw Cuts. Rip teeth cut like vertical chisels. First on one side of the set—small pieces of wood are cut loose across the grain and pushed out. Then on the other side. The tooth following plows out a similar particle to form the cut.

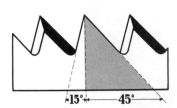

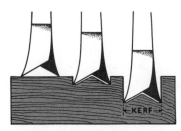

Top View of Cross-Cut Teeth. By sighting along the top of the teeth you will notice a V groove down which a needle will slide when the saw is properly set and filed. Compare these with rip teeth. (*Disston Saw*)

Cross-Cut Saw Teeth. The cross-cut saw is designed for cutting across the grain. The front face of cross-cut teeth have an angle of 15 degrees; the back angle is 45 degrees. Beveling the edges of the teeth about 24 degrees gives the appearance of a series of knife-like points.

Cross Section of Cross-Cut Teeth. Notice the "set" of the teeth—the tooth points protrude out to alternate sides to make the cut or kerf wider than the thickness of the saw blade. For even greater clearance, good quality saws are taper ground. In this view of the saw cutting into the wood notice the knife action, the paring action and the full cut. (*Disston Saw*)

How a Cross-Cut Saw Cuts. The teeth first score the wood like points of two parallel knife blades as the saw is drawn across the grain. Then the edges of the teeth begin paring the groove which is formed and clear the sawdust from the kerf. (*Disston Saw*)

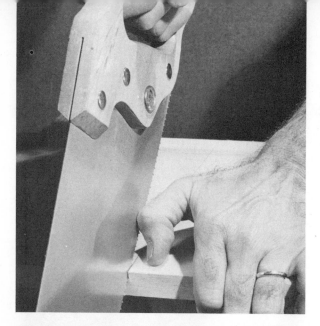

To start a saw cut, brace the saw against the thumb knuckle and draw the saw back a few times before pushing it forward. Saw on the waste side of the guideline.

A small notch made with a knife, one side square on the line and the other slanting on the waste side, will help in starting the saw cut accurately. (*Stanley Tools*)

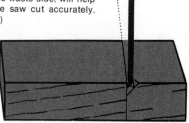

If the saw leaves the line, turn the handle slightly to twist the blade to permit the saw to cut back to the guideline. If the saw is not cutting square to the surface of the work, bend it slightly to gradually straighten the cut. (*Stanley Tools*)

Ripping. With the saw cut started, get the body into position to permit long easy strokes, holding the saw at an angle of 60 degrees. If the saw binds when cutting long sections, insertion of a wedge in the kerf will separate parts and make cutting easier.

Crosscutting. Easiest and smoothest crosscutting will be attained if the saw is held at an angle of 45 degrees to the work. Support the cut off piece as the saw nears the end of the cut to prevent splintering along the edge of the workpiece.

Simple way to guide the saw for an accurate cut: hold a block of wood with a squared end flush to the side of the blade. You can also buy a guide for this.

Trick for cutting a thin slice from the end of a board: place the stock on a piece of scrap. Start the cut in the scrap board and follow through until the end has been trimmed. It's a good idea to clamp the two boards together.

A 2 × 4 clamped near, and parallel to the saw cut guideline will serve as a control for a fairly accurate bevel cut. Position the 2 × 4 so that the saw touches the corner.

Miter boxes are used to obtain accurate straight or angle cuts in handsawing operations. A number of types are available from the simple wooden miter box through several intermediate, moderately priced styles, to the sophisticated professional type which is fully adjustable for a high degree of precision.

Hardwood miter box allows limited cuts at 90 and 45 degrees. Depth of cuts, however, are limited.

All-metal miter box guides saw at 90, 75, 60, and 45 degrees. Maximum depth of cut is about 3 inches.

This advanced design miter box is capable of high precision work at any angle from 45 to 90 degrees.

Miter box settings, left and right, for making various geometric constructions. (Stanley Tools)

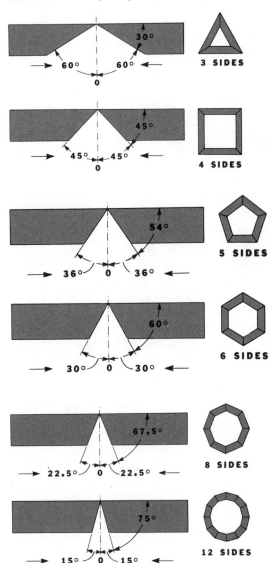

203

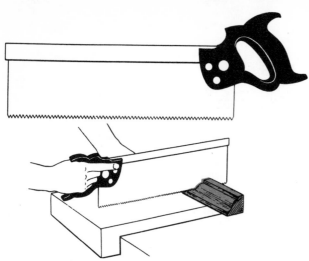

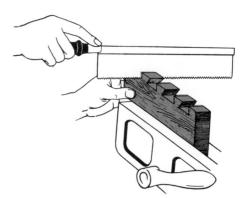

Back Saw. The back saw is similar to the miter box saw but smaller. It is used for fine cutting of molding and other light stock. The stiffened blade makes it invaluable for straight, accurate cutting.

Dovetail Saw. This is a small back saw with a very thin blade and fine teeth which is designed for cutting dovetails, tenoning and other types of precision work. It is also good for modeling projects. (*Disston Saw*)

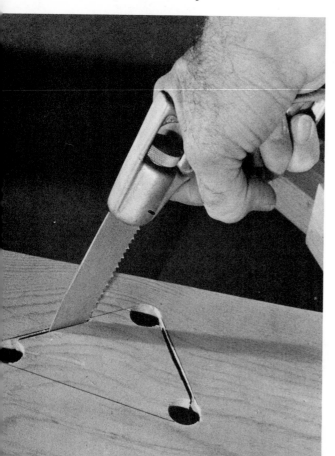

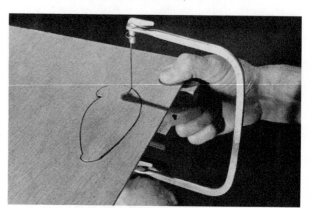

The coping saw cuts curves inside or out. When cutting at a table with the work held flat, the teeth should point downward so that the cut is made on the downstroke.

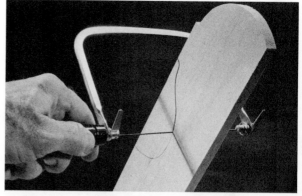

The compass saw is used to make cuts where other saws won't fit. It can make curved as well as straight cuts.

When working with thicker stock held vertically in a vise, the teeth should point away from you so that the cut is made on the push stroke.

Saber Saw

Basically a portable jig saw, the saber saw is designed primarily for making internal and external straight and curved cuts. A relatively fast cutter and quite powerful, the saber saw is especially well-suited for general all-around cutting. It is usually used freehand, but with various means of control through the use of simple jigs, this tool can be used to perform some rather impressive precision sawing tasks.

The ripping fence is a useful accessory which clamps into the saber saw base to guide the saw parallel to the edge for long rip cuts.

Freehand curved cuts can be made with better than reasonable accuracy provided the work is firmly clamped to overcome excessive vibration.

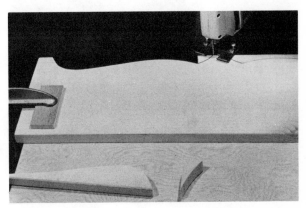

Some curves cannot be cut in one sweep when sharp corners are involved. Make such a cut in several passes. Cut out large portions first to minimize danger of splitting.

Joint-worthy bevel cuts can be made by adjusting the saw to the required angle. A straightedge strip of wood is an absolute must to guide the saw.

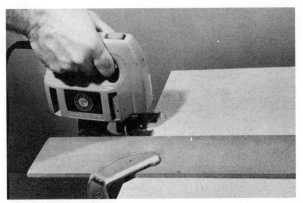

When using a straightedge guide, be sure to have it extend beyond the workpiece. This will insure that the saw is in proper alignment before the blade enters the work.

205

Using the saber saw to rough cut a blank for a gun stock.

A second pass with the saw set for a bevel cut removes additional wood from the edges. When this is repeated on the other side, the blank will be roughly "carved".

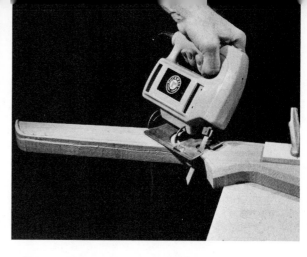

A simple way to clean out a square corner when the width of the opening is too small to allow the blade to turn the corner in the usual manner: Nail a stop strip near, and across the end of the opening. Make repeated cuts up to the stop. The space between the stop and the opening should equal the distance from the blade to the front of the base.

One way to make an internal cutout. Boring four holes at the corners makes a neat, quick job. The cut can be made with only one entry hole also.

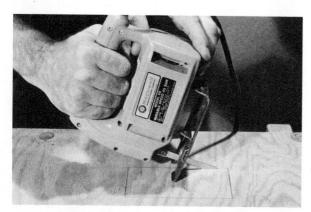

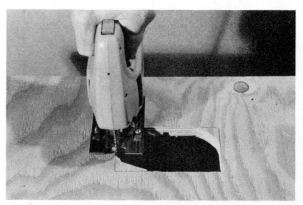

Making a pocket cut without a blade entry hole: Tilt the saw back onto the front of the base. Hold the saw firmly with both hands; start the motor then slowly tilt the saw down allowing the blade to enter the wood. Make straight cuts as far as you can go, turning the corners with curve cuts. Then go back to clean out the curved corners to finish the pocket cut.

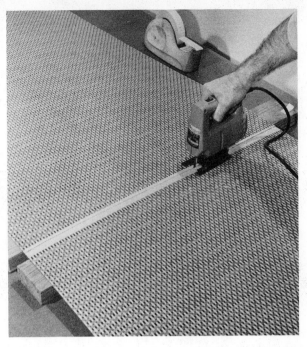

Substituting the saw blade with a knife blade will permit cutting smooth-edged cardboard templates.

The saber saw cuts on the up stroke so that in general, the good side of the material should face down because some splintering results on the top side of the cut. The rule can be broken on occasion as with this piece of plastic laminate if a fine tooth blade and protective masking tape are used. Note how the 2 × 4's bridge the line of cut to support the work.

The door and frame of this end table (left) were cut from the same piece of plywood. Result: no waste and a perfect fitting door. Here's how it is done . . .

. . . A pattern block with rounded corners is tack-nailed to the backside of the workpiece. Several small diameter holes are drilled close together on the cutting line for blade entry. A good place for this is at a hinge location. Make a mark on the base directly opposite the front edge of the blade. When the saw gets to the curve, swing it while advancing it so that the mark is always in contact with the round on the pattern. Note: A blade with set teeth rather than a hollow ground one should be used for any guided saber saw operations for best results.

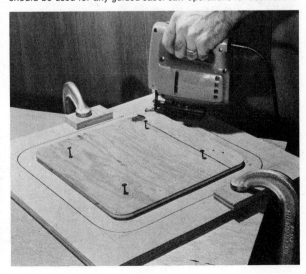

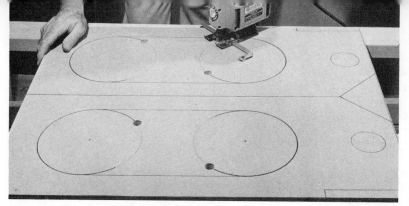

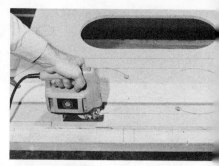

There is no other tool that can make this kind of internal cut with the ease and perfection obtained with the saber saw. Start by drilling blade entry holes in the waste area, then cut out the circles using a pivot guide. Exact placement of the straightedge guide is very important. Position the saw so that the blade is tangent to the line, then put a small mark along the base opposite the blade. Put the blade into the other circle and mark the same way.

Line up the guide to the two marks, clamp it into place and make the straight cut. The resulting opening will need no further machining except for a finish sanding.

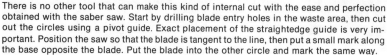

An important note on cutting circles with the saber saw and pivot guides: In order to track perfectly, the pivot point of the guide must be in absolute alignment with the front edge of the blade teeth. Inasmuch as accessory pivot guides have a fixed offset distance, it is essential that you use a blade of a width that is compatible. You can check this out by measuring the distance of both the pivot point and the front of the blade in relation to the front edge of the guide bar.

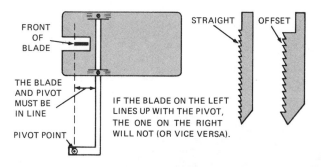

FRONT OF BLADE

THE BLADE AND PIVOT MUST BE IN LINE

PIVOT POINT

STRAIGHT

OFFSET

IF THE BLADE ON THE LEFT LINES UP WITH THE PIVOT, THE ONE ON THE RIGHT WILL NOT (OR VICE VERSA).

The saber saw was used (left) to simplify the otherwise difficult task of cutting out the openings in the side panels of this project. The material is Corian, a tough-to-cut synthetic "marble". The problem—getting a finished cut in one operation.

Sufficiently large curves were incorporated in the design of the openings (right). Holes 1½" in diameter drilled into each corner permitted the saw blade to be positioned tangent to the cutting line. A small starting hole would not allow the saw blade to start off "in line". With the guide clamped in place the cut is made from one hole to the other.

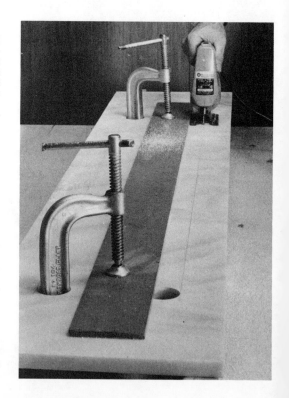

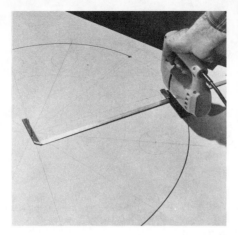

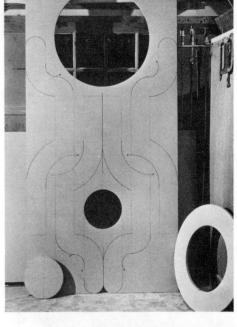

Most accessory circle cutting guides have a maximum diameter capacity of about 24 inches. For larger circles you'll have to make your own. Use a piece of mild steel strip and hammer one end over to form a right angle.

A field day for the saber saw and pivot guide! A close look at this panel reveals how three different "starting" methods were utilized. Some curves were started in holes bored in the waste area. In areas where there was no waste for holes (along the center) the straight cuts were made first. For the reverse curves the blade was simply inserted tangent to the first curve and the pivot repositioned accordingly (upper left and right).

This knock-down desk project further illustrates the degree of precision which is possible with this unique tool. The technique can be applied to many jobs.

The design calls for clean-cut, snug fitting slotted joints. A simple jig and a special trick with the saw blade were required. Precise cutting was a must.

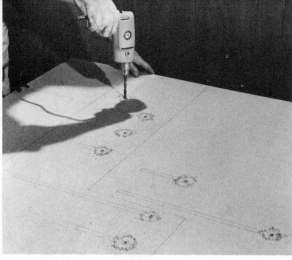

First step — lay out guidelines and drill a hole near one end of each rectangle. The hole can be slightly smaller than the width of the slot.

A jig is made by cutting an opening in a piece of hardboard dimensioned to match the base of the saw plus the amount of the opening to be cut out. (The jig is easier made open-ended with the back piece taped on). A cardboard template helps to line up the jig. When positioned, the jig is tack-nailed into place. The white strip is a tape shim added to correct a slight error in the size of the opening.

Initial cuts are made from blade entry hole along both layout lines. Additional cuts clean out the waste. The end is squared by sliding the saw against the front of the jig.

Slot is nearly complete when all forward cuts have been made but there is a basic problem: The back of this slot cannot be cut out simply by turning the saw around and continuing the cut. There would be an offset in the cut because the base of a saber saw is not centered in respect to the line of cut. On most saber saws it is usually centered over **one** edge of the blade.

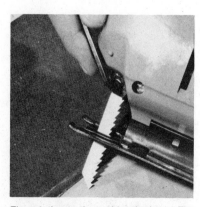

The solution to the problem is simple: The blade is reversed so the teeth point to the rear. Thus the relationship of the blade center to the line is unchanged.

The saw is returned to the slot and is pushed backward, repeating the outline and waste removal cuts and squaring off the end.

Small-radius cuts can be made with extra narrow blades. When a small blade is not available the back can be ground off a regular one.

Portable Circular Saw

The portable circular saw is used extensively for rough carpentry, for cutting large panels and lumber stock to working size, and for general home maintenance and modernizing jobs. It is easy to handle and cuts rapidly, so it is well-suited for this kind of work. But this tool is by no means limited to use for rough cutting only. It can be utilized to perform some of the finer sawing operations as well.

Due to its portability, this saw should be treated with respect and common sense in the interest of safety. Above all, keep it away from children. Form a habit of disconnecting the power cord whenever the saw is not in the process of actually cutting wood, while making various adjustments, or when changing blades.

Always use a sharp blade. A dull one frequently binds in the wood. This can result in an unexpected kickback that can throw the saw over a few fingers (or worse). A bound blade can also cause motor damage, so don't take chances with a dull blade.

An accessory ripping guide can be used to guide the portable circular saw parallel to the edge of stock for ripping. Due to the small area of contact of the "fence", care must be exercised to avoid veering off course.

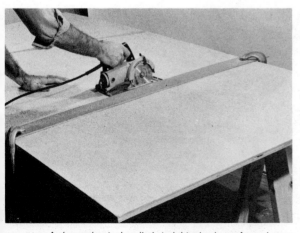

A clamped or tack-nailed straight edge is a safer and more accurate method of guiding the saw.

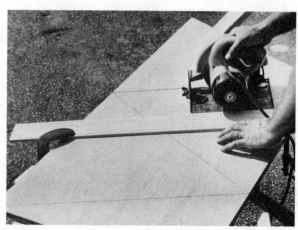

Cutting odd shaped pieces is relatively easy with the portable saw. An important point: always take into consideration the thickness of the blade when setting the guide so the kerf will be on the waste side of the line.

The portable saw (above) cuts smooth on the bottom surface and sometimes splinters the fibers on the top side of the cut so always be sure to cut fancy paneling with the good face down.

A homemade cross-cut guide (above, right) is useful for making quick, accurate cuts across the grain. The other end features an adjustable guide for miter cuts. The secret of a good guide—it must have large and very straight bearing surfaces.

Rabbet cuts (right) are easy: Set the blade to project the required amount then make a series of repeated cuts, moving the tack nailed guide for each pass.

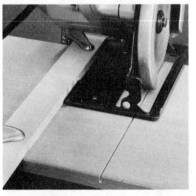

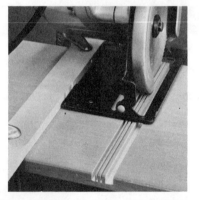

Cutting a dado: Clamp a guide to set one limit of the groove. Set the blade to the required depth and make the first cut . . .

Reset the guide so the second cut is made at the far side of the dado groove. Make a few passes between the outside cuts moving the guide each time . . .

The guide can be dispensed with and the saw guided free-hand to remove the rest of the waste.

An end lap joint is made with a series of kerf cuts through the ends of two pieces of stock. The waste can be removed with a chisel or more saw cuts.

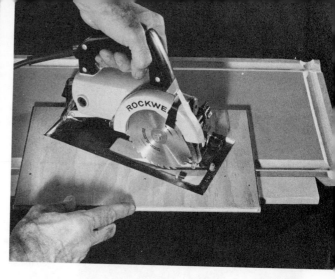

This jig lets you do panel raising. A rectangular opening in a panel which wraps around the base of the saw is attached at an angle to a strip of wood.

The guide is held firmly against the work while the saw is slowly pushed forward. The curved groove must be cut by increments, lowering the blade about 1/16" for each pass. Waste is cut off after the grooves are finished.

This right angle jig is useful for cutting a cross lap joint. Both pieces are clamped together and cut at the same time.

The depth and width for this joint must be carefully measured to obtain a good fit.

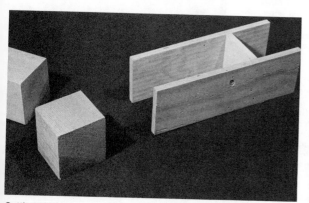

Cutting through extra thick stock requires two passes, one from each side. Accurate alignment of the blade for the second cut is assured with this jig . . .

This is the way the jig is held with a clamp. The whole thing is turned over for the second cut.

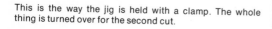

Cutting into the end of stock such as this (left) is difficult because the base of the saw cannot be properly supported. This platform jig supplies the supporting surface for the saw. Photo at right: how the jig is used.

Using the saw to make decorative cuts (left). The saw is tilted for a bevel cut and guided with a clamped strip. Since the saw can tilt in only one direction, the second bevel cuts are made from the other side. At right is a sample of the possibilities.

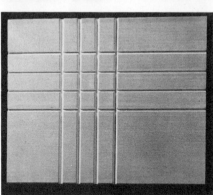

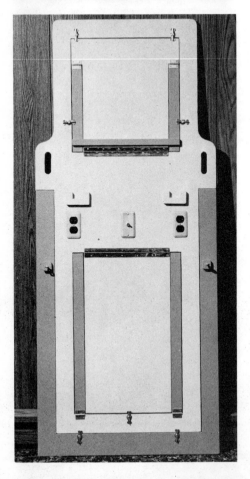

This project (left), a fold-out projector rig, is a good example of the effectiveness of the plunge cut. All the parts were cut in place out of a single piece of plywood.

A high fence (right) is essential for making exacting plunge cuts. This insures that the blade will enter the stock squarely and in proper alignment. Fence is positioned and clamped firmly.

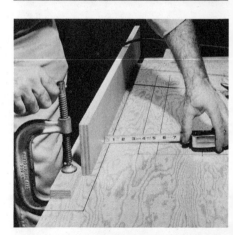

To make plunge cut (right), tape back the retractable blade guard to keep it out of the way. Rest the base against the fence with the back of the saw elevated so the blade clears the work. A pencil mark to indicate the start and stop locations will prevent overshooting. Switch on the motor, then slowly lower the base until it is flat on the board, the blade fully penetrated. Push the saw forward to the end of the cut. Switch off the motor and wait until the blade comes to a full stop before removing the saw. Use a saber saw to clear the kerf to the corners.

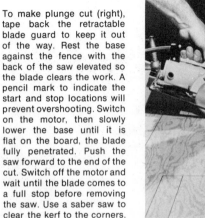

This project (right), a difficult one to tackle with other tools, proved to be a natural for the portable circular saw.

To fit together properly, the numerous geometric shaped parts had to be cut with a high degree of accuracy. A simple jig was devised as shown below.

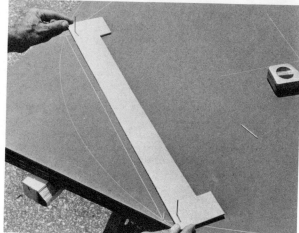

A spacing stick was used for speed and accuracy in setting up the guide for the saw (lower right). The width at each end equals the distance between blade and base edge. The piece is moved into position by lining up a pair of slightly projecting nail points into small holes at each corner of the pattern.

When the nail points find their mark the guide board is moved up to the spacer piece and clamped. This method is quite effective and can be used for any job requiring repeat cuts.

Dense tempered hardboard is tough on regular blades but causes no problems with a carbide tipped blade. Saw is adjusted to cut through four panels at a time. This is the second pass which will complete the cut.

Tack nail a strip of wood to the side to guide the saw for the cut. As each side is cut through, nail a pair of temporary cleats across the opening to keep the lid in alignment while it is being sawed.

To make a box with a perfect fitting lid, construct it completely enclosed. Anticipate where the lid will be cut and be very sure to keep nails or screws out of the path of the saw blade.

The lid can only fit perfectly. Small boxes can be handled on the table saw but large ones are best done with the portable.

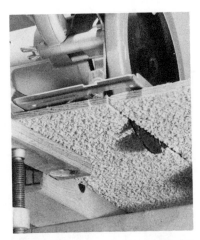

Unusual blade. This one has teeth that point clockwise as opposed to the normal counterclockwise orientation. It is specially designed for cutting plexiglas smoothly.

This special house siding plywood is surfaced with gravel. Only a carbide tipped blade could take on such a brutal chore.

A masonry cut-off wheel permits use of the saw to cut stone, brick or cement. Wear goggles when working with these materials.

ig Saw

The jig saw is particularly useful for cutting curved and irregular shapes. Capable of accepting a wide range of blades sized from 1/64" up to 1/4", it can be used to turn out extremely delicate scroll work in thin stock or for cutting through fairly heavy wood, usually up to 2" thick.

A typical jig saw function. Although not required for cutting a large sweeping curve such as this, an extra fine tooth blade will produce a very smoothly finished edge.

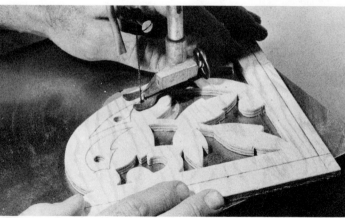

The blade is removed from the chucks and inserted through holes drilled in the waste areas to make internal cuts. A fine blade is essential to execute the small radius cuts in this design. The hold down foot is brought to bear down on the work with just enough tension to keep it from bouncing.

Interchangeable blade guides are available for use with different size blades. The back portion of the blade rides in the groove to prevent twisting and bending.

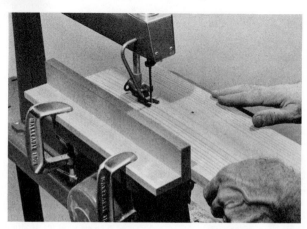

Accurate ripping can be done with a heavy blade and a clamped-on guide fence. For extra long work the blade can be mounted sideways to avoid the overarm at the rear.

217

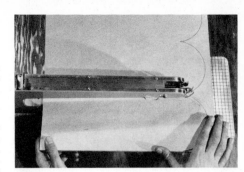

The hold-down (left) must be adjusted to match the angle of the work when doing bevel cutting of any kind.

A special spiral blade (upper right), which cuts in any direction permits this scalloped cut to be made without interference from the overarm. This is a light duty machine used mainly for hobby craft work.

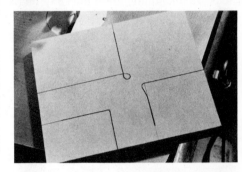

Three methods of cutting an outside corner (right). If a small radius is permitted (bottom) the turn may be made directly. For a sharp corner you must cut into the waste. This can be done by making a reverse loop (center) or by looping past the corner then trimming off the bump with a second cut.

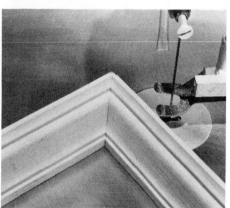

A coped molding joint (left) is one in which one piece is installed with a square cut end and the second piece is cut with a matching profile and butted up against the first. This is easy to do with the jig saw.

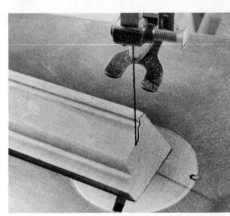

Cut a 45 degree miter first (right). This will reveal the cross section contours on the face of the molding. Now make a straight 90 degree cut following the shape of the top edge. The hold-down is up out of the way for clarity.

This simple jig (left) permits cutting perfect circles. A board with a series of holes drilled along a centerline is clamped to the saw table.

Drill a blade entry hole into the work (right), insert the blade then drive a nail through the center of the work and into the appropriate hole in the jig. Simply pivot the work to cut the circle. In order to track properly the center line of the jig must be lined up at exactly 90 degrees to the blade.

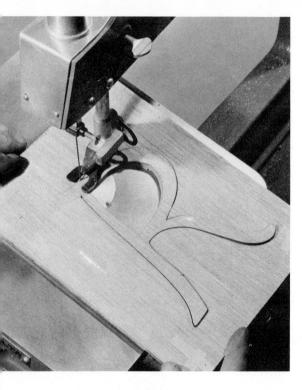

Perfect inlays can be cut with the jig saw. Tape or nail together two pieces of wood of different colors. Tilt the table to cut a slight bevel of 1 or 2 degrees. Insert the blade through as small a hole as possible and cut the design. Keep the work always to one side of the blade so the bevel angle doesn't change.

Separate the cut pieces and reassemble them with the contrasting colors. They will fit together without the kerf showing due to the bevel angle of the edges which cancels out the space.

This illustrates how the bevel angle cancels out the saw cut (kerf) space. The precise amount of bevel required depends upon the thickness of both the blade and the wood. Always make a test to determine the proper bevel angle.

Raised numbers and letters can be cut out of thick stock by angle sawing. Three degrees of bevel is about average for ³/₄″ stock but it should be checked with your blade.

When pressed up from the bottom, the piece will slip partially through until the angled sides touch each other.

BUILDING UP STOCK FOR LATHE TURNING

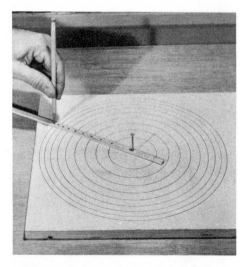

Angle sawing is a novel way to build up stock for lathe turning or carving projects. The piece at left is being marked with rings of varying widths, will take on an asymmetrical form.

The table (right) is tilted for a 4 degree bevel for this particular project. Freehand cutting of the rings is permissible for this kind of work because any slight error will be self-matching.

The reassembled rings (left) will telescope accurately provided they are oriented in their original positions. The drilled blade entry holes in each ring make line-up easy.

Each ring (right) gets a thin coating of glue on each side. Clamping is not necessary since the pieces will bind tightly enough when pressed together. Wipe off excess.

An economy factor (left): each of these units was cut out of boards measuring less than one square foot.

These two sections (right) are joined together to form a special lathe project assembly. (Shown in section on lathe work.)

MAKING PHOTO CUTOUT BOOKENDS

This is a fun type job you can do on the jig saw.

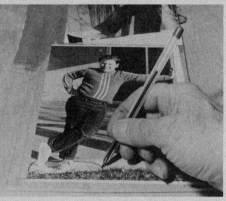

Use contact cement or photo mounting adhesive (left) to mount a picture onto a piece of thin plywood or hardboard. Draw an outline for a cut at the base.

Set the saw table for a slight bevel (right), about 3 degrees. Use a very fine cutting blade to cut around the outline of the figure.

Drill a blade entry hole for inside cuts (left).

The edges will be smooth enough (right) to require no sanding but the corners of the outline should be sanded to remove the sharp edge. Use 220 grit paper with a down stroke only.

Attach a piece of sheet metal to a wood base with a suitable adhesive. The wall paneling type is a good choice.

The cutout is inserted with glue into a groove in the base. A wood filler strip can be used to plug balance of groove.

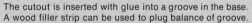

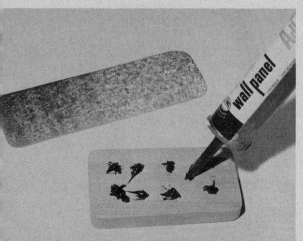

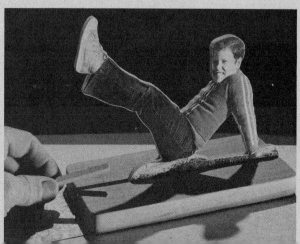

⬤and Saw

The band saw solves cutting problems that cannot be handled by the saber or jig saw. Like these others, it is also used for curve and irregular cutting. It differs in that it cuts much faster and has a greater depth-of-cut capacity. Graceful curves in stock 6″ thick are easily cut with the band saw. When equipped with a narrow blade the saw will turn a fairly small radius, thus permitting work of considerable intricacy. With a wide blade the band saw excels for numerous straight cutting jobs, especially resawing.

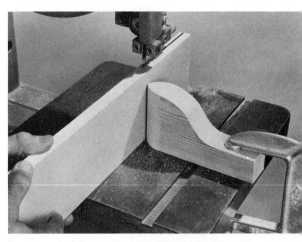

Resawing stock is a common requirement in shop work. This pivot block arrangement is the simplest type of guide for the purpose. The front edge of the block must be positioned directly opposite the blade teeth.

This is a more positive-working resawing jig. The wide upright offers ample bearing surface. The wood "spring" keeps the stock steady. The pressure of the spring should be directly opposite the blade. Accurate resawing is possible only if the blade is sharp and teeth properly set. When nearing the end of this cut a push stick must be used for safety.

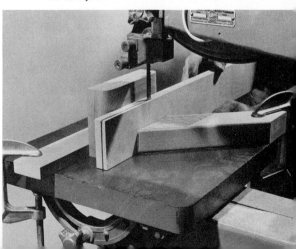

A wide blade is best for cutting long graceful curves with the band saw. Use one hand to push the work, the other to steer it. Move slowly for accuracy.

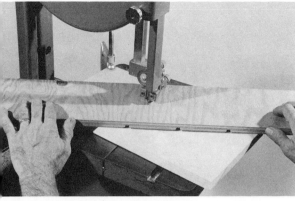

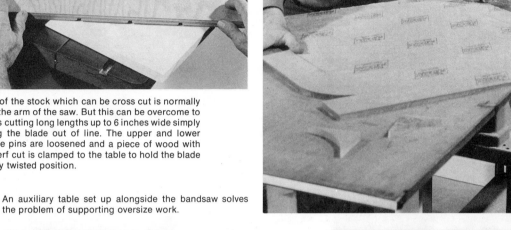

The width of the stock which can be cross cut is normally limited by the arm of the saw. But this can be overcome to allow cross cutting long lengths up to 6 inches wide simply by twisting the blade out of line. The upper and lower blade guide pins are loosened and a piece of wood with a partial kerf cut is clamped to the table to hold the blade in a slightly twisted position.

An auxiliary table set up alongside the bandsaw solves the problem of supporting oversize work.

Kerfing hardwood lathe turning stock to take spurs of the live center. Table is set at 45 degree tilt.

Using the band saw to remove the corners of turning stock. The wood fence is a useful homemade accessory.

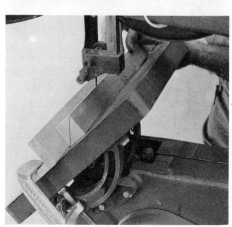

Another method for kerfing the end of a turning block is with the use of a V block. The block is kept from sliding forward by a cleat which butts against the front of the table.

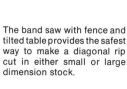

The band saw with fence and tilted table provides the safest way to make a diagonal rip cut in either small or large dimension stock.

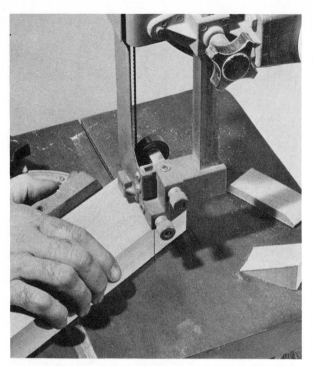

Rip-apart method of making duplicate pieces is done by first cutting a thick piece of wood to the desired shape.

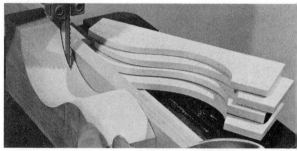

A fence is set up close to the blade to rip the preshaped pieces into a number of duplicate parts.

Miter cuts can be made free hand, but preferably with the aid of a miter gage.

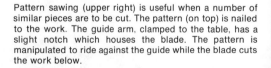

Gang sawing (above) saves time and insures accuracy when multiple parts are required. The stack may be held with carefully placed brads or with masking tape as shown.

Pattern sawing (upper right) is useful when a number of similar pieces are to be cut. The pattern (on top) is nailed to the work. The guide arm, clamped to the table, has a slight notch which houses the blade. The pattern is manipulated to ride against the guide while the blade cuts the work below.

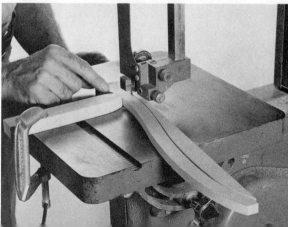

Curved work which is to be ripped to an equal width can be cut with the use of a pivot clamped-on guide. The first cut is made freehand. The parallel cut is then made by riding the stock against the pivot.

224

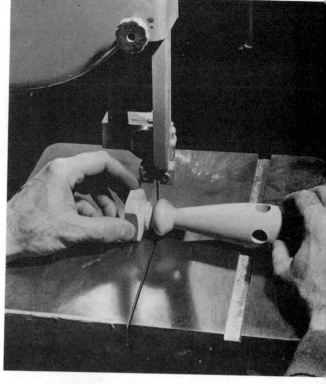

A circle jig for the band saw is similar to the one used for the jig saw. There is a difference in procedure for use. Since the blade cannot be inserted through a starting hole, circles must be started from an outside edge: a flat edge of the work is pressed against the blade while the pivot is driven into the jig.

The steady downward cutting action of the band saw permits this type of cut off with relative safety. A similar cut with a table saw could be hazardous.

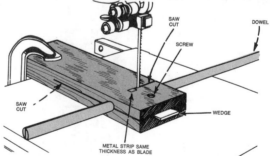

Dowel splitting is ordinarily a difficult job but the band saw equipped with this simple jig makes easy work of it.

The wedge in the saw kerf allows setting of the jig to take the dowel stock with a moderate push fit; the metal strip behind the blade keeps the work square and prevents spiraling. (*Rockwell*)

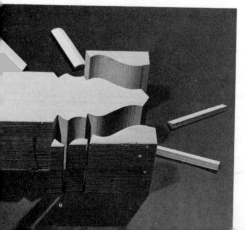

Compound sawing an ornamental finial (left) involves two sets of cuts. The outline on one face is cut with a narrow blade and all the cut-off pieces retained.

The cut-offs (right) are taped back into place to form a level base on the bottom and a marking surface on top. The second cuts are then made to complete the work.

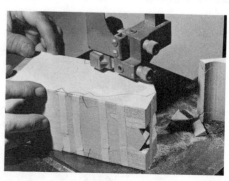

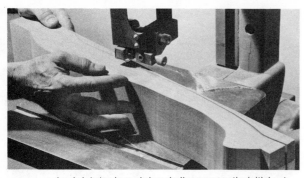

A cabriole leg is made in a similar manner: the initial cut . . .

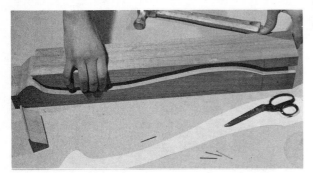

. . . restoring the cut offs . . .

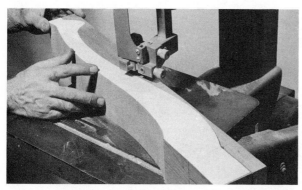

. . . making the final cuts using a cardboard template.

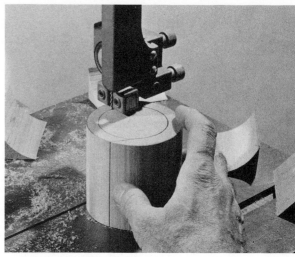

Cylinders of good quality can be cut with the band saw. The outside is cut first, then a lead-in cut is made on a tangent to the inner circle.

Gluing of the lead-in cut can be done with direct contact, or, if accuracy is important, a slip of veneer can be inserted to fill the saw kerf.

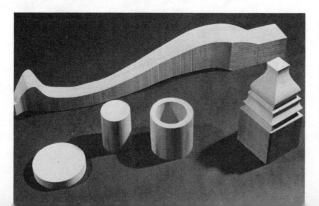

Some of the typical band saw cuttings (left).

Narrow sanding belts are available for use on the band saw. They offer an excellent method of finishing edges and rolling curves. The belt is fitted in place just like a blade using just enough tension to pull the belt tight. (*Sears Roebuck*)

Circular Saw

The circular saw is used to make with the greatest of ease the two basic woodworking cuts: ripping and crosscutting. Long boards can be quickly ripped down the length at any width set by the fence. Crosscutting lengths to size is simply a matter of resting the wood against the miter gage and pushing it past the blade. The resulting edges are straight, square and smooth, and of exacting dimensions.

Precise bevel cuts of any angle up to 45 degrees are obtained by tilting the blade. If the miter gage is also adjusted to cut an angle and used in combination with the tilted blade, a compound miter is produced. A dado or molding head used in place of the blade makes possible the cutting of all sorts of joints or ornamental edges. With easy-to-make jigs this saw can be utilized to its fullest potential in performing many operations quickly and accurately.

For safety use the blade guard and anti-kickback fingers for all operations that permit their use. The photographs on the following pages show the saw being used with the guard removed so that the operations can be seen more clearly.

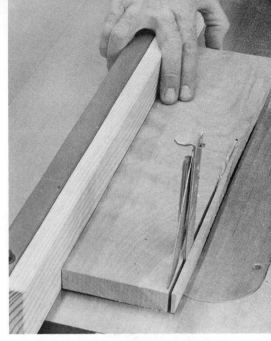

Ripping a board. The fence is set to guide the wood for the correct width of cut. The splitter serves to keep the kerf open to prevent the wood from binding on the blade. Note how the fingers are bridged over the fence as a safety measure.

When ripping a long board without a rear support to hold it up, you can cut about half way through it, walk around to the back and pull it through for the rest of the cut. Do this only if anti-kickback fingers are functioning. They prevent the board from being shot back toward the operator at the front of the saw.

This roller support is quite effective for holding up long boards during ripping operations. Waxed ends of dowel ride freely in the blocks.

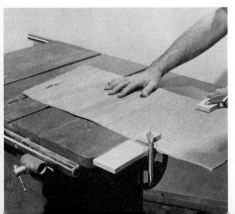

At left is one method of cutting a straight edge on a panel which has none: Clamp a board with a straight edge to the bottom of the panel then let this ride against the table edge.

Another method (right): Tack-nail a straight strip to the top side of the panel a bit beyond the irregular edge. Press the straight strip against the fence in a normal manner.

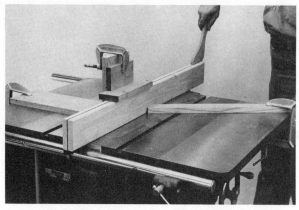

Resawing is best done on the band saw but if necessary it can be done safely with the set-up shown. The job usually entails cutting from both sides. Note how the work is held down and into the fence and the use of a push stick.

Never attempt to guide stock without a properly shaped push stick. This one is good. It rides high, keeping the fingers well away from the blade. Another caution—the next cut, through the knot, would be ill advised.

A wide board attached to the miter gage supports the work better for cross cut operations.

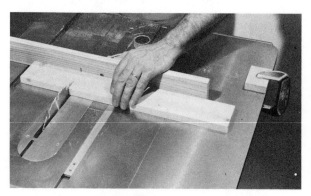

One method of cutting stock to exact length, using a stop clamped at far right. Note that the stop should never be clamped in a line opposite the blade, but well in advance of it to establish position before cutting.

This is a better method for cutting stock to exact length because the stop is always in place at the end of the work.

Use extra precaution with short work. The wide fence and a hold down stick are safety measures.

This is the best way to cut an edge miter. A wood bumper is clamped to the fence. It is then positioned so the distance from the outside of the blade is equal to the thickness of the stock. The blade is lowered below the table, tilted to 45 degrees then turned on and slowly raised until it just enters the bumper (auxiliary fence). Be sure you don't run the blade too far and into the metal fence. If the set up is right the blade will cut exactly into the corner of the stock.

The first cut in making a rabbet should be run with the work on edge . . .

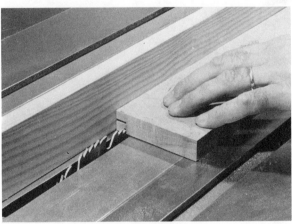

. . . The second cut cleans out the corner.

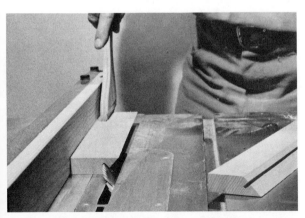

The splined miter is an excellent joint and easy to make. Forty-five degree bevel cuts are first made on the edges. The blade is lowered and another 45-degree cut is made in the opposite direction to form the spline groove.

The spline should be ⅛″ thick by about ⁹⁄₁₆″ wide for standard ¾″ stock.

A jig for cutting wedges.

Perfect miters for frame work can be made with this mitering jig. It's a board with a pair of cleats attached to the bottom which ride in the table grooves. Care must be exercised when setting up the angled cleats on top. Nail them and test for accuracy before gluing.

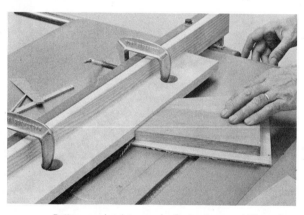

Pattern sawing lets you duplicate pieces quickly and accurately. The auxiliary wood fence is suspended over the blade, its edge flush to the outside edge of the blade. The pattern is tacked to the work. Each edge of the pattern is guided along the fence to cut the exact shape in the workpiece below.

Notched stick, clamped at right, is used as a hold down for small work. Note how the stick is cut short of the fence to allow clearance for the push stick at the end of the cut.

The angled waste piece from the first cut is tacked to the work to guide it safely through the blade for the otherwise difficult job of ripping a triangular-shaped piece.

All work tends to creep slightly during the cutting of a miter thus resulting in an inaccurate cut. The long auxiliary fence attached to the miter gage will prevent this if sharp anchor points (sharpened screws) are inserted from behind and made to project slightly into the work.

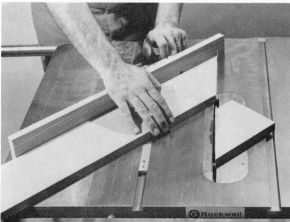

TABLE OF COMPOUND ANGLES

Tilt of Work	4-SIDE BUTT		4-SIDE MITER		6-SIDE MITER		8-SIDE MITER	
	Tilt	Miter Gage	Tilt	Miter Gage	Tilt	Miter Gage	Tilt	Miter Gage
5°	½	85	44¾	85	29¾	87½	22¼	88
10°	1½	80¼	44¼	80¼	29½	84½	22	86
15°	3¾	75½	43¼	75½	29	81¾	21½	84
20°	6¼	71¼	41¾	71¼	28¼	79	21	82
25°	10	67	40	67	27¼	76½	20¾	80
30°	14½	63½	37¾	63½	26	74	19½	78¼
35°	19½	60¼	35¼	60¼	24½	71¾	18¾	76¾
40°	24½	57¼	32½	57¼	22¾	69¾	17	75
45°	30	54¾	30	54¾	21	67¾	15¾	73¾
50°	36	52½	27	52½	19	66¼	14¼	72½
55°	42	50¾	24	50¾	16¾	64¾	12½	71¼
60°	48	49	21	49	14½	63½	11	70¼

Compound miter cut is made by setting miter gage at an angle and the blade tilted. When a number of matching parts are needed it is best to make continuous cuts from one board, turning the work over for alternate cuts.

Compound angles are worked according to the table at right. Angled constructions may be butt or miter jointed. If you wish to cut a four sided butted frame or box with the sides tilted 25 degrees, for example, the settings would be as follows: Blade tilt—10 degrees, miter gage adjusted to 67 degrees. For mitered corners the settings would be 40 and 67 degrees, respectively. Corner blocks are sometimes used to brace 4-sided figures. They are cut with the same settings as for a 4-side butt joint. (*Rockwell*)

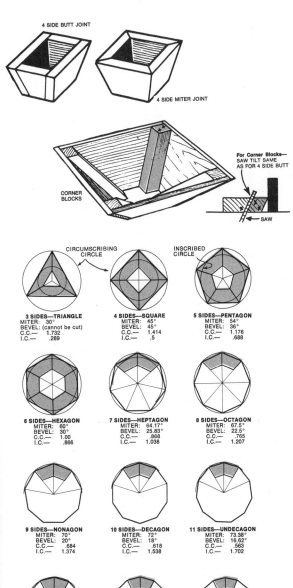

4 SIDE BUTT JOINT

4 SIDE MITER JOINT

For Corner Blocks—SAW TILT SAME AS FOR 4 SIDE BUTT

CORNER BLOCKS

SAW

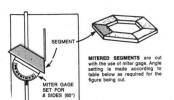

SEGMENT

MITER GAGE SET FOR 8 SIDES (60°)

MITERED SEGMENTS are cut with the use of miter gage. Angle setting is made according to table below as required for the figure being cut.

Segments are frequently required in various woodworking constructions. There are two types: mitered and beveled. Either kind can be cut to perfection if care is exercised in setting the miter gage or blade tilt accurately.

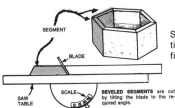

SEGMENT

BLADE

SAW TABLE

SCALE

BEVELED SEGMENTS are cut by tilting the blade to the required angle.

Set the miter gage or blade tilt angle according to these figures with diagrams.

CIRCUMSCRIBING CIRCLE | INSCRIBED CIRCLE

3 SIDES—TRIANGLE
MITER: 30°
BEVEL: (cannot be cut)
C.C.— 1.732
I.C.— .289

4 SIDES—SQUARE
MITER: 45°
BEVEL: 45°
C.C.— 1.414
I.C.— .5

5 SIDES—PENTAGON
MITER: 54°
BEVEL: 36°
C.C.— 1.176
I.C.— .688

6 SIDES—HEXAGON
MITER: 60°
BEVEL: 30°
C.C.— 1.00
I.C.— .866

7 SIDES—HEPTAGON
MITER: 64.17°
BEVEL: 25.83°
C.C.— .868
I.C.— 1.038

8 SIDES—OCTAGON
MITER: 67.5°
BEVEL: 22.5°
C.C.— .765
I.C.— 1.207

9 SIDES—NONAGON
MITER: 70°
BEVEL: 20°
C.C.— .684
I.C.— 1.374

10 SIDES—DECAGON
MITER: 72°
BEVEL: 18°
C.C.— .618
I.C.— 1.538

11 SIDES—UNDECAGON
MITER: 73.38°
BEVEL: 16.62°
C.C.— .563
I.C.— 1.702

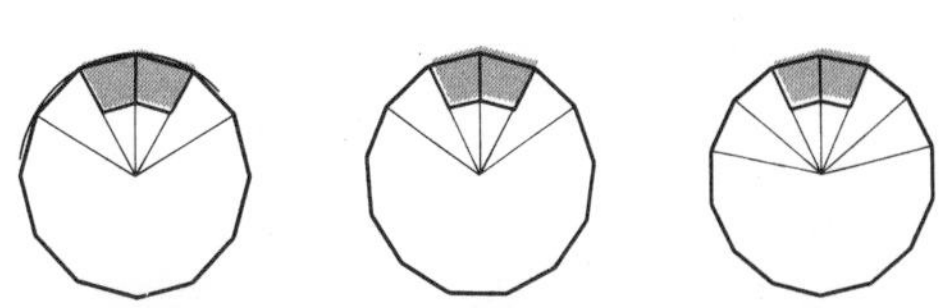

The rules below will enable you to determine the size of segments. (*Rockwell*)

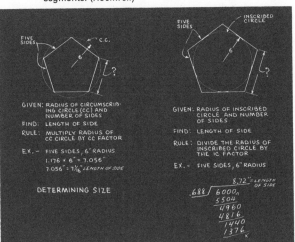

FIVE SIDES

C.C.

GIVEN: RADIUS OF CIRCUMSCRIBING CIRCLE (CC) AND NUMBER OF SIDES

FIND: LENGTH OF SIDE

RULE: MULTIPLY RADIUS OF CC CIRCLE BY CC FACTOR

EX.— FIVE SIDES, 6" RADIUS
1.176 × 6" = 7.056"
7.056" = 7 1/16" LENGTH OF SIDE

DETERMINING SIZE

FIVE SIDES

INSCRIBED CIRCLE

GIVEN: RADIUS OF INSCRIBED CIRCLE AND NUMBER OF SIDES

FIND: LENGTH OF SIDE

RULE: DIVIDE THE RADIUS OF INSCRIBED CIRCLE BY THE IC FACTOR

EX.— FIVE SIDES, 6" RADIUS

8.72" LENGTH OF SIDE
.688) 6.000
5504
4960
4816
1440
1376

12 SIDES—DODECAGON
MITER: 75°
BEVEL: 15°
C.C.— .518
I.C.— 1.866

13 SIDES
MITER: 76.31°
BEVEL: 13.69°
C.C.— .479
I.C.— 2.028

14 SIDES
MITER: 77.14°
BEVEL: 12.86°
C.C.— .445
I.C.— 2.189

When the use of a long fence with anchor points on the miter gage is impractical, some method of preventing the work from sliding must be used. A strip of fine sandpaper rubber cemented to the face of the gage works quite well.

One of the rare occasions when an extra high blade setting is desired: To notch out an inside corner. The high blade produces a minimum kerf on the underside.

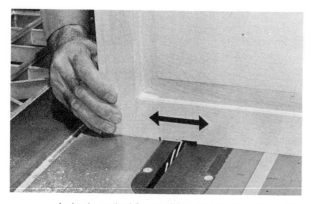

A simple method for mortising the gain for a hinge. The door is advanced a small distance forward after each lateral pass until entire mortise is cut.

When cross cutting a ceiling beam in two passes, make the first cut with the irregular side down to minimize wobble problems due to roundness of shape.

Taper ripping for furniture legs is easily done with this tapering jig which is made up to suit the work. With the work dressed to net size and perfectly square, the fence is set to equal the combined width of the guide board and work. (*Rockwell*)

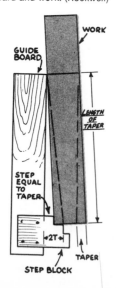

The leg is placed in the first notch of the jig and the combined jig and work are pushed into the saw. An adjacent (not opposite) side is cut in the same manner.

With no change made in the fence setting, the two remaining sides are cut with the work in the second notch.

232

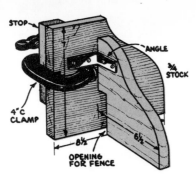

A jig of some kind should always be used when making end cuts such as for this mitered joint. The accessory tenoning jig shown here is an invaluable aid for all sorts of joint cuts. Practical homemade substitutes can easily be made.

A homemade tenoning jig like this lets you avoid risking your fingers attempting free-hand work. Variations can be made as needed to support miters and odd shaped work. (*Rockwell*)

The dado head is in effect a thick saw blade used for making grooves and rabbets of varying widths. Of the two kinds in general use, the one-piece adjustable head is more popular. The other which utilizes individual blades ganged together is shown.

Rabbet and groove joint is popular for drawer joint construction. It is strong, neat and easy to make with a dado cutter.

The miter gage with a stop block is used to cut the dado in the side piece. Two passes are required to form the step. All similar cuts are made before adjusting stop block.

The front piece is held with the tenoning jig to cut the end grooves. A second cut will complete the joint.

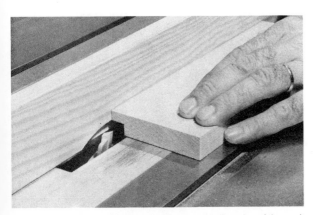

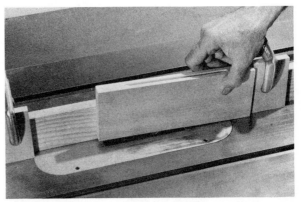

Rabbets are more accurately cut with the edge of the work against the fence. An auxiliary fence is essential for this operation. A recess cut into the fence houses the dado cutter, assures a cut along the edge of the stock that is accurate and keeps fingers away from blades.

The set up for cutting a blind groove is a simple one. Two stop blocks are clamped to the fence. The work is held against the rear stop with front end tilted up. Power is turned on, the piece is lowered into the blade then advanced to the front stop.

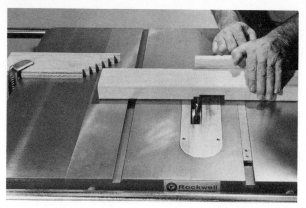

A notched stop block can speed up the making of wide tenons or grooves. Each of the steps advances the work the required amount for each pass over the dado head.

The familiar box joint is a good one because it presents lots of gluing surface. It is easily made with a dado head. A small wood block attached to the fence is used to guide the work for each pass.

Cutting moldings with a molding head in the circular saw is a fast and clean operation. A variety of shapes can be cut with even a limited collection of cutters simply by making multiple passes with slight changes in fence positions, changing knives or even tilting the arbor as was done for one of the passes on this piece.

This jig set up is used to mold the edge of a perfectly circular workpiece. The work is pushed against the cutter and jig, then rotated.

More than 50 molding head shapes available for the circular saw are shown here. Countless other shapes can be developed by combining cuts. (*Rockwell*)

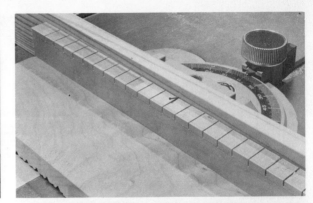

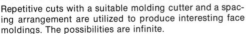

Repetitive cuts with a suitable molding cutter and a spacing arrangement are utilized to produce interesting face moldings. The possibilities are infinite.

The stock is attached to a spacing strip (upper right) which has evenly spaced saw kerfs cut on the top edge. A nail the same thickness as the kerf is driven into the miter gage fence at a slight upward angle.

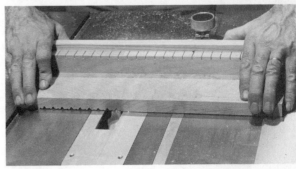

The work is passed over the cutters (right), advancing one notch into the nail marker each time. Setting the miter gage at alternate left and right angles will produce striking effects.

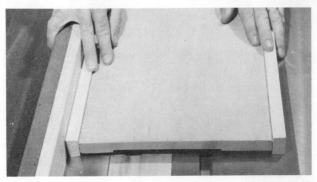

Where better equipment is not available, reasonable planing of warped and twisted boards can be done with straight knives in the molding head. Nail two runners to each edge of the work, being careful that the nails are well out of the area to be cut. The first cut is made at the center of the work, then successive cuts are made out toward edges of either side.

Feeding a board obliquely over a blade produces a cove (curved groove) of exceptional smoothness, shown at left. A temporary fence set at an angle is used to guide the work. The cove cut should not be attempted with one deep pass but, instead, with a number of small cuts made by elevating the blade slightly for each pass. Never use the hands to bear down over the line of cut.

To determine proper fence angle this easy-to-make cove setting jig is helpful. Blade is elevated to height desired. Parallel rule is spread to desired width of cove. Twist the jig until edges touch front and rear teeth of the blade. Set the fence at the angle indicated to obtain a cove which will be of height and width as planned. The fence should be located so the centerline of the work will intersect the center line of the blade.

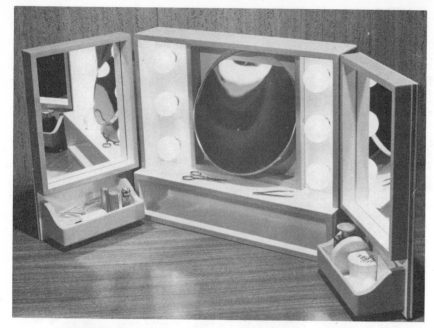

We sometimes make mistakes as was done in the construction of this project—the original design was changed to require a setback on the rear section of the unit—after it was made flush. The problem was solved easily on the table saw, as shown below . . .

. . . First a small cut was made to the depth of the cut off. Then the piece was positioned over the blade . . .

. . . The saw was turned on (upper right), the piece was brought down over the blade. The same cut was next made on the opposite side, feeding straight in up to the small cut . . .

. . . A final cut across the top separated the parts, saved the project.

236

Radial Arm Saw

The radial arm saw is used to make all the basic saw cuts that are possible with the circular saw: crosscut, bevel crosscut, miter, bevel miter, rip, and bevel rip.

Although the circular saw has the edge over the radial saw for ripping operations, the radial saw is better for crosscutting because the work remains stationary while the blade tracks over it. This particular feature is best appreciated when doing the seemingly endless variations of the basic cuts other than straight crosscutting and ripping that can be done with this saw. Because the work can usually remain stationary and even be clamped to the table, there is less dependency on special jigs.

Since the motor and its spindle are exposed and readily utilizable, a few more accessories can be used on this saw than are available for the circular saw. Included are a chuck for holding drill bits, surface planer, sanding drum, a faceplate for turning, and even a saber saw attachment.

The saw is easy to use, especially since it cuts from above the work. The layout marks are made on top of the wood, so they are always in view. In crosscutting the thrust is downward and to the back, thus automatically clamping the work firmly against the guide fence.

In ripping operations the work must **always** be fed **against** the rotation of the saw blade. To do otherwise would cause the saw to shoot the work forward at blade speed. Always work with the blade guard in place and use the anti-kickback fingers during ripping operations. In close quarters use a push stick to feed the work.

There is always a tendency for the work to creep laterally during mitering operations. Therefore it is advisable to install anchor points in the fence to prevent the work from shifting. A few screws with sharpened points projecting slightly through the fence will serve the purpose.

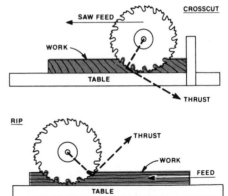

Cross cut and rip cut blade rotation and feed of the radial arm saw. (*Rockwell*)

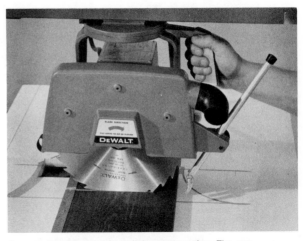

Cross cutting is a basic radial saw operation. The arm is set at the zero position, at right angle to the guide fence. The blade is set at zero vertical position. Hold the stock firmly against the fence and draw the saw blade across for the cut, just far enough to sever the wood. When the cut is completed, return the saw behind the fence.

Gang cutting a stack of 2 × 4's is easily accomplished with the radial saw. Clamped stop block positions all pieces for correct lengths.

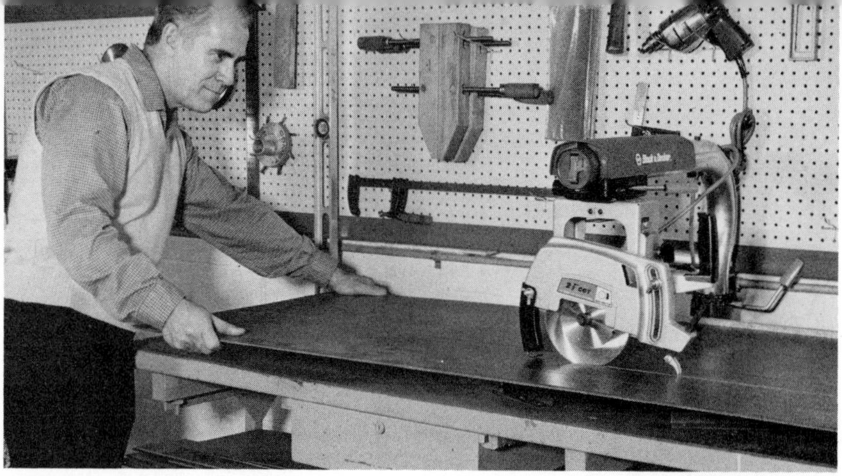

For a ripping operation the yoke is loosened and the blade adjusted to a position parallel to the guide fence. Locate the saw for the desired width of rip then lock the saw carriage against the arm. Feed the work slowly and evenly into the blade. Note how the anti-kickback fingers rest on the work as it moves along. (*DeWalt/Black & Decker*)

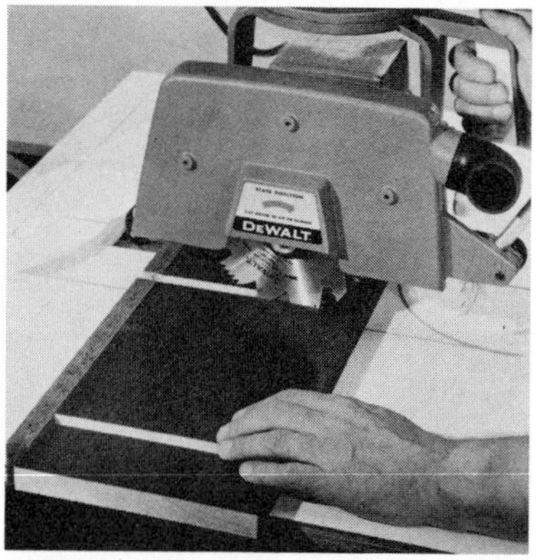

Saw blade is replaced with a dado head for cutting dadoes. Set the blade for proper depth of cut, then pull the saw over the work in the same manner as for cross cutting. Wide dado cuts can be made by making successive passes across the material, cutting in either direction.

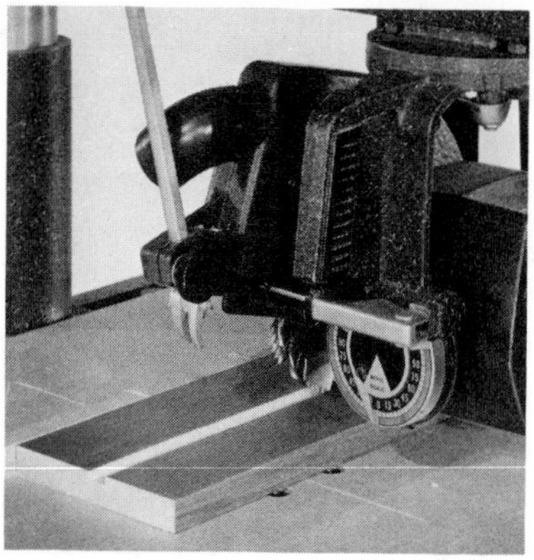

This is a plough cut (a groove the same as a dado but *with* the grain). This operation is done with the dado head in the rip position. Lock the carriage and hold the work firmly down on the table and back against the guide. Can you spot a serious error? (Kickback fingers are not in place).

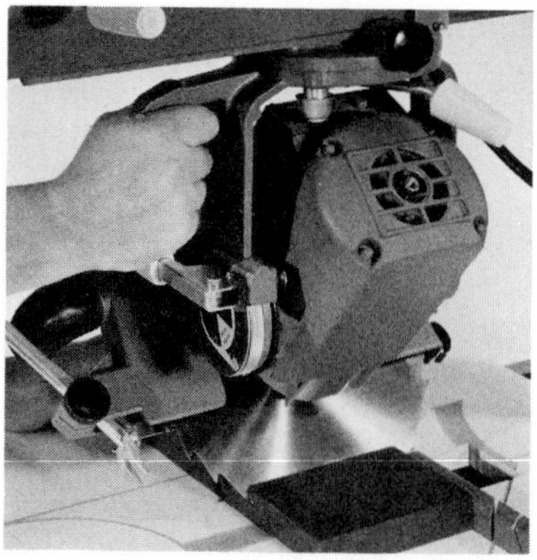

Bevel cuts across the grain are made with the blade at right angle to the table fence. Release the bevel clamp handle and tilt the motor in the yoke to the desired angle which you can read on the bevel scale. Proceed as with a regular cross cut. (*DeWalt/Black & Decker*)

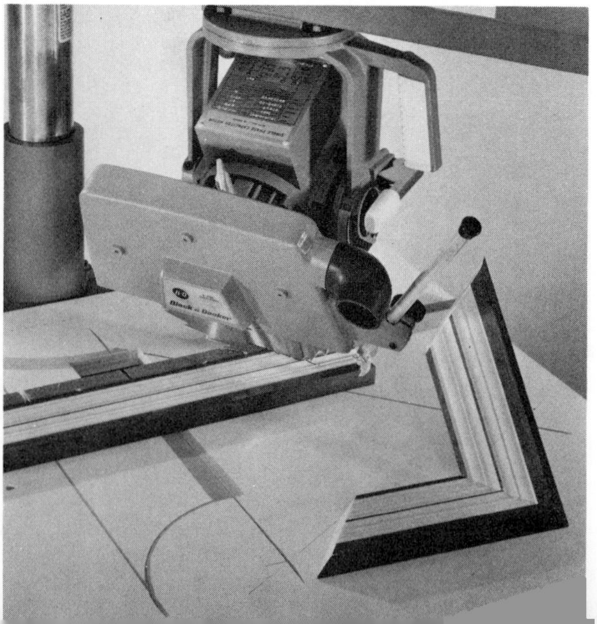

A compound miter cut is a combined miter and bevel. Frequently used to make picture frames or boxes with slanted sides. The arm is adjusted to the desired angle and the blade tilted as required (consult table).

TABLE OF COMPOUND ANGLES

Tilt of Work	4-SIDE BUTT Blade Tilt	4-SIDE BUTT Track-Arm	4-SIDE MITER Blade Tilt	4-SIDE MITER Track-Arm	6-SIDE MITER Blade Tilt	6-SIDE MITER Track-Arm	8-SIDE MITER Blade Tilt	8-SIDE MITER Track-Arm
5°	½	5°	44¾	5°	29¾	2½	22¼	2
10°	1½	9¾	44¼	9¾	29½	5½	22	4
15°	3¾	14½	43¼	14½	29	8¼	21½	6
20°	6¼	18¾	41¾	18¾	28¼	11	21	8
25°	10	23	40	23	27¼	13½	20¼	10
30°	14½	26½	37¾	26½	26	16	19½	11¾
35°	19½	29¾	35¼	29¾	24½	18¼	18¼	13¼
40°	24½	32¾	32½	32¾	22¾	20¼	17	15
45°	30	35¼	30	35¼	21	22¼	15¾	16¼
50°	36	37½	27	37½	19	23¾	14¼	17½
55°	42	39¼	24	39¼	16¾	25¼	12½	18¾
60°	48	41	21	41	14½	26½	11	19¾

Table of compound angles for radial saw operations. Figures are degrees to the nearest quarter-degree. (*Rockwell*)

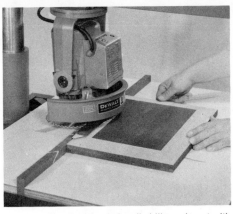

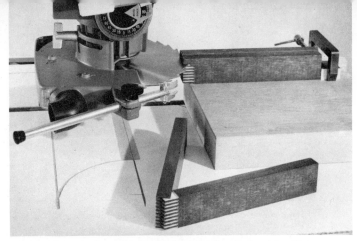

Panel raising is handled like a rip cut with the saw set for horizontal cutting and the blade tilted up a few degrees. The carriage is locked on the arm and the panel is fed past the blade as it is guided against the fence for a smooth cut.

Finger joints for a box are made with the saw set for horizontal cutting. Two adjoining pieces are cut at the same time. One piece is raised the width of the saw kerf above the other and clamped together. Successive cuts are made elevating the blade an amount equal to the width of the groove for each pass. A block is used under the work to allow clearance between saw and table. (*DeWalt/Black & Decker*)

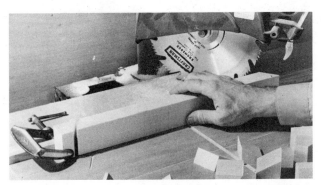

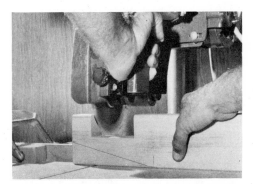

A piece of mitered cut-off scrap is clamped to the fence to serve as a stop block when cutting a number of pieces to identical length. Miter angle is unchanged; stock is flipped end for end to miter both ends.

Stop block is used to line up the first cut when notching out an end on multiple pieces. The stock is shifted freehand after the initial cut.

The first of a series of triangles to be cut is clamped to the table to serve as a precise stop block. The workpiece is flipped over, front to back, after each cut to obtain identical pieces.

Another way to cut angles: Saw arm is set for straight across cutting but the work is clamped to the table at an angle to the guide fence.

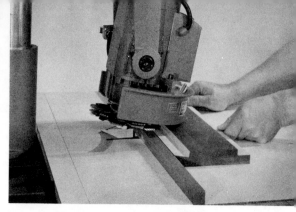

The dado head is used to cut tongue and groove joints. The motor assembly is locked in place and the work is pushed past the blade. (*DeWalt/Black & Decker*)

The saw adjustment for a bevel rabbet cut is the same as for a horizontal rip plus a tilt of the motor.

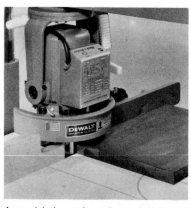

A special shaper fence is required for use when doing molding head operations in which an entire edge is to be shaped. A straight cutter is used here to joint the edge of stock. The infeed side of the fence is set back an amount equal to the depth of cut.

A cabinet door shaper head cutter makes quick work of cutting the quarter-round and rabbeted edge in one pass. As in any shaping operation, the cross grain cuts are made first to eliminate splintering problems.

A circular disk attached to the table serves as a depth collar when cutting a molded edge on a curved workpiece. (*DeWalt/Black & Decker*)

Cutting a circular groove (left) is accomplished by clamping the stock to the table, locking the carriage against the arm, loosening the yoke clamp then rotating the power unit 360 degrees.

Scallops are made with the dado head (right) locked in position for a horizontal cut. The work is fed by pivoting one end against the fence. Feed slowly and hold the stock firmly because there is a tendency for kickback. (*DeWalt/Black & Decker*)

Rosettes for decorative overlaying are made using a strip of wood which is first ripped into a V shape. The blade is then set to cut a 45 degree miter and 45 degree bevel. Make the segments by cutting first with the strip to the left of the blade, then shifting it to the right side of the blade, yielding handsome pieces.

A saucer cut is made by swinging the blade back and forth through an arc while the carriage is locked on the arm and the bevel adjustment lock released. Make repeated passes of about $1/8"$ increments until the desired depth is obtained. (*DeWalt/Black & Decker*)

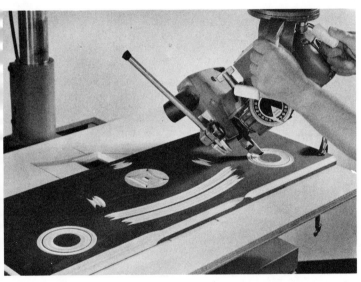

Sample piece shows some of the interesting ornamental cuts which can be made with a molding cutterhead.

Using a drum sanding accessory for contour sanding an edge.

A planer attachment is useful for surfacing the faces of boards. The carriage is repositioned and locked after each pass.

A drill chuck attached to the spindle permits varied drilling operations.

A saber saw accessory attachment can be connected to the motor spindle to further extend the versatility of this tool. (*DeWalt/Black & Decker*)

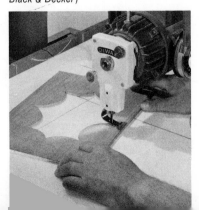

22 Surfacing and Shaping

After sawing to size and shape, wood parts for most kinds of construction generally require additional fabrication with any one or more of a wide variety of tools before they are ready to serve their intended functional or decorative purpose.

Regardless of the complexity of the finished product, its construction is usually the result of applying and combining a variety of basic woodworking operations.

This section deals with the various tools and techniques that are used to smooth, shape, and form the wood beyond the initial sawing. The hand tools will necessitate the development of skills through practice, trial and error. The power tools will enable you to do a better job more quickly and with less effort.

Chisel

Proficient use of the chisel requires practice. Somewhat like the handsaw, it is a tool that depends entirely on manual skills. It is strictly a freehand tool. The depth and shape of cut is controlled only by the amount of pressure applied to the handle and the manner in which the hand on the blade end guides the cutting edge.

Hand pressure can be used on the handle when working with softwood; hammer pressure is usually required for hardwood. Heavy stock removal should be done by sawing whenever possible and the chisel used to make the finish cuts. Always work with a sharp chisel; a dull one is difficult and dangerous to use.

CHISEL

The chisel is a form of knife. Its long shape concentrates the force applied to the handle to a relatively small cutting edge thus permitting it to cut wood with ease. The blade is flat on one side and beveled on the other to form the cutting edge.

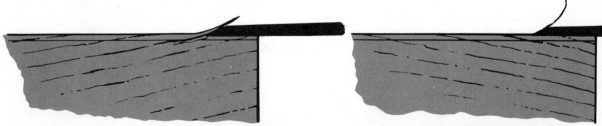

If the chisel is used *against* the grain, in the downhill direction of the fibers, it acts like a wedge splitting the wood instead of cutting it. The result will be a rough, uncontrolled cut.

If the chisel is used *with* the grain, in the uphill direction of the fibers, it will sever the fibers and result in a smooth controlled cut. (*Stanley Tools*)

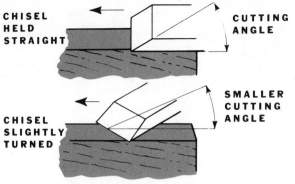

CHISEL HELD STRAIGHT — **CUTTING ANGLE**

CHISEL SLIGHTLY TURNED — **SMALLER CUTTING ANGLE**

When the chisel is slightly turned, it cuts easier and smoother because the cutting angle is smaller. This is a paring cut.

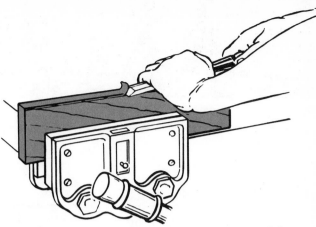

For a smooth, straight finishing cut, keep the bevel up and the straight side of the chisel flat on the work.

To remove wood quickly the chisel may be used with the bevel down. For safety, keep both hands behind the blade.

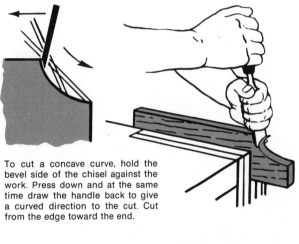

To cut a concave curve, hold the bevel side of the chisel against the work. Press down and at the same time draw the handle back to give a curved direction to the cut. Cut from the edge toward the end.

To cut a hollow curve on edge grain, hold the bevel down and cut halfway from each end of the curve toward the center.

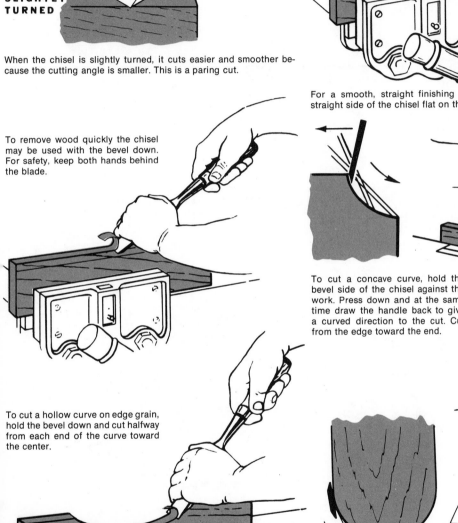

A round shape can be pared vertically. Begin at the edge and work to the center of the end from each side. The flat side of the chisel is held tangent to the curve at each cut. (*Stanley Tools*)

243

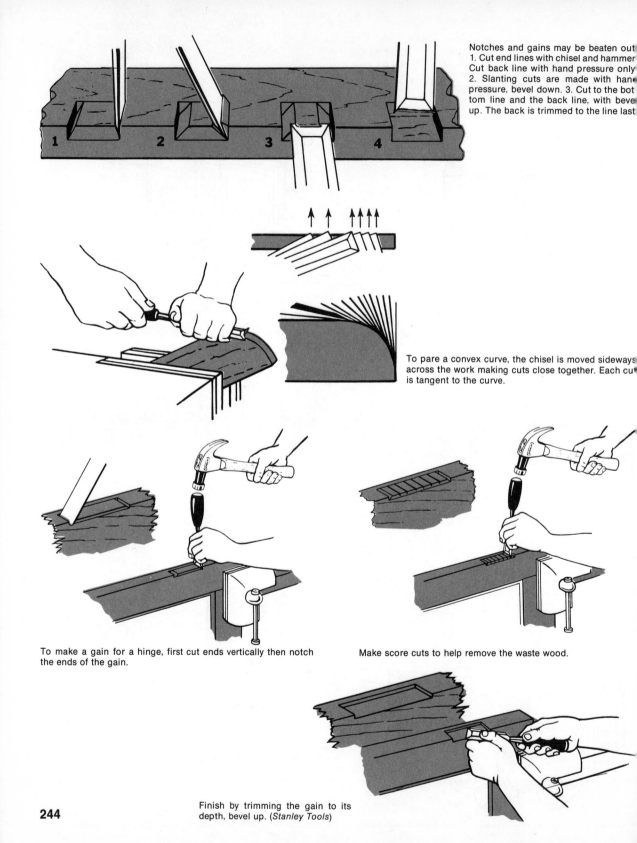

Notches and gains may be beaten out.
1. Cut end lines with chisel and hammer.
Cut back line with hand pressure only.
2. Slanting cuts are made with hand
pressure, bevel down. 3. Cut to the bottom line and the back line, with bevel
up. The back is trimmed to the line last.

To pare a convex curve, the chisel is moved sideways
across the work making cuts close together. Each cut
is tangent to the curve.

To make a gain for a hinge, first cut ends vertically then notch
the ends of the gain.

Make score cuts to help remove the waste wood.

Finish by trimming the gain to its
depth, bevel up. (*Stanley Tools*)

Plane

The plane is actually a form of chisel that is set into a metal base. The blade projects from the base a given amount to control the depth of cut. It is used to trim wood to size, to smooth it, or to cut bevels and chamfers.

Although the thickness of shavings removed with each stroke of the plane is mechanically controlled by the adjustment of the blade projection, the angle of cut obtained on an edge depends on the manner

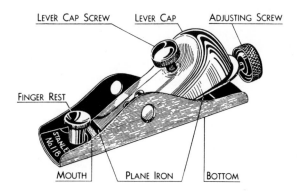

The block plane is designed to be used with one hand. It is especially useful for fine cabinetry and model work. The blade (plane iron) is set with its bevel up, its sharp edge down.

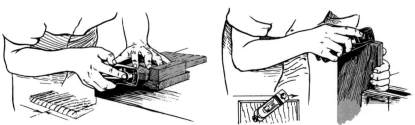

Owing to the low angle at which the blade is set, the block plane is the most effective one to use on end grain. It is also the handiest tool for planing corners and chamfers. (*Stanley Tools*)

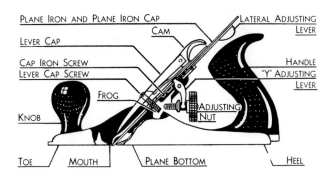

The more commonly used planes, in the order of their average length, are called smooth, jack and fore; measuring about 9, 14 and 18 inches, respectively. All have the same basic parts. They are selected for use relative to he size of the job at hand.

This illustrates why it is easier to plane a long edge straight with a long plane than with a short one. A long plane bridges the low parts and does not cut them until the high spots are removed. (*Stanley Tools*)

in which the tool is applied to the work. To trim or smoothen an edge that is square the plane must be held perfectly flat against the surface. To square an uneven edge the plane is again held on a horizontal plane but made to slice off only the high portions repeatedly until the edge is true.

The cut should always be made in the uphill direction of the grain to obtain the smoothest surface. It is sometimes impossible to determine grain direction by visual inspection. In such cases a thin first cut should be made. If the edge is gouged, the stock should be planed from the opposite direction. On wavy grained wood in which the grain will very likely run in both directions, a very light cut is required.

Parts of the standard double plane iron.

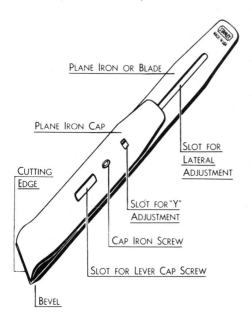

PLANE IRON OR BLADE

PLANE IRON CAP

CUTTING EDGE

SLOT FOR LATERAL ADJUSTMENT

SLOT FOR "Y" ADJUSTMENT

CAP IRON SCREW

SLOT FOR LEVER CAP SCREW

BEVEL

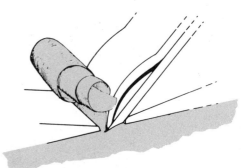

The plane iron cap serves an important function; it breaks and curls the shaving. This prevents the wood from splitting ahead of the cutting edge thus producing a smooth surface. (*Stanley Tools*)

The edge of the plane iron cap must fit tight to prevent shavings from wedging under it, piling up and choking the plane.

To adjust for the thickness of cut, sight along the bottom of the plane and turn the adjusting nut.
To adjust for the evenness of cut, sight along the bottom and move the lateral adjusting lever to the right or left.

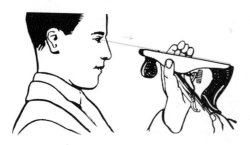

To cut a straight smooth edge the plane is pushed with the grain (uphill direction of the fibers). To keep the plane moving smoothly and straight, press down on the knob at the beginning of the stroke and on the handle at the end of the stroke. (*Stanley Tools*)

If you plane all the way across an end grain, the corners will split and ruin edge of board.

Plane half way from each side towards the center to prevent splitting when planing end grain.

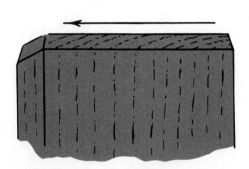

An alternate method of planing end grain if there is sufficient excess wood: Cut a chamfer on the second edge then plane in one direction. The angled end will not split. (*Stanley Tools*)

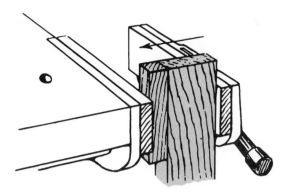

Another method of planing end grain without splitting the corners of the work. Clamp a scrap of wood tightly against the second edge then plane all the way across.

Spokeshave

The spokeshave is a special plane with a short base and wide blade that is used to shape and smooth curved surfaces. A flat base spokeshave is used for convex curves and a curved base version is used for concave work. It is adjusted in the same way as a plane: the amount of blade projection controls the depth of cut.

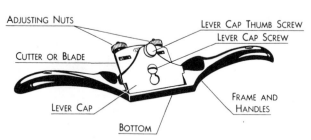

The spokeshave is a form of plane which has a base short enough to allow it to follow curves. It is a useful tool which is easily mastered.

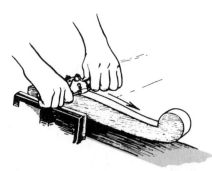

The tool can be pushed or pulled; it works equally well in either direction. The flat bottom tool is used on convex or concave edges where the curves have a long sweep.

The convex bottom spokeshave is used to cut concave curved edges having small sweeps. (*Stanley Tools*)

The spokeshave is the ideal tool to use to smooth carve a free form shape which has been rough cut on the band saw. As with planing, direction of cutting action should always be made with the grain.

When shaping long curves with the spokeshave, it is good practice to make long, uninterrupted cuts in order to develop the shape with as few bumps as possible.

Work which has been shaved with a properly sharpened tool with a keen edge will need very little final sanding.

The spokeshave was the most-used tool in the carving of this graceful decorative piece, shown on the following pages.

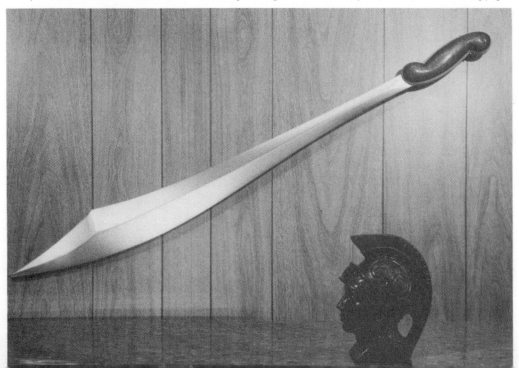

This tool should be held at a slight angle and the cut made in the uphill direction of the grain. When the grain changes direction, so should the direction of the stroke be changed. Deep cuts may be made for quick stock removal, but the final cuts should be light ones in order to obtain smooth finished contours. The spokeshave is frequently used to smooth the surfaces of band sawed wood that has the characteristic "washboard" ripples.

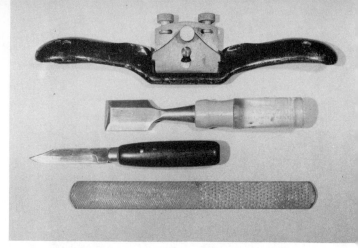

The spokeshave can't do it all. Here are some of its helpers. The chisel and rasp are used to work the small curves in the handle. The knife takes care of whittling off the waste ends which are used to clamp the work in progress.

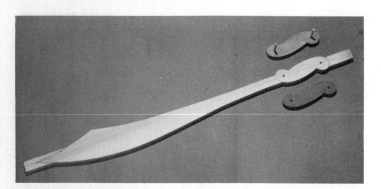

Blank for the carving can be cut by hand or power saw. Handle is made up of darker wood, glued with dowels which go all the way through and give the effect of rivets.

Pencil lines are used to guide the tool for the initial bevel cuts; the rest is done by eye. A lamp placed directly over the work accentuates the contours, makes it easier to see the results of each cut.

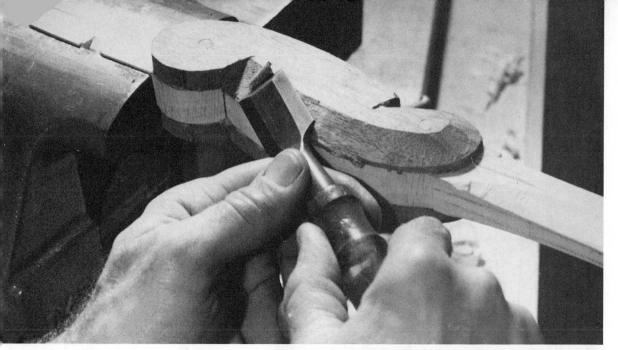

Paring cuts are made with chisel to rough form the handle. Note how the waste end is used to clamp the work.

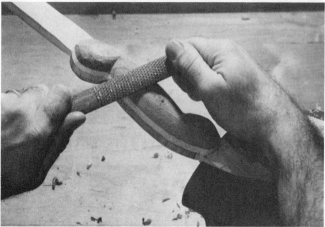

The wood rasp is used to smooth out the bumps left by the chisel. This section is a bit too small to work with the spokeshave.

The effectiveness of the overhead skim lighting is well illustrated here during the final sanding.

Surform Tool

The Surform tool has a cutting surface that looks much like a cheese grater. The cutting surface has hundreds of tiny, sharp teeth that work like so many individual planes. It is an excellent tool to use for general stock removal, for shaping, and for smoothing operations.

The tool is available in a variety of shapes and is handled like either a rasp or a plane. The depth of cut is fixed by the nature of the

The Surform tools are used for all kinds of general shop work. They are unexcelled for sculpturing wood because they cut smooth and fast. This is an example of the kind of shaping work which can be done with the Surforms.

The tool is handy for forming cylindrical shapes on the lathe. Grasp it with both hands and keep it continuously moving across the work.

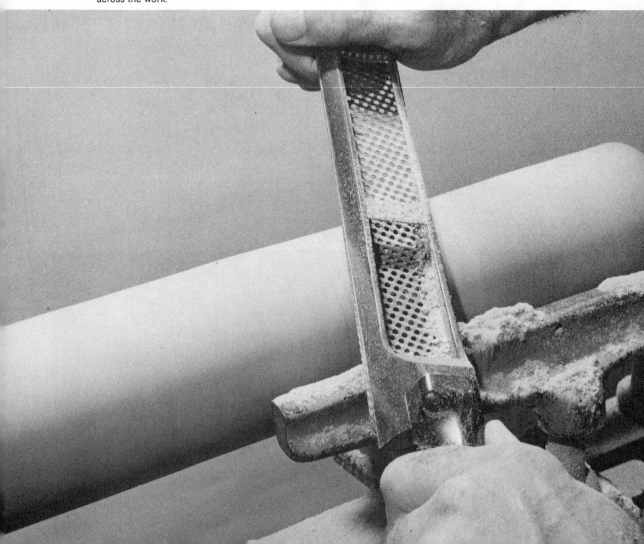

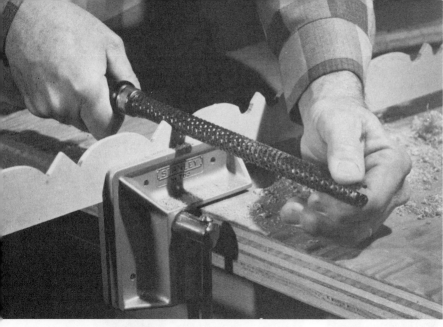

The tool is used exactly like a rasp; it cuts on the forward stroke. Small work should be firmly supported to keep it from vibrating.

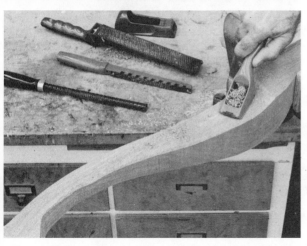

The small convex curved Surform is a natural for shaping the inside curve portions of a cabriole leg. This tool can be used with one hand.

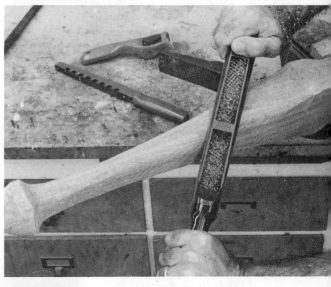

The amount of stock removed can be controlled by varying the angle of the stroke. All the shaping of a cabriole leg after bandsawing can be done with these tools. Sanding will complete the work.

To round an edge, first make heavy cuts to form a bevel then light cuts at varying angles. (*Stanley Tools*)

253

cutting surface. Each pass of the tool over the work will remove just so much stock. Although it cuts fairly rapidly due to the great number of cutting edges, the depth of each total cut is not excessive due to the shallowness of the teeth. This is advantageous when used for shaping intricate curves because it allows gradual progress to occur. Mistakes are hardly possible.

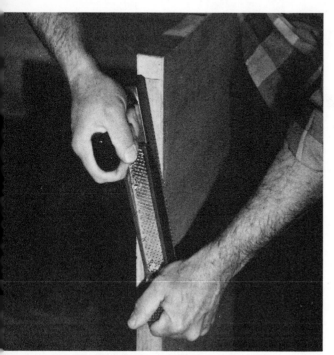

Work from both ends towards the center to trim the end of a door. Apply equal pressure with both hands to keep the tool flat on the work. Slight sideways motion helps cut faster.

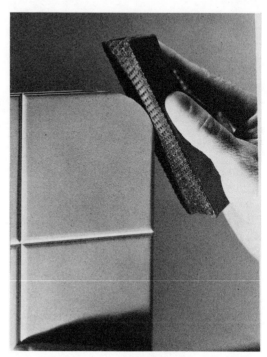

Use the Surform on tough hardboard materials. It won't dull as readily as a plane or chisel. (*Stanley Tools*)

FORMING SPIRALED CYLINDERS·

The round tool is especially well suited for forming spiraled cylinders. Here's the way it's done: Wrap a strip of paper around a cylinder at an angle leaving a slight space to allow tracing between the windings.

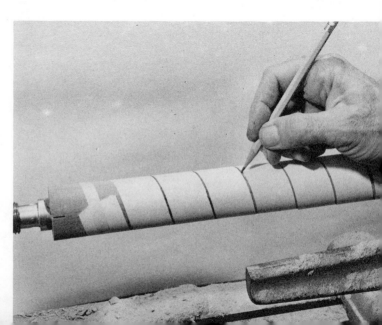

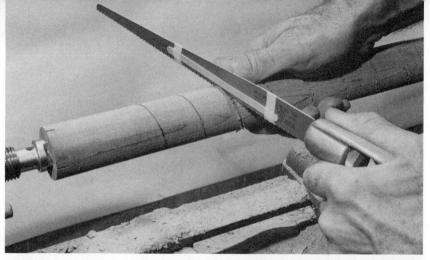

Make a partial saw cut along the line, about 1/8" deep. A stick taped to the blade serves as a depth gage.

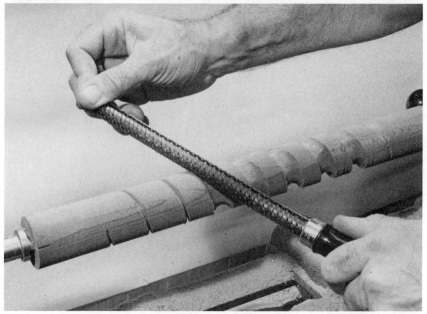

The lathe is used only as a very convenient holding device. Do not use power for this operation. Run the tool along the sawed guide line with a slightly rocking motion. Turn the work manually when the desired depth is reached at each turn in the work.

Go over the groove to work out any small flats then sand with a thin strip of abrasive cloth using both a rocking and side swinging motion.

ointer

The jointer is essentially a mechanized counterpart of the hand plane. It is used mainly to square and smooth the edges of stock in preparation for joining by gluing (hence the name).

In a routine shop procedure one edge of a board that is to be sawed is first jointed smooth and square on the jointer. This produces a finished edge

The proper method of feeding the work: Suitable downward pressure is exerted on the front of the board so the newly-formed surface makes good contact with the rear table. The hand at the rear of the work exerts no down pressure, but simply pushes the work to the knives.

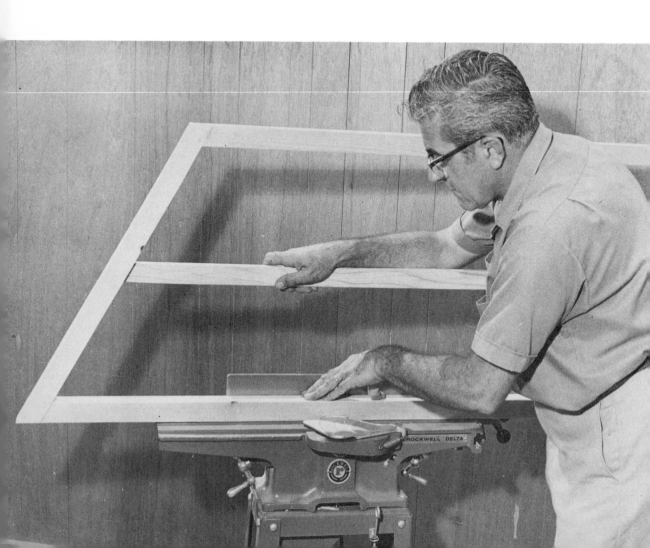

As the work advances, the front hand is repositioned so that it continues to bear down over the rear table. The back hand continues to push steadily from behind.

Nearing the end of the cut, the back hand bears down slightly while pushing to help prevent the board from tipping up as it overhangs the outfeed table.

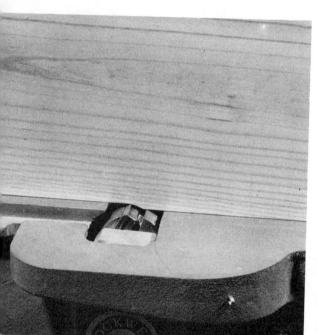

In order to do satisfactory work, the rear or outfeed table (left), must be adjusted so that it is at exactly the same height as the cutterhead knife at its highest point.

When handling wide work it is advisable to fasten an auxiliary high fence to the regular one in order to provide a more positive support for the work. Side pressure is always required to keep the work in contact with the fence and is especially important when jointing wide stock.

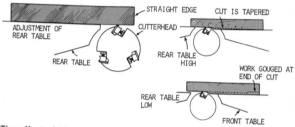

The effect of high and low rear table on jointer cuts. The proper adjustment is easily made by sighting with an accurate straight edge. (*Rockwell*)

that rides against the fence of the saw. The stock is cut slightly oversize, then passed through the jointer on the second side to trim and smooth it to size, making it ready for gluing.

If the jointer were capable only of planing edges of stock, it would nevertheless be a worthwhile tool because of its time and labor-saving advantages over hand planing. But the jointer

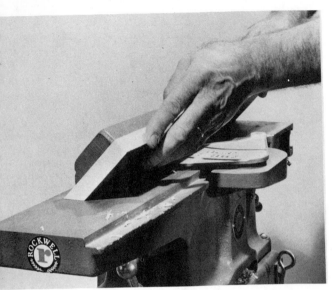

Bevel cuts are made by tilting the fence to the required position. The fence can be tilted in or out as desired. It is generally safer, however, to work with the fence tilted **in** like this.

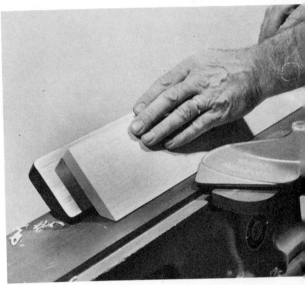

There is sometimes a tendency for the wood to slide away from the fence when beveling with the fence tilted **out.**

A homemade push block is an absolute necessity for safety during surfacing operations. This one utilizes old plane handles. A small cleat across the rear bottom grips the work.

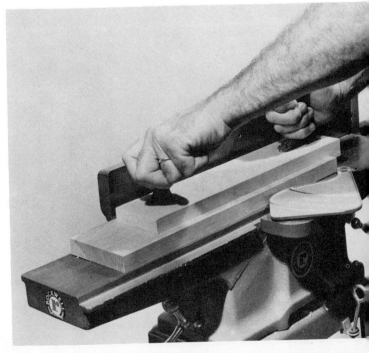

In use the left hand grasps the knob and bears down while the right hand holds the handle and pushes forward slowly and smoothly.

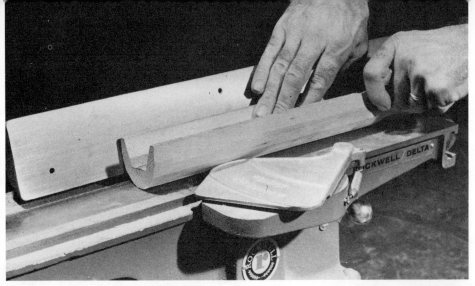

Rounded contours can be formed by making repeated passes while continually changing the angle of the work after each pass. The fence is kept in one slightly out tilted position to guide the work in a straight line. The operation is essentially done free hand.

Rabbets are accomplished by setting the fence for the width of cut, and the front table for the depth. Cutting an end rabbet on narrow stock is done with the aid of a backing block which is used to push the work.

An L shaped jig clamped as shown permits cutting round tenons on round stock. The work is slowly pushed into the revolving cutterhead and is then slowly revolved in the same direction as the rotation of the knives.

259

can be used to accomplish many basic woodworking operations, including surfacing, beveling, rabbeting, and tapering. Special, simple techniques may be used to produce round tenons, stop chamfers, raised panels, and ornamental molding.

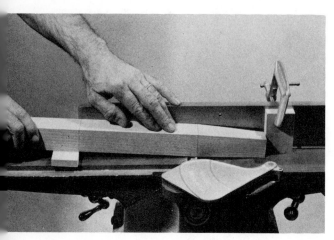

The jointer is well suited for making taper cuts for furniture legs. The front table is lowered for the desired depth of cut. A stop block is clamped to the fence to positon the stock for the start of the taper. A block is bradded into the stock at a point where it will support it at an angle that allows the front end to contact the table while the point at which the taper is to start contacts the knife. The cut is made by pulling the work back over the cutter. The block is re-bradded for each side.

To further shape a leg a stop chamfer may be cut. This is done by lowering both the front and rear tables equally. A start and stop block are clamped to the fence to control the length of cut. The work is held against the rear stop with the front end tilted upwards. With the power on, the work is lowered into the cutter then advanced. There is always a strong kickback tendency at the start of the cut therefore the stop block must be very firmly clamped to the fence.

The bevel stop chamfer is a widely used cut for built-ins and furniture. It is made in the same way as a straight one but with the fence tilted. The piece is shown in the up-tilted position for the start of the cut.

Decorative moldings can be produced by making a series of stopped cove cuts in the surface of a board. The procedure is rather simple.

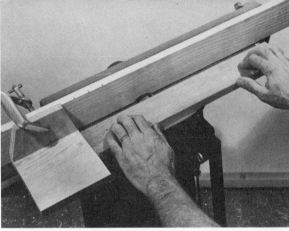

A wide stop is clamped to an auxiliary wood fence which is marked with equally spaced indexes. The end of the work is fed squarely against the stop then pushed into the rotating knives. Both the front and rear tables are lowered an equal amount.

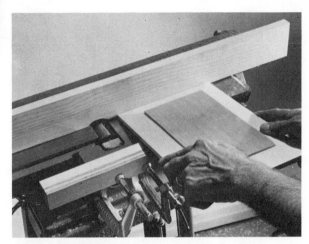

Panel raising can be done by clamping a board to the rabbeting ledge in order to position the work at an angle. Set the rear table level with the knives as for a normal jointing operation. Take small cuts, increasing the depth of cut about $1/16''$ after each pass. Make the cross-grain cuts first to prevent splintering problems.

The stop block doing its job at the end of the cut. Use **both** hands for these operations. One hand is pictured here only for clarity. Note that the blade guard is removed for this operation so watch the fingers.

Router

The router is used for edge and surface shaping and joinery. With various cutters, some of which are self guiding, or with simple jigs, this portable shaper can perform an unlimited variety of operations. This home workshop project illustrates the nature and quality of work that can be done with the router. It was used to form the basic lap, rabbet and dado joints required in the construction of this piece. The router was also used to cut the trim molding and to make the raised panels.

The router bit rotates clockwise therefore when cutting straight edges, the router must be moved left to right (as you face the work) so that the cut is made against the rotation of the bit. *(Black & Decker)*

The router can be used to break sharp corners. It does this with more accuracy than would be obtained with a sander.

Cutting to the corner of end grain will usually split a bit of wood at the end of the cut. If the cut is not to be continued around the corner, a piece of scrap wood should be temporarily added to the emerging corner so the router will cut into it and avoid splitting the corner of the work.

If the edge is to be shaped completely around, then simply rout the end grain portions first. The cuts along the sides in the direction of the grain will clean up the splintered ends and create a neat, molded corner.

Routing the edges of this unit after temporary assembly results in a continuous molded edge with a pleasing small radius in the corners. A self piloting bit with a non-cutting tip controls the sidewise movement of the bit so that the operation is safely and accurately performed freehand. When it is necessary to repeat the cut on the other side, the depth of cut should be such that it will leave about $1/8$" of uncut area at the center to provide a guiding edge for the pilot during the second pass.

One of the main advantages of the router over the shaper is its ability to work into tight corners. This assembly for a door insert has angled corners which are too sharp to be molded on the shaper. See photo at right.

The router is one of the easiest of the power tools to use and it will do an excellent job if the bit is sharp and if the proper rate of feed speed is used. The correct feed is easily checked by looking and listening: Look at the cut edge for burn marks indicating that the feed is too slow. Listen to the sound of the motor. If it sounds as though it is slowing down, it signals a forced feed—too fast! This slowing will build up heat, dulling the cutter and perhaps damaging the motor. Experiment with some scrap wood, both soft and hard. They react differently. You will soon acquire the "feel" for the correct rate of feed.

The router equipped with a flush trimming bit is excellent for trimming large boards to size. In this application the router is being used to plane the edges. To insure perfect final fit, the doors of these storage units were made a bit oversize then temporarily nailed into position. The slight overhang making up for any errors which may have developed. The ball bearing guide of the bit rides against the side wall while the bit shaves the edge of the door absolutely flush to the side panels.

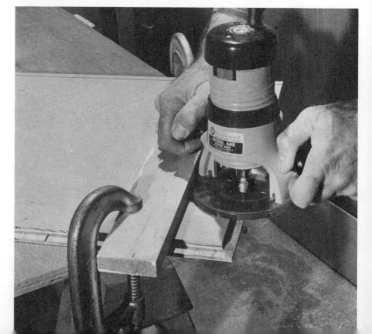

A rabbeting bit with pilot tip is generally used to cut rabbets. However, if an extra wide rabbet is required, a straight bit can be used. A guide is clamped to the work to control the width of cut. If the bite is too much for the bit to take in one pass (as it usually is) just make a few free hand passes before making contact between the base edge of the router and the guide.

Using the router to cut perfect dadoes requires a very simple set up. Clamp two straight boards parallel to each other and centered over the proposed dado. Space them equal to the diameter of the router base. Use a straight or mortise bit of the appropriate size and push the router through the channel.

As can be seen by the size of this cabinet, the router was the only practical tool useable to cut the dado joints. Panels of this size cannot be properly worked with a stationary circular or radial saw.

Top quality lap joints can be made using only a hand saw and the router. Saw cuts are first made to set the width of the joint. The router with a straight bit set to the required depth is used to clean out the waste.

This type of joint is exceptionally strong and among one of the easiest to make. Note that the glue will be spread evenly before assembly of the parts.

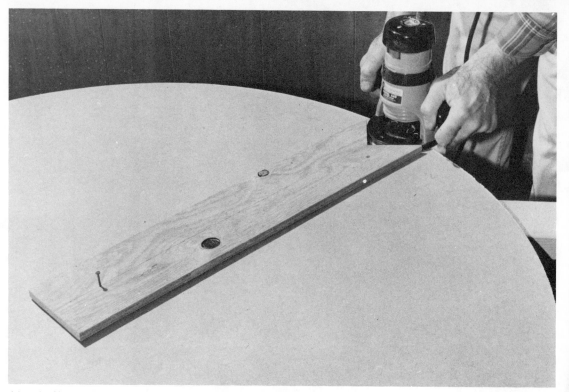

A length of board with a V cut notched into one end to house the router base is an effective jig to use for trueing up or edge finishing circular work of any size. The piece shown is 4' in diameter. A nail driven into the center of the work forms the pivot. Any kind of bit may be utilized with this set up.

Attractive, deep cross sectioned moldings can be made by utilizing the built-up method: Cut two or more boards with parallel outlines then mold the edge of each.

Glue the parts with the required amount of offset to creat a continued molded pattern.

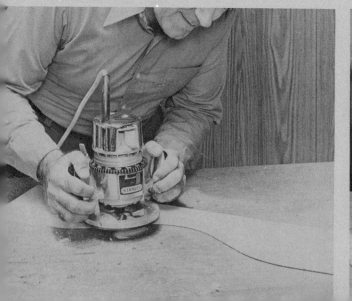

A routing tip: Some veneer panels of certain wood species have a tendency to splinter along the end grain edge. The problem can be avoided by pre-scoring the inside edge of the anticipated line of cut with a sharp knife.

Small work such as this railing could present a problem because there is too little surface to support the router base properly. A scrap of wood of equal height and a clamp to hold a second scrap over both to keep them in place solves the problem.

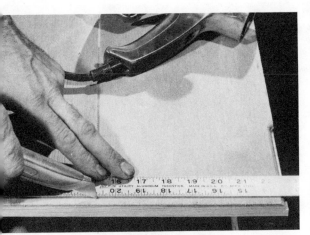

The cut must be made (below) in exactly the right place so make careful measurement before scoring.

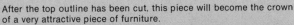

After the top outline has been cut, this piece will become the crown of a very attractive piece of furniture.

Carbide tipped router bits are available and should be used for trimming plastic laminates which are very wearing on ordinary bits. The standard procedure for working with laminates is to cut the pieces oversize then trim flush or beveled as required. The holes in the wood were bored before application of the laminate.

Shaper

The shaper is used to make decorative cuts and to form joints on the edges of wood. It does much the same type of work as the router but is much more powerful, and in some applications, faster. Most work can be fed through the shaper as routine operations without the need for special jigs.

Very little skill is required to produce quality work with the shaper. As with many of the power tools, the skill is built-in. You need only select any one of the several basic set ups

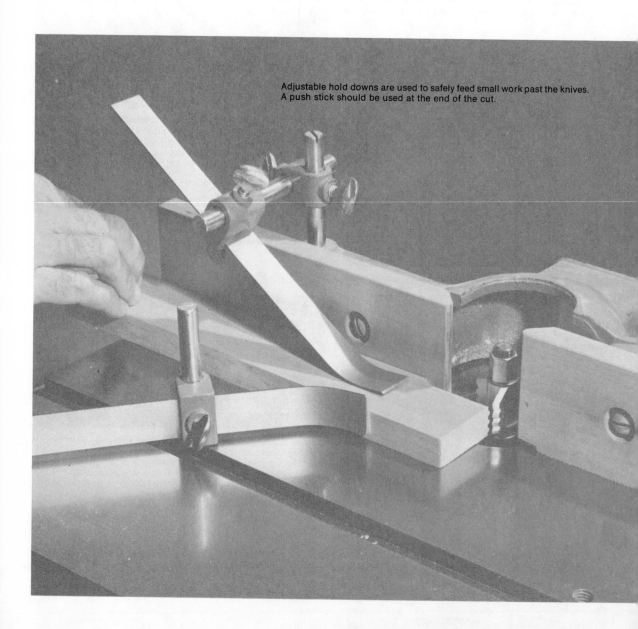

Adjustable hold downs are used to safely feed small work past the knives. A push stick should be used at the end of the cut.

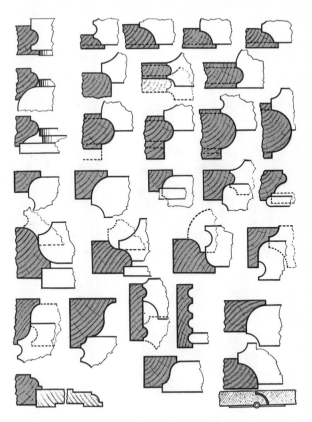

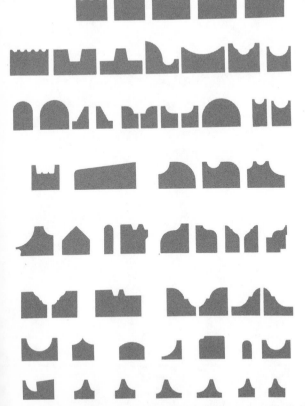

These are some of the many shaper cutter knives commonly used.

In many cases two or more passes with different parts of the same cutter may be made to vary the design. By using more than one cutter shape for an edge an endless variety of contours are possible.

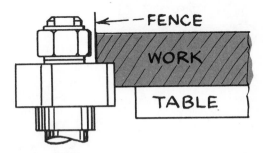

There are four basic methods of working with the shaper. Each one is adapted for a particular type of work. The safest and most satisfactory operation is in working with a fence to guide the work. This method is the one most used for straight work, the fence limiting the depth of cut. (*Rockwell*)

For average work where a portion of the original edge of the work is not touched by the cutter, both the front and rear fences are adjusted to be in line.

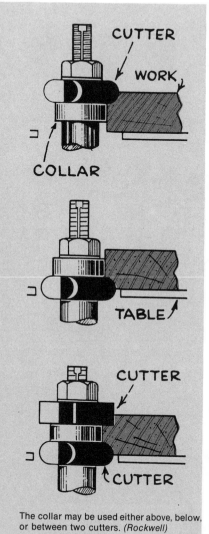

CUTTER

WORK

COLLAR

TABLE

CUTTER

CUTTER

The collar may be used either above, below, or between two cutters. *(Rockwell)*

Where the shaping operation removes the entire edge of the wood the rear fence must be adjusted so that it will make contact with the new edge. The adjustment is made by making a partial cut then advancing the fence to lightly contact the new edge.

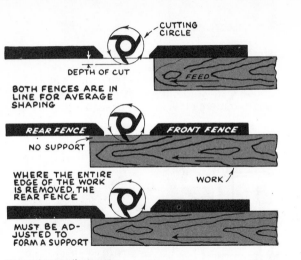

CUTTING CIRCLE

DEPTH OF CUT

FEED

BOTH FENCES ARE IN LINE FOR AVERAGE SHAPING

REAR FENCE FRONT FENCE

NO SUPPORT

WORK

WHERE THE ENTIRE EDGE OF THE WORK IS REMOVED, THE REAR FENCE

MUST BE ADJUSTED TO FORM A SUPPORT

Shaper fence adjustments.

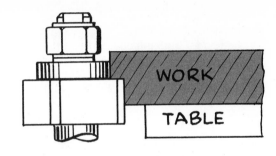

WORK

TABLE

Work which cannot be shaped against a fence is usually shaped against a collar. In this method of working, the rim of the collar rides against the work and limits the depth of cut. The diameter of the collar controls the cut. *(Rockwell)*

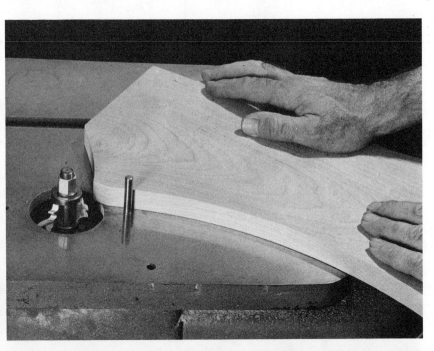

A steel fulcrum pin is used to support the work for the start of the cut when working against a collar. This reduces the possibility of kickback.

After the cut has been started, the work is swung free of the starting pin and rides only against the collar.

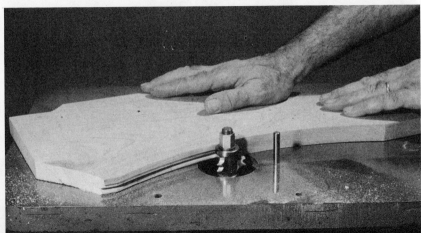

271

according to the requirements of the job, make the necessary adjustments, then apply the work to the cutting edge.

Whenever possible, shaping should be done against the fence because it is the safest method for both the operator and the work. The fence provides a positive support for the work and at the same time serves as a partial guard over the cutters. With the fence removed as is required for some operations, the cutters are fully exposed, so extra care must be exercised to keep the hands well out of the danger area. Use sharp cutters at all times because a dull

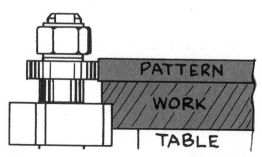

When making a number of like pieces a pattern may be used. This is similar to shaping against collars, except that a pre formed pattern and not the work rides against the collar. This method permits shaping the entire edge of irregular curved work, an operation which is impossible in any other manner. (*Rockwell*)

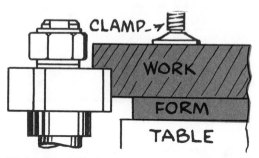

The fourth method of shaping is with a form. A form is any device in which the work is held so that it can be advanced to the cutter. (*Rockwell*)

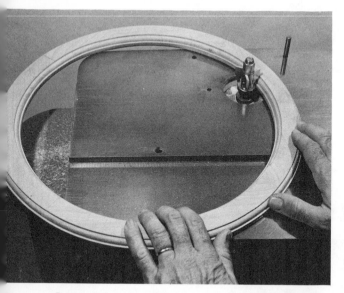

Extra care must be exercised when shaping with the cutter uppermost because accidental lifting of the work would gouge the wood. This could easily happen here if the grip on the work was momentarily relaxed.

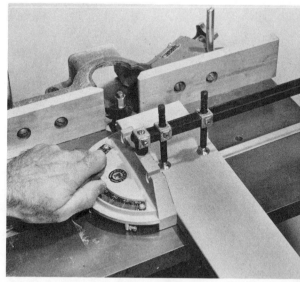

The sliding jig is the most common form used on the shaper. The miter gage with accessory hold down clamps is useful for guiding the ends of narrow work.

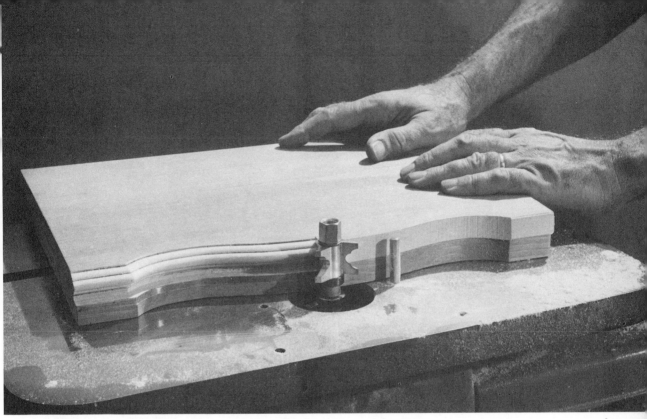

Working an entire edge with a pattern. The collar and pattern are in the lower position. The work is held to the pattern with several brads driven through the bottom of the pattern.

A straight cutter used with a collar and a thin plywood pattern is used to plane a curved edge true and smooth.

one can cause kickback that could result in a hand being thrown into them.

The work should always be fed against the rotation of the cutters and never forced rapidly into them. When the work involves cutting both end and edge grain, make the end grain (cross grain) cut first because it tends to splinter the wood slightly at the end of the cut. The cut with the grain will usually clear the area that was damaged. When very deep cuts are required, it is ad-

A circular saw tenoning jig can be used to advantage for numerous jointing operations where the work must be held in a vertical position.

A convex jig is used to shape an inside curve. The jig is cut to the same size curve as the work. This method can be used only when the curve is part of a true circle.

A simple miter fence can be constructed for advancing the work past the cutter at an angle.

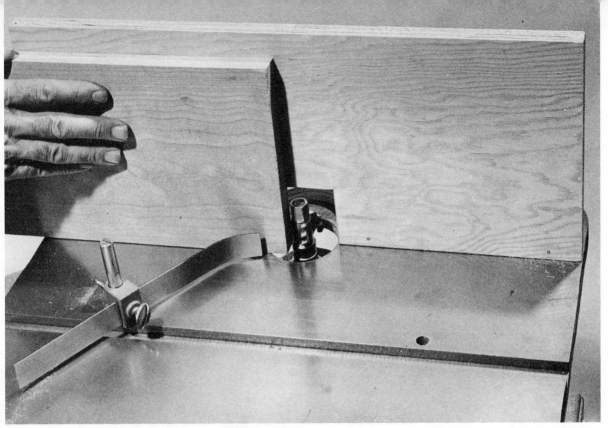

Wide stock which must be shaped on the face is difficult to guide along the comparatively low standard fence. An auxiliary high wood fence should be used for this kind of work to provide a proper bearing surface.

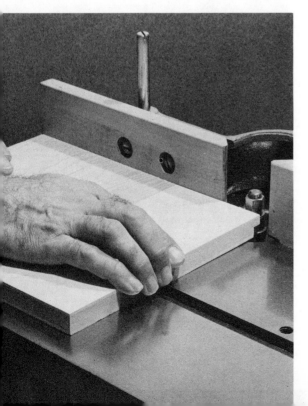

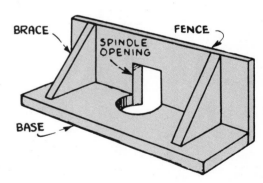

A typical homemade high auxiliary fence. (*Rockwell*)

Use of a wide back-up board is a simple means of advancing a narrow piece of stock squarely across the cutter. A tight grip on both pieces is essential.

visable to make several passes to achieve the full shape. This applies when working with or without the fence.

Cutters can be positioned to operate above or below the work. When used above, the cut is clearly visible while in progress, but the work can easily be damaged if it is accidently lifted during the cut. When cutting from below the work, accidental lifting or tilting will not harm it in any way. The progress of the cut may not be visible, but this is unimportant, since it serves no purpose to be able to see the cut until it is completed. In some of the accompanying photographs a top cutter position is shown. This is done for clarity.

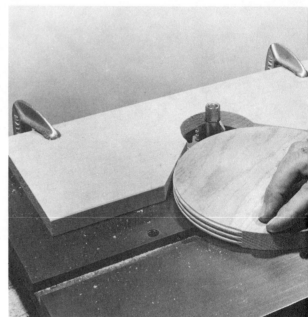

A piece of wood with a V cut and an opening for cutter clearance can be used to shape the edge of a circular workpiece.

A wood rip fence clamped to the table permits planing stock to exact width. A clamped hold-in is essential, positioned behind the cutter.

When narrow molding is needed it is best made by shaping the edges of wide stock then in turn ripping the strips to size on a table saw. Two sides may be worked each time to speed up the operation.

276

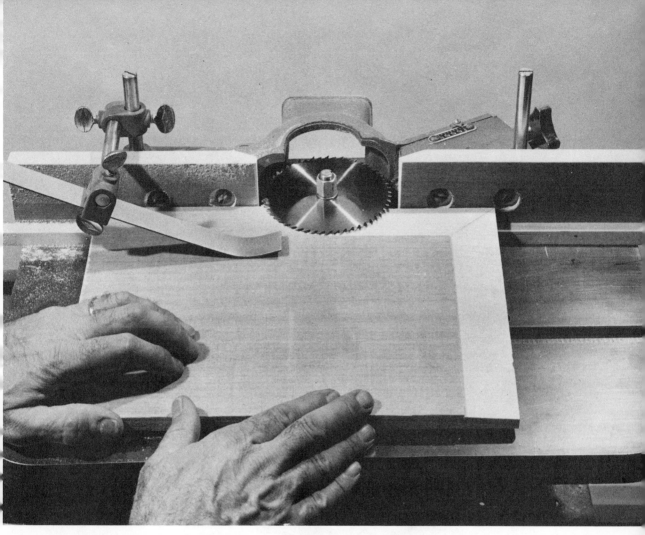

A small diameter saw blade may be used for making raised panels. A strip of wood is attached to the fence in order to support the work at a slight upward angle as shown.

Stops are clamped to the fence to control the length of a stopped mold cut.

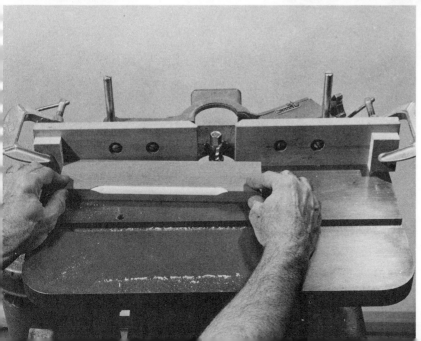

25 Drilling

Drilling holes is one of the most common and important operations performed in the workshop and in general maintenance and repair work around the house and property. Some work requires holes drilled with a high degree of precision, while other operations can tolerate holes made with somewhat less accuracy.

Holes bored for the installation of dowels or round tenons in joint construction must be quite exacting. Precision in pinpoint alignment, uniform spacing, and true perpendicularity are essential. Accurate angle drilling may also be required. This kind of work is best done on the drill press. Doweling jigs for use with hand drilling tools are available. They permit drilling holes accurately in the edge or end of stock.

Holes with less exacting requirements can be made with the hand tools, manual or electric. Pilot holes for screws and holes for numerous other purposes of construction and design are usually made by hand. Large work that cannot fit on the drill press or out-of-shop work must be done by hand. There is no other choice.

Hand Drill

Hand-operated drills are less frequently used in this age of power tools, but if you prefer manual drilling, or have no choice in the matter, there are three basic types available: the geared crank hand drill, the bit brace, and the push drill.

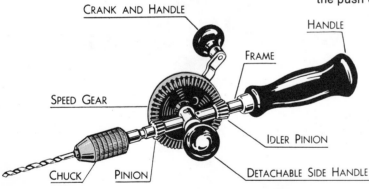

CRANK AND HANDLE

HANDLE

FRAME

SPEED GEAR

IDLER PINION

CHUCK PINION DETACHABLE SIDE HANDLE

The hand drill has a three jawed chuck which holds straight shank drills up to $\frac{1}{4}''$ diameter. Some models have a $\frac{3}{8}''$ capacity and two speed gear setup. (*Stanley Tools*)

The hand drill is used to drill holes up to $\frac{1}{4}''$ or $\frac{3}{8}''$, depending on the chuck capacity. A gear ratio of about 3 or 4 to 1 provides the necessary speed for drilling holes in wood. The pressure applied to the handle should be varied according to the diameter of the drill bit. Small drills are easily broken or bent if too much pressure is applied. When drilling deep holes, retract the drill occasionally to allow the chips to clear out of the flutes.

Pierce a small starting hole with an awl to prevent the drill point from starting in the wrong place. The drill may be held with the back handle or pushed with the stomach while steadied with the side handle. Vertical drilling is usually easier. Hold the drill straight and steady. Wobbling will enlarge the hole and may break the drill bit.

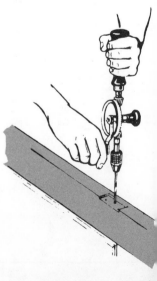

278

The bit brace with auger bits is used to bore holes larger than ¼″ up to 1″. For holes up to 3″ in diameter the expansive bit is used. There are differences in the design of the twist in auger bits, but they all work the same way. The feed screw penetrates the wood and draws the body of the bit into the wood. A pair of spurs (some bits have only one) score the perimeter of the hole in advance of the lips or cutters, which slice through the surface of the wood to make the hole. The shavings climb up the twist portion of the bit and out of the hole.

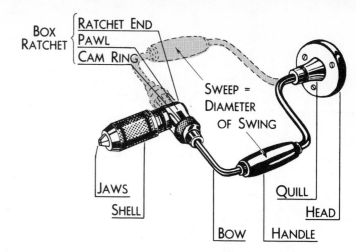

The bit brace with its large crank supplies plenty of leverage for easy and fast boring of large holes. Torque is increased in proportion to the sweep. (*Stanley Tools*)

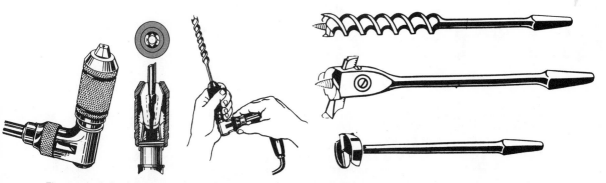

The standard chuck holds square shank bits. The square tapered socket of the jaws automatically centers the bit. The ratchet assembly permits working close to a corner or in a small space where a complete turn cannot be made. Adjusted for a counter-clockwise rotation, the brace can be used for removing screws.

Three basic types of bits used to bore holes with the brace. The standard twisted auger is used to bore holes ³⁄₁₆″ up to 1″. The expansion bit (center) is adjustable for cutting holes from ⅞″ up to 3″ in diameter. The Forstner bit (bottom) does not have a feed screw; it bores a hole which is flat on the bottom. (*Stanley Tools*)

A hole may be bored all the way through the work without splintering the other side by clamping a piece of waste wood against the back. (*Stanley Tools*)

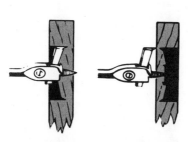

An alternate method of boring through the work without splintering is to bore until the feed screw point shows on the other side. The drilling is then continued from *the other side*. (*Stanley Tools*)

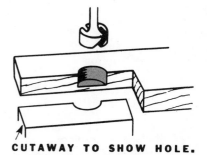

CUTAWAY TO SHOW HOLE.

The Forstner bit is used to bore holes partway through where the feed screw of an auger bit would spoil the other side, or where the spurs would weaken the bottom of the hole. It can be used very close to the edge of a board. (*Stanley Tools*)

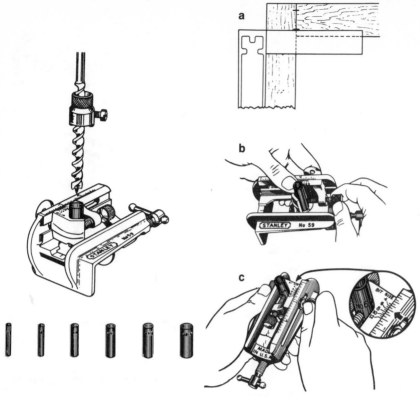

The doweling jig is used to locate and bore matching holes accurately on the edges of jointed work which is to be reinforced with dowels. Special guides are used for various sized dowels from $3/16''$ to $1/2''$. (*Stanley Tools*)

a. Using a doweling jig is quite easy: A center line is marked on the face of the work for the number of dowels desired.
b. A guide of suitable size is clamped into the jig.
c. A sliding adjustment is made to position the guide the required distance from the face side of the work.

d. The jig is clamped firmly to the work after aligning an index mark with the center line on the wood.
e. A bit is placed into the guide and the hole bored.
f. Dowels are inserted into the holes to complete the joint.

The push drill is handy for drilling very small holes for nails or screws. That it is operated with one hand is sometimes an advantage when the other hand is needed to hold the work.

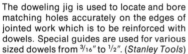

MAGAZINE HANDLE

ENCLOSED SPIRAL SPINDLE AND SPRING

CHUCK SLEEVE

MAGAZINE LOCK RING

CHUCK

1/16''   3/32''   1/8''   5/32''
5/64''   7/64''   9/64''   11/64''

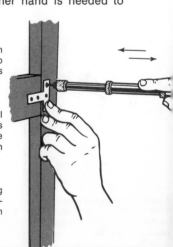

The automatic push drill can be used with one hand to drill small holes for screws and brads.

Drill points for the push drill are sized by sixty-fourths from $1/16''$ to $11/64''$. They are stored conveniently within the magazine handle.

This drill operates on a spring action. The return stroke reverses the drill point to clean away chips. (*Stanley Tools*)

Portable Drill

The portable electric drill is the happy medium between the manual drills and the drill press. Hardly any physical effort is necessary to drill holes with this tool other than to apply moderate pressure on the handle to drive the bit into the work. A need for heavy pressure indicates that the bit is dull.

The only skill you need to develop in the use of the drill is in aiming it straight or at a required angle. For much of the work for which the portable is used, aiming by eye will suffice. For more exacting results, the use of a square or T bevel resting alongside the drill will help in aligning the bit.

When drilling large holes, be sure to clamp the stock securely to the table and back up the work with a scrap board to keep from drilling into the table. This also prevents the bottom of the hole from splintering. On deep cuts, back out frequently to clear the waste and to give the bit enough time to cool.

The electric hand drill is far superior to the manual drills because it bores holes much more quickly and with practically no physical effort. In many situations the portable is better than even the drill press simply because it can be taken to the work.

Sometimes it is necessary to make special jigs (left) in order to hold odd shaped assemblies together for drilling. Alignment is improved if the eyes are sufficiently removed from the work to allow an overall sighting.

Drilling holes for screw joints (right) can be speeded up considerably with the use of a combination screw pilot drill bit. It drills the pilot, shank and countersink hole in one operation. Temporary nails should be driven part way for easy later removal.

When drills of two sizes are to be used for the same hole (left), bore the larger hole first. The smaller drill bit will always center itself at the tapered bottom of the large hole whereas a large bit may not always do so in a pre-drilled smaller hole.

Sighting along a square (right) helps to align the drill for more accurate drilling. Sometimes the use of a second one set at a right angle may be desirable for more critical work.

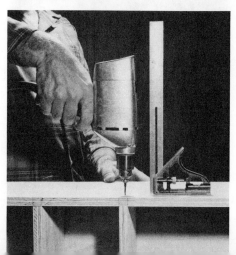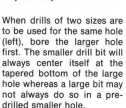

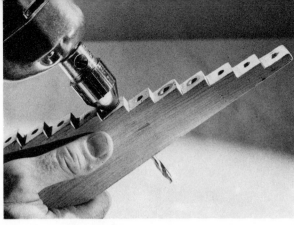

A handy drilling depth gage can be made by cutting a series of steps in a small board with a band or saber saw, then drilling a hole through the center of each step. In use you simply select the step which allows the drill to project through the bottom the desired amount. The jig is placed over the work to stop the drill at the right depth.

When you have a number of holes to bore at the same angle a jig can help obtain uniformity. Nail two pieces of wood at right angles and carefully drill a hole at the required angle. The jig is held tightly against the board to drill the holes at each location. Hardwood should be used for the jig.

Oversize holes are best cut with a hole saw accessory. Running a variable speed drill at highest speed results in the smoothest cut, beginning at a moderate speed.

Using a drill bit extension in a difficult spot. A set screw holds the bit.

A right angle attachment (left) is useful in many situations where space is limited.

A disk sanding attachment (right) for the drill is especially suited for quick paint removal. The drill should be tilted so only the outer third of the sanding disk makes contact. Otherwise the disk will bounce out of control and gouge the work. (3M Co.)

Using a drum sanding attachment (left) to smooth a curved edge. The drill must be held firmly with two hands and kept continually moving. Light or medium pressure should be used, never heavy.

Miniature grinder tool (right) can be used for the most delicate drilling jobs.

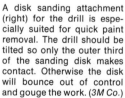

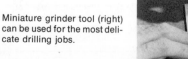

Drill Press

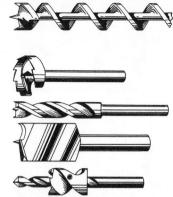

The drill press is an essential piece of equipment for precision drilling. It provides a simple, practical means to accomplish professional results for many woodworking chores. In addition to drilling, this machine will do routing, shaping, surface planing, sanding and mortising with the same degree of accuracy as it can drill holes.

The spindle and chuck to which the boring tool is attached is set perfectly perpendicular to the table. Consequently the drill press routinely makes holes that are perfectly straight and true. A variety of special jigs and set ups are employed to drill holes that are accurately spaced, at any angle, or on irregular or curved surfaces. All are rather simple devices that can be readily made and applied.

When using the drill press, be sure to secure the drill bit or other tool properly and firmly in the chuck. Check the path of the bit to make sure that it will pass through the center hole in the table. Always work on a back-up board when boring through-holes. Clamp the work firmly to the table, particularly when using large bits or hole cutters. Never, under any circumstance, use the fly cutter without clamping the work. Finally, adjust the spindle speed as required for the work to be done. As a general rule, the softer the wood and the smaller the bit, the higher the permissible speed. Bits up to $3/4''$ in diameter should be operated at about 2000 rpm. Bits larger than this should be run at about 700 rpm. If a tool begins to smoke, this indicates too high a speed or too fast a feed, or both.

These are some of the common hole boring bits used on the drill press. From top to bottom: Auger bit, multi-spur bit, spur machine bit, speed bit, twist drill with counterbore. Auger bits for use on power drills must have a solid point without threads. The multi-spur cuts smoothly, can be used at an angle. The spur machine bit produces the cleanest hole for dowels, is fast cutting. Flat speed bits are made in many styles, range from $1/4''$ to $1\frac{1}{2}''$. The twist drill with counterbore is used to drill the shank and counterbore hole for recessing screws in one operation.

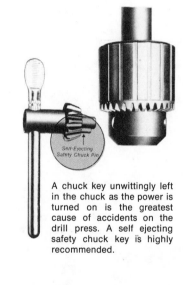

A chuck key unwittingly left in the chuck as the power is turned on is the greatest cause of accidents on the drill press. A self ejecting safety chuck key is highly recommended.

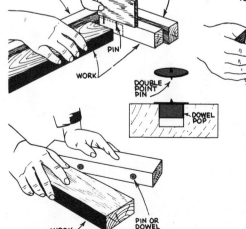

Holes for dowel joints must match up perfectly between mating pieces. These are the simplest and most accurate methods of marking the hole centers. The pin method utilizes two ordinary pins stuck in a block of wood which is positioned to come between the joining members. When pushed together, the pin heads make an impression on each piece. Double pointed tacks or dowel pops (centers) are the more standard method. When using the pops, one hole is drilled first. The pop is inserted in this hole then pressed against the second piece. When used carefully, a template will work quite well. (*Rockwell*)

283

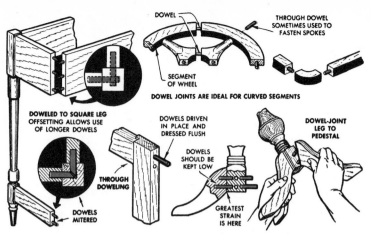

Typical dowel joints. To obtain maximum strength when doweling a rail to a leg, the dowels should be either offset or mitered. Offsetting is best but not always possible on narrow work. Through doweling is strong because maximum dowel length can be used. (*Rockwell*)

The depth stop adjustment assures equal and correct depth of holes. Always make a test boring in scrap when hole depth is critical.

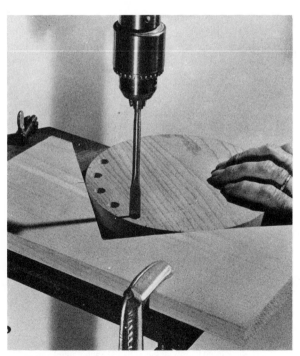

A V cut in a board clamped to the table is a useful jig for drilling holes uniformly around a circle. An index mark on the jig is used as a reference to line up equally spaced marks on the edge of the work.

The same V block is used with the table adjusted to a vertical position to bore holes around the outside of a circular piece.

284

Boring a Deep Hole
The average drill press has a four-inch stroke. This means that holes deeper than four inches must be made by boring from opposite ends of the work. This will increase the capacity to double that of the quill stroke. Positive alignment of the second hole is accomplished in this manner: A hole is drilled partly into a scrap board clamped to the table (left). The table is lowered to accommodate the work (right). To align the hole in the scrap so that it is centered directly under the spindle, the bit is removed and a longer dowel of the same diameter is inserted into the chuck. The table is adjusted so the hole lines up with the dowel.

The first hole is bored (left) in the work to the maximum depth. Insert a short piece of dowel (right) into the hole in the scrap stock. Turn the work over, insert the first hole into the dowel then bore the second hole, which should line up perfectly.

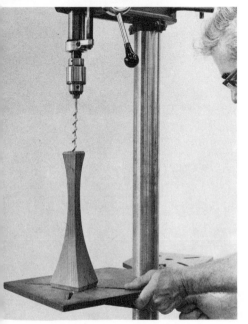

A simple device for holding work which is to be bored at an angle. Note that the waste end at the bottom of this turning, with its flat portion, was left on in anticipation of this drilling operation.

Another method of boring a deep hole is possible if an extra long drill bit is available: Lower the table sufficiently and bore as deeply as possible into the work. Then raise the table and make a second boring, and so on, until the hole is complete.

285

A curved workpiece is supported at the correct angle between a pair of 2 × 4's to solve the problem of boring holes for spindles at a uniform angle.

The drill table is adjusted to the vertical position for end boring a long piece of work. This method is safer and more accurate than resting the bottom of the work on a lowered table or on the floor.

This is a good method of boring dowel holes for a miter joint. The table is set at the vertical position and a wood guide is clamped to the table at 45 degrees.

Pocket holes (left) provide a simple method of attaching rails to table tops or shelves to side members with screws.

POCKET HOLE

A block of wood (right) with a 15 degree bevel angle is used to support the work. Both the guard and the work must be firmly clamped. The first cut makes the pocket and the initial hole is the guide. The guide can remain in place and only the work shifted for subsequent pocket drilling. The smaller body holes for screws should be drilled before the guide is removed.

One method of drilling holes in round stock (left). The table is set at 45 degrees and the guide block clamped in a position that will center the point of the drill in the corner. If a through hole is to be made, a scrap board should be used below.

Another method for drilling into round stock is with the use of a V block. The point of the bit must line up with the center of the V.

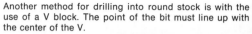

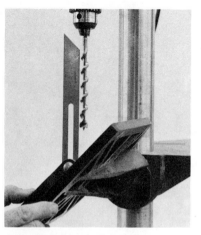

Drill tables have built-in stops for horizontal, vertical, and 45 degree settings. For other angle settings the T bevel is used against a long drill bit for accuracy. A smaller bit can be substituted after the table is adjusted.

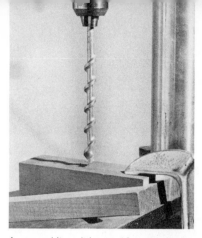

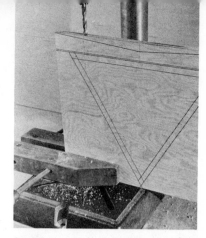

A work piece is butted up to a scrap block and both clamped firmly in order to drill a partial hole in the edge of stock. The arc can be varied by shifting centerline.

An auger bit can't be used for angle boring because the spurs contact the wood before the point does. The problem is solved by clamping a wedge over the work to provide a flat surface for the bit to enter.

Sometimes it is advantageous to drill the holes in advance of the cutting operation. Note how the clamp is used to hold the work in position.

Cutting large holes (left) with a hole saw usually requires a second cut from the other side. This type of rotary cutter is smooth operating, generally doesn't require clamping of the work.

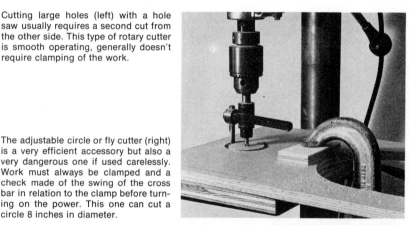

The adjustable circle or fly cutter (right) is a very efficient accessory but also a very dangerous one if used carelessly. Work must always be clamped and a check made of the swing of the cross bar in relation to the clamp before turning on the power. This one can cut a circle 8 inches in diameter.

The fly cutter's business end (left) is practically invisible while it is turning; keep hands well away and make sure the tool has come to a full stop before handling it.

Plugs cut from the same stock (right) as the work are used to conceal dowels and screw heads in finer constructions. They can be pried out by splitting with a small screwdriver or they may be cut out as shown at right, below.

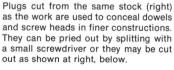

How plugs may be retrieved by cutting. (Stanley Tools)

SAW HERE →

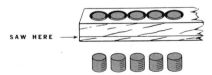

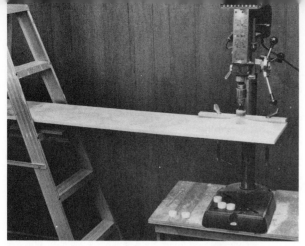

A step ladder makes a handy support for drilling oversize work. Blocks are used on the step to obtain level.

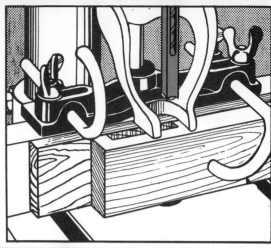

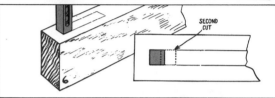

A mortising attachment for a drill press uses a hollow square chisel with a matching drill bit (upper left). The bit cuts a round hole while the chisel cleans out the corners. A series of overlapping holes are bored in the stock to form the mortise. (*Rockwell*)

Various applications of mortising in making joints.

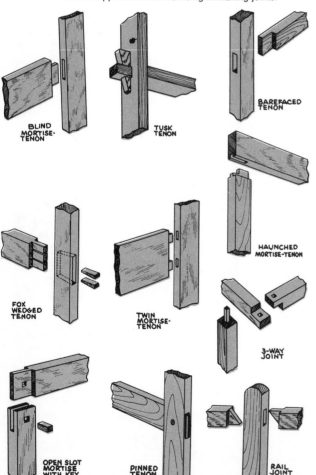

BLIND MORTISE-TENON

TUSK TENON

BAREFACED TENON

HAUNCHED MORTISE-TENON

FOX WEDGED TENON

TWIN MORTISE-TENON

3-WAY JOINT

OPEN SLOT MORTISE WITH KEY

PINNED TENON

RAIL JOINT

Precision pattern sanding (right) can be done on the drill press by attaching to the table a smooth disk of hardboard or wood of the same diameter as the sanding drum, perfectly centered.

The work to be sanded is cut slightly oversize (below) and tacked to a smoothly sanded pattern of the exact size and shape required. The pattern rides against the disk thus controlling the sanding cut on the work. This procedure is of value when a number of similar pieces are to be made.

A drum depressed into a hole cut into a wood table allows the full edge of the work to come into contact with the sander for free hand contour sanding. (*Sears Roebuck*)

Custom made sanding cylinder is easily made for odd size sanding chores: A piece of abrasive paper is rubber cemented around a dowel inserted in the chuck.

Using the drill press to do a tricky job—cutting a series of concave depressions (beginning at left). Holes are drilled to allow clearance for the pilot tip of a quarter-round router bit. The cuts are made to the required depth.

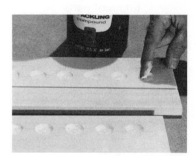

The pilot holes are filled with spackle (right).

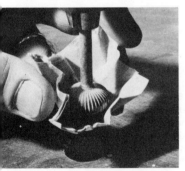

A rotary rasp (left) with approximately the correct shape is used as a sanding fixture. A piece of abrasive paper is "conditioned" by continued folding and wrinkling to remove some of its stiffness. It is then wrapped around the rasp and taped around the neck.

A quick pass (right) at high speed smoothens the depressions as no other method could.

The drill press can be used as a router. Highest possible spindle speed should be used. (*Sears Roebuck*)

Inasmuch as the drill press spindle is not designed to take abusive side pressures, it is wise to remove as much waste material as possible before routing. A honeycomb of shallow holes was first drilled into this dense material to make the job of routing a lot easier.

24 Sanding

Sanding is primarily a smoothing operation performed after the wood has been cut and shaped with various tools. Through the use of abrasive materials of varying degrees of grit size, the fibers of the wood are worn away to a point where the surface becomes microscopically even and smooth to the touch and in appearance. But sanding is not limited only to the function of smoothing wood. Efficient power sanding equipment is used extensively for shaping wood, for rapid stock removal, and for making fine touch-up cuts for the final fitting of parts.

Coated Abrasives

The designations "sanding" and "sandpaper", although technically incorrect, are commonly used when referring to the operation and to the material. The term "coated abrasive" is more properly descriptive of the material used for smoothing or shaping wood, but obviously it would be a bit awkward to say, "coated abrasiving a piece of wood." So, sanding wins out.

There are four principal kinds of abrasive minerals that are applied to a paper or cloth backing with various adhesives to form a coated abrasive: flint, garnet, aluminum oxide, and silicon carbide. Flint (another misnomer) is actually quartz, the mineral used on the common sandpaper sold in hardware stores. It has little value for use in woodworking because it lacks toughness. Although it costs less than the other abrasives, it is actually more expensive to use because it wears out very rapidly. Garnet, a reddish-brown mineral much harder than flint, is a very good abrasive and is widely used in woodworking.

Aluminum oxide, a man-made abrasive of brownish color is extremely hard. It cuts faster and wears longer than garnet. Silicon carbide, also man-made, is identified by its distinctive blue-black color. It is the hardest, sharpest and fastest-cutting of all the abrasives. It is almost as hard as diamond. When purchasing coated abrasives, the name of the mineral is used as the reference: garnet paper, aluminum oxide paper, and so forth.

Abrasive grains are applied to the backing in what is described as **closed** or **open** coat formation. The closed coat abrasive has grains that are closely packed together covering the entire surface of the paper (or cloth). This results in a fast-cutting and durable sheet but with the disadvantage of clogging readily when used on relatively soft wood. Open coating leaves some space between the particles so that only about 70 percent of the surface is covered. This produces a sheet material that is not quite as fast-cutting as the closed coat, but it is less prone to clogging up. In general, open coat is suggested for use with soft or resinous wood and closed coat for general sanding.

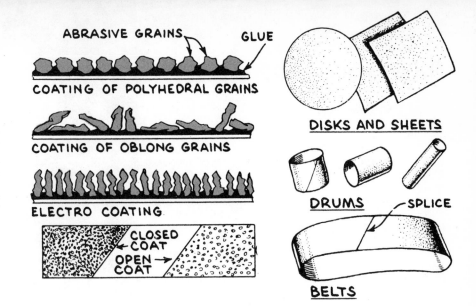

ABRASIVE GRAINS   GLUE

COATING OF POLYHEDRAL GRAINS

COATING OF OBLONG GRAINS

ELECTRO COATING

CLOSED ←COAT

OPEN → COAT

DISKS AND SHEETS

DRUMS

SPLICE

BELTS

Abrasive grains are graded by passing through screens and are then made into various abrasive products through special coating processes. Polyhedral grain shape is ideal for gravity type coating methods where grains are dropped onto glued surface. This method is not satisfactory with oblong grains because they would fall over into the glue. Special electrocoating method stands oblong grains on end for a superior modern abrasive. *(Rockwell)*

rading

COMPARATIVE GRADING

SIMPLIFIED GRADES	GRIT NUMBER	SYMBOL NUMBER
VERY COARSE	12	4½
	16	4
	20	3½
	24	3
	30	2½
COARSE	36	2
	40	1½
	50	1
MEDIUM	60	½
	80	1/0
	100	2/0
FINE	120	3/0
	150	4/0
	180	5/0
EXTRA FINE	220	6/0
	240	7/0
	280	8/0
	320	9/0
	360	—
	400	10/0
	500	—
	600	—

Abrasives are graded according to the size of the abrasive grains. Two systems of grading are generally used. An older method uses grit symbols from 4½ (coarsest) to 10/0 (finest). The newer system grades the abrasives by mesh numbers which refer to the openings per inch in a screen through which the grains can pass. Grit numbers in this system range from 12 (coarsest) to 600 (finest). Listings of abrasive grades usually include both numbering designations. Manufacturers use either one of the systems.

The grade of abrasive you select will depend on the work to be done. An open coat coarse aluminum oxide paper will work well for rough stock removal on soft pine. For the same treatment on hardwood, a closed coat paper of a slightly coarser grit would be a good choice. For paint removal an open coat coarse grit is the best choice. For a finish-ready sanding on a piece of hardwood construction with smooth planed surfaces a 180 grit paper may be sufficient. If this same construction has considerable tool marks on the surface, three successive sandings with 80, 120 and 180 grit paper may be required. The 80 grit would certainly remove the tool marks but in doing so, it will have left its own deep scratches. The moderately fine 120 grit paper would leave proportionately smaller scratches. And so on down the line with each successively finer grit. In general, a quicker job will be accomplished if no more than two grade sizes are skipped between changes.

Hand Sanding

Despite the availability of the various power sanders, hand sanding is frequently required in the application of coated abrasives. Tight spots, odd shaped pieces, and molded edges sometimes can be sanded in no other way than by hand. Sanding between finishing coats is always done by hand. Then, too, there are certain sanding operations that require the "feel" of the hands on the abrasive sheet to achieve the wanted result.

The important consideration in sanding irregular surfaces is in getting the paper to reach every part of the surface as evenly as possible so that no one part is over- or under-sanded. This is best done by finding some means of supporting the paper in such a way that it takes a shape that matches the part to be sanded. There are many ways that this can be accomplished. A few ideas that work quite well are shown in the accompanying photos.

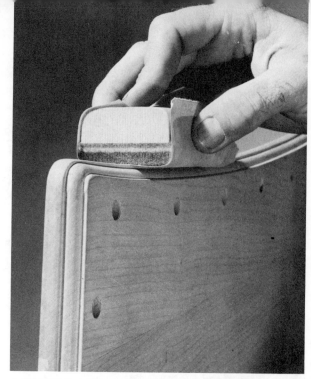

A piece of felt glued to a block is used as a sanding pad to produce a "softened" molded edge.

A scrap of indoor-outdoor type carpeting has just the right amount of "body" for inside curve sanding. When held this way with a slight downward pressure, the pad flexes to form the proper matching contour.

A hole of suitable diameter is bored in a block of wood which is then cut to form a quarter-section for use as a form fitting sanding block for quarter-round surfaces. Many molding shapes have partial rounds which can be handled this way.

Nylon mesh coated with abrasive particles is excellent for contour sanding. This remarkable new type abrasive can be washed and re-used over and over.

Odd shaped sanding blocks are easily made of wood. Rubber cement is coated to both surfaces to make a quick bond, and allows easy replacement of sandpaper.

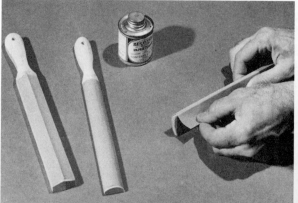

Power Sanding

The finishing sander is used primarily for the final sanding of components or assembled work. It is sometimes the only sander needed for a project or it may be used in conjunction with any of the other types of sanders. It is quite easy to use: simply bring it to the surface and move it slowly back and forth in the direction of the grain.

The portable belt sander is designed for sanding flat surfaces, but it is also very useful for fast stock removal and general shaping of large curved surfaces. This is strictly a two-handed tool. Grasp it firmly and hold it away from the work until the motor has been turned on, then gently lower it, allowing the rear of the machine to contact the work first. Move the sander slowly back and forth, shifting it sideways about half the belt width after each stroke. Do not press down on the sander because its own weight supplies the necessary cutting pressure. Although sanding with the grain is the general rule, the belt sander is frequently used cross-grain to level an uneven surface.

The stationary disk sander is not especially recommended for surface sanding, but it is excellent for smoothing end grain, dressing up miter cuts, and general sanding of outside curves on the edges of stock. Irregular-shaped pieces are usually guided freehand with very good results. The miter gage and various other guides are used for precision work.

The drum sander is particularly useful for sanding inside curves and for freehand shaping. A small drum inserted in the chuck of a portable electric drill is used mainly for smoothing a surface. For precision sanding of curved parts the drum is used on the drill press or other suitable stationary machine, such as the radial arm saw or the lathe. The large drum sander, usually mounted on the other end of a stationary disk sander spindle, can be used for freehand shaping of small or large work. A drum sander with an auxiliary fence attached can be used for precision sanding.

The stationary belt sander is an excellent machine for all kinds of shaping and smoothing operations. With various jigs attached it can do precision work of top quality.

The finishing sander is rolled over an edge to produce a softly rounded edge. A medium fine paper is sufficiently abrasive for this kind of cutting. This should be followed by a fine, 220 grit paper for a glass-like surface.

The individual parts of any project should be thoroughly finish-sanded before assembly. This is particularly important for the surfaces which would be hard to reach after assembly.

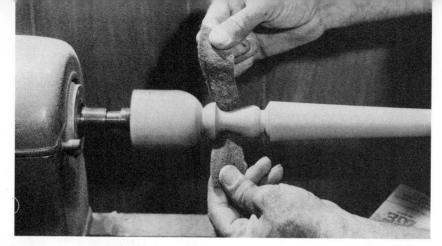

The nylon pad type abrasive cut into strips is very effective for lathe work smoothing. It won't burn the wood as paper abrasives sometimes do.

The brush-backed sanding wheel (left) has strips of abrasive extending from the hollow core to just a bit past the ends of the brushes. In operation the brushes press on the strips to follow wood contours.

The brush-backed wheel is quite safe to use even for small work like this (right).

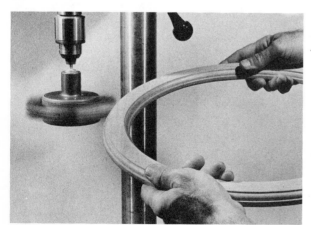

Only a very light touch should be used when sanding shapes with relatively sharp corners to avoid eroding them.

Using the sander-grinder to handle a large piece of work. Note how the far end is supported on the workbench.

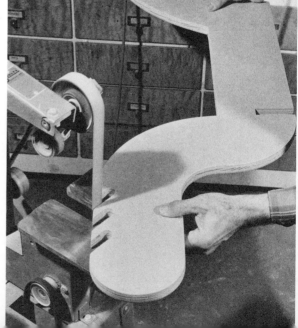

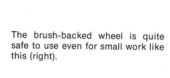

An auxiliary wood table centered over the axis of the drum is used to sand the curve for a furniture leg which is to be fitted to a round column. The piece is moved back and forth on the table.

Wood fence set up to straddle the drum helps to keep the work in proper attitude for perfect right angle sanding.

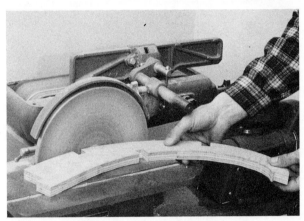

Work is fed only to the "down" side of a disk sander. Most work of this nature can be handled free hand with exceptionally good results.

Accurate bevels are sanded with the aid of the miter gage. Work should be fed with light pressure to avoid burn marks. Sliding work along disk prevents overheating.

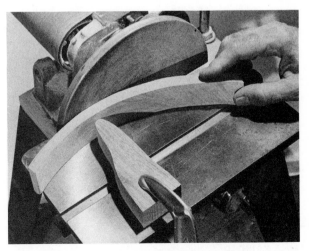

Sanding to uniform width is accomplished by clamping a block with a rounded nose to the table. Band sawed piece with its inside smoothened rides against the nose.

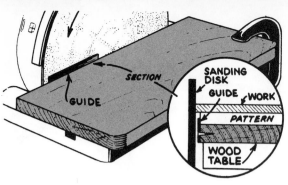

Pattern jig for Disk Sander.

Sanding with a pattern insures perfect work every time. A wood table, to one side of which is screw-fastened a thin rigid strip of metal, is clamped over the regular sanding table. The guiding edge of the strip should be about 1/8" from the surface of the disk and the pattern should be made 1/8" undersize to correspond.

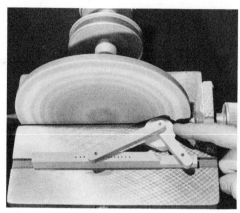

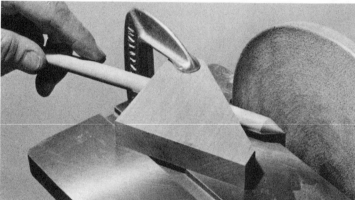

Pivoting arms of this little jig help to sand perfect miniature disks. Shifting the left arm to a new nail position will alter the size of the disk.

Dowels can be accurately pointed with a jig. A hole of the same diameter as the dowel stock is drilled in a scrap of wood which is clamped to the table at the required angle. The dowel is pushed through the hole until contact is made with the disk, after which it is rotated.

While the disk sander is not particularly suited to sand long straight edges, good work can be done with this set-up (right). A wood fence with a hold down is clamped to the table at a slight angle to prevent the work from touching the disk at the "up" side.

Jig for sanding long, straight edges.

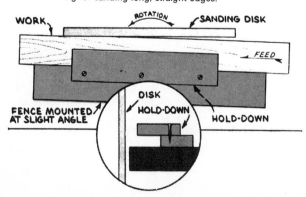

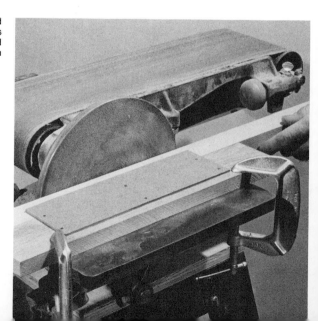

A handy hint for the disk sander: Cut out the center of a sandpaper disk and replace it with a disk of a different grit. This gives you grit options and saves changing disks for different grits.

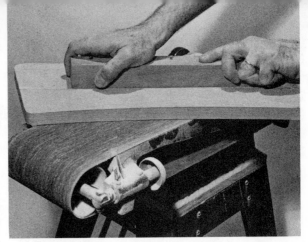

Attach a gripping block to the back of the work to permit safe and efficient sanding of a surface. If work is wider than the belt, use a diagonal feed like this.

Inside corners can be sanded if the belt is tracked so that it runs exactly flush with the edge of the table.

A compound miter is cut by tilting the table and setting the miter gage to the required angle. The work is pushed in along the miter gage.

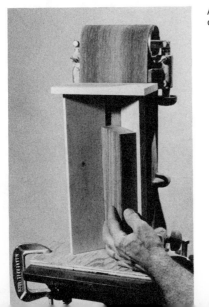

A V shaped jig makes quick work of cutting clean accurate chamfers on short pieces and end grain.

Chamfering jig is made by forming a V groove with two boards fitted at right angles with a suitable space between them to allow the corner of the work to project.

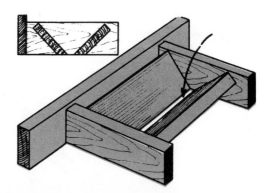

297

A board clamped to the table with a nail driven through the center of the work is a necessity for sanding various kinds of circular pieces accurately.

A pivot arm jig is useful for accurate sanding of segments. A series of holes in the arm of the Y allows setting the pivot at different distances to vary the size of the arc.

The end drum can be used to sand inside curves. The sander can be either vertical, horizontal or set at an angle depending on what is the most convenient position.

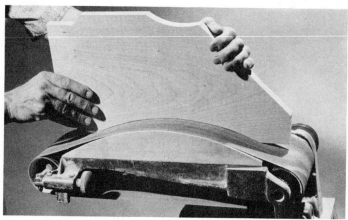

A curved form screwed to the regular table is used to sand irregular curves. There is usually enough adjustment play to allow a shallow form like this to fit.

These are typical belt sander forms.

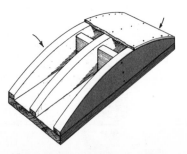

A slightly loose belt adjustment permits free hand curve sanding against the bottom of the sander.

298

Tungsten carbide sanding accessories are great for the economy-minded craftsman. Tough abrasive chips embedded in metal cut rapidly and last indefinitely. They're made for hand and power tools as well.

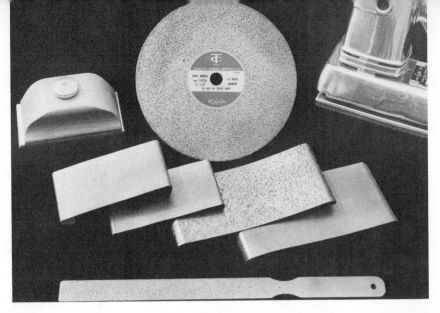

A special hand sanding block is used. It has a thumbscrew adjustment for locking the pad firmly in place. Pads are available in fine, medium and course grits.

If pad clogs up with wood dust it is easily cleaned with a wire brush. This one is on a portable sander.

The disk type sander is remarkably safe when used as a sawing tool. Illustration shows that moving disk causes no kickback.

Grits of abrasive are embedded in the edge of the disk thus permitting it to be used for cutting coves.

25 Fastening

There are three common methods of fastening or assembling wood: with nails, with screws, and with glue. Nailing is the simplest way to join wood and the hammer is among one of the easiest of all tools to use if handled properly.

Hammers

The standard curved claw hammer is the one most frequently used for all–around work. Hammer size is designated by the weight of its head which varies from 7 to 20 ounces. Weight selection depends on the intended use; average shop work is usually handled best with a 16-ounce hammer. For heavy framing or construction work with large nails a 20-ounce head would serve better.

An important feature of a nailing hammer is the shape of its face; it may be flat or bell faced. The striking surface of the bell face hammer is slightly convex. This permits driving the nail flush to the surface without leaving hammer marks on the wood. This is a desirable feature, but this type hammer must be handled a bit more carefully than the flat faced one because the rounded face can more easily slip off the nail head or bend it. The flat face hammer is generally used for rougher types of construction where a hammer head dent doesn't much matter.

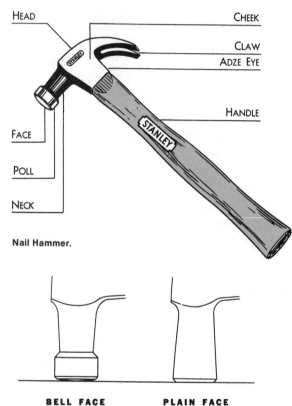

Nail Hammer.

HEAD · CHEEK · CLAW · ADZE EYE · HANDLE · FACE · POLL · NECK

BELL FACE **PLAIN FACE**

A bell face hammer will drive a nail flush with the surface of the work with less chance of marring it.

The hammer head should be tightly fitted to the handle. Never use a hammer with a loose head.

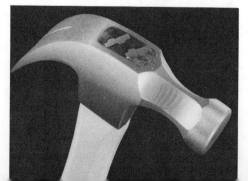

When it becomes necessary to replace the handle, secure it properly with a wooden wedge and two metal ones. (*Stanley Tools*)

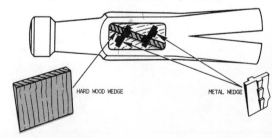

HARD WOOD WEDGE · METAL WEDGE

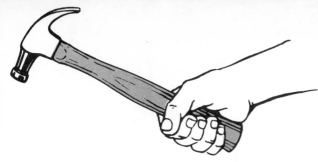

Grasp the hammer firmly near the end of the handle for most kinds of work.

For controlled, light blows, grasp the handle of the hammer closer to the head.

ailing

Practice swinging a hammer squarely on the nail head using a scrap board and a handful of nails. Hold the hammer near the end of the handle and use a wrist movement with light taps to start the nail. Then take full swings using the wrist and arm to put power into the stroke. If a nail begins to bend slightly, you'll discover that you can steer it back to center by slightly changing the striking angle. But if a nail bends more than 7 or 8 degrees, remove it and start with a new one. Ease up on the power as the nail head nears the surface.

Nails can usually be driven into soft wood without difficulty, but hardwood frequently requires a drilled pilot hole. If a pilot hole is used, it should be slightly smaller than the diameter of the nail and about $2/3$ of its length.

When nailing near the end of a board, try blunting the point with a hammer blow to prevent splitting. This allows the nail to shear the wood fibers instead of wedging them apart, thus reducing the possibility of splitting. Driving nails in the same grain line causes splitting when the nails are spaced too closely. This should be avoided, but if it can't be, then drilling pilot holes will solve the problem.

Nails should be three times longer than the thickness of the wood they are to hold. When nailing a T joint where access is not possible through the cross member, toe-nailing should be utilized. Drive the nails at an angle from both sides of the center piece. The use of a temporary stop, tack nailed against the center member, will keep it from sliding. Butted joints can be strengthened considerably by driving the nails in at a slight angle to each other.

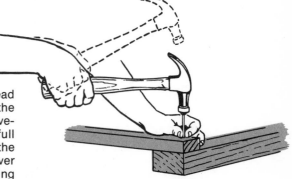

Rest the hammer face on the head of the nail to set the aim. Then give the nail one or several light taps to start it.

Swing the hammer so the head meets the nail head squarely to avoid bending the nail.

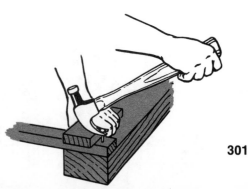

When removing nails slip a piece of wood under the head to protect the surface and to keep the pull more in line with the nail. (*Stanley Tools*)

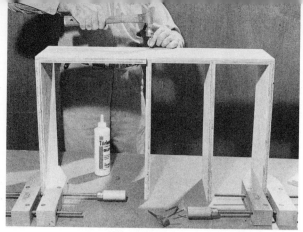

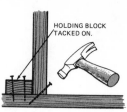

HOLDING BLOCK TACKED ON.

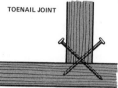

TOENAIL JOINT

Clamps are most helpful for holding the parts of an assembly in place because they permit the use of both hands for starting nail joints.

Toenailing is used when nails cannot be driven from the outside surface. Nails are driven at opposing angles, positioned to be offset.

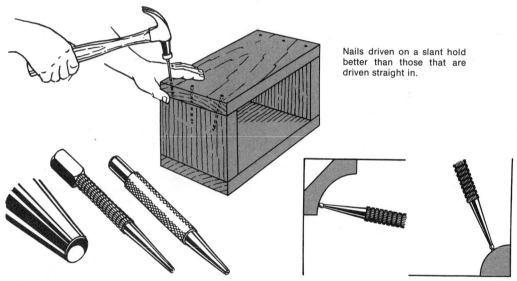

Nails driven on a slant hold better than those that are driven straight in.

Nail sets are used to drive nail heads below the surface. They are made with round or square heads and with several sizes of tips.

Heads are left projecting slightly on finished work to avoid hammer marks. The nails are then set below the surface with a nail set.

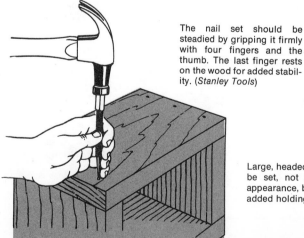

The nail set should be steadied by gripping it firmly with four fingers and the thumb. The last finger rests on the wood for added stability. (*Stanley Tools*)

Large, headed nails may also be set, not necessarily for appearance, but to give them added holding power.

ails

The variety of nails that are available is large, but the types used for general construction and woodwork are the common and finishing nails. The difference between the two is in the head size and shape. The common nail has a broad flat head that is usually driven flush with the surface of the wood. The finishing nail has a much smaller head by comparison and is usually driven below the surface so that it may be concealed with some form of wood filler. The common nail with its wider head has greater holding power than the finishing nail.

Nail length is designated by two systems: inches and "penny", an antiquated term probably related to the cost by weight. The term is still used, abbreviated with a small letter d, but it indicates length only. Nails range in size from 2d (1″) to 60d (6″). Common nails have a slightly heavier cross section than finishing nails of equal length. Brads are similar to finishing nails in appearance but are much thinner. They are specified by length in inches and a wire gauge number from 11 to 20. The higher gauge number indicates a smaller diameter. Finishing nails range from 2d to 20d; 1″ to 4″.

PENNY SIZE	LENGTH INCHES	
2 d	1	
3 d	1 - 1/4	
4 d	1 - 1/2	
5 d	1 - 3/4	
6 d	2	
7 d	2 - 1/4	
8 d	2 - 1/2	
9 d	2 - 3/4	
10 d	3	
12 d	3 - 1/4	
16 d	3 - 1/2	
20 d	4	
30 d	4 - 1/2	
40 d	5	
50 d	5 - 1/2	
60 d	6	

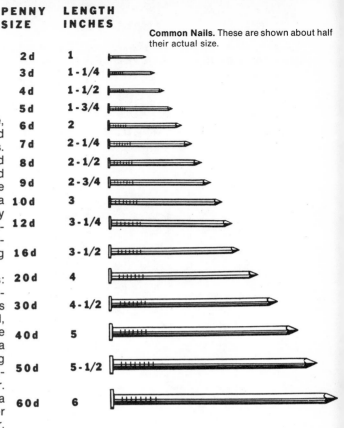

Common Nails. These are shown about half their actual size.

Finishing nails are available from 2d (1″) to 20d (4″). They are slightly smaller in diameter than common nails that are of equal length.

LARGE FLAT HEAD

LARGE FLAT HEAD CHECKERED

FLAT HEAD COUNTERSUNK

DUPLEX HEAD

OVAL HEAD

OVAL HEAD COUNTERSUNK

There are many variations in sizes and shapes of heads.

BLUNT POINT

LONG DIAMOND POINT

NEEDLE POINT

DUCK BILL POINT

CHISEL POINT

Nail points are also varied to meet special needs.

BARBED NAILS

NAILS WITH RINGS

RESIN COATED NAILS

These nails are designed to hold better than ordinary smooth sided nails. (*Stanley Tools*)

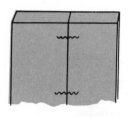

PLAIN EDGE PARALLEL

PLAIN EDGE DIVERGENT

SAW EDGE PARALLEL

SAW EDGE DIVERGENT

Corrugated fasteners are made in four types. They're used for making light duty joints. (*Stanley Tools*)

Corrugated fasteners can sometimes be used on large frames which are to be surfaced with paneling. They hold the parts together prior to reinforcing.

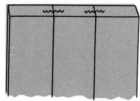

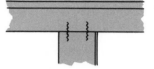

Corrugated fasteners can be used for rough joining and to reinforce glue joints.

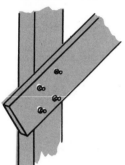

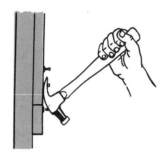

DUPLEX HEAD NAIL

These nails are used for temporary enclosures, scaffolds and concrete forms. They are driven up to the lower head. The upper head projects for easy removal. (*Stanley Tools*)

Clamp nails are used to force glue joints together. The flat flanged edge is shaped to draw the parts together when the nail is driven into a thin kerf cut into the joint. On some work they can be used without glue.

A thin saw kerf is all that's needed to join two pieces with a clamp nail. For this application a second nail is driven into the other end. For picture frames and other small work only one nail is required per joint.

Rust proof nails are available and should be used on outdoor construction. Rust stains here betray a builder's desire to save a few dollars on the cost of nails. Non-rusting aluminum or galvanized nails would have cost only little more.

crews

Wood screws are threaded fasteners designed to join wood to wood. They have far greater holding power than nails and several other advantages: They can be readily turned to draw parts tightly together, they are more attractive than nails, and they can easily be withdrawn to disassemble parts. They are, however, more expensive than nails and require more time to install, so screws are usually used for jobs of better quality.

Wood screws are threaded for two-thirds of the length and have either slotted heads which are driven with a regular flat-bladed screwdriver or cross-slotted heads that require a Phillips-head screwdriver. Common screws have flat, round, or oval heads and are available in steel, brass, copper, aluminum, or stainless steel. Flat head screws are used for application where the head must be flush to the surface or below it. Round heads project completely above the surface, while oval heads project slightly. Oval head screws, the most decorative, are usually used to install hinges and other exposed hardware.

SCREW SIZES

Screw sizes are indicated by length and diameter (gauge). The length of any screw is shown in the number of inches or fractions of an inch. Lengths range from 1/4″ to 6″. The diameter is expressed in gauge numbers from 0 (about 1/16″) through 24 (approximately 3/8″). The most commonly available sizes are numbers 2 through 18. Note that with screws the higher gauge number indicates a greater diameter, while nail wire gauge sizes run the other way: higher numbers for smaller diameters.

BODY DIAMETER IN SCREW GAUGE NUMBER →

Screw sizes are measured across the diameter of the shank (unthreaded portion) and the length, from the widest part of the head to the point. (*Stanley Tools*)

LENGTH

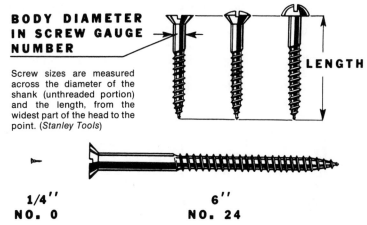

1/4″ NO. 0

6″ NO. 24

There are many sizes of screws from 1/4″ No. 0 to 6″ No. 24 (shown half size). Screw lengths increase as follows: Screws from 1/4″ to 1″ increase by 1/8″; 1″ to 3″ increase by 1/4″; 3″ to 6″ increase by 1/2″.

SCREW SIZE LENGTHS MADE IN EACH GAUGE

Screw Gauge No.	Length Range Inches	Screw Gauge No.	Length Range Inches
0	1/4 — 3/8	9	1/2 — 3
1	1/4 — 1/2	10	1/2 — 3 1/2
2	1/4 — 3/4	11	5/8 — 3 1/2
3	1/4 — 1	12	5/8 — 4
4	1/4 — 1 1/2	14	3/4 — 5
5	3/8 — 1 1/2	16	1 — 5
6	3/8 — 2 1/2	18	1 1/4 — 5
7	3/8 — 2 1/2	20	1 1/2 — 5
8	3/8 — 3	24	3 — 6

DETERMINE SCREW SHANK SIZES BY COMPARISON BELOW

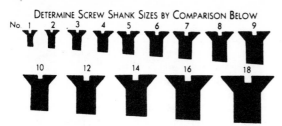

Outlines show comparative screw gauge sizes.

The label on a box of screws gives all the necessary information:

Kind of screw:	Wood Screw
Shape of head:	Flat Head
Finish:	Bright
Material:	Steel
Length in inches:	1¼"
Diameter in screw gage:	No. 6
Quantity:	1 Gross

INSTALLING SCREWS

For maximum holding power the entire length of the threaded part of the screw should penetrate the base piece of wood whenever possible. In general, screws installed in end grain should be slightly longer because end grain doesn't hold screws too well.

Very small screws can sometimes be installed in soft wood without need of pre-drilled holes. A starting hole made with the point of an awl may be sufficient. Ordinarily, however, two different size holes must be drilled into the wood to install a screw. One hole equal to the shank diameter of the screw is drilled into the upper or outside member. This hole should allow the screw to slip through freely.

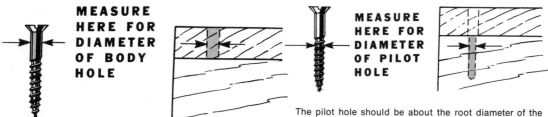

MEASURE HERE FOR DIAMETER OF BODY HOLE

The smooth part of the screw should pass easily through the body hole so the head can draw both pieces of wood tightly together.

MEASURE HERE FOR DIAMETER OF PILOT HOLE

The pilot hole should be about the root diameter of the screw. In soft wood, about 30 percent smaller; in hardwood, about 10 percent smaller. When using softer brass screws in very hard wood the pilot hole should be slightly **larger** than the root diameter.

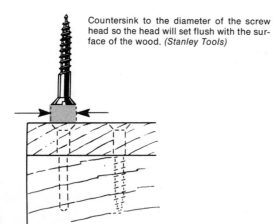

Countersink to the diameter of the screw head so the head will set flush with the surface of the wood. (Stanley Tools)

The pilot hole is drilled next. This should be a little smaller in diameter than the root, or smallest diameter of the screw (the flat section between the threads). For hardwoods the pilot hole diameter should be about 10 percent less than the root and it should be drilled as deep as the screw will go. For softwoods the pilot diameter should be approximately 30 percent less than the root and it should be drilled to a depth of about one-half the length of the screw.

Flat head and oval head screws require a third hole, the countersink. This allows the screw to recess flush to the wood at the rim, the widest part. This is a beveled hole drilled to a diameter equal to that of the screw head.

In order to insure accurate alignment of the holes, the larger shank hole is drilled first, then the pilot hole. The pointed bottom of the larger hole forms a self-centering seat for the smaller drill. The wider, beveled countersink drill will readily center itself in the shank hole. This is drilled last.

A fourth hole is sometimes necessary to conceal a flat head screw with an inserted wood plug or filler material. This is the counterbore hole. It is drilled in a diameter slightly larger than that of the screw head and to a depth sufficient to recess the screw the desired amount. The counterbore hole is always drilled before the shank hole.

Much time and effort can be saved in drilling screw holes by using the combination drill bits that will form the pilot, shank, countersink or counterbore holes in one operation. They have a built-in depth stop so that the correct depth of hole is always assured. Screw-mate, as one popular brand is called, is available in many sizes. The gauge size and length is stamped on each bit's rim.

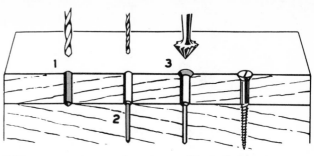

Drilling sequence for a countersunk screw. (*Stanley Tools*)

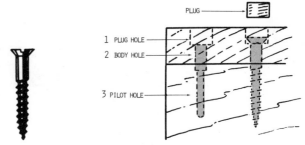

When the screw head is to be covered with a plug, bore the plug hole first then the body and pilot holes.

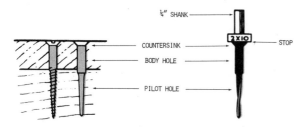

Combination wood drills and countersinks are made in 24 sizes to match the most commonly used flathead screws. They are used in power drills.

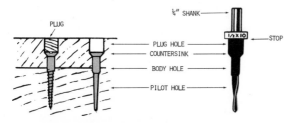

This Screw-mate is used to drill holes to allow for body of screw and plug. (*Stanley Tools*)

DRILL SIZES FOR WOOD SCREW HOLES

Screw Gauge Size	Shank Hole	Softwood Pilot Hole	Hardwood Pilot Hole	Counterbores In $^1/_{16}$ ths For Plugs
0	$^1/_{16}$	—	$^1/_{32}$	—
1	$^5/_{64}$	$^1/_{32}$	$^1/_{32}$	—
2	$^3/_{32}$	$^1/_{32}$	$^3/_{64}$	3
3	$^7/_{64}$	$^3/_{64}$	$^1/_{16}$	4
4	$^7/_{64}$	$^3/_{64}$	$^1/_{16}$	4
5	$^1/_8$	$^1/_{16}$	$^5/_{64}$	4
6	$^9/_{64}$	$^1/_{16}$	$^5/_{64}$	5
7	$^5/_{32}$	$^1/_{16}$	$^3/_{32}$	5
8	$^{11}/_{64}$	$^5/_{64}$	$^3/_{32}$	6
9	$^3/_{16}$	$^5/_{64}$	$^7/_{64}$	6
10	$^3/_{16}$	$^3/_{32}$	$^7/_{64}$	6
11	$^{13}/_{64}$	$^3/_{32}$	$^1/_8$	7
12	$^7/_{32}$	$^7/_{64}$	$^1/_8$	7
14	$^1/_4$	$^7/_{64}$	$^9/_{64}$	8
16	$^7/_{64}$	$^9/_{64}$	$^5/_{32}$	9
18	$^{19}/_{64}$	$^9/_{64}$	$^3/_{16}$	10
20	$^{21}/_{64}$	$^{11}/_{64}$	$^{13}/_{64}$	11
24	$^3/_8$	$^3/_{16}$	$^7/_{32}$	12

Screwdrivers

Driving a screw into wood is a simple operation provided the proper screwdriver is used. The important requirement is that the screwdriver be matched to fit the shape, width, and length of the slot of the screw.

There are a number of screwdriver styles and sizes. The size of a flat tip screwdriver is specified by the length of the blade, while Phillips screwdriver tips are made to fit specific sizes of Phillips screws. A selection of about a half dozen plain screwdrivers would normally be adequate to fit the varied slotted screw heads.

For cramped quarters a short or stubby screwdriver is used. Several styles of offset screwdrivers are available for other difficult working situations. A parallel tip screwdriver, which has straight sides, is used for driving screws into counterbored holes.

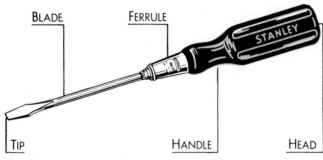

Parts of a standard screwdriver.

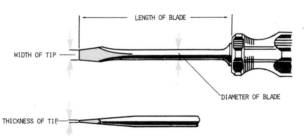

Generally, the width of the tip is the same as the diameter of the round blade. The tip thickness is in proportion to the width to fit properly in the slot of the screw. Size is specified by length of blade.

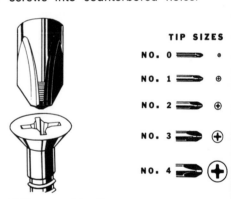

Phillips screwdriver tips are made in five sizes.

TIP SIZES

NO. 0
NO. 1
NO. 2
NO. 3
NO. 4

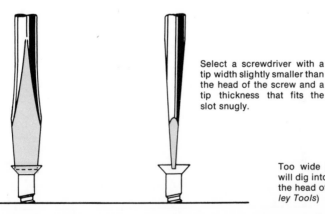

Select a screwdriver with a tip width slightly smaller than the head of the screw and a tip thickness that fits the slot snugly.

Too wide a screwdriver tip will dig into the wood around the head of the screw. (Stanley Tools)

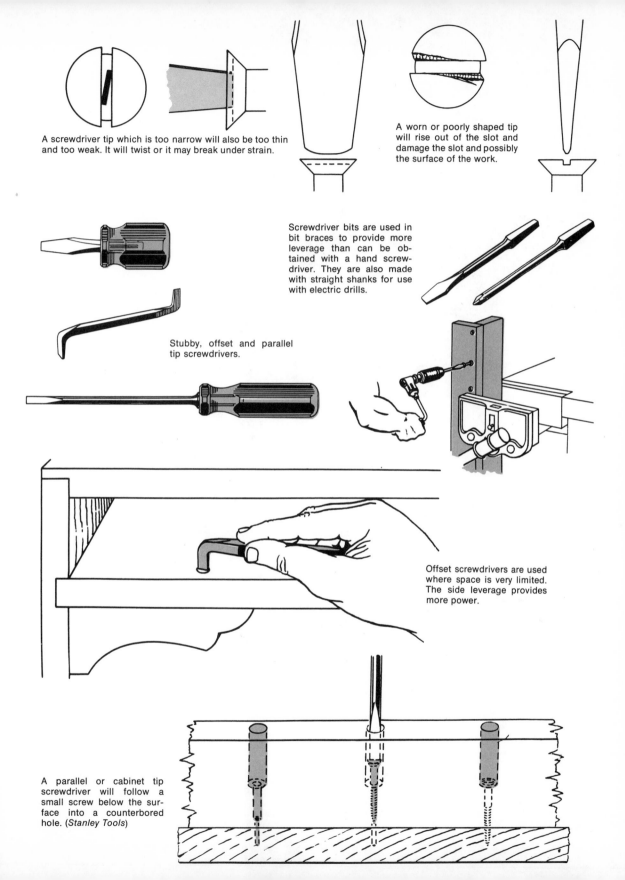

A screwdriver tip which is too narrow will also be too thin and too weak. It will twist or it may break under strain.

A worn or poorly shaped tip will rise out of the slot and damage the slot and possibly the surface of the work.

Screwdriver bits are used in bit braces to provide more leverage than can be obtained with a hand screwdriver. They are also made with straight shanks for use with electric drills.

Stubby, offset and parallel tip screwdrivers.

Offset screwdrivers are used where space is very limited. The side leverage provides more power.

A parallel or cabinet tip screwdriver will follow a small screw below the surface into a counterbored hole. (*Stanley Tools*)

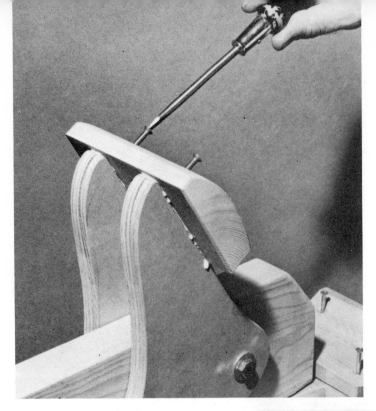

Screws are frequently used as substitutes for clamps on odd-shaped assemblies that are glued together.

Clamps, cardboard spacers and tape are utilized to assure accurate installation of a strip hinge. The cardboard spacers between the boards are used to separate the boards the proper amount for clearance.

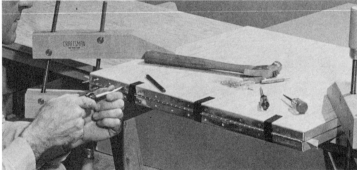

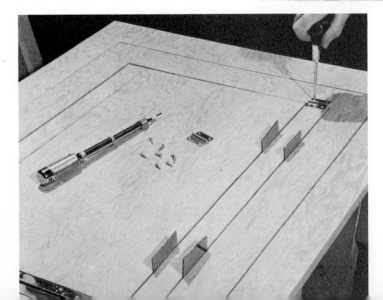

Another trick for installing hinges accurately: Cardboard spacers can be used in numerous hinge installation applications for doors and cabinets.

ther Fasteners

In addition to nails and screws, there are various other fastening devices used for joining wood to itself or to some other material. These include nuts and bolts, anchors, rivets, and other miscellaneous items. Heavy constructions, such as workbenches, outdoor furniture, or framed structures, are often assembled with nuts and bolts or lag screws. Wall cabinets and built-ins are secured to hollow walls with toggle bolts or collapsible Molly bolts. Masonry nails and various masonry anchor screw and bolt devices are used to make attachments to all types of masonry walls and floors.

Heavy cabinets and built-ins are hung or secured to hollow walls with toggle bolts. For a removable installation Molly bolts would be better.

VARIOUS FASTENERS

MOLLY BOLT

CARRIAGE BOLT

TOGGLE BOLT

MACHINE BOLT

MASONRY ANCHOR

STOVE BOLT

LAG SCREW

HANGER BOLT

DOWEL SCREW

A device for holding and driving special masonry nails insures quick and safe penetration into even the toughest concrete. A sliding washer steadies the nail while being driven, then seats against the head for extra holding power. Threaded studs are also available.

NAIL DRIVER

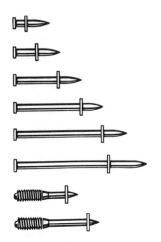

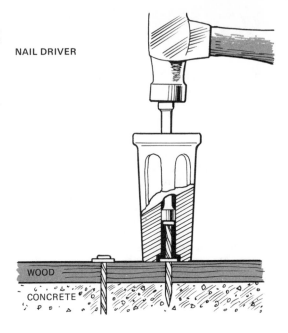

WOOD

CONCRETE

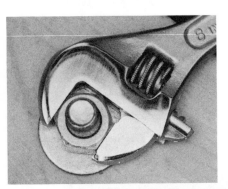

Machine bolts are used to join wood members in heavy constructions or where maximum holding power is required.

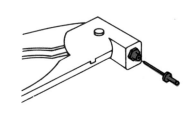

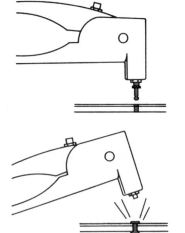

Pop riveters are handy for joining thin wood or hardboard parts. They are especially advantageous for riveting items which have no access from the back. (*U.S.M. Co.*)

Lag screws and glue are used to make good strong joints.

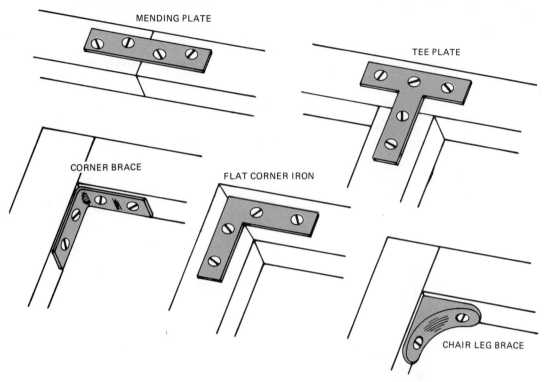

MENDING PLATE

TEE PLATE

CORNER BRACE

FLAT CORNER IRON

CHAIR LEG BRACE

Repair plates of various shapes are used to make or reinforce simple joints with screws.

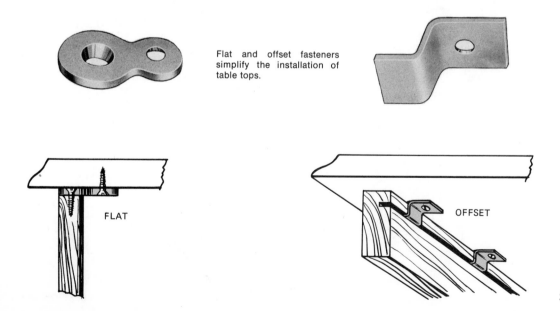

Flat and offset fasteners simplify the installation of table tops.

FLAT

OFFSET

iscellaneous Hardware

There are many kinds and styles of common and special hardware products used in wood-working. Some of them are illustrated here. It is advisable to obtain a particular piece of hardware before beginning a construction or repair in order to be better able to figure out special dimensions or clearance allowances that may be required. Hinges, lid supports, drawer slides, and countless other items frequently influence the basic design of a project. Some specialty hardware fixtures are not always available at local dealers but are obtainable through woodworker's mail order supply houses. Their catalogues should be consulted.

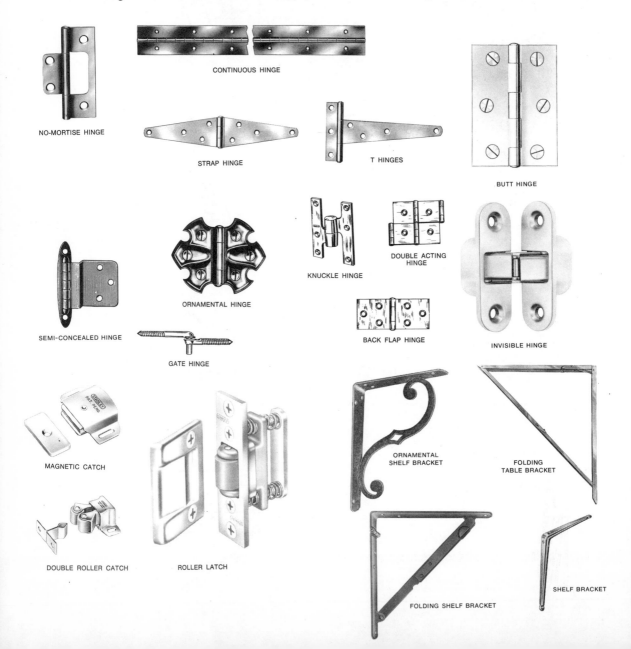

NO-MORTISE HINGE

CONTINUOUS HINGE

STRAP HINGE

T HINGES

BUTT HINGE

ORNAMENTAL HINGE

KNUCKLE HINGE

DOUBLE ACTING HINGE

SEMI-CONCEALED HINGE

GATE HINGE

BACK FLAP HINGE

INVISIBLE HINGE

MAGNETIC CATCH

DOUBLE ROLLER CATCH

ROLLER LATCH

ORNAMENTAL SHELF BRACKET

FOLDING TABLE BRACKET

FOLDING SHELF BRACKET

SHELF BRACKET

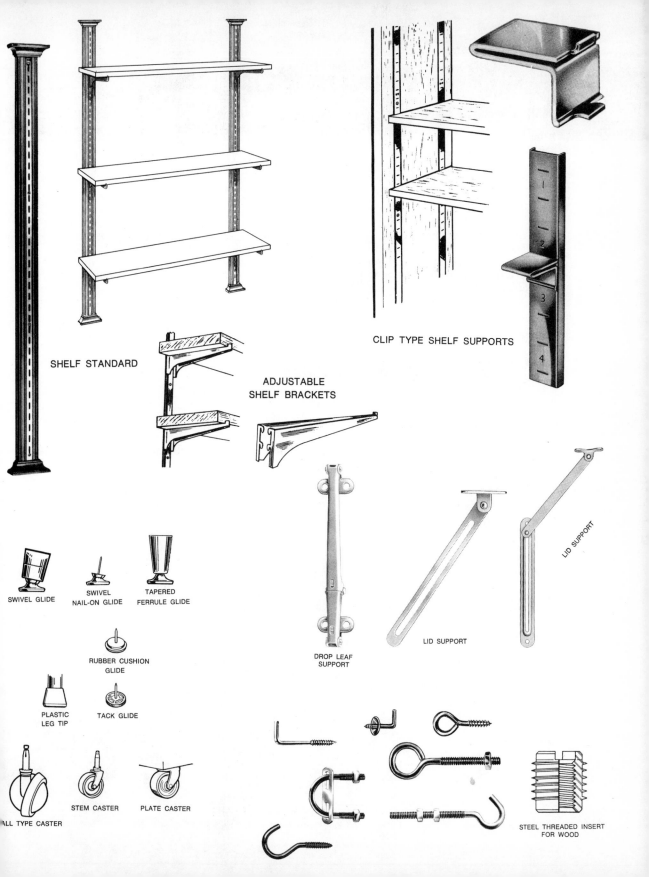

SHELF STANDARD

CLIP TYPE SHELF SUPPORTS

ADJUSTABLE
SHELF BRACKETS

SWIVEL GLIDE

SWIVEL
NAIL-ON GLIDE

TAPERED
FERRULE GLIDE

RUBBER CUSHION
GLIDE

PLASTIC
LEG TIP

TACK GLIDE

DROP LEAF
SUPPORT

LID SUPPORT

LID SUPPORT

BALL TYPE CASTER

STEM CASTER

PLATE CASTER

STEEL THREADED INSERT
FOR WOOD

Many of the fanciful things that can be produced on the lathe may tend to suggest to the uninitiated that wood turning is a very difficult craft. This is not so; lathe work is actually relatively easy. Expert wood turning skills cannot be developed on the first attempt, of course, but the fundamentals can be learned in short order. Speed and accuracy will come with practice and experience as you work with the tools.

Cutting Actions

Wood turning involves very few basic cuts that are used to form an infinite variety of shapes through the use of hand manipulated chisels. There are two basic methods of turning: by a scraping action or a cutting action. In scraping, the tool is held horizontally and fed forward into the work to scrape away particles of wood. The cutting method involves holding the tool edge at an angle that allows it to pierce the surface of the wood to shave off material somewhat as is done with a hand plane.

The scraping action is very safe and produces cuts that are completely satisfactory, while the cutting method is very difficult and to a certain extent, dangerous; a wrong move can cause the chisel to jam into the work and be thrown from the hands and ruin the work, too. Many expert wood turners, amateur and professional alike, work almost exclusively with the scraping method. There is no difference whatsoever in the final result of the work done by either method. The various finished turnings shown in following pages were all done by scraping procedures.

Lathe Chisels

The standard set of wood-turning chisels comprises five different shapes. The gouge is used for rough cutting the stock to cylindrical shape, for fast stock removal, and for cove cutting. The skew chisel is used for smoothing cylinders, for cutting shoulders, beads and V's. The parting tool is used for making sizing cuts, straight incisions, and cut-offs. The spear or diamond point is used to form recesses or corners and general scraping cuts. The round nose is used to scrape concave curves and coves. A flat or square nose is also sometimes used for straight surface scraping. The gouge and skew can be used for both scraping or cutting, while the other chisels are used strictly for scraping.

THE COMMON TYPES OF TURNING CHISELS AND GOUGES

GOUGE

The gouge is used for making roughing cuts. It should be held firmly but not rigidly. The cutting edge should contact the work slightly above center.

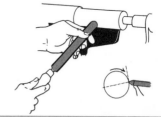

SKEW

The large skew is used for smoothing the surface after roughing with the gouge. Small skews are used for squaring ends, cutting shoulders; V grooves and beads. The angle of contact shown is for cutting rather than scraping.

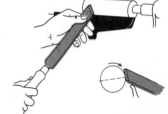

PARTING TOOL

The parting tool is used for cutting diameter grooves and cutting off stock. It is strictly a scraping tool which is held on edge.

SPEAR POINT

The spear point is used mainly for cutting V grooves and beads and general shaping. The point or either side of the chisel can be used for cutting. Cutting edge should be slightly above center.

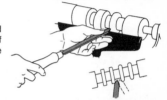

ROUND NOSE

The round nose is used for rounding out concave curves. It is a scraping tool which is held flat on the tool rest with edge slightly above center. (H. K. Porter)

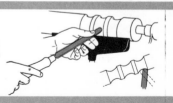

asic Cuts

The following procedures outline the steps involved in forming the basic shapes in wood turning. Practice these few cuts and you'll soon acquire the know-how required to turn finished products.

Start by selecting a solid piece of stock of sound quality without cracks or knots. Cut it square and mark a center on each end. Two crossed diagonal cuts on one end will help to seat the live center spur that spins the work. A small hole at the other end seats the dead center. If the stock is over 3″ square, it is advisable to bevel the corners so that you start with an octagonal-shaped piece that is more easily turned to a cylinder. Mount the piece on the lathe between the centers.

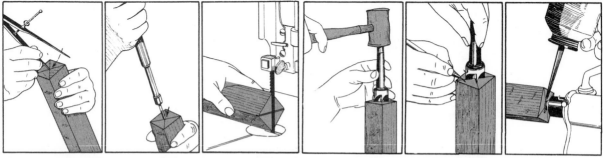

Preparing stock for turning: **a.** Use dividers to mark center on soft wood. **b.** Drill the center if wood is hard. **c.** Also saw diagonals for hardwood live center. **d.** Use mallet to set spur center. **e.** Mark the work for re-centering. **f.** Always oil or wax the dead center. (*Rockwell*)

Stock which is over 3 inches in diameter will rough turn to cylinder shape a lot easier if it has the four corners beveled in advance.

MEASURING TOOLS FOR LATHE WORK

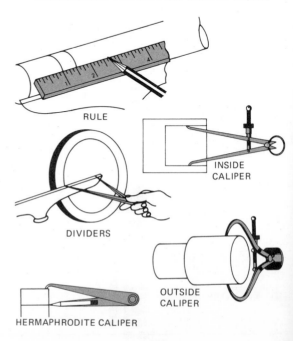

RULE

INSIDE CALIPER

DIVIDERS

OUTSIDE CALIPER

HERMAPHRODITE CALIPER

ROUGHING A CYLINDER

Adjust the tool rest to about ⅛″ away from the work and ⅛″ above the centerline. Run the lathe at low speed and use the gouge for the first or roughing cut to form the cylinder. Either hand can be used to hold the handle, which should be grasped firmly. The other hand holds the tool near the blade with thumb on top and the index finger resting on the curved ledge of the tool rest. All tools can be held this way. The handle hand provides the movement and cutting angle of the chisel, while the tool rest hand serves to control the depth of cut and to manipulate the tool into the various positions along the work.

The roughing cut is always started from the inside and continues towards an end. Bites of two or three inches at a time are made in both directions towards each end until the round is formed to within ⅛″ of the finished size. The gouge is rolled slightly in the direction of the feed for roughing with a cutting action, otherwise it is held in a constant position as it is moved across the work.

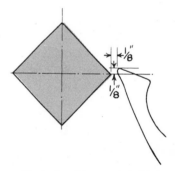

The tool rest is mounted about ⅛″ away from the work and about ⅛″ above the work centerline for best results.

LATHE SPEEDS

DIA. OF WORK	ROUGHING OFF	GENERAL CUTTING	FINISHING
Under 2 In. Diameter	900 to 1300 R. P. M.	2400 to 2800	3000 to 4000
2 In. to 4 In. Diameter	600 to 1000 R. P. M.	1800 to 2400	2400 to 3000
4 In. to 6 In. Diameter	600 to 800 R. P. M.	1200 to 1800	1800 to 2400
6 In. to 8 In. Diameter	400 to 600 R. P. M.	800 to 1200	1200 to 1800
8 In. to 10 In. Diameter	300 to 400 R. P. M.	600 to 800	900 to 1200
Over 10 In. Diameter	300	300 to 600	600 to 900

Speeds for wood turning are adjusted according to the diameter of the work, using lower speeds for larger diameters.

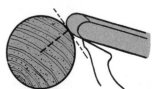

GOUGE IN SHEARING OR CUTTING POSTION

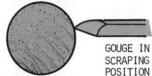

GOUGE IN SCRAPING POSITION

Positions of the gouge for cutting and scraping methods of turning the work. *(Rockwell)*

The large gouge in use for making the initial roughing cut. The tool is always worked from the center outward with a slight rolling motion.

SMOOTHING A CYLINDER

The skew is used to smooth the cylinder and to take it down to the required size. Set the outside caliper and check the diameter constantly as you slide the tool along the work in a scraping action to level any irregularities made by the gouge.

Smoothing a cylinder with a skew in a scraping position. Push tool into work then move from side to side. Never start at the end. Lathe speed can be increased after the roughing cut.

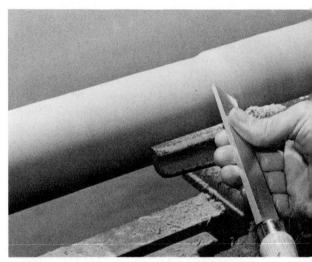

Using the skew to size a cylinder with the cutting method. Only the mid-section of the cutting edge must make contact with the wood. This method is somewhat difficult.

PARTING CUT

The parting tool serves most importantly for making sizing cuts. Although lathe work can be done strictly "by eye", it is seldom done this way. The parting tool is used to cut grooves at various locations along the cylinder which set the rough limits or guidlines for the desired shape. The procedure is quite simple: A full size drawing of the turning is marked off at locations where distinct changes in the profile occur. These points are transferred to the rounded cylinder by marking with a pencil. The caliper is set for the diameter at a given location on the drawing. The parting tool is pushed straight into the work to form a groove to the required depth indicated by the caliper setting. This is repeated for all the locations. With this done it will simply be a matter of removing the waste stock between each groove with various chisels to produce the basic form of the turning.

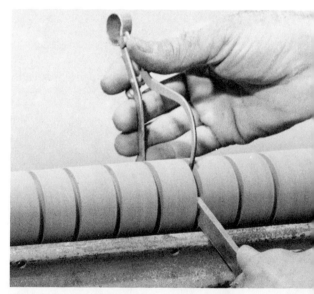

Using the parting tool to make a diameter sizing cuts. This tool is easy to use. It may be held with one hand while the caliper is held with the other.

CUTTING V'S AND BEADS

V cuts are made with the spear point chisel held flat on the tool rest and pushed into the wood at evenly spaced intervals. Beads are also readily cut with the spear point. The parting tool can be used to cut to depth between the beads if a flat division is desired between each bead. The bead is made by scraping with the left or right edge of the chisel that is rotated slowly to form the curve.

COVE CUT

Cove cuts can be made with the gouge or round nose. Set the caliper to the smallest diameter and check constantly. If working with the round nose, force it into the center of the cove location, then swing it from side to side using the thumb and forefinger as a pivot. To cut a cove with the gouge, hold it vertically with its edge resting on the tool rest. Start at the outside limit of the cove rolling and pivoting the tool as the cut is made. Work from both sides towards the center. When coving, the center should first be roughed to size with a parting cut.

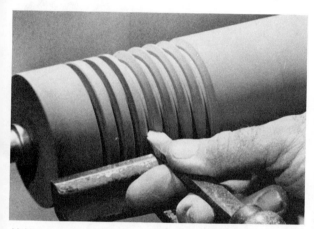

Making V cuts with the spear point tool. Parting tool was used first to form flat grooves but this cut can be made without grooves to obtain a true V shape.

Cutting a cove with a round nose is quite simple. Pivot the tool at the thumb while making wide sideways movements of the handle in both directions.

Cutting a cove with the gouge is quicker but more difficult. Gouge is held with edge on tool rest (cutting edge vertical) and positioned at outer limit of cove. It is then fed in and rolled to the horizontal position as it nears center. Step is repeated from other side.

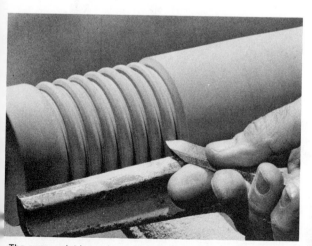

The spear point is used to cut beads. The cutting edge is rotated by pivoting at the thumb while the handle is moved sideways.

SHOULDER CUTS

When a turning has a square section, the cut from square to round can be made with a skew or spear point. A nicking cut is first made to prevent the square corner from splintering. The parting tool is then used to cut a groove to the required depth. The curved shoulder is then shaped with the spear point starting at the nick on the square corner and slowly pushing it forward while swinging the handle in a slight arc. A square shoulder can be cut in the same way as a square section except that the chisel is fed straight in instead of being swung.

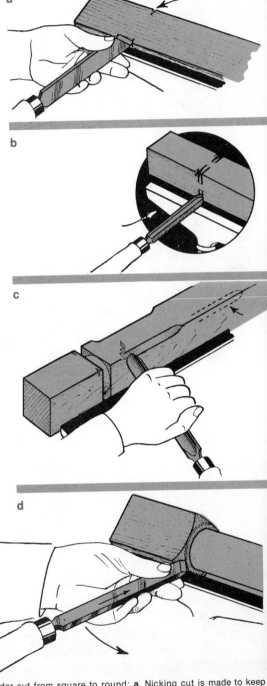

a

b

c

d

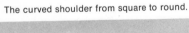

Making a shoulder cut from square to round with the skew in a scraping operation. The spear point could also be used.

The curved shoulder from square to round.

Shoulder cut from square to round: **a.** Nicking cut is made to keep work from splitting. **b.** Parting cut to depth required. **c.** Roughing with the gouge. **d.** Toe of skew is used to scrape the curve. (*Rockwell*)

LONG CUTS

To cut a long taper the parting tool is used first to make grooves to the depth of the smallest, largest, and several in-between diameters. The waste is removed to the guiding diameters with the gouge. This is followed by the skew to smooth the cut.

The skew, round nose, and spear point are variously used to cut long concave or convex curves. The spear point in particular, with one edge against the work and the point leading into the waste, can be used for much of both convex and concave curve cutting.

Any turning, however complex in shape, is comprised of a combination of the individual basic cuts. You will discover that there is considerable overlap of function among the different chisels, so there are no definite rules on which tool to use for a specific cut.

Long straight or curved cuts can be made with skew, round nose or spear point. Spear point is shown moving across the tool rest with the point leading into the waste.

A half pattern template is used to check the accuracy of the work when multiple spindles are in progress.

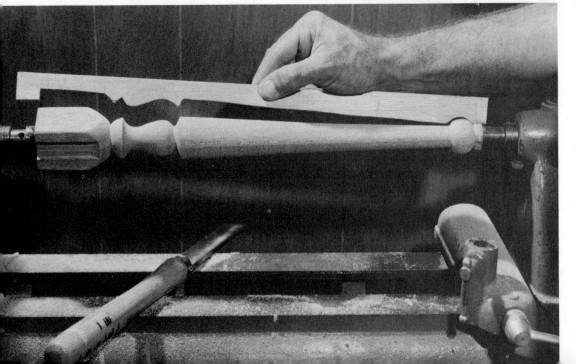

Face Plate Turning

Turnings that cannot be worked between centers must be mounted on a faceplate or screw center. Projects such as bowls, wheels, rims and the like are turned on the faceplate. Screws are inserted through the back of the faceplate and directly into the work. If normal screw fastenings interfere, the work may be mounted on an auxiliary backing block. Small work can be mounted on a single screw center.

The block to be turned should first be cut with a saw to circular shape and approximate diameter. All faceplate turning must be done by the scraping method. An attempt to use a

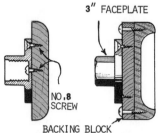

3″ FACEPLATE

NO. 8 SCREW

BACKING BLOCK

ALLOW EXTRA STOC CUTTING OFF

DIRECT MONTING ON 3″ FACEPLATE

MOUNTING ON BACKING BLOCK

MOUNTING ON SCREW CENTER

Various faceplate mounting methods. (*Rockwell*)

Direct mounting a 3″ faceplate on a glued up block for a bowl project. Stock for faceplate work should be pre-cut into disk.

The first step in faceplate turning is to trim the outside diameter to size. This is generally done by making a bite at one edge and continuing it right across the surface.

cutting technique on the edge grain of large work would prove disastrous. The tool rest should be positioned to bring the cutting edge of the tool on the centerline of the work. Although most of the tools can be used, much of the shaping in faceplate work can be done with the spear point and round nose chisels. The gouge is used for heavy stock removal on the face of the turning.

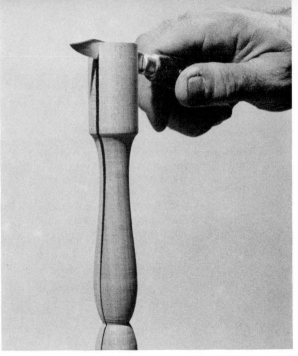

Split turnings are made by various methods. The simplest is to glue two pieces of stock together with a piece of slick paper between the joint. When the full round turning is completed and sanded smooth it is split apart at the joint.

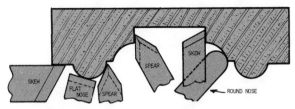

Some of the typical scraping cuts in faceplate work. (*Rockwell*)

Using the round nose to make an inside curve.

Trimming the inside curves with a round nose. Caliper checks must be made frequently to avoid cutting too deeply.

325

Lathe Techniques Applied

Lathe projects need not be run-of-the-mill candlestick-type productions. When you've learned the basics, you can spend your leisure time most enjoyably turning out many kinds of things. An important aspect of lathe work is that beautiful, finished products can be made with relatively small expenditure for material.

The sequence on how the chess set was made is shown particularly because it illustrates quite clearly how easy such detailed work can be. The tricks used to solve special problems should be noted. They may prove useful to you in varied lathe projects.

This handsome maple and walnut set was made with some standard turning tools and a few simple homemade ones which were necessary to manipulate some tight spots.

This turning project requires a screw center mounting to permit working on ends. Drilled holes are tapped to make threads for a machine-screw center. Most centers have regular wood screw ends which don't require tapping.

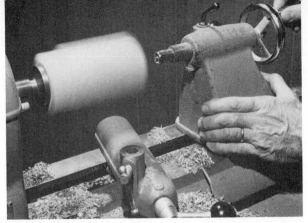

Squared and centered block is threaded onto the screw. The deep hole is OK, it doesn't interfere. Roughing and parting cuts can vibrate the work considerably and cause lopsided work. To avoid problems, the dead center is used for part of the work (see right).

To obtain a true axis, the tailstock is moved into the spinning work, then locked. This insures that the stock will **maintain** the **same axis** when the dead center is removed for later operations.

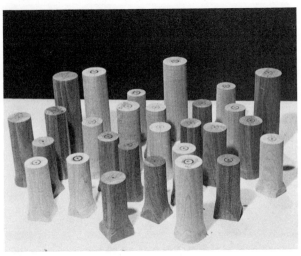

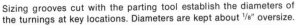

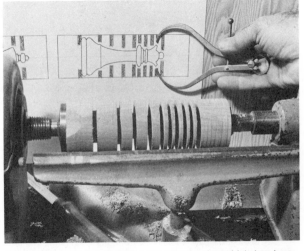

Mass production methods are essential to speed up the job. All pieces are first roughed out to cylindrical form with the gouge.

Outside caliper is set against a full size drawing which has been marked with the diameters required at various points.

Sizing grooves cut with the parting tool establish the diameters of the turnings at key locations. Diameters are kept about 1/8" oversize.

This is the secret of successful lathe work. When the blanks are sized this way, the main contours are virtually formed. The parting tool and calipers are very important tools.

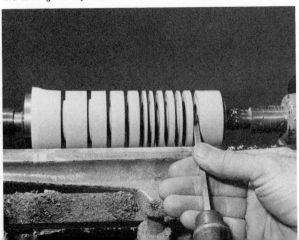

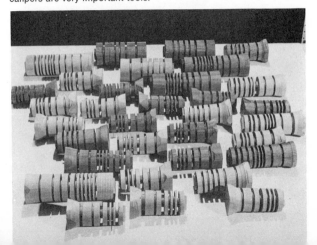

The turnings quickly begin to take shape when the waste wood between grooves is scraped away.

Regular lathe tools are used as far as they can go, then the homemades take over. Here an old file end was ground to the exact contour needed for a particular section. The cutting edge is not sharpened to a severe angle, only to a slight bevel.

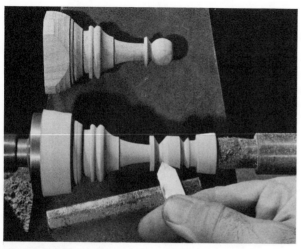

The ball ends of the pawns are formed with the spear point. The first partly finished sample is placed near the work for use as a guide.

Lathe is operated at high speed for small diameter work like this but sharp tools and small bites are the rule.

A hack saw is utilized to form the very narrow grooves required in a "neck". Note how the tool rest is used to keep the saw under control. A very fine blade is used.

A small screwdriver ground to just the proper shape makes easy work of cutting extremely fine detail. No regular lathe tool could do it. This illustrates why the dead center is used as much as possible.

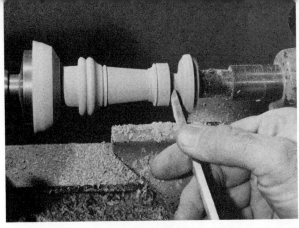

This figure is being separated at the end with the parting tool. It will remain in place on the live end screw center.

Tailstock is moved out of the way to permit working on top end details. The screw center holds piece firmly.

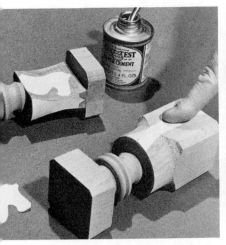

Paper patterns of the horse's profile are cemented to the blocks for easy following in cutting. Flat section is used for gripping work in vise (right).

Note how ample waste is allowed on the ends of figures. A second cut on the side will fairly well form the horse's head.

A sanding drum attached to the lathe is used for a good part of the "sculpturing". Some hand sanding is also required.

Another lathe accessory, the chuck with a saw blade mounted is used to cut the tricky slots. Note how the work is guided past the blade against a slanted jig. Watch the hands on a set up like this!

Another innovation: a rat-tail file chucked in the lathe shapes the scallops in the queen's crown.

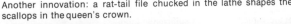

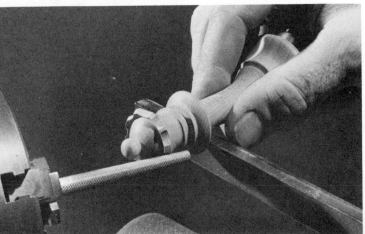

TURNED CHANDELIER

An attractive lamp like this can be turned in a couple of hours using a few of the basic scraping cuts. Advance planning is required, however, concerning the hole through the center for the power cord. It should be drilled before starting the turning.

How to solve the problem of the hole to contain the electric wire: If a drill bit sufficiently long enough is available, bore the hole then plug the end (or ends) with dowel.

Another method is to cut the block in half, run a groove down each center, plug up the ends then glue the halves together.

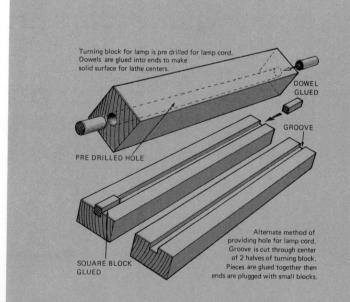

Turning block for lamp is pre drilled for lamp cord. Dowels are glued into ends to make solid surface for lathe centers.

DOWEL GLUED

GROOVE

PRE DRILLED HOLE

Alternate method of providing hole for lamp cord. Groove is cut through center of 2 halves of turning block. Pieces are glued together then ends are plugged with small blocks.

SQUARE BLOCK GLUED

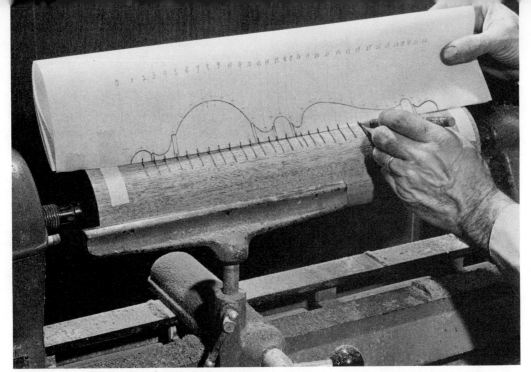

Marking the cylinder for parting cuts. Full size drawing is folded in half and placed on the work to transfer the marks accurately. Lines are made heavy so they'll show as the wood spins.

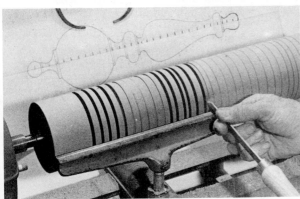

A quick series of sizing cuts with caliper measurements . . .

. . . and the spindle is ready for the "fun" work.

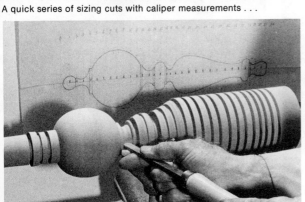

The round nose shapes the concave curves . . .

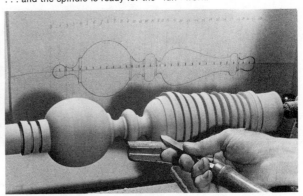

. . . while the spear point shapes the convex ones.

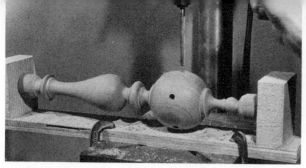

This jig holds the turning in perfect alignment for precise hole drilling on the press. Nails in the ends allow the piece to be rotated.

The spindle end is separated with a saw cut to allow boring a large hole in the ball end for wiring. Cut is made part way then finish coats are applied while the work is still lathe-bound. The cut is completed after finish is dry.

The end spindle is glued back in place after the wiring is complete. Lamp hardware such as this is available from woodworker's mail order houses or electric supply stores.

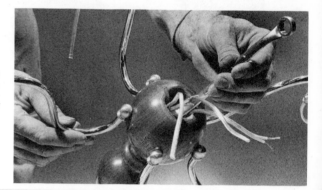

MIXED WOOD TURNING

It is important to use species of similar hardness and turning characteristics when selecting woods for gluing into a block. Centers and wood are marked for later repositioning.

Glued up stock of contrasting woods forms interesting patterns when turned. There are no set rules but long slender turnings should have thin mixed sections through center.

PRE-HOLLOWED TURNING BLOCK

Jig saw set at a slight bevel angle produced this "telescoping" turning block for a lamp. Pre-hollowed sections are glued together to form a complete, enclosed unit. (More information on the rings can be found in section on Jig Saw.)

A limited amount of lathe work is required because the main shape is basically pre-formed.

After the steps are leveled off the work is sanded then the bottom is cut away to reveal the hollowed out lamp fixture.

The finished product makes a unique conversation piece.

CONSTRUCTION TECHNIQUES

27 Woodworking Joints

Any woodworking project consisting of more than one part will require some form of joint to fasten the components into a subassembly or a completed unit. Innumerable joints have been devised and are commonly used in woodworking. Some are quite simple and can be made with hand tools, while other more complicated ones, especially those involving grooves and dados, require the use of various power tools.

This miniature greenhouse project required the use of many kinds of joints including dadoes, rabbets, butts and miters.

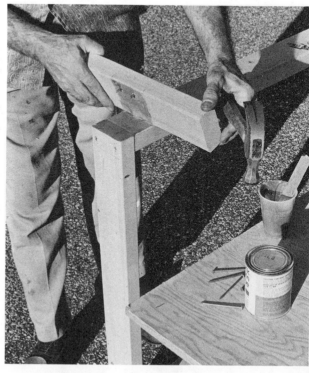

A joint need not be complicated if it will serve the purpose. This simple butt joint with a cross-over member will be quite strong.

The selection of a particular joint is usually dictated by several factors: strength requirement, appearance, and ease or difficulty of fabrication. In general, the easiest to make joint that will do a satisfactory job is the one to choose. For example: a mortise and tenon is a good strong joint but somewhat more difficult to make than a simple doweled butt joint. Yet the latter is equally as strong as the mortise and tenon.

The most commonly used joints may be classified into several basic groups: butt and edge, rabbets, dadoes and grooves, lap joints, miters, mortise and tenon, and dovetail joints.

A proper fit is essential for good joints, so whenever possible, the parts for a joint should be marked by direct contact. Lay one part over the other and use a sharp knife to scribe the cutting lines. Identify mating pieces for easy matching during assembly. When possible use dowels, splines, cleats and corner blocks to strengthen joints. Gussets, braces, nails, screws, bolts, and numerous metal brackets are also useful for making joints stronger.

BUTT JOINT. Butt joints are the easiest to make, but are very weak when not reinforced. They can be strengthened by adding any of the above-mentioned reinforcements. Blind dowels require exacting alignment, so they are best made with the aid of a doweling jig or on the drill press. An easy way to make good dowel joints using other than a drill press is by through-drilling. In this method the parts are held together and the holes for the dowels are drilled into them from the outside. Slight errors in the perpendicular may occur but not in alignment. The dowels are driven in the same holes, so alignment of the parts is absolutely assured. If

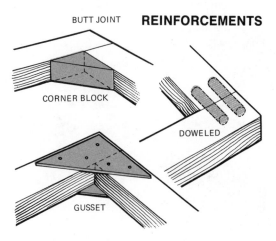

BUTT JOINT   **REINFORCEMENTS**

CORNER BLOCK

DOWELED

GUSSET

Plain butt joints can be strenghtened in many ways. Several methods are shown.

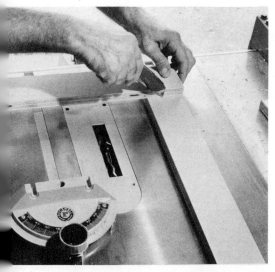

Accuracy is of prime importance in the making of good joints. The best way to make an accurate layout for cuts is to superimpose the parts, then scribe the lines directly to the mating pieces. Here a sharp blade is used to scribe the line. It makes finer line than pencil.

Through-doweling is the easiest way to make a doweled butt joint when a drill press is not available. Hold tool straight and drill carefully at right angle to the work.

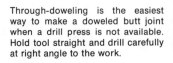

appearance is important, the holes can be counterbored and plugs cut from the same stock can be used to conceal the dowels.

The edge joint is used to join narrow widths to form larger workpieces, such as table tops and cabinet members. There are several variations of the edge joint. Dowels, splines, rabbets, tongue and groove, and other milled shapes produce joints that are stronger than a plain edge joint. When joining boards edgewise, the annular rings should be alternately reversed to counteract warping tendencies.

RABBET JOINT. The rabbet joint is used extensively for drawer construction, boxes, and case making. It is an easy joint to make with the circular saw, router, shaper, or jointer. It is a groove cut into the edge or end of one member into which the other piece is fitted.

The width of the rabbet should equal the thickness of the material and the depth should be one-half to two-thirds the thickness. If the joint is to be glued, the depth of the shoulder should be two-thirds of the stock thickness, but if it is to be assembled with nails or screws then the depth should be one-half the thickness.

The rabbet joint is the most suitable one to use for recessing the back panel of cabinets and cases. When set into a rabbet cut a bit deeper than itself, the panel will be concealed.

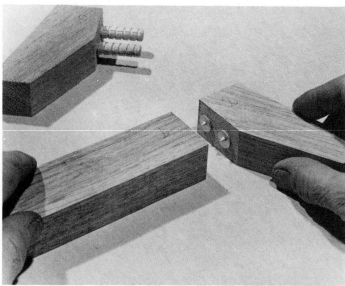

Dowel buttons are sometimes used to conceal dowel ends while at the same time adding an interesting design feature.

Dowel centers are used to lay out the center marks for drilling dowel joint holes. They are inserted into holes drilled in the first piece which is then pressed against the other to make pointed impressions. They're available in common dowel sizes.

This gate leg table assembly made entirely with doweled butt joints is quite strong.

Homemade dowel centers can be made by cutting a dowel about 1/2" long, then glueing thumbtack precisely on center of the dowel piece. Point can be filed down a bit.

Varied edge joint treatments

A special shaper cutter is used to make this popular glue joint cut.

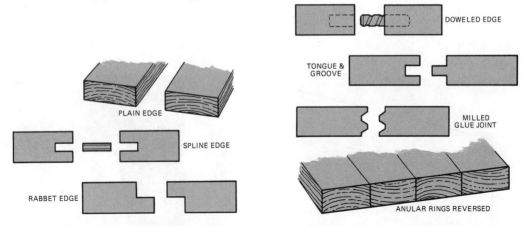

PLAIN EDGE

SPLINE EDGE

RABBET EDGE

DOWELED EDGE

TONGUE & GROOVE

MILLED GLUE JOINT

ANULAR RINGS REVERSED

Varied Edge Joint Treatments. Splines should be made with ⅛″ plywood rather than with solid stock. Note the increased surface of shaped joints. They result in more glue area and stronger joints.

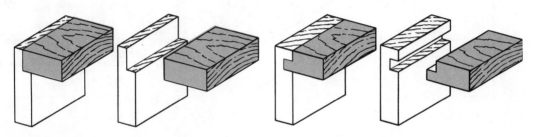

The rabbet joint is strong and easy to make with power tools. It is used in drawer and cabinet construction.

The rabbet can be combined with a dado to make an even stronger joint. This is better for drawers.

337

On certain veneer plywood projects a deep rabbet is utilized in order to minimize the end grain that would otherwise mar the appearance of the work.

DADO AND GROOVE. The dado joint is used to join the end of one board into the surface of another. It is used in furniture and all forms of cabinet and shelf construction. When the joint is cut across the grain of the wood, it is called a dado. A groove joint is exactly the same as a dado with the exception that it is cut along the grain.

There are two main types of dado: the plain dado and the blind or stopped dado. In the plain dado the groove continues completely across the board, while in the stopped dado the groove is made only partly across the surface. The cross member is notched out to fit into the partial groove. The blind dado is used when neat appearance is important.

LAP JOINT. The lap joint is one in which an equal amount of material is removed from each member so that the pieces assemble flush. There are many variations of this joint, including the half, end, cross, and edge cross lap. The common forms of this joint are used to splice the ends of boards, for frame construction, to join cross-rails and bracing, and to join pieces in "egg crate" fashion.

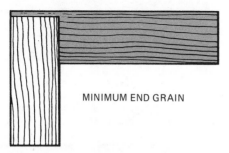

MINIMUM END GRAIN

A rabbet with a deep shoulder can be used to minimize end grain exposure in hardwood veneer plywood construction.

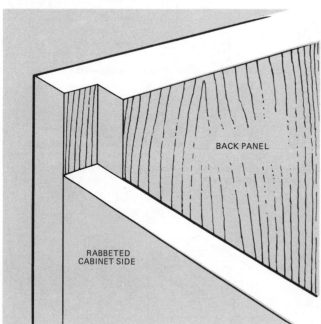

BACK PANEL

RABBETED CABINET SIDE

Detail of rabbet joint used in attaching back panels.

Setting a back panel into a rabbet for concealment and added strength.

338

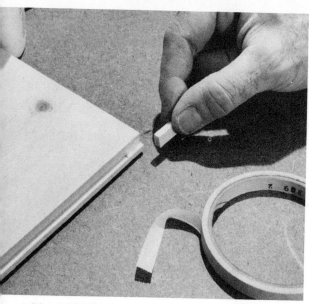

A handy trick for concealing the opening at the end of a rabbet which would be exposed to view when butt joined with an end member: Cut small filler block and glue it into end of rabbet.

The prime purpose of the deep rabbet on this piece is for appearance rather than strength. It conceals the raw plywood edge.

The corner joints on these pieces are rabbets of a sort. Joints are frequently "invented" to meet the needs of a particular job.

An angled joint such as this cannot be made with a wide cutting dado. Repeated passes with a thin blade was required. Note use of corner block to reinforce miter joint.

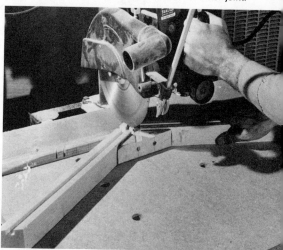

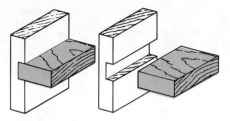

The plain dado joint is a rectangular recess which runs across the grain of the wood.

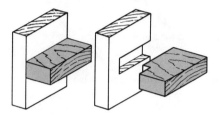

The blind dado is used when appearance of the edge is important.

A blind dado joint is frequently used to join rails to legs. Addition of a corner block will add much strength. Note how the rail ends are rounded to fit the curved shape of the groove which is formed by the dado cutter.

Dado joints for this large cabinet assembly were easily made with the router.

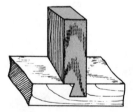

The half-dovetail dado makes a strong lock joint.

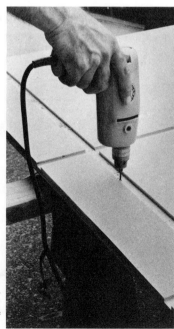

Screws must be used on large dado jointed assemblies in order to pull the parts tightly together for proper gluing. Screw pilot holes are bored throughout in the centers of each of the grooves.

When the cut is made in the direction of the grain the joint is called a groove instead of a dado.

MITER JOINT. The miter is an angled joint used primarily to conceal end grain in picture frames and molding applications, on furniture and cabinet work. Edge miter joints are used to conceal the edge grain of structural members in furniture and cabinet work particularly when hardwood veneer panels are used. The miter joint is not too strong unless reinforced with dowels or splines.

There are many styles of lap joints. These are the types most frequently used.

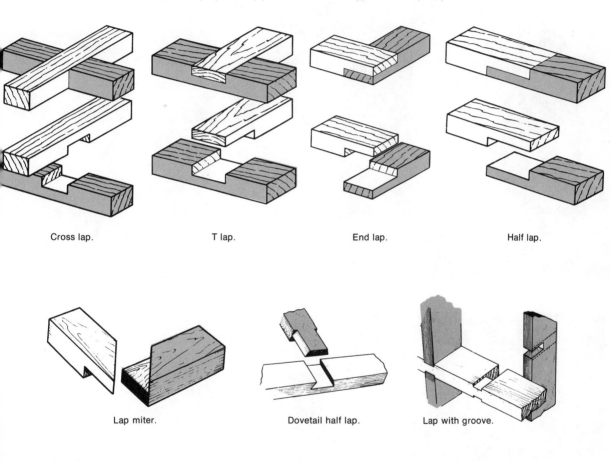

Cross lap.

T lap.

End lap.

Half lap.

Lap miter.

Dovetail half lap.

Lap with groove.

Three way cross lap.

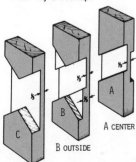

C OUTSIDE

B OUTSIDE

A CENTER

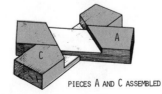

PIECES A AND C ASSEMBLED

PIECE B ADDED

This joint is particularly useful for making hexagonal constructions where each 'spoke' is required to radiate from a common plane. Although it looks complicated, it really isn't; all cuts are made with the miter gage (or radial arm) set to 30 degrees, alternately, to left and right of zero. The dado head projection is set equal to ⅓ or ⅔ of the stock thickness, as indicated.

341

The edge cross lap joint, used in projects at left and below, offers a strong union of pieces in a variety of assembly applications. It eliminates the need for cleats.

The edge cross lap joint is used vertically in these two pieces.

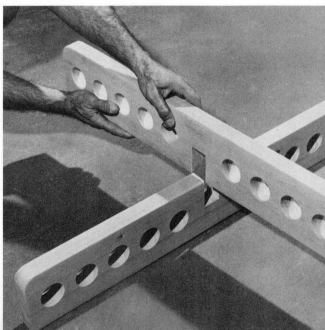

MORTISE AND TENON. This joint is strong and is frequently used to join legs to tables and chairs and for better frame constructions and other types of assemblies. It is made in a number of forms, the simplest one being the open mortise and tenon. It can be cut easily with a dado cutter on the circular or radial arm saw.

The blind mortise and tenon can be made in several styles. It may be square-cornered, round-cornered, or round. The square corner version is most easily made with a mortising attachment on the drill press. This drills square-cornered holes. The round-cornered mortise can be cut with a router. The round mortise is made by simply drilling a hole of the required size. Any of these joints can be made with hand tools in which case the mortise is formed with a chisel after boring a series of adjoining holes to clear out much of the waste. As a general rule, the thickness of the tenon should be about one-third the thickness of the mortised member.

DOVETAIL JOINT. The dovetail is a strong and highly ornamental corner joint. It is one of the most painstaking of all the joints to make by hand. It can easily be made, however, with the router and a dovetailing accessory fixture. The box joint, which is a simpler form of the dovetail, can easily be made on the circular or radial arm saw.

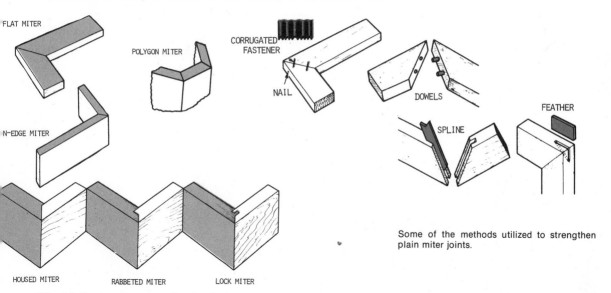

FLAT MITER

POLYGON MITER

CORRUGATED FASTENER

NAIL

DOWELS

SPLINE

FEATHER

N-EDGE MITER

Some of the methods utilized to strengthen plain miter joints.

HOUSED MITER   RABBETED MITER   LOCK MITER

Miter joints are used to conceal end and edge grain and for angular constructions.

The roof framing sections of this unit have a plain miter at the base and a compound miter at the meeting point.

MORTISE AND TENON JOINTS

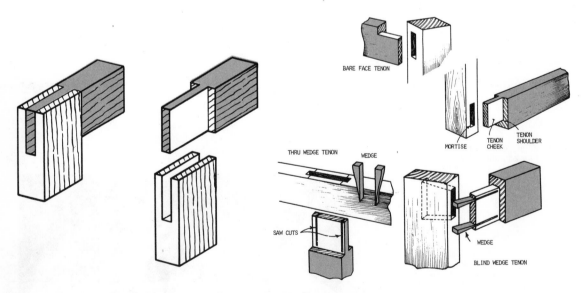

ROUND TENON

SQUARED TENON

THRU MORTISE TENON

STUB MORTISE TENON

BLIND MORTISE TENON

Some of the more common mortise and tenon joints.

BARE FACE TENON

MORTISE

TENON CHEEK

TENON SHOULDER

THRU WEDGE TENON

WEDGE

SAW CUTS

WEDGE

BLIND WEDGE TENON

More mortise and tenon joints.

Round mortise and tenon joints were used to join the legs of this hassock to the base. Round tenons are easy to make on the lathe.

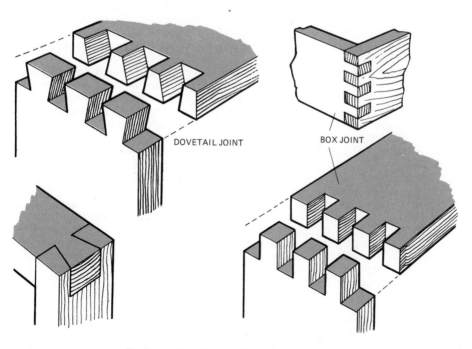

DOVETAIL JOINT

BOX JOINT

The box or finger joint is a variation of the dovetail.

20 Gluing and Clamping

The gluing operation is a very important phase of woodworking. Regardless of how much time and effort you may put into the fabrication of nicely made parts for a project, the success of the finished piece of work will depend not only on how well it goes together but of more importance, perhaps, how well it stays together.

Glue Selection

Good lasting joints, stronger than the wood itself, are possible and relatively easy to accomplish provided that the proper glue is selected and is correctly applied.

There are many modern glues and adhesives available for woodworking. While most of them have remarkable holding power, the question as to which one to select will depend on specific characteristics of the glue and the nature of the job. There are variables in both areas that must be considered.

Some glues are very quick-setting, others are not. If an assembly is relatively small, a quick-setting glue would be quite·suitable. However, the use of the same glue on a large, complex glue assembly could prove disastrous if the glue begins to dry on one part, while it is still being applied to another section. The problem of premature drying during assembly is one of the prime causes of joint failure. It can also occur with other glues that are not inherently quick-setting types. Most glues will set faster at higher temperatures, so it stands to reason that working temperature is an important factor. Conversely, it should be noted that some glues do not work well at low temperatures.

The condition or quality of a joint will influence the choice of glue. Some glues have good gap-filling properties. If a joint is poor fitting, such a glue would be advantageous. There are times when joints must necessarily be made loose-fitting in order to permit assembly at all. A typical example would be a chair with numerous turnings set at compound angles. Certain tenons would have to be made undersized so that they could be nursed into place. A good gap-filling glue is used to assure success.

The difference between a water resistant and a waterproof glue could make the difference between life and death. A boat assembled with water resistant (instead of waterproof) glue wouldn't stay afloat very long at all. There is also a big difference in the cost between the two types of glue. If a project can get by with a water resistant glue, by all means use it instead of the more costly waterproof kind. A picnic table, if it were to be glued, would require waterproof glue. A table to be used on a porch would be satisfactory with a water resistant glue.

Another factor to consider in glue selection is its heat resistance qualities in terms of the project. Thermoplastic glues, such as polyvinyl resin (white), become soft at temperatures of about 165 degrees. Therefore such a glue would be a poor choice for the construction of a TV cabinet or a radiator enclosure.

Some jobs may very well require the use of two or even three different kinds of glue. An example would be a plywood cabinet that is to be surfaced with plastic laminate and trimmed with wood molding borders on the surface of the laminate. The plywood is assembled with white glue. The lamination process is handled with contact cement, while the trim is attached to the laminate with one of the new super adhesives. This last step, attaching wood to a smooth plastic surface would have been quite a problem in the days before the development of the space age adhesives.

Kinds of Glue

POLYVINYL RESIN GLUE. This is the familiar "white" glue widely used for general woodworking. It is available in the convenient plastic squeeze bottle, always ready to use. This glue sets up quite rapidly at room temperature, dries colorless, leaving an invisible glue line.

It is not water resistant and tends to soften at high temperatures. It has good strength and fairly good gap-filling properties.

HIDE GLUE. This is the old fashioned animal glue made from hooves, hides, and bones of cattle. It was the favorite of the professional cabinetmaker for many years and is still used to some extent in the furniture industry. It has lost some ground since the development of the synthetics, but it is still available in liquid form in plastic squeeze bottles. It is extremely strong and slow-setting thus allowing plenty of time for assembly. It is not waterproof, but it is a good gap filler.

CASEIN GLUE. Made from milk curd, this glue is available as a tan powder that must be mixed with cold water to a heavy cream consistency. It is quite strong and can be used at any temperature above freezing. Though it is not waterproof, casein is highly water resistant. It is excellent for gluing oily woods and is a fair gap filler. It is a bit rough on tool edges and stains some woods, such as maple, oak and redwood.

PLASTIC RESIN GLUE. A urea-formaldehyde adhesive that comes in powdered form. It must be mixed with water for use. It makes extremely strong joints that are highly water resistant. It is not a good gap filler, so joints must fit well. It sets in 4 hours and is non-staining.

ALIPHATIC RESIN GLUE. A cream-colored ready-to-use liquid available in plastic squeeze bottles. It is very strong, sets in about ¾ hour at room temperature, but it can be used at 50 degrees F. It is not appreciably water resistant, but it does have good heat resistance.

RESORCINOL RESIN GLUE. A two-component completely waterproof glue available in a unit consisting of one can of liquid resin and one can of powered catalyst. It sets with heat generated when the catalyst hardener is added to the resin. It is very strong and excels for boat building, outdoor furniture, or any structures subjected to water or tropical or sub-zero temperatures. It is quite expensive, leaves a dark glue line, is slow setting, and it fills gaps.

EPOXY RESIN ADHESIVE. A two-part resin and catalyst adhesive that will make a very strong waterproof bond. Excellent for joining wood to almost any other material, such as metal, masonry, glass, ceramics or plastic. It is an excellent gap filler and requires no clamping.

CONTACT CEMENT. A neoprene rubber-based liquid ready to use. It is the ideal medium for bonding sheet plastic laminates to wood. It is also excellent for applying thin veneer edging to plywood constructions. It is applied to both surfaces and allowed to dry for about 30 minutes before assembly. Parts bond immediately upon contact. The regular type is highly volatile, but a latex base non-flamable contact cement is also available.

Assembly should be checked during clamping for squareness. It will be too late once the glue has set.

Pre-planning the sequence of assembly is important even on simple projects. The uprights on this one would be difficult to insert without messing up the glue if they were left until last.

347

Gluing Procedure

The wood surfaces to be glued should be dry, clean and smooth, and the pieces should fit together with good contact. A trial assembly without glue should always be made in advance of the application of the glue on large assemblies. This dry run will afford the opportunity to determine the best sequence of assembly. Glue can be applied to the wood directly from a squeeze bottle in a wavy line or a series of beads, then properly spread. This can be done with a brush or by joining both pieces and sliding them back and forth to get an even spread. Brush application is best.

End grain usually requires more glue than edge grain because the hollow ends of cut off

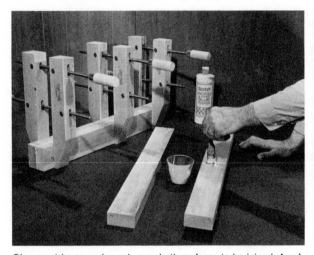

Glue must be spread evenly over both surfaces to be joined. A sufficient number of clamps will distribute the pressure evenly.

Spiral grooved dowels are the best to use; they allow excess glue to escape. They're available in several sizes.

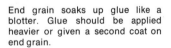

End grain soaks up glue like a blotter. Glue should be applied heavier or given a second coat on end grain.

wood fibers are more absorptive. The best way to handle this is to coat the ends first then apply a second coat after the edges have been coated.

Glue squeeze-out from a joint will be minimal if the proper amount of glue has been applied. The problem can't be avoided, but it can be solved. While the glue is still damp, use a sharp chisel to carefully scrape off the any excess. Then wipe the surface with a cloth dampened with warm water before the glue sets. Never use sandpaper to remove excess glue while it is still wet as this will force the glue deeper into the wood. Excess glue removal is very important because even the slightest trace of glue on a finished surface will act as a sealer, preventing stains or other finishing materials from penetrating evenly.

To hold parts square while you work, you can fasten a temporary brace with nails. But take care not to mar exterior surfaces.

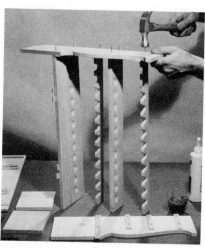

Temporary cleats are most helpful for obtaining perfectly aligned butt joints. They must be removed before glue sets so they won't stick.

In some nail or screw and glue operations a bar clamp can be used to hold the pieces in line.

Spacing cleats are especially important on butt jointed large assemblies. The glue may be deposited in a bead but it should be spread out evenly with a brush.

The best assembly sequence for a job like this is to attach the shelves to the back first, then add each side. Top and bottom which are to be butted over the ends go on last.

Some pieces like these angled stacking tables require a simple jig set-up for proper gluing assembly.

A level is used to check the plane to avoid a twisted assembly. The work is checked and adjusted properly only if the work table has **first** been leveled.

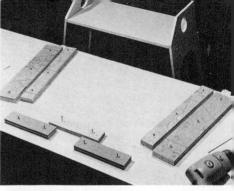

Cleats are nailed into the work surface in order to hold the parts in proper relation to each other for assembly

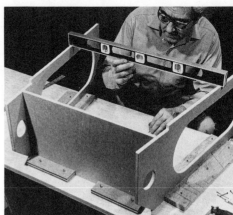

(lamping

Proper clamping pressure is important in gluing and it must be applied while the glue is still fluid. Excessive clamp pressure will cause a starved joint that will be weak because too much glue was removed from the contact surfaces. Insufficient pressure will also result in a weak joint because the parts will not make proper contact. Common sense must be your guide.

In order to tackle a variety of gluing operations it is necessary to have a variety of clamps on hand. The quantity will depend on the nature of the work. Some jobs will require only a few clamps, while others may need everything you own plus a few makeshift ones. When clamps are lacking or if their use is impractical, wood screws are excellent substitutes.

C clamps and adjustable hand screws (parallel clamp) are used for small assemblies and bar clamps for large work. With C and bar clamps, cawls (small blocks of wood) should be used to protect the surface of the work from becoming indented. The hand screws have wooden jaws, so they don't require the use of protective cawls.

When using the hand screw, it is important to adjust the jaws parallel to the work so that the pressure is distributed over a wide area. The greatest pressure is obtained by tightening the outer screw because it provides greater leverage. When necessary, the jaws can be adjusted out of parallel to match an odd-shaped piece of work.

When gluing stock edge-to-edge to make up wide panels, the bar clamps should be placed on alternate sides to equalize the pressure. A minimum of three clamps should be used for this work, but four would be better.

A special note about working with dowels and mortise and tenon joints: Liquid cannot be compressed. Provision must be made to allow excess glue to escape from a closed joint; otherwise any one of several things will happen. If glue is trapped in the bottom of a joint, it may prevent the joint from closing. If excessive clamp pressure is used to close the joint under an extreme condition, the wood will split. A third possibility is that the clamp will break. Therefore it is very important to allow extra space in the bottom of an enclosed joint. In the case of dowels, the spiral grooved type should always be used. The grooves allow the excess glue a means of escape. If ordinary dowels are used for a joint, two flats should be cut on the sides to serve the same purpose. All dowels and tenons should be given a slight bevel on the ends to permit easy insertion into the openings.

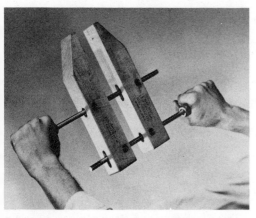

Rough adjustment of a hand screw is made by swinging it in this manner. The face must be kept well away! *(Adjustable Clamp Co.)*

The deep throat and the ability to "lean" forward enables this type of clamp to reach into awkward positions.

Protective cawls need not be used if the work is to receive a final jointing and the wood is hard. Wood of a soft variety which could dent easily would need cawls (wood blocks between clamp jaws).

351

Gluing four segments which will be used for a round cut out. The shaped edge joint provides increased glue surface. Step notches have been cut to facilitate clamping.

Squeezed out glue should be scraped off before the glue dries. On finished joints the scraping should be followed by wiping with a damp cloth to remove all traces of glue. Note how the bar clamps help to bring in the centers while the C clamps pull in the ends to produce a good tight joint.

When gluing up large panels, use two small brads at two corners only to prevent the piece from sliding. Nails should never be used in four corners in order to allow the panel to spread to its proper position during the clamping.

Many clamps are needed for an assembly of this size. Note how a high cleat is used across the center to cause the center hold-down to bend thus providing downward pressure at the hard to reach mid section. Two more hold-downs will be added.

Some joints such as at the top of this unit are very difficult to clamp properly. Epoxy resin glue was used to advantage because it is a good gap filler and requires no clamping. Note the use of wax paper to keep adhesive off adjoining members which will be part of a hinging unit.

Using wood bar clamps for edge gluing. Note how the clamps are reversed to help equalize the pressure.

Pipe clamps are economical because one set of fittings can fit pipes of any length. *(Adjustable Clamp Co.)*

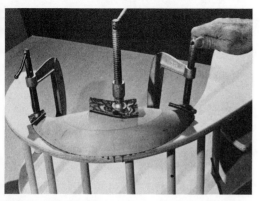

C clamps with swivel jaws and scraps of carpet work quite well for gluing irregular shapes. Run-off glue will be scraped off and cleaned with water before it sets.

A band clamp has many applications in gluing irregularly shaped pieces.

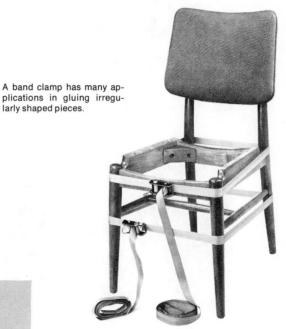

A picture frame clamp is easily made with a few pieces of scrap hardwood. *(Adjustable Clamp Co.)*

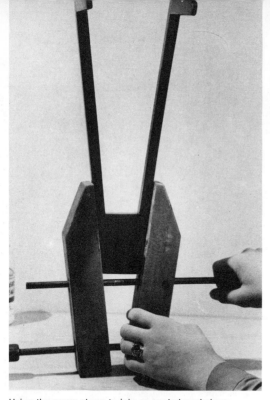

Using the screw clamp to join an angled workpiece.

Another application of the rope clamp trick.

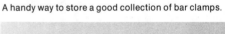

A handy way to store a good collection of bar clamps.

When time is of the essence the heat of a closed car can be used to accelerate the glue set up time.

Contact cement is spread evenly with a serrated spreader. It is applied to both surfaces and allowed to dry before joining the parts. (See section on plastic laminates)

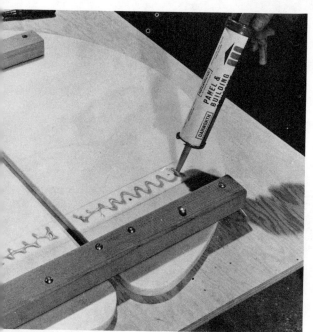

Wall panel mastic adhesive is useful for joining wood to various kinds of non-porous surfaces.

Silicone sealant is effective for setting plastic panel inserts. It remains flexible, prevents expansion.

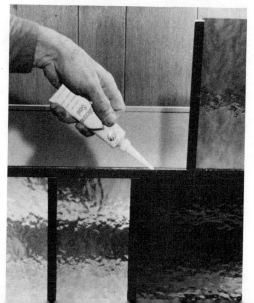

This wood turning is unique because it contains a glass vase. It illustrates a novel glue assembly.

Beveled segments are made with a profile of the vase cut out of each section. Shallow saw kerfs in each end accept wood feathers which help to keep the pieces in place.

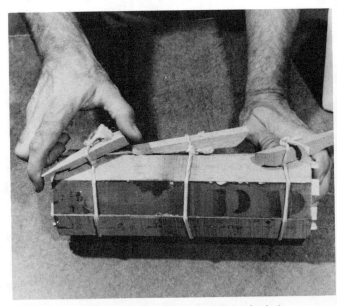

The only practical method of clamping the work is the simplest — strong cord applied like a tourniquet.

Hot melt adhesives are good for small, quick jobs. Not practical for a sizeable assembly because adhesive sets in 10 seconds. Holding power is very good and the bond is waterproof. *(U.S.M. Corp.)*

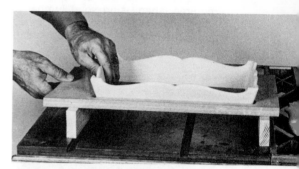

A simple jig for applying pressure to a construction with tapered sides. The work is forced down into a board with a rectangular opening.

Spray adhesive is not good for joining wood to wood but excels for attaching cloth to wood.

Resorcinol is the glue to use for outdoor projects such as this paneled garage door. If sun is shining, big jobs should be done on cool days; otherwise glue will set too rapidly.

22 Working with Plywood

Due to its many advantages, notably strength, stability, economy, and ease of workability, plywood is the ideal construction material for home workshop or handyman projects. It is well-suited for remodeling, making furniture, cabinets and built-ins, shelving, indoor and outdoor storage units, decking, and many other applications.

The large sheet size of plywood eliminates the need for making the many joints ordinarily required when using solid lumber for construction. Douglas fir plywood is the kind most commonly used for general construction and also the least expensive. Here are some basic techniques of working with this versatile material.

LAYOUT AND CUTTING

When planing plywood never work off an end; plane from both ends toward the center to avoid tearing out plys at the end of the cut.

Plan the layout carefully to avoid waste and simplify your work. Be sure to allow for the thickness of the saw blade between adjacent pieces. Grain direction should normally run the long way of the wood.

The type of saw determines which side of plywood to face up. The good side should face up when using hand, table, radial, jig or band saw. The good side should be face down when using the portable circular saw because it cuts from the bottom up.

A saber saw also cuts from the bottom up so here, too, the good side of the panel faces down.

CONSTRUCTION JOINTS

Butt joints like the one at left are simplest to make, suitable for ½ or ¾ inch plywood. For thinner panels, use a reinforcing block to make a stronger joint. (American Plywood Assn.)

Frame construction makes it possible to reduce weight by using thinner plywood.

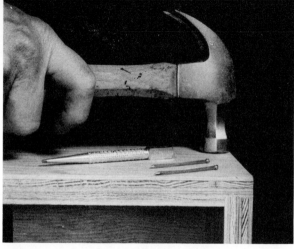

Rabbet joints are neat and strong, easy to make with power tools. This is a good joint for drawers, boxes or cabinets.

Dado joints can be quickly made with a power saw to produce neat shelves. The grooves should be sized accurately to provide a snug fit.

PLYWOOD FASTENERS

The thickness of plywood determines nail size. Used with glue, the following nails will produce good strong joints: For $3/4''$ plywood, 6d casing or finishing nails. For $5/8''$, 6d or 8d finishing nails. For $1/2''$, 4d or 6d. For $3/8''$, 3d or 4d. For $1/4''$, use $3/4''$ or $1''$ brads, 3d finishing nails or $1''$ blue lath nails.

Holes should be pre-drilled where nails must be close to an edge. Drill bit should be slightly smaller in diameter than the nail to be used. *(American Plywood Assn.)*

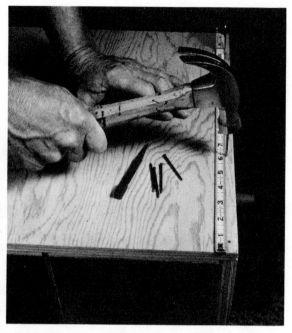

Nails should be spaced about 6″ apart for most work. Glue should be used with nails for durable joints.

Corrugated fasteners can be used to reinforce miter joints in 3/4″ plywood. They add much strength to a joint.

Screws provide more holding power than nails. Sizes indicated are minimums; longer screws should be used whenever possible. The following gives plywood thickness, diameter and length of smallest screws recommended, and size of pilot hole to drill: 3/4″ plywood No. 8, 1 1/2″, 5/32″ hole; 1/2″ plywood, No. 6, 1 1/4″, 1/8″ hole; 3/8″ plywood, No. 6, 1″, 1/8″ hole; 1/4″ plywood, No. 4, 3/4″, 7/64″ hole.

Screws and nails can be countersunk and the holes filled with wood filler applied slightly higher than the surface of the plywood then sanded flush. *(American Plywood Assn.)*

GLUING

Before applying glue make sure of a good fit of the joint by testing. Both pieces should make contact at all points for lasting strength.

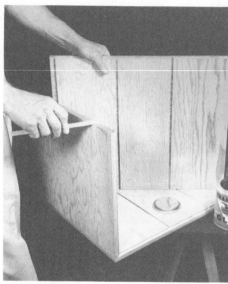

Spread glue over entire surface of joint. End grain absorbs glue rapidly so it should be given a preliminary coat. Apply a second coat after allowing the first to soak in for a few minutes.

Clamp the joints tightly with clamps, nails or screws. *(American Plywood Assn.)*

ASSEMBLING

Plan the steps of assembly. It is frequently easier to break down complex projects into sub-assemblies which make joints more accessible. Clamps should be applied with full jaw in contact. When jaws are not parallel, parts of the joint receive less pressure.

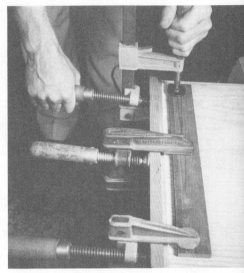

Special clamps help to do a better job. Edge clamps are used here to glue a facing edge to plywood. Bar clamps grip the panel, edge clamps bear against the edge banding stock.

A handy trick for clamping miter joints. Triangular blocks are glued to the ends of each miter, with paper in between. This will allow easy removal. Pull glued miter joint together with clamps. When joint has set pry blocks away and sand off the remaining paper. *(American Plywood Assn.)*

INSTALLING

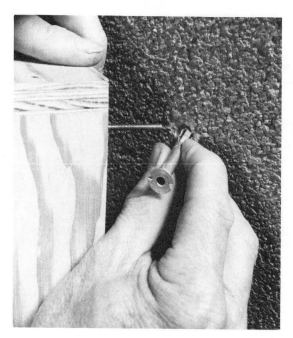

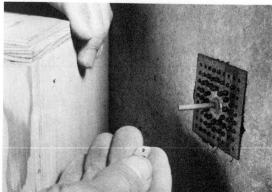

Solid masonry walls call for anchor bolts which are fastened with mastic. The square metal base is squeezed into blob of adhesive and allowed to set.

Hollow walls permit installing cabinets with screws driven directly into studs. If studs don't coincide, toggle bolts or Molly fasteners (shown) must be used. First drill hole in wall, insert Molly and tighten. Bolt is then removed and used to hang the cabinet.

DRAWER CONSTRUCTION

This drawer shown upside down is easily made with hand tools. Butt joints are glued and nailed. The bottom should be $3/8"$ or $1/2"$ plywood. The drawer front extends down to cover the front edge of the bottom. (American Plywood Assn.)

Another type of drawer made with hand tools. Additional strip of wood glued and nailed to front panel reinforces the bottom which can be made of economical ¼" fir plywood.

Drawer with extended bottom is easy to make. The overhangs serve as runners to support and guide the drawer in grooved or cleated side of cabinet.

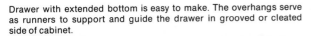

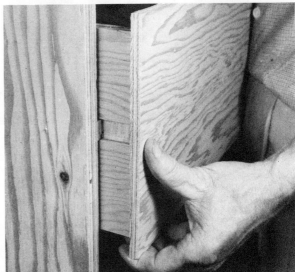

Sturdy drawers (above, left) are easy to build with power tools. Picture shows one side being put into place (it is dadoed on outer face for drawer guide). Rabbet drawer front (at right) to take sides; dado sides to fit drawer back. All four parts are grooved to take ¼" plywood bottom.

With power tools, drawer sides can be grooved (above, right) to fit over a strip of wood glued to the side of the cabinet. For a reversed procedure the strip can be attached to the drawer side and the groove made in the cabinet side before assembly.

One of the simplest methods of drawer-and-guide construction which can be made with power tools. The drawer slides in slots dadoed into the ¾" plywood cabinet sides. (American Plywood Assn.)

SHELVES

Inexpensive shelf supports. These fittings plug into blind holes drilled into the plywood sides of a cabinet. Additional holes permit moving shelves when desired. Be careful not to drill holes through. *(American Plywood Assn.)*

Combination slot and dado joints can be used for more elaborate compartmented shelves which nest in the vertical members.

Nails and glue need be used only on the side members. This type of built-in shelving requires carefully measured cuts.

CABINET BACKS

When hand tools are used, attach strips of 1/4" quarter-round molding for the back to rest against. Glue and nail the back to the molding.

Rabbeted sides are the standard method of applying backs to cabinets. Cabinet at left has rabbet just deep enough to take the plywood back flush. The version at right shows a deep set rabbet which is better for uneven walls. The lip can be trimmed wherever necessary to get a good fit between the unit and the wall.

Two methods of applying cabinet backs without rabbets or moldings. One by nailing the back flush with outside edge. Second by setting the back 1/2" from the edge.

Nail cabinet back into rabbet by driving nails at a slight angle. Use 1" brads or 4d finishing nails. (American Plywood Assn.)

EDGE TREATMENTS

There are many ways to finish plywood edges. You can achieve handsome, solid results by cutting a V groove and inserting a matching wood strip, but this method is comparatively difficult. Other suggested edge treatments are shown. *(American Plywood Assn.)*

Butt edging fir plywood construction with $1/8'' \times 3/4''$ solid wood strips. Glue and finishing nails are used.

A watered down coating or two of white glue makes an excellent sealer for exposed edges of MDO plywood which is to be painted. Edge is lightly sanded before painting. This treatment prevents the edge plies from showing through the paint.

V shaped strip of solid oak is shown being placed into a V groove cut into the edge of an oak surfaced veneer panel. Groove is made with special cutter on shaper.

Thin strips of real wood edge-banding are available, with or without pre-coated pressure sensitive adhesive. Contact cement is used to apply the non-coated strips. They're available for ordinary and cabinet species panels. *(American Plywood Assn.)*

30 Working with Hardboard

The uses for this material are quite diverse. As was mentioned earlier, there are several types of hardboard of two general kinds: plain panels that lend themselves ideally for handyman or workshop projects and the decorative wall panels. Working methods are basically similar for both kinds with a difference only in installation procedures.

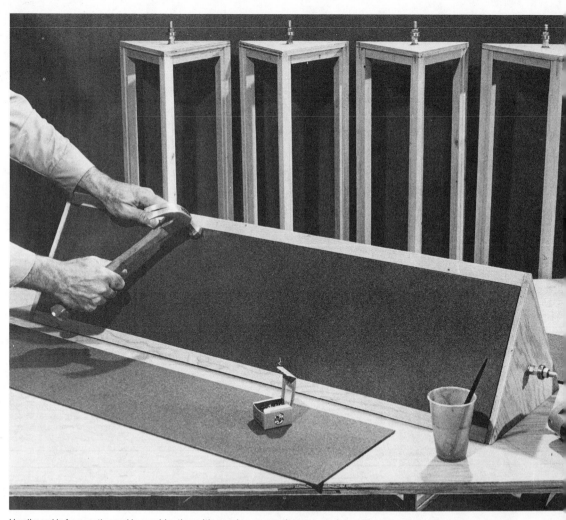

Hardboard is frequently used in combination with wood to economize on material costs.

Sawing

Hardboard can be cut with any hand or power saw using a crosscut or combination blade. Cut with the face or exposed surface up when using a hand, table or radial arm saw, and face down when using a saber or portable circular saw. For extensive cutting a carbide-tipped blade is suggested with power saws because hardboard is somewhat abrasive and a bit rough on edged tools.

Machining

Hardboard can be planed, routed, or otherwise shaped without concern about splintering or chipped corners, since it is grainless. If tools are sharp and operated at sufficiently high speed with a moderate rate of feed, smooth edges and sharp corners will result. Ragged or torn edges in the board are usually the result of dull tools. High speed drill bits will do a satisfactory job for drilling hardboard. Drill the panel face up and provide a solid backing to obtain clean holes. A block plane, with its low-angle blade, works well with hardboard. A surform tool is better; it cuts faster, and doesn't dull as quickly.

Sanding

Edges machined with sharp tools generally need little, if any, sanding but sharp edges can be eased by hand or power sanding. Sanding is also useful for slight stock removal for final fitting. Rounded or beveled edges are best done with a plane, Surform or other cutting tools then finished by sanding. Tempered hardboard presents no problem, but standard grade board becomes a bit fuzzy when sanded. If this is objectionable, apply a coat of thinned shellac after the preliminary sanding, then re-sand with a finer grade of abrasive.

Bending

Hardboard can be readily bent in one direction. Thin $1/8''$ panels can be bent to a smaller radius and with less chance of breaking than thicker boards. Also, tempered board can be bent to smaller curves than non-tempered board of equal thickness. The bendability of hardboard can be increased if it is soaked with water prior to installation. For normal application a curved form must be provided around which the panel can be bent and fastened. Start at one end and permanently fasten the panel as it is wrapped around the form.

Fastening

Hardboard can be fastened with nails, screws, glue, or adhesives. It should be fastened to a solid, continuous support at the perimeter or wherever rear supports occur. Nails or screws can be inserted as close as $1/4''$ from the edge, but $3/8''$ is better. Large panels should be fastened at the center first, then progressively toward the edges. When panels butt against a fixed member, fastening should start at the edge closest to the fixed member, then continued toward the opposite edge.

Nails should be driven perpendicular to the panel surface to avoid fiber distortion that will cause puffing or puckering around the nail. Pre-drilled holes will result in a neater job when using finishing nails that are to be sunk and filled. Holes must always be drilled for screw insertion.

Glues take quite well to standard grade hardboard that has a screened back. When applying glue to the smooth face or to tempered board, a light sanding to slightly roughen the surface will provide a better adhesion. Clamping pressure should be applied when using glues but not when installing hardboard with panel adhesives. Clamping would squeeze out the adhesive resulting in a poor bond.

Whatever the method of fastening, a slight gap should always be left between butting panels to allow for expansion that occurs during periods of high humidity. Tightly fitted panels can buckle under extreme conditions.

Some practical applications for this low cost sheet material are shown.

PERFORATED PANEL INSTALLATION

Perforated panels must be installed with fixture clearance in back. For $1/8''$ panels minimum space is $3/8''$; $3/4''$ for $1/4''$ panels. For installation over a solid wall, a $3/4'' \times 3/4''$ furring strip is required. Panels may be secured with adhesive, nails or screws.

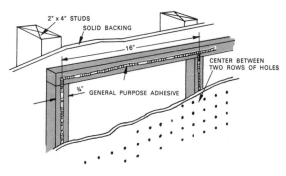

FURRING STRIP APPLICATION

Small panels may be installed free-standing, without furring. Stand-offs should be spaced at 6″ intervals along the edges and every 12″ over intermediate supports. Panels are attached directly to the studs in open-frame installations. Nails, screws or adhesive may be used over studs.

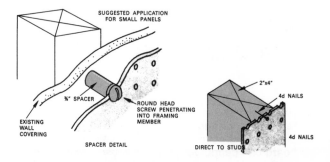

SPACER DETAIL

DIRECT TO STUDS

INTERIOR PARTITIONS

When surfacing a partition wall, nails should be spaced 4″ apart around the edges and at 8″ intervals on intermediate supports. Thin walled partitions may be constructed with 2″ x 2″ framing or studs on edge. Thin partitions do not support loads well.

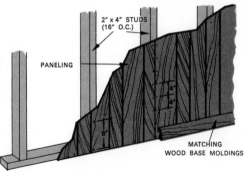

2″ x 4″ STUDS
(16″ O.C.)

PANELING

MATCHING
WOOD BASE MOLDINGS

INTERIOR PARTITION DETAILS

2″ x 4″ STUDS ON EDGE
TO REDUCE WALL THICKNESS

2″ x 2″ FRAMING MEMBERS

THIN WALL PARTITIONS

SHELF CONSTRUCTION

For sturdy construction, fasten shelves to framing with nails or screws and glue. For short span shelves $^1/_8$″ or $^3/_{16}$″ tempered hardboard is suitable. For longer spans and heavier objects, use $^1/_4$″ tempered hardboard. Note: Masonite and Presdwood are manufacturer's trade names.

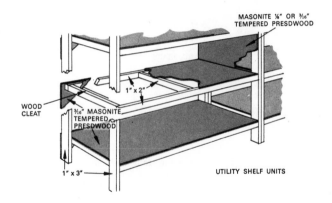

MASONITE ⅛″ OR ³⁄₁₆″
TEMPERED PRESDWOOD

1″ x 2″

WOOD
CLEAT

³⁄₁₆″ MASONITE
TEMPERED
PRESDWOOD

1″ x 3″

UTILITY SHELF UNITS

CABINET CONSTRUCTION

Cabinet framing should include a nailing or gluing surface around the perimeter of the base to support the lower panel fully. Added-on cleats may be used for this. *(Masonite Corp.)*

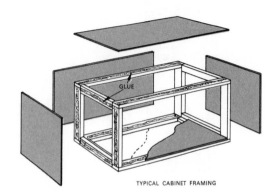

GLUE

TYPICAL CABINET FRAMING

FLUSH UTILITY DOOR

Sturdy, flush doors may be made by gluing $1/8''$ hardwood panels to both sides of a simply constructed 1" x 4" softwood frame. The frame joints may be butted, glued and held with corrugated fasteners. The door will be quite rigid if a full coating of glue is applied to both surfaces and clamped. Brads can be used in lieu of clamps.

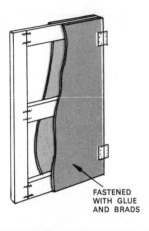

FASTENED
WITH GLUE
AND BRADS

CABINET DOORS

Several methods of cabinet door construction. The panel door at top can be made by grooving $3/4''$ stock. Note that the panel does not butt tightly in the joint to allow for expansion. Hollow and solid core doors are usually made with $1/2''$ stock. Edges can be rabbeted for semi-concealed hinge installation or they can be molded the same as any wood edge.

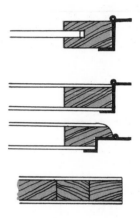

FLUSH DOOR FROM OLD PANEL DOOR

An old panel door can be salvaged and modernized by surfacing with hardboard. All exposed edges should be eased with a plane, file or sandpaper. Both surfaces must be finished in an identical manner to avoid warping. *(Masonite Corp.)*

OLD DOOR WITH ALL PAINT
OR VARNISH REMOVED

CASEIN GLUE

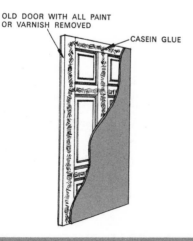

COUNTER TOPS

Counter tops may be surfaced on one side only if suitable anchoring support is provided. Otherwise both sides should be surfaced. Edges can be rounded and finished or treated with metal or plastic banding.

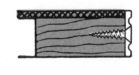
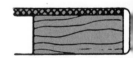
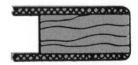

CONCRETE FORM

Complex curved forms for poured concrete footings are easy to make and inexpensive if hardboard is used for the construction.

Strips of hardboard 6″ wide by 8′ long are overlapped about 10″ and nailed together to form a long continuous strip. A brick is placed below the joint as a backstop for clinching the nails.

Detail photo shows how the long hardboard strips (some over 48′ in length) were utilized.

The resultant concrete footing would be the envy of any professional contractor. The cost for form material was about 9 dollars.

Working with particleboard is in some ways similar to working with both hardboard and plywood combined. Like hardboard, particleboard is a grainless material that can be machined with excellent results, but it too is rough for extensive usage on non-carbide tools. As for its similarity to plywood, particleboard is generally available in the same large panel sizes and in standard thicknesses of ³/₈″, ¹/₂″ and ³/₄″. Therefore it can be used like plywood as a self-supporting structural material. The similarity ceases there because particleboard costs considerably less than plywood.

TYPICAL PARTICLEBOARD JOINTS

Particleboard parts may be joined in much the same manner as lumber or plywood. Shown are a few of the joints which work well with this material. (*U. S. Plywood*)

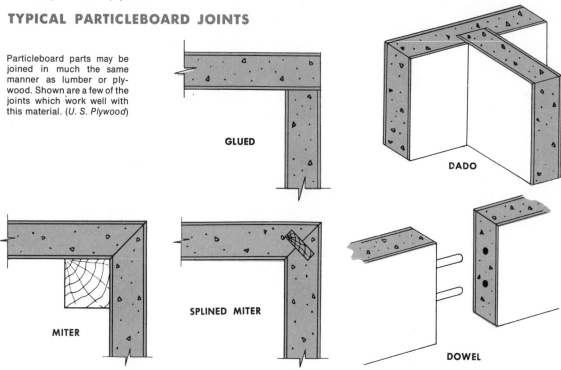

GLUED

DADO

MITER

SPLINED MITER

DOWEL

USES. Particleboard has fine characteristics of strength and durability and is widely used in industry to manufacture many of the things that surround you in your own home—doors, cabinets and furniture, to name a few. However, it has never caught on strongly as a do-it-yourself construction material. The reasons why are difficult to pinpoint, but it may be due to the fact that particleboard is not easily worked with hand tools and it is very abrasive on tool edges.

If economy is of interest to you, these are some of the possibilities for its use: The ³/₈″ thickness is especially suitable for wall paneling and wainscoting and for small cabinet doors and sliding cupboard doors. Panels of ¹/₂″ thickness can be used for drawer construction. The huskier ³/₄″ material is useful for partitions, sliding passage doors, and stable, warp-resistant core stock under wood veneers, and decorative plastic laminate surfaces. It is also suitable for shelving. 30″ span is the recommended maximum, but adding the support of rigid bracing greatly increases the strength of the shelf. The following are the few facts you need to know about working with this inexpensive manufactured wood that is stronger than wood.

PARTICLEBOARD EDGE TREATMENTS

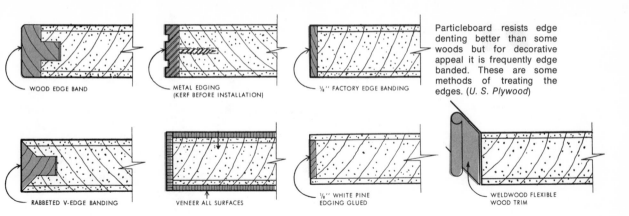

WOOD EDGE BAND

METAL EDGING
(KERF BEFORE INSTALLATION)

1/8'' FACTORY EDGE BANDING

Particleboard resists edge denting better than some woods but for decorative appeal it is frequently edge banded. These are some methods of treating the edges. (*U. S. Plywood*)

RABBETED V-EDGE BANDING

VENEER ALL SURFACES

1/8'' WHITE PINE EDGING GLUED

WELDWOOD FLEXIBLE WOOD TRIM

SAWING. Much of what was said about working with hardboard also applies to particleboard. Completely grainless, knot-free wood having no flaws, cracks or imperfections, it can be cut with either crosscut or rip saw blades. Blades that make smooth cuts in wood will similarly produce smooth edges in this material. A sharp blade properly aligned will cut 45 degree bevels along an edge with no appreciable chipping.

EDGE MACHINING. Any shape that can be routed or shaped on wood can be made on particleboard. Although fairly smooth cuts can be accomplished, some porousness will result in the exposed edge. This can be remedied by filling if the edge is to remain exposed.

DRILLING. Drilling particleboard will present no problem if the work is properly backed up to prevent chipping when the tool breaks through the back of the panel. Clamp the back up block firmly for trouble free results. Fly cutters and hole saws usually cut better holes than spade bits.

EDGE TREATMENTS. Edges of particleboard are very rarely left exposed. They can be concealed in much the same manner as is done with plywood edges. This includes the use of natural wood veneers, solid wood strips, molding, metal T molding, or strips of plastic laminate. Contact cement is used to apply laminate edging or thin wood veneer and regular glue with good gap-filling quality for attaching the heavier wood edges.

FASTENING. Nails should be used only with glue, never alone. Glue should also be used with screws for lasting joints because the screw-holding properties of particleboard closely approximate those of soft pine lumber. While ordinary wood screws are adequate, much better results are obtained with sheet metal screws. Pilot holes should always be drilled for screws; however, unlike with ordinary wood, they should be of minimum diameter—about 1/4 the root diameter of the screw. Avoid overturning screws as they are driven. A drop of glue in the screw hole is always helpful.

FINISHING. Particleboard generally requires very little sanding to render it ready for finishing. A finishing sander equipped with 220 grit paper will usually suffice. A filler and sealer application should be used before painting, enameling, or clear finishing.

SIMPLE PARTICLEBOARD CONSTRUCTION

A simple toy chest made inexpensively with particleboard. It is quite tough and can take much abuse.

The material is rather heavy so it is a good idea to cut it down to working size before taking it to the table saw for further machining. If necessary, it can be worked completely with portable tools.

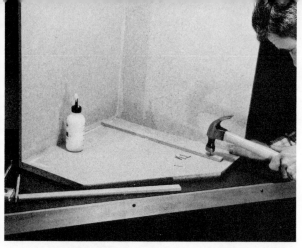

Nails don't hold particularly well in this material so glue must always be used for lasting joints.

Although other joints are stronger, ordinary butt joints, glued and reinforced with screws, prove quite serviceable.

Screws can be inserted close to the edge of the board. Small, 1/4" screws have very little bite here but will hold because of their number. A drop of glue on each screw helps considerably. With regular small hinges, through bolts would be much better.

The Surform tool is a good one to use for rounding off corners. An ordinary plane would become dull quite rapidly on this material. The tooled edges require sanding but not the surfaces; they're factory sanded to perfection and ready for finishing.

The back and front of this drawer are made of 3/4" particleboard, the sides and bottom are 3/8". Note how the front has been treated with a deep rabbet.

Moldings provide the finished touch to work. They are used to the greatest extent in interior remodeling around windows and doors and to conceal the seams and joints in wall paneling work. They can be used to break up the monotony of large, plain walls or surfaces or to add dimension to small ones.

Moldings also serve a major decorative purpose in furniture construction and many molded shapes can be formed directly on the work in a shop equipped with the necessary tools. There are situations, however, which require the use of added-on molding regardless of the availability of shaping tools. A typical example would be a raised outline molding on a cabinet door or drawer front. There is no simpler nor more practical way to accomplish this than with molding added on.

Molding treatments may vary from simple base and casing applications to more elaborate wall and ceiling treatments. Machine carved moldings are relatively inexpensive and easily installed. (Armstrong Cork)

The simplest and most practical way to obtain a recessed panel effect such as this is by adding molding around the front edges of each of the doors.

Plain edges can be readily transformed into fancy ones with the use of common moldings. This project utilized ready made moldings throughout.

A scrap of wood and some picture frame molding are combined to make an interesting wall clock, quickly and at low cost.

Ready-made molding can prove advantageous to you if you don't have the necessary equipment to shape fancy edges. A simply constructed table or cabinet made with plain edges can suddenly be transformed into a fancier piece with the addition of molding. Many otherwise ordinary projects can be given the final touch of professionalism with the use of molding.

For shop projects, molding joints are usually cut quickly and accurately on a table or radial arm saw. Involved jobs of molding fitting, such as are encountered in room remodeling projects, are tackled by hand sawing with the aid of a miter box. It would be too inconvenient to make the countless trips to the shop to make the many cuts required. So, regardless of how well your shop is equipped with power tools, keep a handsaw ready; you may have to rely on it when you decide to panel some walls.

Commonly available hardwood molding with matching curved corner sections which are pre-mitered are generally used for cabinet doors and drawer fronts. Here's another use for them. Miters need be cut only on the straight strips to the desired length.

This frame combines shop work and ready made molding. The main frame was made with basic table saw cuts then painted. The delicate trim molding was cut to fit, painted in contrasting color then glued in.

MITERING A MOLDING

Mitering a Molding. For accuracy, set miter box saw at 45 degrees, trim each of the two mitering members in opposite cuts so together they form a tight right angle. This method is used to miter moldings that are applied to one-plane surfaces such as doors, windows and picture frames. (*Western Wood Products Assn.*)

COPING A MOLDING

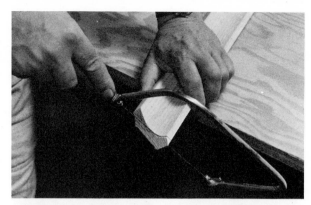

Coping a Molding. A coped joint is usually used where moldings meet at inside corners. It's preferred over a miter joint because it conceals irregularities better. Set the molding in the miter box in the position that it is to be installed on the wall; upright against the backplate. Trim at a 45 degree angle. Remaining profile serves as a guideline for the coping saw. Follow the contour on the face to trim away the mitered wedge. Fit the profile against the face of adjoining molding, imperfections in sawing will be invisible except at closest inspection. This method is used for moldings applied to two-planed surfaces, such as cornices, chair rails and baseboards (*Western Wood Products Assn.*)

The coped cut is effectively made with the coping saw regardless of how complex the shape. The side of a pencil point passed over the end will make the line of cut easier to follow.

BLENDING MOLDINGS

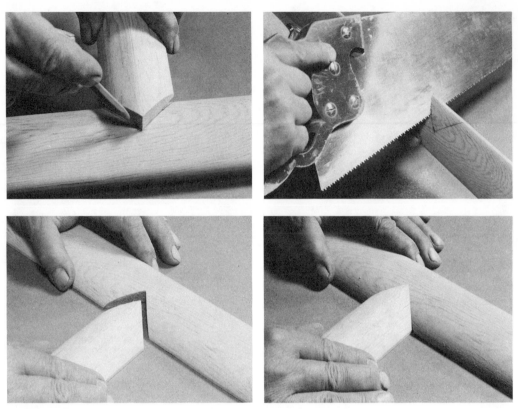

Blending a Molding . . . at right angle. The intersecting molding must be one that is of symmetrical design such as half rounds or other moldings which have both halves of the pattern balanced in design. Trim the intersecting (middle) molding to a point with two 45 degree cuts. Use the point as a pattern to trace the cutout on the molding to be intersected. Carefully saw out the V and install. Where sharp edges still remain, soften with sandpaper. (*Western Wood Products Assn.*)

A variation of the intersecting cut. The middle piece is cut to a point as above. The upper moldings require first a 45 degree miter cut which allows them to meet, then a 45 degree bevel cut at mid-point to form the V.

BLIND NAILING

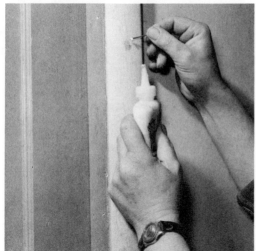

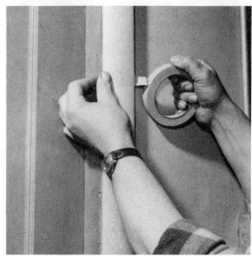

Blind Nailing. This is a novel method of installing molding which is to be clear-finished. Carefully gouge up a sliver wide enough so that the head of a finishing nail can be buried in the cavity. Drive the nail and set it then glue the sliver back into place. Use tape to hold it until glue dries. A touch of sandpaper will remove all traces of the fastening method. (*Western Wood Products Assn.*)

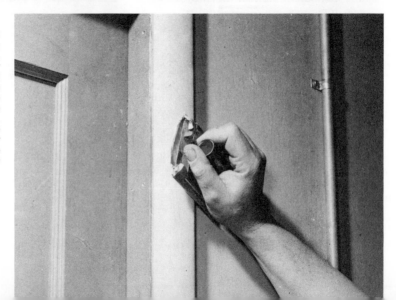

There are several useful techniques for bending wood with which you should become acquainted. They will enable you to expand the scope of your woodworking activities considerably. The methods include lamination, kerfing, and self-forming of skin plywood. Wood can also be bent by steaming, but this method is not covered here due to its difficulty of handling and the necessity for special equipment.

The wood-bending procedures shown are practical because they require no special equipment and are easily accomplished in the home workshop. The three methods are quite varied, each one being best-suited for a particular kind of application. The possibilities are almost unlimited.

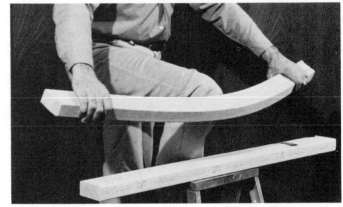

It doesn't require too much muscle to bend a piece of heavy stock if you prepare it for the purpose.

Lamination

The curved chair frame illustrated is a good example of the advantage of bending wood to shape by the lamination method. Each of the curved side members are made from a relatively small board. To make these same parts by band sawing out of a solid board would be impractical and disadvantageous for several reasons. It would be virtually impossible to obtain a solid board of sufficient width. The alternative of edge-joining several boards to make a wide one would be a poor solution because it would result in a tremendous amount of cut-off waste and, more important, the cut out part would be very weak at the end grain portions that would occur in several places.

Bending wood by the lamination process simply involves cutting a board into a num-

This chair was made with the bent lamination method which keeps material costs down and produces curved parts with high structural strength.

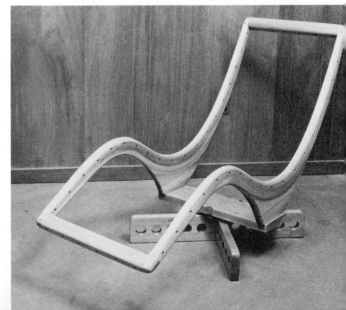

ber of thin, flexible strips, then gluing them back together again in a bent shape. The resultant curved piece has great strength primarily because the grain of the wood runs exactly parallel to the curve, thus there are no end grain portions along the contour. Also, it is actually stronger than the original board due to the stiffening effect of the glue layers and tensions caused by compression and expansion of the wood fibers along both sides of the individual strips.

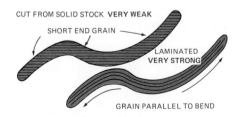

Comparison of grain direction between a part cut from a solid board and a laminated one. Note weak end grain areas on the cut out piece.

The procedure is relatively simple: the wood is cut into thin flexible strips then reassembled with glue into a bent bundle in a form jig.

While both hardwoods and softwoods can be bent, hardwoods are better suited for the purpose. Ash, birch, elm, hickory, maple, oak, sweet gum, and walnut are the hardwoods commonly used. Among the softwoods, Douglas fir, redwood, southern yellow pine, and white cedar work best.

Slow-setting hide glue that has good gap-filling properties is suitable for laminating wood for interior projects. Resorcinol resin waterproof glue should be used for outdoor constructions.

LAMINATING PROCEDURES

1 Thin strips $3/32''$ or smaller are ripped with a fairly smooth cutting blade. The stock should be straight grained, knot-free and without cracks or other flaws. Work from a single board when possible to maintain a continuous grain pattern if the piece is to be clear finished.

2 All strips should be kept in their original positions. This is important because grain characteristics vary throughout a board. Mis-matched grain could cause some difficulty in obtaining a close fitting bundle. Number each strip in sequence.

3 An outline of the desired curve is drawn full size on wrapping paper. Make tracings for forming blocks at key locations along the curve.

6 Glue is applied to both surfaces of each strip in full coats and the strips stacked one atop the other until all have been coated. Glue should by no means be of the quick setting type —plenty of assembly time is needed.

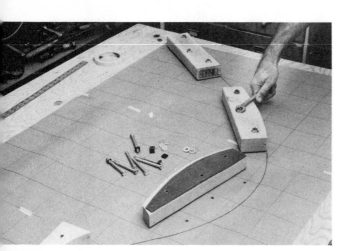

4 Forming blocks are cut from 2 x 4 lumber about 12 inches long. Locate the curve through the blocks so that sufficient cut-off remains to produce a matching clamping block. Bolt the main formers into the work surface. The dark piece is a ⅛" hardboard spacer.

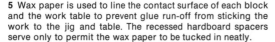

5 Wax paper is used to line the contact surface of each block and the work table to prevent glue run-off from sticking the work to the jig and table. The recessed hardboard spacers serve only to permit the wax paper to be tucked in neatly.

7 Clamping starts at one end and progresses towards the other. Note the clamping block behind the former. This is put into place before the clamp is applied.

8 A thick bundle like this requires some help when making the return curve (assistant is out of view). Lessened leverage at this stage necessitates bending only several pieces at a time and clamping temporarily.

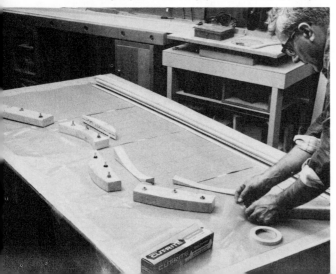

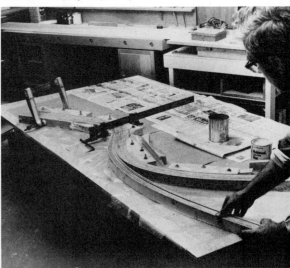

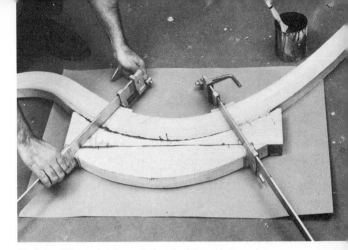

9 Clamps should not be spared for a job of this size. Work remains clamped for twice the usual time to allow the glue to dry thoroughly and to gain full strength.

12 One nail is used at the end of each of the added-on pieces to prevent slipping. They're driven in only part way to facilitate later removal.

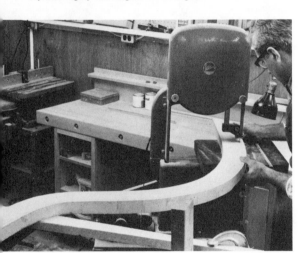

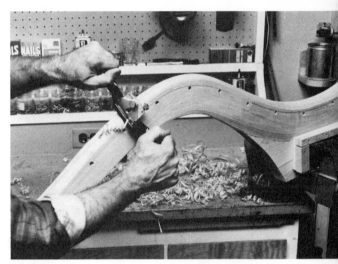

10 After removing excess surface glue with a belt sander the piece is band sawed to the precise shape. The lamination should be made oversize to allow for trimming.

11 Small sections need not be laminated. Note how the cut-off is added to the bottom to economize on lumber.

13 Final touches include rounding with spokeshave and sanding surfaces smooth.

14 Cross members are joined with strong doweled lap joints.

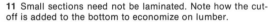

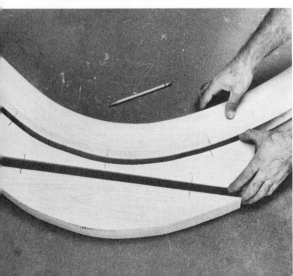

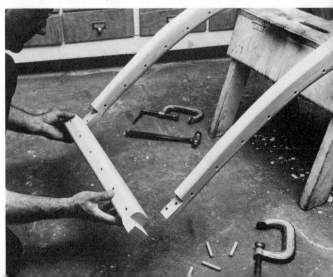

KERFING

A solid board can be rendered quite flexible by sawing into it a series of kerfs close together to within about $\frac{1}{16}''$ of the outside surface. The spacing between kerfs and their depth are variables which depend on the kind of wood used and the complexity of the bend desired. They can be closely approximated by making a simple measurement as shown in the diagram.

The graceful sweeping curves of this all-wood construction are its main attraction. It illustrates what can be done by means of the kerf bending method.

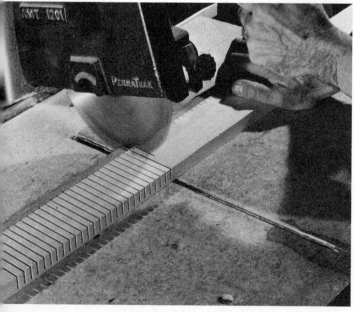

Kerfing (deep saw cuts) is done across the grain. The depth of the grooves and the spacing between them control the degree of bend that can be obtained.

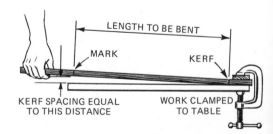

To determine spacing distance between kerfs: Make one test kerf, bend the wood until the kerf closes then measure the distance from the mark to the table. This dimension is what the spacing should be.

When a wide board (about 1') is to be bent, it is advisable to make an actual test on a narrow strip of the same material. This will fairly well reflect how a wider piece will react.

Kerfs need not be equally spaced. If the curve required includes small and large bends, the spacing can vary accordingly: the closer the spacing, the sharper the bend.

If the piece is to be free standing, it may be strengthened by filling the kerf spaces with thick glue or wood putty forced into the grooves prior to bending. Another means for stiffening the piece is by gluing on a facing or backing of thin flexible plywood.

The kerfing method is useful for forming the aprons on circular or round cornered tables, curved drawer fronts, and varied projects of a diverse nature.

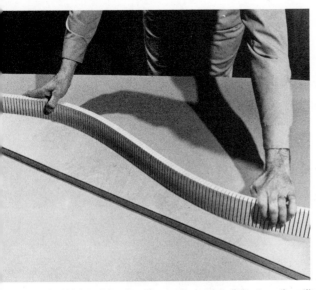

A kerfed board bends quite readily but has little strength until it is supported as it will be against this solid member. A mixture of fine sawdust and glue worked into the grooves will add rigidity.

Ready made grooved oak molding used for installing hardboard filigree panels can be kerfed to permit edgewise bends. This approach makes possible novel curved installations. Kerfs must be very thin, made with a band or jig saw. Glue filler plus a thin plywood facing on the rear surface make it sufficiently strong.

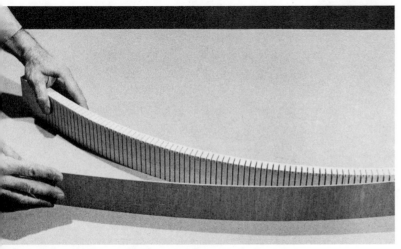

Another method of reinforcing the strip is by gluing on a thin layer of flexible plywood.

A KERF-BENT PROJECT

Due to the unusual nature of the workshop-built car body shown on page 390, some of the key points of its construction are shown. The intent is not to induce you to build your own (although it is a lot of fun), but it is felt that some of the related procedures of construction may prove useful to you in other projects.

1 The job starts off with a laminated bend: doubled up 1″ x 6″ boards glued and clamped while in a curved position will form the basic frame. A temporary stringer bows the sides.

2 Waterproof glue, lag screws and nuts and bolts are used to make a sturdy frame.

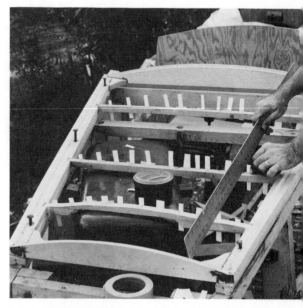

3 A straightedge and paper tabs solve a tricky problem. Paper tabs are taped to temporary sticks to obtain outline shape for ribs. Papers are moved up to ruler's bottom edge then taped. Sticks are then lifted out, and the outline formed by the papers is transferred to wood panels and then cut out.

4 Ribs with varied curvature turn out just right with the paper tab method. Accuracy is essential here in order to obtain a good glue contact surface overall.

5 Plywood hood panel is set into rabbet and clamped. A block plane is used to make final adjustments for a perfect fit.

8 Kerfing one of the fender sections. The depth of the grooves can be deepened with a second pass if the part doesn't bend sufficiently on the first try.

6 Protective wood strips help to distribute the clamping pressure evenly. The number of clamps is not excessive. They're needed because the skin in this case is $5/16''$ thick. This is quite heavy for a dry, self forming bend without kerfs.

7 Cardboard mock-up can be most helpful in working out basic design details.

9 Note how the kerf spacing has been varied so that the board is not weakened unnecessarily where only a moderate bend will be required.

10 Sufficient clamp pressure is essential for this kind of a glue-up. Skin being glued to the kerfed section is $1/4''$ marine grade mahogany veneer plywood. Waterproof glue but no nails or screws were used on any of the surfacing veneers.

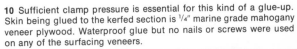

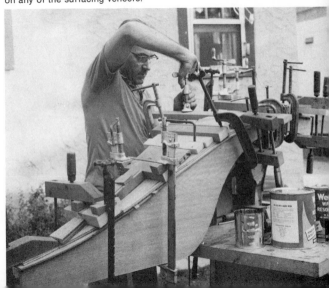

11 Veneer plywood is glued on beyond edges of project sides, then trimmed flush with the router.

12 Detail view of a rear fender kerfing before addition of skirt and plywood surfacing. When completed the unit is remarkably strong. Sawdust and glue will be pressed into the grooves.

Detail view of engine housing shows another kerf-bent section. Kerfing offers unlimited design possibilities.

elf Forming

Thin three-ply ⅛″ plywood, usually referred to as "skin", is flexible enough to bend into curves of relatively small radius. These panels will not bend equally as well in both directions, however. The greatest flexibility occurs on the axis of the surface grain direction, as indicated in the diagram.

The skin is bent and glued into place directly on the work, which can be of open, ribbed construction. Ribs or supports must be built in at various locations to provide ample gluing surfaces. Clamps should be used whenever possible but small, headed nails can be used to make gluing contact if clamping is not feasible. Finishing nails or brads should be avoided because the wood may pop through the small heads.

Non-supported free standing small parts, such as curved chair backs, can be made by laminating a number of pieces of skin plywood between a form. The form for a typical chair back is made by nailing three lengths of 2′ x 6′ construction lumber into a thick block. A band saw cut is made through the block in the desired curve. The glued bundle of plywood is clamped between the two halves of the form. The maximum number of pieces of about 18″ in length that can be handled comfortably by this method is five or six.

Skin plywood is easy to bend provided the grain runs in the proper direction. Glue and nails spaced about 1 inch apart are OK for a bend like this. Clamps are needed to keep the front end from popping out.

1/8″ BENDABLE PLYWOOD (3 PLY)

This drawing shows grain direction for bending skin plywood.

This is how the skin treatment shapes up on the front end of this early automobile model, a novel project.

This is a well constructed framing for bent wood installation. It affords ample gluing surface and the panel will not be exposed at the edges.

Piece is carefully test fitted before application of glue.

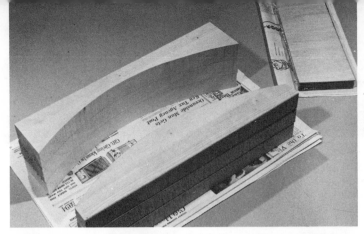

This is a simple form made with triple stacked 2 x 6 lumber. It can be used to laminate ⅛" plywood for curved drawer fronts or chair backs.

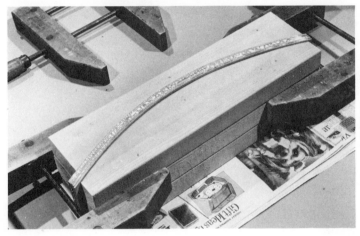

The plywood is well coated with glue on both sides and sandwiched between the two halves of the form. This is a handy, quick method for small jobs.

The floor section must support weight. Therefore a heavier, ⅜" plywood is used. This requires kerfing to form the bend.

A deep wide dado is another method used to make sharp bends for some applications. After a piece like this has been installed, the weakened corner should be backed up with glue blocks or packed with spackle.

54 Paneling Walls

Attractive and maintenance-free paneling offers the ideal solution to problem walls or those that are just plain boring. The almost infinite variety of wall paneling that is available will enable you to transform an ordinary room into a distinctive interior with relative ease. If you can measure accurately and use a saw and hammer properly, you can panel a wall.

Prefinished hardwood veneer paneling is good looking and handsomely at home in any room of the house. (*U.S. Plywood*)

This deeply textured hardboard paneling faithfully duplicates the charm of weathered barnwood. Large 4' × 8' panels go up quickly. They're washable and almost indestructible. *(Masonite Corp.)*

Existing Walls

Test the wall with a scrap of paneling (or wood) and a dab of adhesive to determine whether the adhesive will hold when contemplating a direct-to-wall installation. Adhesives may not stick to certain paints.

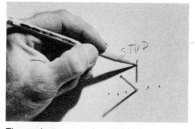

The easiest way to locate hidden studs is by probing with a nail, or using a stud finder available at hardware stores. Studs are not always evenly spaced so they should be located and marked.

Paneling can be applied directly to an existing wall, to furring strips, or on open studs. It can be readily installed against any dry, even wall without special preparation. If the wall is very old and broken or very uneven, furring will be required. Eveness can be checked out by sighting with a long, straight board.

Masonry walls should always be furred to provide an air space between their damp surface and the panel. If dampness is excessive, especially on below-grade portions, a coating with waterproofing cement paint is recommended before attaching the furring. Special hardened masonry nails can be used, but the easiest way to attach the furring is with adhesive.

Open studs can be used as a direct base for panels provided they are spaced properly at 16" on center so that a panel joint will fall on the center of a stud every four feet. If only a few discrepancies exist, extra studs where needed will solve the problem. Otherwise furring strips should be employed.

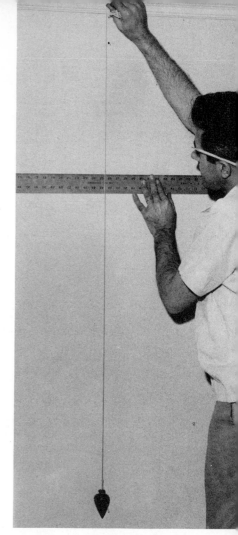

It is absolutely essential that the first panel be started perfectly plumb to insure that the following ones will also be true. Use a plumb line to mark a guideline for the placement of the first panel.

FURRING

Furring refers to strips of wood, usually 1" × 2", that are attached horizontally around the walls spaced 16" apart with vertical members applied at 48" centers. Furring, shimmed at low spots on the wall to establish even planes, provides a suitable base for the panels. Furring is also applied around doors, windows, and other openings.

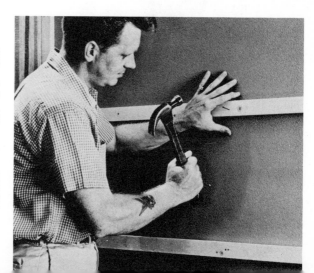

Furring strips, 1" × 2", are nailed into the old wall at stud locations, horizontally around the room. They're spaced 16" apart. Vertical furring must also be applied where panel edges are to be attached. Furring may also be attached with adhesive. (*Masonite Corp.*)

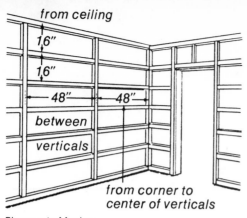

from ceiling

1,6"

1,6"

←— 48" —→|←— 48" —→

between

verticals

from corner to
center of verticals

Placement of furring.

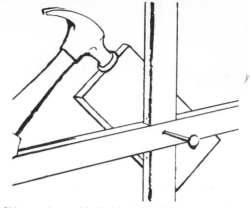

Shims are inserted behind furring to bring out a low spot.
Nail must be driven through the shim to secure it.

HOW MANY PANELS?

Determine your panel needs by adding the length of the walls and divide by 4, assuming the panels are standard 4' wide. For example, for a 16' × 24' room you add 16' + 16' and 24' + 24' which totals 80'. Divide by 4 and you'll find that you will require 20 panels. The cutouts which you'll make for doors and windows can be used to panel above and below the windows and above the doors.

ACCLIMATING PANELS

Allow the panels to become conditioned to the temperature and humidity of the room in which they are to be installed by storing them there for a few days before use. Also, since natural wood panels have variations in color and graining, it is advisable to stand the panels around the room in the sequence that gives the most pleasing effect. Number the panel backs in the order they are to be installed.

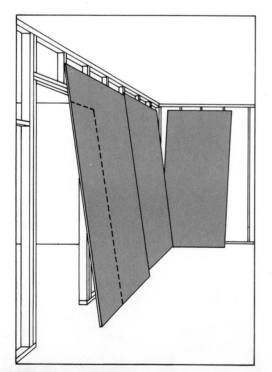

Place the panels around the room to judge the most desirable sequence of installation. Use crayon to mark the order on the back of each panel.

Stack the panels for a few days in the room to be decorated to acclimate them to the new surroundings. Furring in between allows air circulation. *(U.S. Plywood)*

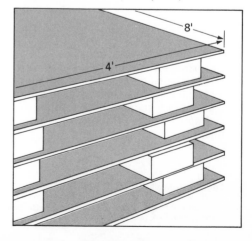

8'

4'

Installing Panels

Paneling generally starts at a corner but not always. If there is a fireplace or picture window, you may want to start on either side or at the center of it. Regardless of where you start, the first panel is the important one because it will establish the vertical alignment of the others. Most corners are not perfectly true, thus necessitating trimming of the first panel to fit. A compass or divider is used to transfer the outline of the corner to the panel. Place the panel a few inches from the corner using a level to get it perfectly plumb vertically. A few temporary nails at the top will hold it in place. Run one point of the divider along the corner while the other scribes a line on the panel. Trim the panel to fit. The total amount trimmed off should allow the other edge of the panel to fall on the center line of the vertical furring or stud. If the corner is only slightly irregular or out of plumb, it may not be necessary to trim at all if molding is to be used.

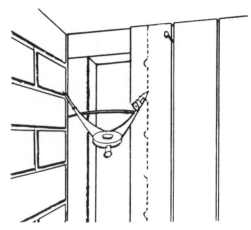

Use a compass to scribe the outline of an irregular or out of plumb corner to the first panel. This is not necessary for small irregularities which can be covered with molding.

Panels may be installed by nailing or with adhesive. The adhesive method results in a neater job with no nails showing on the surface. If nails are used with plywood paneling, they should be set and filled with matching putty. Special matching-colored nails are available for hardboard paneling if you prefer nailing. A caulking gun is used to apply the adhesive in a continuous ribbon around the entire perimeter area about $1/2''$ in from the panel edge. Three-inch beads are applied 6 inches apart on all horizontal furring or at $16''$ intervals down a plain wall. Methods of applying adhesives vary with the product. Always check the manufacturer's instructions on this.

Butt the edges of plywood paneling against the previously installed panel and continue around the room. If you are installing hardboard paneling, you must leave a slight space between joints to allow for expansion—about $1/16''$. For the same reason, hardboard panels should never be tightly fitted between the ceiling and floor.

Panels can be cut with hand or power saws. Drill saw entry holes at corners of cutout areas. Use fine tooth blade to prevent excessive chipping.

Cartridge packed adhesive is applied to furring with a caulking gun. Three inch beads are spaced about 6 inches apart. (*U.S. Plywood*)

401

Panels are half-nailed at the top to allow necessary hinge action for setting the adhesive. Nails are driven into grooves when possible.

Panel is pressed into adhesive (right) then pulled away and held for about 10 minutes with a prop to allow the solvent to partly evaporate. Some adhesives work differently; they should be checked out in the instructions.

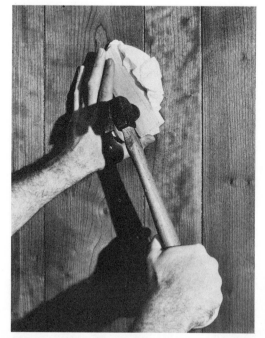

Panel is pressed (left) into place firmly, then tapped gently with a block of wood wrapped in cloth to assure overall contact of the adhesive and wood surfaces.

Cardboard templates are very handy for obtaining the cutting pattern for hard-to-fit pieces.

 # Molding

The regular-type of molding is applied after all the paneling has been installed. Extruded moldings, commonly used with hardboard paneling, must be applied as the job progresses, since they fit around the edge of the panel. When paneling completely around four walls of a room, however, the first corner panel goes up without a vertical molding. The last panel on the fourth wall gets the molding instead, so that it butts up against the edge of the first panel to conceal the joint.

TYPES OF MOLDINGS AND THEIR USES

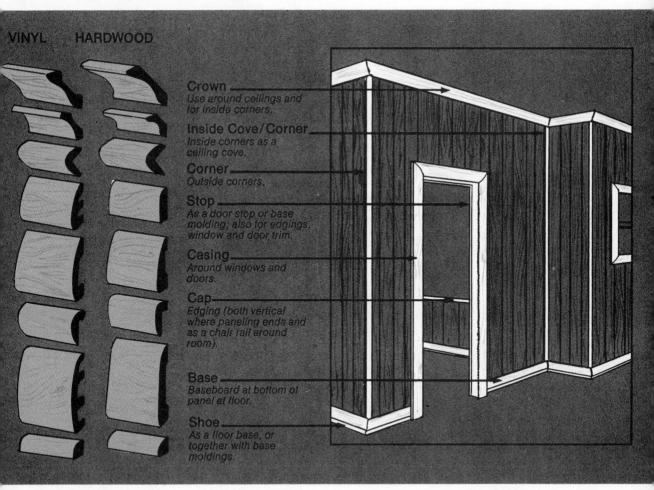

VINYL   HARDWOOD

Crown
Use around ceilings and for inside corners.

Inside Cove/Corner
Inside corners as a ceiling cove.

Corner
Outside corners.

Stop
As a door stop or base molding; also for edgings, window and door trim.

Casing
Around windows and doors.

Cap
Edging (both vertical where paneling ends and as a chair rail around room).

Base
Baseboard at bottom of panel at floor.

Shoe
As a floor base, or together with base moldings.

Types of moldings and their uses. Moldings are made in natural wood and matching vinyls for hardwood and hardboard panels. (*U.S. Plywood*)

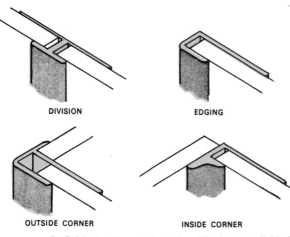

DIVISION

EDGING

OUTSIDE CORNER

INSIDE CORNER

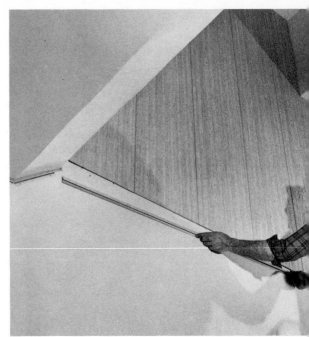

Prefinished color coordinated moldings are available in aluminum or plastic designs that fit all kinds of wall paneling. (*Masonite Corp.*)

Aluminum divider strip molding permits installation of panels over panels on a tall wall. It forms a very neat joint.

Corner moldings are used in this installation to terminate the paneling. The last two sections will slide into the grooves.

Vinyl-covered wood baseboard molding matches the paneling; is used in conjunction with the extruded aluminum molding.

Other Paneling

All paneling doesn't measure 4' × 8'. Solid wood paneling is available in regular or random widths with various joint treatments. This is generally installed to furring by toe-nailing at an angle through the tongue of each panel into the furring. The nails must be countersunk to allow the next panel to fit without obstruction. The nails are concealed by the groove of the next panel.

Hardboard paneling is also available in plank size, which is 16" × 8', with interlocking tongue and groove edges. Three such panels measure 4' wide so that the furring arrangement detailed for standard 4' × 8' panels also applies. Special metal clips are supplied with these panels to facilitate automatic spacing between joints. Although these planks are smaller, thus requiring more handling to cover a given area, they are also lighter and easier to handle than the large panels.

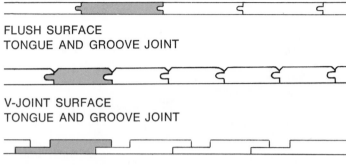

**FLUSH SURFACE
TONGUE AND GROOVE JOINT**

**V-JOINT SURFACE
TONGUE AND GROOVE JOINT**

**CHANNEL SURFACE
LAPPED JOINT**

A number of solid wood paneling profiles are available. Three typical types are shown.

TONGUE AND GROOVE

Tongue and groove paneling up to six inches in width should be blind nailed through the base of the tongue into the cross-blocking or nailing strips of the supporting wall. The nails should be countersunk to allow for flush application of the next panel.

Tongue and groove paneling more than six inches in width requires surface nailing as illustrated below. Countersink all surface nails. Since wood tones vary with the type of finish selected, nail holes are best concealed with a matching putty *after the final surface finish has been applied*.

LAPPED

Lapped paneling less than six inches wide should be surface nailed using the standard countersink-and-fill method.

For lapped paneling more than six inches wide, use an additional surface nail taking care to avoid nailing through the underlying lap. Both nails should be countersunk below the surface of the paneling. Since wood tones vary with the type of finish selected, nail holes are best concealed with a matching putty *after the final surface finish has been applied*.

Solid lumber paneling nailing techniques. Finishing nails should be long enough to penetrate at least an inch into the framing members. For all paneling up to ¾" thick, 2" nails are recommended.

35 Applying Plastic Laminate

Among the many advantages of plastic laminate as a surfacing material is the ease with which it can be applied. Laminate is no longer used primarily for sink and counter tops, as it once was. Smart furniture, book shelves, and built-ins can also be durably and decoratively surfaced with this versatile material.

The basic steps of working with laminate are simple and few, involving cutting, coating with adhesive, applying to the work, and trimming. The base material to which the sheet is bonded needs no special preparation with the exception that it should be clean, dry and smooth, and with no holes or voids.

Plastic laminates can be used for many applications other than sink and counter tops. This laminate-surfaced chair is an example.

CUTTING

Laminate sheet is generally cut $1/8''$ to $1/4''$ oversize. This allows some leeway for alignment with the part to which it is to be applied, while at the same time providing the means of obtaining accurate joints through flush trimming procedures. There are situations when the laminate is to be applied in an enclosed area, in which case it must be cut to exact size.

Cutting can be done with a handsaw, any of the power saws, or by scoring with a knife or awl. Fine-toothed saw blades should be used to avoid chipping. The decorative surface faces up for all but the saber and portable circular saw. Score cutting is better suited to the $1/32''$ sheet, but it can also be used with $1/16''$ laminate. The line should be made with several passes of the knife or awl, especially on the heavier sheet, to insure cutting through deeply enough. The piece is then carefully bent to break it free. After cutting and before applying adhesive, the edges should be lightly sanded or filed to remove any loose chips that could cause a poor bond if they get onto the bonding surfaces.

When cutting plastic laminate with a saber saw the decorative side should be face down. A paper pattern is a helpful guide when cutting an odd shaped piece which has a surface design that must be properly oriented. Ordinarily a penciled line will do.

APPLYING CEMENT

Contact cement is the adhesive used to bond the laminate. There are both flammable and non-flammable types. They work equally well, but extreme caution is advised when working with the former. It should never be used near open flame, sparking motors, or without adequate ventilation. The cement can be applied with a paint brush, roller, or a special serrated spreader. An even, full coat is applied to both surfaces, then allowed to dry, usually about one-half hour. Sufficient drying is important for a good bond and this is easily determined by lightly touching the surface with a scrap of kraft paper. It will pull away clean without sticking when the cement is properly dry.

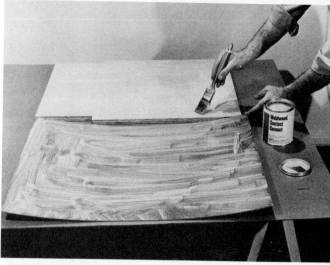

Applying contact cement with a brush. Full coats are put on both surfaces and allowed to dry thoroughly before joining. There is no urgency to assemble the parts because they'll bond up to an hour after drying.

APPLYING THE LAMINATE

Once the two coated surfaces touch, they bond immediately and no further adjustment of position is possible. Therefore the laminate sheet must be accurately positioned before contact is made. This is best done with the kraft paper slip sheet method.

Cut two pieces of kraft (brown wrapping paper) and place them on the wood surface so that they overlap each other several inches at the center, making sure they cover the entire glued area. Place the laminate sheet on the paper and position it as required. While holding the laminate in place at one end so it doesn't shift, lift the other end and slip out the first sheet of paper. Allow the laminate to make contact, then remove the remaining sheet of paper.

No clamping is required with contact cement, but momentary pressure should be applied to insure total contact. Pressure can be applied with a small roller or by tapping a small block of wood firmly with a hammer.

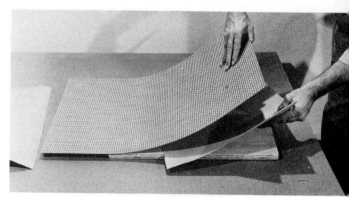

Cemented surfaces cannot be shifted after contact is made so they must be accurately aligned. Slip-out paper method is fool proof. The second sheet of wrapping paper is removed after the laminate has made contact.

Block and hammer are used to insure intimate contact between cemented surfaces. A smooth block is usually used but when working with a deeply embossed sheet like this, a block with felt padding is a good idea.

A router makes easy work of trimming off the excess material flush to the edge. A plane can be used but the blade will need frequent sharpening. A mill file can be used as an alternate.

TRIMMING

The excess laminate overhanging the edges can be trimmed flush with a block plane or file, but a router equipped with a flush-trimming bit will do a better and much faster job. The special router bit has a rolling pilot tip that automatically controls the depth of cut. The router is moved along the surface, while the pilot rides against the edge of the work cutting the sheet absolutely flush to the edge. A second bit is used to produce a beveled edge after two pieces have been joined at right angles. This bit, usually available with a 25 degree bevel, is also self-piloted.

Butt joints at corners are made by trimming the first piece of laminate flush to the work edge, then applying the second sheet, again slightly oversized. A pass with the bevel cutter completes the joint. When applying laminate to a counter or table top with matching laminate edge, the edge banding should be applied first so that the joint line appears on the side rather than on the top. This is not a hard and fast rule with all edge banding treatments. On certain pieces of furniture and built-ins it is sometimes desirable to have the joint line on the side rather than on the edge.

After trimming, the beveled corners should be slightly eased with a 400 grit abrasive paper held over a block of wood. Care should be exercised to avoid rubbing the abrasive on the surface.

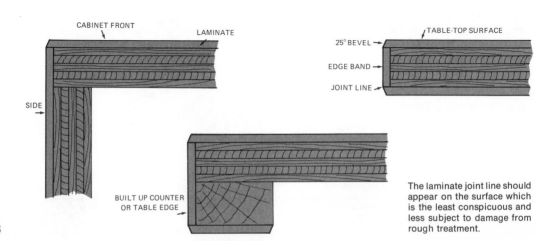

The laminate joint line should appear on the surface which is the least conspicuous and less subject to damage from rough treatment.

pecial Treatments

Laminating a plain, flat surface presents no particular problems, but built-ins, bookshelves, and some kinds of furniture require a certain amount of advance planning. Such projects, with hard to reach areas, are best handled by pre-surfacing some of the components before assembly.

If a project such as a bookshelf, for example, is to be surfaced completely both inside and out, ill-fitting joints would surely result if an attempt is made to surface the insides after assembly. Not only would precise fitting and trimming be difficult, but remember that cemented surfaces bond on contact, allowing no opportunity for a second try. Also, if screws are to be used for assembly, they would need to be inserted before the outside surface is covered.

The accompanying photographs illustrate the techniques of handling projects that require surfacing prior to assembly. The methods will serve as a guide for practically any job you're likely to tackle.

Plastic laminate in exquisite teak wood pattern was used for this project for two good reasons: to keep costs down and to avoid the necessity of making difficult miter joints to conceal dissimilar edges which would otherwise occur with a hardwood veneer or lumber core plywood. Ordinary fir plywood was used for the basic construction.

Certain disciplines must be exercised when surfacing projects with hard to reach inside areas. This project has plenty of them.

409

When cutting laminate by scoring it is advisable to clamp the straight edge firmly in place to avoid a costly mishap. Note how the far end of the guide is held in a place where a clamp can't reach.

It is important to plan the cuts so that grain patterns will match and continue through adjoining sections of a construction. Masking tape labels indicating the location and "top" of each piece can be important.

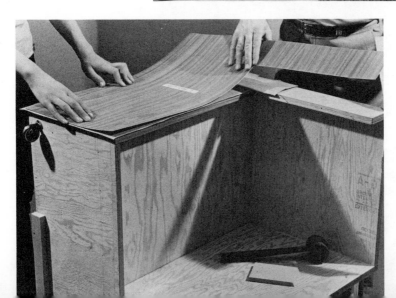

Four hands are better than two when applying the laminate to the wood. This is $1/32''$ vertical grade material which is quite suitable for many applications except table or counter tops.

Dado joints are the best to use for bookshelf type constructions. The grooves should be cut after the laminate has been applied to the piece for a neat job. Dado head can be used to make the grooves in one pass. Otherwise use a regular saw blade (with fine teeth) and make a series of cuts after kerfing the outer borders of the groove.

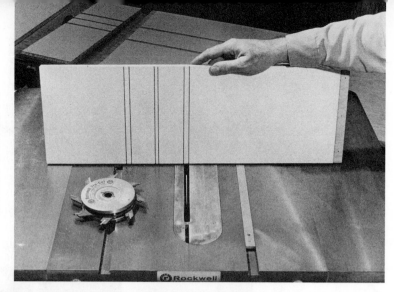

Large back panels frequently cannot be dado grooved too easily. The raw wood areas which are necessary for a proper glue joint are formed by spacing the laminate inserts. Nails and wood blocks help to accurately align the panels which are pre-cut to exact size.

When fabricated this way, with the laminate applied before final assembly, all joints are bound to turn out just as intended.

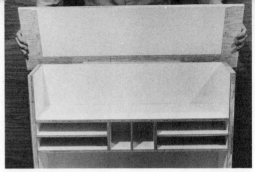

Test fitting the top before gluing it into place. Note the nail holes along the center of the joint areas. They are made in advance to guide the drill for making the screw pilot holes from the outside.

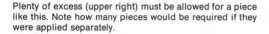

Glue must be applied sparingly to the wood joint surfaces and evenly brushed out to avoid excess squeeze-out.

Laminate cannot be applied to outside surfaces until the joints are fastened with glue and screws. Front edges can be applied after final assembly.

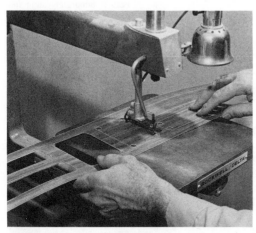

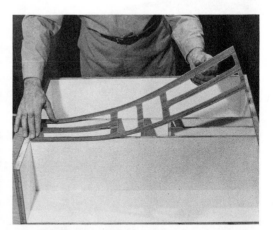

Numerous butt joints can be avoided on an application such as this by cutting a network of edging out of a single piece of laminate. Holes drilled through the waste at corners are for jig saw blade entry.

Plenty of excess (upper right) must be allowed for a piece like this. Note how many pieces would be required if they were applied separately.

The router is used to clean off the excess. The small radius which is left in the corners is easily squared with a file. When filing, apply pressure only on the down stroke.

Natural hardwood trim molding can be applied to the surface of non-high gloss laminates. Masking tape is used for accurate layout. Corners are marked with tape to guide the reassembly with glue.

The molding is stained and finished before installation to eliminate an otherwise very tedious task. Most adhesives will not serve too well in an application like this. This one, Scotch Super Strength, works very well. Be sure to test different adhesives for holding power before use.

In making the chair illustrated earlier, similar techniques of pre-surfacing certain parts was necessary but with slight variations. Photo shows how a close fitting joint is made by temporarily assembling the chair with screws. The angled piece is then bonded in place to butt up against the adjoining panel.

Chair is disassembled to permit unobstructed use of the router to trim the excess from all the outer edges. All inside edges of the laminate pieces are slightly beveled in advance to permit easier insertion of the various members during final assembly. Again, glue and screw joints are made before applying the outside laminate.

413

Prefabricated parts provide you with one of the quickest and easiest ways to enrich your craftwork. They can be especially advantageous if you lack certain skills or the necessary equipment to make a special component for a project. On the other hand, you may want to use them simply to save time, even if yours is a fully equipped shop and your talents equal to the task.

Shown are a few examples of some practical applications of ready-made parts. If you want to go pre-fab all the way, you might be interested in a kit-type project such as the grandfather's clock.

QUEEN ANNE STOOL

The construction of a stool such as this can easily be a one-evening project. The handsome legs are purchased ready made and they are easy to install. They're available in several distinctive styles and sizes suitable for cabinets, tables and many other uses. Mail order houses sell them at relatively low cost.

1 A simple box frame is made with butt joints, nails and glue. Cleats provide a support for the base panel and a partial support for the legs.

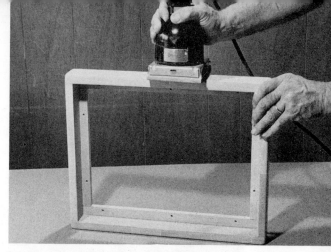

2 A finishing sander is used to smooth the surfaces and to ease all corners to obtain a soft look.

3 The legs come without screw holes and with only a preliminary sanding thus requiring a light once-over with fine grit paper.

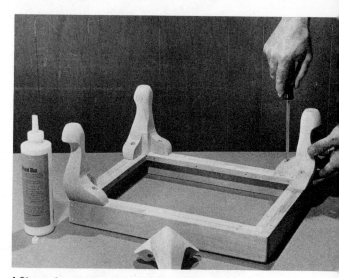

4 Glue and screws are used to secure the legs to the frame. Carefully wipe any excess glue from joints.

5 A plywood panel and a block of foam just about complete the job. For a distinctive finish see procedure in the section on finishing.

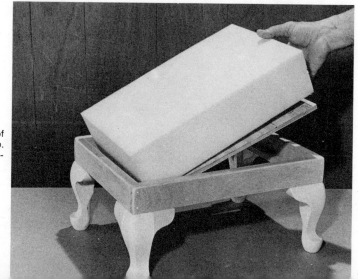

FIDDLEBACK STOOL

A scrap of wood cut into a fiddle back shape with a saber saw becomes an instant stool with the addition of screw-on ready-made legs.

CONSOLE SET

Another use for store bought legs in combination with hardboard filigree panel. The result is a handsome console set.

Grooves cut into the flat of the legs permit neat installation of the decorative panel. The table top is a piece of plywood surfaced with laminate and edged with molding.

METAL LEG CHAIR

This box construction is similar to the stool shown on opposite page. It has metal legs which are attached in the same way as the wooden screw-on type.

DOWEL TABLE/CHAIR

Dowels and ready-made legs simplified the construction of this piece.

Dowels are well suited for a job like this because they're made of strong maple.

The legs are reinforced with dowels. Metal brackets are screwed on to legs to maintain a true plane.

LEG TOP-BRACKETS

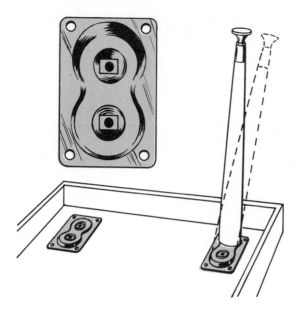

Leg top plate brackets are available in two-position combinations which permit a choice of either straight or flared installation.

SMALL SPINDLES

Although you may have the capability to turn your own spindles, a project requiring many of them can be simplified by using ready-made ones.

SCREEN POSTS

Ready-made legs fitted with pivoting pins and adjustable glides serve in this novel way.

The method used to align the holes for the spindles may be of interest: The ring is secured to the base with masking tape.

The holes are then enlarged in each piece to accommodate the spindle ends. The pilot holes which go through the bottom of the base section are plugged with spackle to keep glue from running out.

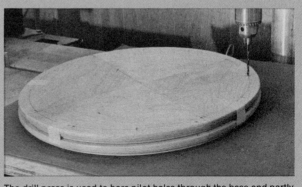

The drill press is used to bore pilot holes through the base and partly into the bottom of the ring.

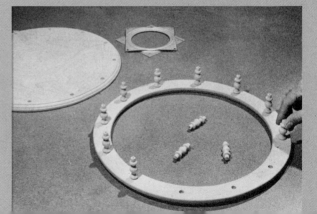

DRAWERS

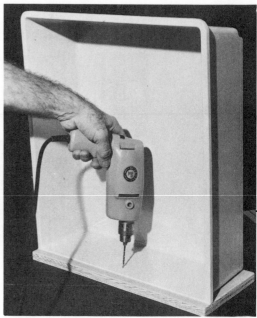

These drawers (below) are specially designed with a straight lip projection at the front which permits easy installation of a wood facing. A thin groove is cut into the wood to receive the lip. Sliding fixtures come with it.

Ready-made smooth cornered drawers (left) made of high impact plastic are a big help on major cabinet constructions which need many drawers.

Another type of ready-made drawer which is suitable for installation in existing cabinets, this one attaches with just four screws.

CARVED PLAQUES

Carved plaques made of durable composition molded wood add a fine touch to this homemade bar. They're carried by most lumber dealers.

CEILING BEAMS

This ruggedly textured surface gives the appearance of a heavy hand-hewn timber but it is actually a hollow plywood, easy to install beam.

The beam is a novel fold out construction with pre-mitered edges which are easy to assemble. The "hewn" surface is on the inside, well protected from manufacture to installation. (*U.S. Plywood*)

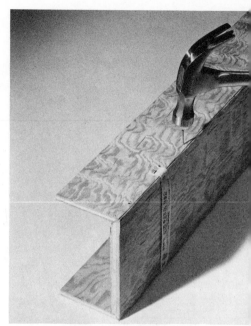

A factory installed cloth tape holds the components together while the miter joint is nailed. The tape is then discarded.

Installation is quite simple with this lightweight beam. It is placed over a previously attached nailer strip and nailed into it.

GRANDFATHER'S CLOCK

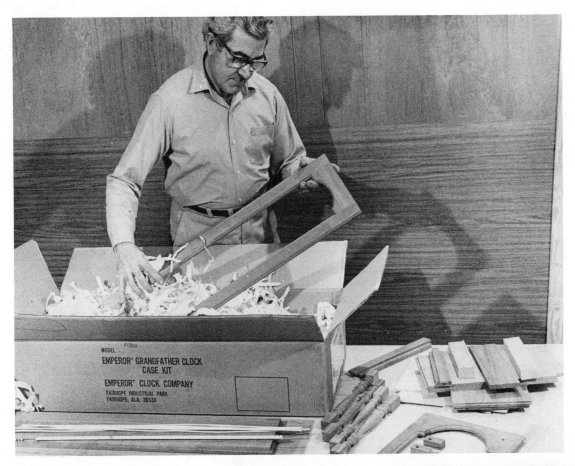

This little package contains all the parts required to assemble a complete grandfather's clock case. The cost for such a kit is quite reasonable due to mass production manufacturing methods.

Most of the joints are pre-cut and require only gluing for assembly.

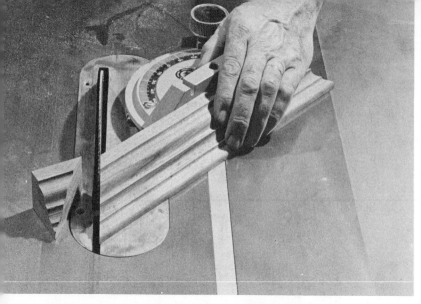

Mitered corners of the trim molding must be cut by the user. This makes good sense as a safety measure: Any slight errors resulting from an out of square glue up of the case can be adjusted by altering the angle of the miters.

Although the parts in the kit are machined to close tolerances, careful workmanship is essential in the assembly stage if professional results are to be obtained.

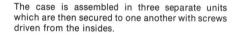

The case is assembled in three separate units which are then secured to one another with screws driven from the insides.

Store bought moldings and turnings can be used in many ways. This fixture provides another example.

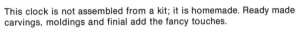

This clock is not assembled from a kit; it is homemade. Ready made carvings, moldings and finial add the fancy touches.

When finished the solid walnut clock looks every bit as good as any that could be bought at considerably higher cost.

The application of a finish can enhance the beauty of a fine wood or greatly improve the appearance of a less attractive, ordinary wood. It is not difficult to obtain a good finish if the surfaces of the wood are first prepared by sanding and undercoating properly.

A nicely constructed project deserves a good finish.

Sanding

A finish coat will not cover defects such as scratches or dents; on the contrary, it may intensify them. Before sanding fill any nail holes, gouges, or other indentations with a wood-patching compound. If the wood is to be clear finished, use a color compound that matches the wood as closely as possible. Shallow dents can sometimes be removed by swelling the grain with water. Before filling a small dent try wetting it with a few drops of water. This will usually raise the grain sufficiently so that it can be sanded flush.

The smoother the piece of wood, the better the final finish will be. Therefore it is essential

426

that the wood be sanded thoroughly before any finish is applied. Sand each individual piece *before* assembly because it is very difficult to do a proper job of sanding inside corners or other obstructions. Sand with the grain using progressively finer grits until the surface is satin smooth. Veneers require very special care to avoid sanding through to the core stock. After assembly, the work should be given a final sanding by hand with very fine paper to remove any roughness developed in handling. Dust off the wood with a brush or vacuum cleaner, then follow up with a tack rag to remove the last traces of dust. A tack rag is a cloth that has been impregnated with a sticky substance that picks up dust and lint. It is available at nearly all paint stores.

If most of the sanding is done before assembly, the final sanding will be less demanding. *(3M Co.)*

leaching

Bleaching is the process of lightening the color of wood with chemicals. It is used to obtain a "blond" finish or to remove undesirable stains. Most bleaches are two-solution preparations. Some are applied in two separate solutions, while others are intermixed immediately before use and applied in one coat. Both types contain chemicals that are harmful to the skin and clothing, so it is important that rubber gloves and old clothing be worn when working with bleaches.

Procedures for bleaching vary with brands. Read and follow the manufacturer's instructions carefully. The operation is usually quite simple: The bleaching agent is applied with a brush and allowed to dry. The maker's directions will tell you whether or not a neutralizer need be applied. If not, a water rinse is used followed by sanding after the wood is dry.

illing

Woods such as oak, mahogany, walnut and chestnut have open-grained structures with large pores that make it difficult to achieve a smooth, even finish. A paste wood filler is used to fill the pores and smooth the surface. This material is not to be confused with hole-patching filling compounds, such as Plastic Wood and the like. Paste wood filler is a heavy-bodied

427

material that must be diluted to brushing consistency before use. Turpentine or mineral spirits are the usual thinning agents used.

Filler is available in various wood-matching colors or in a natural, non-colored tint. It can be applied to the bare wood or to wood that has been stained. The colored fillers have a slight staining effect, therefore stains may not be needed before filling. This should be checked out on scrap wood.

Brush the filler over a small area at a time, working it well into the pores of the wood. Allow it to set until it starts to lose its "wet" look. To test for proper dryness drag a finger across the surface. If a ball is formed, it is time to wipe. If the filler slips under the pressure of the finger, it is still too wet. Wiping too soon will pull the filler out of the pores. Allowing it to set too long will cause great difficulty in wiping off the excess.

When the filler is ready, wipe off the excess from the surface with burlap or other coarse cloth. Wipe across the grain to pack the filler into the pores until practically all of the excess is removed, then finish off by wiping with a clean soft cloth in the direction of the grain. Let it dry overnight, then sand very lightly to remove any excess filler. When filling is complete, spread the rags out to air. Do not leave them in a pile, they may ignite from spontaneous combustion. Take this precaution with any finish-impregnated rags.

When the filler has set the excess is removed by wiping across the grain with a coarse rag or burlap.

Color matched paste wood filler is worked into the open pores with a stiff brush.

ealing

A sealer coat is used to "secure" the filler and stain that has been applied and to reduce absorbency of the finish coats into the wood. On close-grained wood that is not to be stained, the sealer is the first coat of finish to be applied. Otherwise it goes on after the filler and stain. A coat of sealer should be applied to all surfaces of a project, even the ones that are out of view and not intended to receive finish coats. This serves to prevent moisture absorption.

Shellac diluted with denatured alcohol makes a good sealer. It dries quite rapidly and can be rubbed and ready for coating in several hours. Fine steel wool is used to smooth the shellacked surface because it clogs abrasive papers.

A lacquer-based sealer called sanding sealer can also be used. It dries in ten minutes and can be sanded in about thirty minutes. It sands off as a powder and does not clog the paper.

A coat of sealer is used as a buffer between filled or stained surfaces and the finish coats. It forms a non-porous base.

Lacquer-based sanding sealer cuts off as a fine light powder which wipes off easily. Sanding of finish materials should always be done by hand. (*3M Co.*)

429

taining

Stain is used to color and to bring out the beauty of nicely-grained woods. Frequently the clear finish coats will do this too, so staining is not always necessary.

Get into the habit of pre-testing stains and finish coats together and separately on scraps of wood of the same species as the finished work. Depending on the particular piece of wood, stains sometimes absorb more in some areas than in others. The application of a sealer before staining will help to prevent blotchy and uneven results.

There are several types of stains: penetrating and pigmented oil stain, and water stain. The oil stains are easier to use than the water-type. Penetrating oil stain is not advised for use with lacquer-based materials because it will bleed through. Therefore a shellac sealer rather than a sanding sealer should be used over or under this stain.

Penetrating oil stain is applied with a brush or cloth pad. Work on one full section or panel at a time, allow it to stand a few minutes, then wipe with a lint-free cloth so that a uniform color results. The longer the wait before wiping, the deeper the penetration. After drying a shellac sealer coat is applied.

Pigmented oil stains are effective in uniforming wood or for staining a piece of work made from different wood because the pigments are somewhat opaque. For heavy effects these stains should be allowed to dry without wiping. Otherwise, they're applied in the same manner as the penetrating stains.

Water stains are readily absorbed by the wood resulting in greater contrast in the grain or figure of the wood. This is an advantage that is offset by the fact that the water swells the wood and raises the grain. It can warp wood and sometimes affects glue joints. For this reason stains are not generally used in the home workshop.

Stain is applied in the direction of the grain with a cloth or brush. It should always be tried on waste stock first.

opcoats

The final step in finishing is the application of a topcoat to protect the surface and to produce the desired effect, such as a high gloss, satin, or flat finish. There are many kinds of topcoat finishes available, including regular varnish, synthetic (polyurethane) varnish and lacquer, as well as penetrating finishes.

VARNISH. Usually, at least two, and sometimes three coats of varnish are required. A full-flowing coat of varnish will ordinarily level itself, but an excessive deposit, especially on vertical surfaces, may run or sag. Brush the varnish first across the grain, then follow with light strokes with the grain to even it out. Always brush from the dry area into the wet. Work a small section at a time and get to the new one as quickly as possible before the edges begin to dry. Light sanding is required between coats after paint has been allowed to dry thoroughly.

Quick-drying finish coats should not be overbrushed. Good lighting is essential. *(3M Co.)*

POLYURETHANE. Polyurethane varnish is fairly quick-drying, very durable, and highly water resistant. It is brushed in the same way as regular varnish but differs in the follow up. Sanding between coats is not required if each coat is applied within the time specified by the manufacturer. The time element is important because chemical fusing occurs between coats only for a certain period. If too much time lapses between coats, sanding will be required in order to obtain the bite necessary for adhesion. This kind of finish is not fussy about weather. It actually hardens more rapidly under humid conditions. Special sealers may be required with some synthetics, so this must be checked out in advance.

LACQUER. Regular lacquers are very fast-drying and are suitable only for use with spraying equipment. Brushing lacquer is available for brush application. This, too, is rather quick drying; therefore it must be applied differently than varnish. Brush the lacquer only in the direction of the grain and do not go back over the part that has been coated. Several coats with fine sanding between them is standard practice.

431

RUBBING. It is sometimes necessary to rub down the final coat to remove brush streaks, runs, or dust specks. Or this step may be employed to obtain a soft sheen. A 600 grit waterproof silicon carbide paper is used for this, lubricated with water or rubbing oil. If a higher luster is desired, rubbing is done with a felt pad charged with oil and pumice, a very fine abrasive. For still finer work rottenstone powder is used instead of pumice.

Sanding operations on final coats should be done "wet". Rubbing oil or soapy water can be used to lubricate the abrasive paper.

Paste wax is frequently used to obtain a soft sheen after the final coat has been rubbed down. *(3M Co.)*

PENETRATING FINISH. There are a number of modern wood finishes that penetrate deeply into the wood, then solidify to protect the surface from within. Some are quite easy to use because they are complete finishes requiring no pre-sealing or priming and dry very rapidly. It is not unusual to completely finish a piece of work with three coats in as many hours. Danish oil finish is another type of penetrating, all-in-one finishing material. It seals, finishes, and preserves the wood and imparts the popular rich appearance commonly seen on modern Danish furniture.

PAINTING. The surface of wood to be painted does not require the extra-careful attention that is needed for wood that is to be clear finished. It must be sanded smooth and clean nevertheless. An undercoater is applied first to seal the wood and to provide a suitable base for the finish coats. Nail or screw holes and dents can be filled after the undercoater has dried. A coat of shellac is applied to knots or sap streaks to seal them. For easier and better covering the undercoater should be colored to about the same color as the final coat.

Sand the undercoat after it is thoroughly dry, remove all dust, then apply the paint or enamel using the same brushing techniques as for varnishing. If a second coat is required, the first one must be lightly sanded. The final coat is not sanded.

Certain woods like Douglas fir plywood have a "wild" grain caused by the difference in grain density between the hard summer growth and the softer, more porous spring growth. Paints absorb unevenly on such surfaces, thus accentuating the grain pattern. This is nor-

432

mally not desirable, so a special "grain-taming" undercoater is used before painting such wood. White Firzite is a commonly used undercoater that is designed to neutralize the uneven absorption characteristics of fir plywood. A clear version is available for use as a sealer for clear finishing. Both these materials are for interior use only.

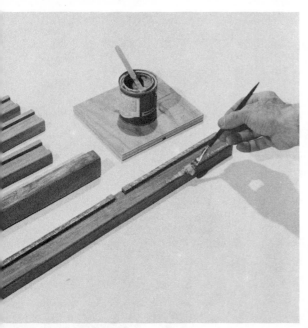

It is sometimes advantageous to apply paste filler to hard-to-reach parts before assembly. Oily filler must be kept off joints which are to be glued. This insures a continuous bond.

One-step modern finishes are especially useful for projects which are tricky to handle. The edges of the frame adjoining the non-wood surface were treated with filler before assembly.

Small nails driven into the underside support the work to allow easier application of the finish.

The back panel has been temporarily removed from this work to facilitate finishing, and will be glued on later.

A small bevel purposely cut into the trim during construction permits easier painting up to a sharp corner. The shield's edge sits in the slight groove.

Plastic foam "brush" is used to apply paint to an edge on a two color paint job. This type of applicator produces clean, sharply defined edges.

Heavily pigmented stains are work savers on outdoor projects. They cover in one coat and need nothing under or over.

WOODGRAINING. You can economize on woodworking projects by using a lower grade, less expensive lumber that can readily be grain-finished to conceal the flaws while at the same time giving it the appearance of an attractive, more expensive wood. It is done with antiquing or woodgraining finish (they're both the same). The process is easy, effective, and almost foolproof. The materials come in kits consisting simply of a base and glaze coat.

The kits are available in many wood-matching tones with either latex or oil base coats. The latex-type is usually preferred because it dries quickly and cleans up with water.

The procedure consists of three basic steps. Apply the base coat after only minimal wood surface preparation. Since the base is relatively heavy bodied, you won't have to worry too much about super fine sanding. Holes and dents should of course be patched. When the base coat is dry apply a thin coat of glaze color tone to a complete area. While still wet use a dry paint brush and lightly run it through the coated area. If your hand shakes in the process, so much the better: this will give the grain effect a natural character. Go over the entire area this way, wiping the brush occasionally. That's all there is to it. If it doesn't look just right, you merely wipe off the glaze with a cloth and start over. You can't miss and the results may amaze you, even on the first attempt.

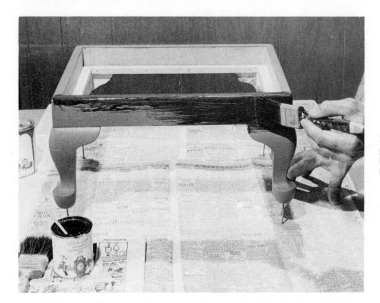

Woodgraining. A thin glaze is applied to the work which has first been coated with a quick-drying latex base color.

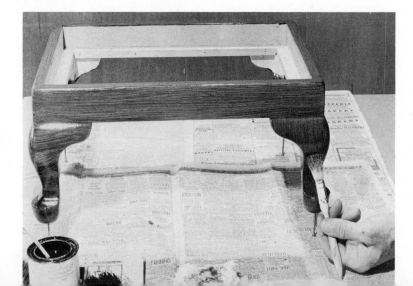

Grain pattern is formed by passing a dry brush, steel wool, or other object over the glaze while it is still wet. The technique is very easy and the results always quite good.

Mail Order Catalog Companies
for the Woodworking Enthusiast

Brookstone Co., Peterborough, N. H. 03458. Brookstone specializes in hard-to-find tools, many of them for small and delicate jobs. Catalog comes out three times a year. Price is 50 cents a year.

Caldwell Industries, Luling, Tex. 78648. Here you'll find tools and castings—mostly for the machinist/tinkerer. Catalog is priced at $1.

Colonial Workshop, Box 41611, Sacramento, Calif. 95841. Plans are the specialty here—most of them for colonial-style furniture. They also have a few modern designs, and plans for outdoor furniture. Catalog is free.

Constantine, 2050 Eastchester Rd., Bronx, N. Y. 10461. An indispensable source for specialty woods and veneers, furniture hardware, finishing materials, inlays, shop books, specialty tools and supplies. Also plans and kits. Catalog is 50 cents.

Craftsman Wood Service, 2729 S. Mary St., Chicago, Ill. 60608. A line of products similar to those of Constantine. Craftsman is handier for midwestern orders especially. Catalog is 50 cents.

Defender Ind., 255 Main St., New Rochelle, N. Y. 10801. Defender's Marine Buying Guide is primarily a catalog of marine supplies, but much is useful around the home. Good selections of fiberglassing supplies, marine hardware. Catalog/manual is 75 cents.

Edmund Scientific Co., 300 Edscorp Bldg., Barrington, N. J. 08007. Edmund Scientific is known best for its telescopes and kits and other scientific equipment, but their catalogs also feature materials you can use in home-improvement projects. Catalog is free.

Furniture Designs, 1425 Sherman Ave., Evanston, Ill. 60201. Full-size furniture plans. Catalog is $1, lists 150 plans.

Gaston Wood Finishes, Box 1246, Bloomington, Ind. 47401. Finishing materials you won't find in a store. Stains, lacquers, varnishes, oil finishes, pigments, toners, dryers, fillers, sealers, shellacs, wood bleaches, along with clock parts, furniture hardware, etc. Catalog is 50 cents.

Minnesota Woodworkers Supply Co., 925 Winnetka Ave., N. Minneapolis, Minn. 55427. Another catalog along the lines of Constantine and Craftsman, without the specialty woods. Veneers, inlays, carved moldings, framing supplies, lamp parts, and finishing supplies. Catalog is 50 cents.

Popular Science Plans, 380 Madison Ave., New York, N. Y. 10017. PS has a wide assortment of plans for canoes, boats, domes, outdoor storage buildings, sail car, man-carrying kite, etc. The catalog is 25 cents.

Sears, Roebuck and Co., In addition to the general catalog, Sears has a pair of specialized catalogs of great help to the homeowner: The Sears Home Improvement Catalog and the Sears Suburban, Farm, and Ranch Catalog. Both catalogs are free from Sears. Write to the regional distribution center nearest you: Sears, Dept. 139AF, Atlanta, Ga. 31935; Chicago, Ill. 60607; Columbus, Ohio 43228; Dallas, Tex. 75295; Greensboro, N. C. 27480; Kansas City, Mo. 64127; Los Angeles, Calif. 90051; Memphis, Tenn. 38140; Minneapolis, Minn. 55407; Philadelphia, Pa. 19132; Seattle, Was. 98184.

Woodcraft Supply Corp., 313 Montvale Ave., Woburn, Mass. 01801. Good honest woodworking tools. Carving tools are excellent, as are their sharpening supplies. Specialty items include wood-threading kits and hand planes of all types. Catalog is 50 cents.

index

Adhesives, *see* Glues
Air drying lumber, 24, 25
Aliphatic resin glue, 346
Aluminum oxide, 290
American Lumber Standards, 65
Annual rings, 16–17, 23
Ash:
  identifying, 27, 36
  suitability tables, 30, 31
Aspen, 34, 36
Auger bit, 110
Avodire, 36
Awls, 112, 196

Back saws, 109, 204
Back-stamp, 69
Ball peen hammer, 111
Band clamps, 353
Band saws, 152–155, 222–226
Bar clamps, 350, 353, 363
Basements, shops in, 83–84
Basswood:
  identifying, 27, 34
  suitability tables, 30, 31
Bayonet saws, *see* Saber saws
Beech:
  identifying, 27, 34
  suitability tables, 30, 31
Belt sanders:
  portable, 127, 128, 293
  stationary, 164–166, 293, 297–298
Bench grinders, 182–183
Bench rule, 108, 190
Bench sanders, 164–166, 293–299
Bench saws, *see* Circular saws
Bench tops, 90
Bending wood, 386–397
  comparative strengths, 30
  kerfing, 390–394
  lamination, 386–389
  self-forming, 395–397
Benge, 36
Bent needle nose pliers, 113
Birch:
  classified, 18
  identifying, 34
  suitability tables, 30, 31
Bits, 110
Blackwood, 36
Bleaching wood, 427
Block plane:
  hand, 109
  power, 134–135
Board foot (bd. ft.), 63
Bolts, 311, 312
Box wrench, 111
Boxelder, 27

Brackets, 314–315
Brad driver, 111
Brush-backed sanding wheel, 294
Budinga, 36
Buckeye, 31
Butt joint, 335–336, 359, 364
Butternut, 30

C clamps, 112, 350, 352, 353
Cabinet backs, plywood, 367
Cabinet catches, 314
Caliper rules, 108, 190
Calipers, 108, 181, 197, 318
Carbide tipped saw blade, 144
Carpenter's level, 108, 197
Carpenter's pencil, 112
Carpenter's square, 108
Carriage bolt, 311
Carving chisels, 109
Casein glue, 346
Casters, 315
Cedar:
  classified, 18
  identifying, 32
  suitability tables, 30, 31
Ceiling beams, ready-made, 422
Cement, contact, 347, 355, 407
Center punch, 112
Chairs, ready-made, 417
Chandelier, turned, 330–331
Check arbors, 181
Cherry, 28
  classified, 18
  identifying, 34, 36, 37
  suitability tables, 30
Chess set, turned, 326–329
Chestnut, 28, 30, 31
Chisels, 5, 109, 242–244, 250, 251
  impact tool, 136
  wood-turning, 317
Circular saws:
  portable, 117–121, 211–216
  stationary, 137–145, 227–236
Clamp nails, 304
Clamp-on vise, 113
Clamps, 112, 350–357
  for hardboard, 372
  for plywood, 362–363
Coated abrasives, 290–291
Cocabola, 37
Coffeebean, 37
Combination square, 108, 192
Combination wood rasp, 110
Compass, 108
Compass saws, 109, 204
Compound angles, table, 231, 238
Contact cement, 347, 355, 407

Coped joint, 383
Coping saws, 109, 204
Corrugated fasteners, 304, 361
Cottonwood:
  identifying, 27, 34
  suitability tables, 30, 31
Countersink, 110
Crosscut saw, 109
Curves, drawing, 199
Cut-off saws, *see* Circular saws
Cypress:
  identifying, 27, 32
  suitability tables, 30, 31

Dado head, 144, 145
Dado joints, 338, 339–340, 360, 366
Diagonal cutter pliers, 113
Disc sanders, 164–166, 293, 295–297, 299
Dividers, 108, 181, 196, 318
Double jaw vise, 113
Double-end wrench set, 111
Douglas fir, 28
  plywood, 44, 358
  suitability tables, 30, 31
Dovetail jig, 133
Dovetail joint, 343, 345
Dovetail saws, 109, 204
Dowel centers, 112
Dowel screws, 311
Drawer construction:
  plywood, 364–365
  with ready-mades, 420
Drawing irregular shapes, 198–199
Drill press, 160–163, 283–289
Drills:
  hand, 110, 278–280
  power:
    portable, 122–126, 281–282
    stationary, 160–163, 283–289
Drum sanders, 164–166, 293, 295

Edge-grained wood, 23
Edge-mark, 69
Edges:
  particleboard, 377
  plywood, 368–369
Ellipse, drawing, 198
Elm:
  identifying, 27, 34
  suitability tables, 30, 31
End cutting nipper, 113
Epoxy resin adhesive, 347
Expansion bit, 110

Face plate turning, 324–325

Fasteners, 300–313
  bolts, 311, 312
  corrugated, 304, 361
  flat, 313
  hardboard, 372–375
  nail driver, 111, 312
  nail sets, 112, 302
  nails, 300–304, 311, 312
    clamp, 304
    comparative holding power, 30
    hammering, 300–302
    hardboard, 372
    masonry, 311, 312
    paneling, 405
    plywood, 360–361
    splitting of wood by, 31
    types of, 303
  offset, 313
  for particleboard, 377, 379
  repair plates, 313
  screws, 305–312
    hardboard, 372
    installing, 306–307
    particleboard, 377, 379
    plywood, 361
    screwdrivers, 308–310
    sizes, 305–306
Faux Satine, 37
File cabinet, hardware, 96–97
Files, 110
Filigree hardboard, 52, 54
Filling, 427–428
Finishing, 426–435
  bleaching, 427
  filling, 427–428
  sanding, 426–427
  sealing, 429
  staining, 430
  topcoats, 431–435
Finishing sanders, 127, 129, 293
Fir:
  classified, 18
  identifying, 32
  suitability tables, 30
Flat fasteners, 313
Flat-grained wood, 23
Flint, 290
Fly cutter, 287
Folding rules, 108, 191
Framere, 37
Framing square, 194
French curve, 108
Furring, 399

Garnet, 290
Gauges, 108, 195
Glides, 315
Glues, 346–350
  application of, 348–350
  clamps, 112, 350–357, 362–363, 372
  hardboard, 372, 373, 374

kinds of, 346–347
  particleboard, 377, 379
  plywood, 362
Goncalo Alves, 37
Grading lumber, 65–69
  hardwood, 66, 67, 68
  plywood, 68–69
  softwood, 66, 67, 69
Grandfather's clock, ready-made, 81, 423–425
Grinders, bench, 182–183
Growth rings, 16–17, 23
Gum:
  identifying, 27, 35, 37
  suitability tables, 30, 31

Hackberry:
  identifying, 27
  suitability tables, 30, 31
Hacksaw, 109
Hammers, 111, 300–302
Hand tools, 108–113
  cutting, 109, 242–255
    chisels, 5, 109, 136, 242–244, 250, 251, 317
    planes, 109, 245–247
    saws, 109, 200–204
    spokeshave, 109, 248–250
    surform tool, 252–255, 379
  drills, 110, 278–280
  fastening:
    hammers, 111, 300–302
    mallets, 111
    rivet tool, 111
    screwdrivers, 111, 308–310
    stapler, 111
    wrenches, 111
  holding:
    clamps, 112, 350–357, 362–363, 372
    pliers, 113
    vises, 113
    wrenches, 113
  layout, 108, 190–197
  measuring, 108, 181, 190–197, 318
  miscellaneous, 112
  shaping, 110, 250, 251
Hanger bolt, 311
Hardboard, 47–54
  fasteners for, 372–375
  paneling, 398, 401, 403, 405
  perforated, 53, 93
  specialty, 51–54
  types of, 49–50
  working with, 370–376
Hardware, miscellaneous, 314–315
Hardware file cabinet, 96–97
Hardwood:
  bending, 387
  cells, 15
  cutting, 23
  defined, 18
  domestic, 34–35

fine, 27, 36–39
  grading, 65, 66, 67, 68
  identifying, 34–35
  lumber yards, 77
  plywoods, 68
Heartwood, 15, 17
Hemlock, 30, 31, 44
Hermaphrodite caliper, 318
Hexagon, drawing, 198
Hickory, 30, 31
Hide glue, 346
Hinges, 314
Holly, 27
Home improvement centers, 75

Impact tool, 136
Ipi, 37
Iroko, 37

Jig saws, 156–159, 217–221
Jointers, 168–170, 256–261
Joints, 334–345
  butt, 335–336, 359, 364
  coped, 383
  dado, 338, 339–340, 360, 366
  dovetail, 343, 345
  lap, 338, 341–342
  miter, 341, 343, 382
  mortise and tenon, 343, 344, 345, 351
  particleboard, 376
  plywood, 359–360
  rabbet, 336–338, 339, 360, 367

Kelobra, 37
Kerfing, bending wood by, 390–394
Keyhole saw, 109
Kiln drying wood, 24, 25, 67
Knives, 110, 112, 145

Lacewood, 37
Lacquer, 431
Lag screws, 311, 312
Laminates, plastic, 57–59, 406–413
Lamination, bending wood by, 386–389
Lap joint, 338, 341–342
Larch:
  identifying, 33
  suitability tables, 30, 31
Lathes, 176–181
  basic cuts, 318–325
  chisels, 317
  cutting actions, 316
  face plate turning, 324–325
  measuring tools, 318
  techniques applied, 326–333
Layout tools, 108, 190–197
Leg top-brackets, ready-made, 418
Levels, 108, 197
Light fixtures, 98
Linear foot measure (lin. ft.), 64
Line-up punch, 112

Locust:
   identifying, 27, 34, 35
   suitability tables, 30, 31
Long nose pliers, 113
Lumber, 22–26
   cutting methods, 23
   defects, 26
   determining needs, 70–72
   dimensions, 61–64
   economizing, 71–72
   grading, 65–69
   marks, 67
   milled, 62–63
   ready-made items, 78–81
   rough, 62
   seasoning, 24–25
   sizes, 60–64
   sources of, 74–78
   storage, 95
   surfaced, 62
   terms, 73
   units of measurement, 63–64
Lumber supply houses, cut-rate, 75
Lumber yards, 74, 77
Lumber-core plywood, 43

Machine bolts, 311, 312
Madrone burl, 37
Magnolia:
   identifying, 27
   suitability tables, 31
Mahogany, 38
Mallets, 111
Manufactured woods, 46–59
   hardboard, see Hardboard
   particleboard, 55–56, 376–379
   plastic laminate, 57–59, 406–413
Maple, 28
   bench tops, 89, 90
   classified, 18
   identifying, 27, 35
   suitability tables, 30, 31
Marking gauge, 108, 195
Marks, lumber, 57
Marnut, 38
Masonry nails, 311, 312
Measuring tools, 108, 181
   lathe work, 318
   techniques, 190–197
Milled lumber, 62–63
Mini hacksaw, 109
Miter boxes, 109, 203
Miter gage, 295
Miter joint, 341, 343, 382
Molding cutter knives, 145
Molding heads, 144, 145, 234
Moldings:
   for paneling, 403–404
   working with, 380–385
Molly bolt, 311
Mortise and tenon joints, 343, 344, 345, 351

Multipurpose tool, 102, 184–189
Myrtle Burl, 38

Nail drivers, 111, 312
Nail sets, 112, 302
Nails, 300–304, 311, 312
   clamp, 304
   comparative holding power, 30
   hammering, 300–302
   hardboard, 372
   masonry, 311, 312
   paneling, 405
   plywood, 360–361
   splitting of wood by, 31
   types of, 303
Narra, 38
National Hardwood Lumber Association, 66
New Guinea, 38
Nuts, 311

Oak, 9, 28
   classified, 18
   identifying, 35, 38
   suitability tables, 30, 31
Offset fasteners, 313
Orbital sanders, 129
Oriental Wood, 38

Padouk, 38
Painting, 432–434
Paneling walls, 398–407
   existing walls, 399–400
   installing, 401–402
   moldings, 403–404
   solid wood paneling, 405
Particleboard, 55–56, 376–379
Paste wood filler, 427–428
Pecan:
   identifying, 27, 38
   suitability tables, 31
Pencil, carpenter's, 112
Penetrating finish, 432
Perforated board, 53, 93
Peroba, 38
Phillips point screwdriver, 111
Picture frame clamp, 353
Pine, 28, 44
   classified, 18
   identifying, 33
   suitability tables, 30, 31
Pipe clamps, 353
Piqua, 39
Pitch pocket, 26
Plain-sawed wood, 23
Planes:
   hand, 109, 245–247
   power:
      jointers, 168–170, 256–261
      power block, 134–135
      uniplane, 171–172
Plaques, ready-made, 421
Plastic laminates, 57–59, 406–413

Plastic resin glue, 346
Plastic-faced mallet, 111
Platina, 39
Pliers, 113
Plumb bob, 197
Plywood, 40–45
   classification of, 44–45
   defined, 40
   grading, 68–69
   hardwood, 68
   kinds of, 43
   skin, 395–397
   textured, 45
   working with, 358–369
      assembling, 363
      cabinet backs, 367
      construction joints, 359–360
      cutting, 359
      drawer construction, 364–365
      edge treatments, 368–369
      fasteners, 360–361
      gluing, 362
      installing, 364
      layout, 358
      shelves, 366
Plywood saw blade, 144
Polyurethane varnish, 431
Polyvinyl resin glue, 346
Pop riveters, 312
Poplar:
   classified, 18
   identifying, 27, 35
   suitability tables, 30, 31
Poplar Burl, 39
Power block plane, 134–135
Power tools:
   portable, 100, 109, 114–136
      circular saws, 117–121, 211–216
      drills, 122–126, 281–282
      impact tool, 136
      power block plane, 134–135
      routers, 130–133, 262–267
      saber saws, 114–116, 205–210
      safety, 107
      sanders, 127–129, 293
   stationary, 100–101, 137–189
      band saws, 152–155, 222–226
      belt sanders, 104–166, 293, 297–298
      bench grinders, 182–183
      circular saws, 137–145, 227–236
      disc sanders, 164–166, 293, 295–297, 299
      drill press, 160–163, 283–289
      drum sanders, 164–166, 293, 295
      jig saws, 156–159, 217–221
      jointers, 168–170, 256–261
      lathes, see Lathes
      multipurpose tool, 102, 184–189
      radial arm saws, 100–102, 146–152, 237–241
      sander/grinder, 167, 294

Power tools (con't.)
    sanders, 164–166, 293–299
    shapers, 173–175, 268–277
    uniplane, 171–172
Prefabricated parts, see Ready-mades
Preservatives, 11
Prima Vera, 39
Protractor, 108, 197
Punches, 112
Push drill, 110
Putty knife, 112

Quarter-sawed wood, 23

Rabbet joints, 336–338, 339, 360, 367
Rabbet plane, 109
Radial arm saws, 100–102, 146–152, 237–241
Rasps, 110, 250, 251
Ratchet bit brace, 110
Ready-mades, 78–81, 414–425
  ceiling beams, 422
  chairs, 417
  drawers, 420
  Grandfather's clock, 81, 423–425
  leg top-brackets, 418
  plaques, 421
  spindles, 78, 79
  stools, 79, 414–416
Redwood:
  classified, 18
  grade marks, 67
  suitability tables, 30, 31
Repair plates, 313
Resin glues, 346–347
Resorcinol, 346
Rip saw, 109
Rivet tool, 111
Rosewood, 39
Rough lumber, 62
Round file, 110
Routers, 130–133, 262–267
Rubber mallet, 111
Rubbing, 432
Rules, 108, 190–191, 318

Saber saws, 114–116, 205–210
Sander/grinders, 167, 294
Sanders:
  portable, 127–129, 293
  stationary, 164–166, 293–299
Sanding:
  hand, 292
  power, 293–299
Sandpaper, 290–291
Sapele, 39
Sapwood, 15, 17
Sassafras, 27
Saw horses, 90, 92
Saws:
  band, 152–155, 222–226
  circular:

    portable, 117–121, 211–216
    stationary, 137–145, 227–236
  hand, 109, 200–204
  jig, 156–159, 217–221
  radial arm, 100–102, 146–152, 237–241
  saber, 114–116, 205–210
Scale drawing, enlarging, 198
Scraper, 112
Scratch awls, 112, 196
Screen posts, ready-made, 419
Screw centers, 181
Screw driving bits, 110
Screw hooks and eyes, 315
Screw mate bits, 110
Screw starter, 111
Screwdriver set, 111
Screwdrivers, 111, 308–310
Screws, 305–312
  hardboard, 372
  installing, 306–307
  particleboard, 377, 379
  plywood, 361
  screwdrivers and, 308–310
  sizes, 305–306
Sealer coat, 429
Seasoning, 24–25
Self-centering punch, 112
Service hardboard, 49, 50
Shapers, 173–175, 268–277
Shelf brackets, 315
Shelf standards, 315
Shelves, plywood, 366
Shop, 82–99
  cleanup tips, 99
  hardware file cabinet, 96–97
  lighting, 98
  location, 83–85
  lumber storage, 95
  planning, 86–88
  tool storage, 93–94
  wiring, 99
  workbench, 89–92
Shure-set nail driver, 111
Silicon carbide, 290
Single jaw vise, 113
Skin plywood, 395–397
Sliding T bevel, 194
Slim blade knife, 110
Slip joint pliers, 113
Smooth plane, 109
Softwood:
  cells, 15
  cutting, 23
  defined, 18
  domestic, 32–33
  grading, 65, 66, 67, 69
  identifying, 32–33
  plywoods, 69
  veneer descriptions, 69
Specialty hardboard, 51–54
Spindles, ready-made, 78, 79

Spokeshave, 109, 248–250
Springwood, 16, 71
Spruce:
  identifying, 33
  suitability tables, 30
Spur bit, 110
Square foot measure (sq. ft.), 64
Squares, 108, 192–194
Staining, 430
Standard hardboard, 49, 50
Stapler, 111
Steel square, 194
Steel tape rule, 191
Stools, ready-made, 79, 414–416
Storage:
  lumber, 95
  tools, 93–94
Stove bolt, 311
Straight-line sanders, 129
Summerwood, 16, 17
Surfaced lumber, 62
Surform tool, 252–255, 379
Sycamore:
  identifying, 27, 35
  suitability tables, 30, 31

T bevels, 108, 194, 195
T squares, 108
Table saws, see Circular saws
Tamo, 39
Tape rule, 108
Teak, 39
Tempered hardboard, 49, 50
Templates, 199
Toggle bolts, 311
Tools:
  construction of, 105–106
  design of, 104
  finish of, 104
  hand, see Hand tools
  power, see Power tools
  quality of, 103
  safety and, 107
  selection of, 100–103
  storage of, 93–94
Topcoats, 431–435
Trammel points, 108, 197
Triangle, 108
Try square, 108, 192, 193
Tupelo:
  identifying, 27
  suitability tables, 30, 31
Turning, see Wood turning
Twist drills, 110

Uniplane, 171–172
Utility knife, 110

Varnish, 431
Veneer descriptions, 69
Veneer-core plywood, 43

INDEX

Vise grip plier-wrench, 113
Vises, 113

Wall paneling, 398–407
  existing walls, 399–400
  installing, 401–402
  moldings, 403–404
  solid wood, 405
Walnut, 28
  identifying, 35, 39
  suitability tables, 30, 31
Warp resistance, 28, 31
Willow, 27
Wiring, shop, 99
Wood:
  availability, 13
  beauty, 12
  bending:
    comparative strengths, 30
    kerfing, 390–394
    lamination, 386–389
    self-forming, 395–397
  cells, 15
  color, 12, 21
  decay resistance, comparative, 31
  grain, 12, 19–21
  growth rings, 16–17, 23
  hardness, 28, 30
  hardwood:
    bending, 387
    cells, 15
    cutting, 23
    defined, 18
    domestic, 34–35
    fine, 27, 36–39

grading, 65, 66, 67, 68
  identifying, 34–35
  lumber yards, 77
  plywoods, 68
identification, 32–35
kinds of, 27
lumber, 22–26
  cutting methods, 23
  defects, 26
  determining needs, 70–72
  dimensions, 61–64
  economizing, 71–72
  grading, 65–69
  marks, 67
  milled, 62–63
  ready-made items, 78–81
  rough, 62
  seasoning, 24–25
  sizes, 60–64
  sources of, 74–78
  storage, 95
  surfaced, 62
  terms, 73
  units of measurement, 63–64
manufactured, 46–59
  hardboard, see Hardboard
  particleboard, 55–56, 376–379
  plastic laminates, 57–59, 406–413
plywood, see Plywood
selection, 28–31
  considerations, 28–29
  suitability tables, 30–31
shaping, comparative difficulty of, 31
softwood:
  cells, 15

cutting, 23
  defined, 18
  domestic, 32–33
  grading, 66, 67, 69
  identifying, 32–33
  plywoods, 69
  veneer descriptions, 69
splitting in nailing, comparative, 31
surface characteristics, 12, 19–21
texture, 19, 21
warping, 28, 31
workability, 10
Wood chisel, 109
Wood graining, 435
Wood handle hammer, 111
Wood rasp, 250, 251
Wood screws, see Screws
Wood turning, 316–333
  basic cuts, 318–325
  cutting actions, 316
  face plate turning, 324–325
  lathe chisels, 317
  measuring tools, 318
  techniques applied, 326–333
Woodworking, basic operations in, 5–8
Workbench, 89–92
Workshop, see Shop
Wrenches, 111, 113

Yardstick, 198

Zebrano, 39
Zig zag rules, 108, 190, 191

$1\frac{1}{2}''$

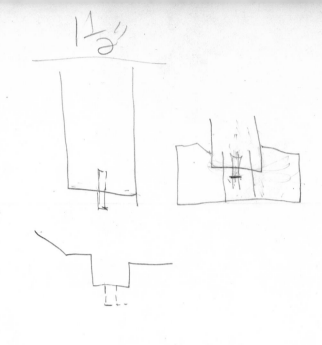